Ethics, *Love,*

and faith *in*

Kierkegaard

Indiana Series in the Philosophy of Religion

Merold Westphal, editor

Ethics, Love,

and Faith in Kierkegaard

Philosophical Engagements
Edited by Edward F. Mooney

Indiana University Press
Bloomington & Indianapolis

This book is a publication of

Indiana University Press
601 North Morton Street
Bloomington, IN 47404-3797 USA

http://iupress.indiana.edu

Telephone orders   800-842-6796
Fax orders   812-855-7931
Orders by e-mail   iuporder@indiana.edu

© 2008 by Indiana University Press

The paper used in this publication meets the minimum requirements of American National Standard for Information Sciences—Permanence of Paper for Printed Library Materials, ANSI Z39.48-1984.

Manufactured in the United States of America

Library of Congress Cataloging-in-Publication Data

Ethics, love, and faith in Kierkegaard : philosophical engagements / edited by Edward F. Mooney.
    p. cm. — (Indiana series in the philosophy of religion)
  Includes bibliographical references and index.
  ISBN 978-0-253-35141-8 (cloth : alk. paper) — ISBN 978-0-253-21995-4 (pbk. : alk. paper) 1. Kierkegaard, Søren, 1813–1855. I. Mooney, Edward F., date
  B4377.E84 2008
  198'.9—dc22

                     2007051953

1 2 3 4 5   13 12 11 10 09 08

Contents

Preface

These explorations of ethics, love, and faith in Kierkegaard first saw the light of day in Copenhagen, mid-August 2004. They were the centerpiece of a celebration held for Alastair Hannay, a philosopher who has devoted his life to bringing Kierkegaard into the open. Author of *Kierkegaard* in the Routledge *Arguments of the Philosophers* series (1982), and of the landmark achievement *Kierkegaard, A Biography* (2001), Hannay is also translator of a number of texts for Penguin, including *Fear and Trembling, Either/Or, Papers and Journals, Sickness unto Death,* and *A Literary Review.* Niels Jørgen Cappelørn graciously offered the facilities of the Kierkegaard Research Center for the late-summer event, attended by the writers represented here and by many others, who read and discussed versions of these chapters.

Kierkegaard research has been a community venture among students and scholars from a number of sub-disciplines (philosophy, theology, literary studies, history, psychology) and countries. Because Kierkegaard wrote in a minor European language, many arrive in Copenhagen not only to delve into the archives but to learn Danish, or to improve their facility. Thus it is entirely fitting that the papers included here were delivered first, not in Chicago, New York, London, Paris, Oslo, or Sydney, but in Copenhagen.

The collection is presented in parts by theme, each part followed by an appreciative and critical response by Hannay. Thus the volume delivers an active conversation among a dozen-plus distinguished scholars, broadcast for an international audience from that marvelous site where one hundred and fifty years ago a prodigious writer set out those works without which today's intellectual cultures of Paris, Sydney, New York, London, and Kyoto would be unrecognizable.

Ethics, *Love,*

and Faith *in*

Kierkegaard

Introduction: A Socratic and Christian Care for the Self

Edward F. Mooney

My task is a Socratic task, to revise the definition of what it is to be a Christian.

The essays gathered here display Kierkegaard's thoughts on ethics, faith, and love refracted through the prisms of over a dozen contemporary scholars. They are vivid testimony to the ongoing power of Kierkegaard's texts to pull new circles of unexpected readers from successive generations; only writers of great depth have that power to repeatedly regenerate their readerships. Of course, the topics are irresistible: neighbor love and despair, a self free of affectation, refiguring ethics, charting the place of God and sovereign goods, preserving the spirit of one's thought through irony, a theater of pseudonyms, and various styles of indirection. These topics fall under the broad purview of philosophy of religion where love and faith and ethics will intersect. That is the fertile site where Kierkegaard engages his time and where these essays in turn engage Kierkegaard.

In its own small way, this collection continues a tradition of Kierkegaard interpretation vigorous and growing through the century and a half since his death in 1854. The world of philosophy and religion today is unthinkable without Heidegger and Wittgenstein, Barth and Tillich, and more recently, Derrida or Habermas or Cavell.[1] The worlds of these writers rest in turn, and to a greater and lesser extent, on Kierkegaard, as they each avow. He is one of the select and indispensable few who leave us endlessly instructive works. In Robert Brandom's phrase, Kierkegaard gives us "tales from the mighty dead," tales that won't be buried, that we can't help retelling and recasting. The Kierkegaard who emerges from these essays is committed equally to Socratic inquiry and to the inflections of a Christian faith. He tries both a Socratic and a Christian source for self.

By his consummate literary skill—which is equally his underrated capacity for both intimate and collective connection—Kierkegaard draws his reader into restaging, retelling, and reliving his explorations of the moral and religious center of a life. The moral center here is that set of aspirations toward the good, true, and beautiful that inform a worthy life, and it clearly overlaps a religious center. Kierkegaard engages us dialogically as Socrates did, laying out a claim or provocation and sometimes an extended view, in ways to draw us in—and draw us out. He draws his reader toward his labyrinth, toward and into some portion of his written world, then steps aside to let her write or speak—or worry for her voice. The address is often intimate, singling out a reader not accidentally addressed as "my reader." We're not allowed to back into anonymity, to become "just anyone in general," say, "any rational mind," or to retreat to a vacant look. He aims to change, or turn, attentive listeners toward the good. So we're all excused from giving just an impersonal *report* on his work. He challenges us to engage at the level of passion as well as intellect.

Both Socrates and Kierkegaard give us a mix of dialogical interrogation and lyric vision—the vision, for both, being simultaneously philosophical and religious. They provide the sting of provocation but also words that move and dart and soothe, that shape a world we could inhabit while also reaching back to intimate a soul or self that's *ready* to inhabit such a world. The self we could become, and the world that we could concomitantly welcome, are saturated by moral, religious, and aesthetic energies that make demands on our subjectivity. To believe that truth is subjectivity, in Kierkegaard's famous words, is to believe that there are such demands that we are subject to, to which we are answerable. Words call on us religiously and morally to square accounts, and there's an aesthetic to the way we hear and answer those appeals. Those like Alcibiades who fell in love with Socrates felt they had to change their lives, and Kierkegaard can have a similar effect. We trace the sort of appeal his writing makes and simultaneously feel that attraction as a deep demand on our lives.[2] Socrates and Kierkegaard make *existential* demands. It might seem that we're straightforwardly challenged to take on the writer's words as our own, to appropriate them, as one says, but that's only half the story. The writer's words take *us* on, *claim* us, *challenge* us to be our next and better self, to become, as one might say, who we are. We read the text, but the text is also designed by Kierkegaard to read *us,* and in light of what it sees, call us to be anew, to be as someone new.

Kierkegaard addresses a unique individual, "his reader," but this most intimate engagement also has a wider, social relevance. Passages resonate outward from their immediate voicing with the promise of a resonance of indefinitely wide appeal—of potentially universal bearing. Although I may be a unique recipient of his intimate address, a wider community is also, equally addressed. A simple private-public contrast breaks down here, by design. There's a kind of little-noticed incipient sociality built into the structure of such intimate address.

He does not drop community to one side, as tradition often has it. He writes explicitly in *Works of Love* and *A Literary Review* of social issues in a way that brings out our reliance on others. His polemics against Christendom take on a social, institutional, and cultural target as wide as any Marxist or Nietzschean target might be. Early Frankfurt School critics, Adorno and Marcuse, and in the next generation, Habermas, assimilated much of the broad social dimension of Kierkegaard's critique. In addition, and less obviously, even the most personal writing, addressed to the reader quiet in her solitude, intimates an indefinitely expanding circle of those who can hear this personal address, and take heed. So Kierkegaard does not oppose his withering institutional critiques to his more intimate dialogical address. He harbors, so I'd argue, a utopian hope that one by one the transfiguring resonance of his address might radiate unstoppably, enacting continued couplings or communions. Perhaps this outward spread might even found a city (as Plato envisioned), or a biblical kingdom of persons of goodwill. To put it in a phrase, for Kierkegaard, community, communication, and communion arise linked in interpretations of potentially universal resonance.

Of course, the possibilities of such success rest on our capacities to hear and take to heart and are notoriously prone to failure. Our grip on a world and on the worlds of others in some ways is just another aspect of our uncertain, always provisional, grip on ourselves. Yet there's hope inherent in both Kierkegaard's and Plato's unfinished polemics and more personal intimations. Plato adumbrates an unfinished struggle with his mentor Socrates and with Athens. Kierkegaard plays out a similar struggle—with Socrates and Christ, with Copenhagen, and with himself. Kierkegaard's polemics with Church, Academy, cultural decay, and the Press are attacks on what he calls Christendom, and his dialogues and soliloquies bear against his own acknowledged tendencies to backslide.

However undeniable his literary and religious genius, some have doubted that Kierkegaard measures up specifically as a philosopher. If he's valued as a philosopher, it's often in terms of his local battle with fashionable Hegelianism. A critic of Hegelian philosophy, it's assumed, must be philosophically adept. But this tentative concession to a narrow philosophical relevance overlooks a more central and powerful philosophical center to his writing. His self-conception as a Socratic figure, evident from his early dissertation (*The Concept of Irony, with Constant Reference to Socrates*), on to his deathbed witness that his vocation had "always been Socratic," grounds his philosophical vocation at its proper depth. His legacy as a critic of Hegelian fashions pales beside his powerful legacy as the gadfly of Copenhagen and of our time.

Kierkegaard took to heart a Socrates who was much more than a rational, interrogating critic of Athenian piety. Socrates' interrogations were partly reason-based, but also, as we might say, faith-based, or based on nonintellectualized commitments. His vocation is instigated and confirmed by a temple oracle, his conduct is guided by a god or *daimon,* his last wish is to make a religious offering, his devotion to love is articulated in terms relayed by a mysterious priestess. Significantly, he does not interrogate his primary informer on the nature of love, but submits to being interrogated and corrected by Diotima—out of earshot of anyone who might dispute her account. All this sounds strangely like religious revelation, or at best, a knowledge of love acquired *through* religious-philosophical instruction and then relayed as revelation.

Kierkegaard's religious vocation is interwoven with his philosophical calling—just as Socrates' philosophical vocation is seamlessly interwoven with his religious calling. Kierkegaard could hardly fail to notice that as his life came more and more to assume a trajectory culminating in Christian martyrdom, it also came to assume the trajectory of a Socratic martyrdom.

Kierkegaard mocked a philosophy that let reason overpower the worlds of faith and moral life. He *didn't* mock philosophy in its Socratic incarnation. He assimilated the practice of Socratic interrogation and saw the religious-philosophical concerns of Socrates as a prime exemplification of the ancient view of philosophy as healing, as ministering to what Kierkegaard would call "a sickness unto death." Philosophy is not a merely academic pursuit but a therapeutic practice that employs critique both for diagnosis and as a corrective exercise. Critique removes obstacles a city or a self might maintain in an ignorant or perverse furtherance of spiritual disease. One symptom of disease, as Kierkegaard saw it, was an exorbitant indulgence in useless learning, learning that paraded theatrically and left life aside. In the voice of Anti-Climacus, he cries, "Socrates, Socrates, Socrates! What the world needs, absorbed as it is in so much learning, is a new Socrates!" Socrates could provide skeptical corrosives, but also the vision of Diotima, a witness to love as a mediator linking selves to each other and to the divine.

Early on, Kierkegaard pleads in his journal for an "idea for which he could live and die," an "idea" or inspiring model he succeeded in finding in the lives of Christ and Socrates. He would be a writer who could be true to their living and their saying, in part by depicting the many ways a person and one's city could *fail* to be thus true. Christ and Socrates, he saw, are put on trial because they put others on trial by their words. But they also tried others by their example, by how they lived their words. They let themselves be subject to their words so thoroughgoingly that they were the truth they spoke. Person and speaking became as one. The truth they lived was subjectivity. They lived subject to words, to ideals, to the ideas they spoke; they were truthful to them.

Kierkegaard chides the systematic philosophy of his day for neglecting this dimension of the human—the necessary yielding to ideals of worth, of taking up with them (and being taken by them) as a condition of finding life. He would have scorned the idea that philosophy is the endeavor to find solutions to a number of technical set-piece puzzles, say, "the problem of evil" or "the existence of God," which ought to name existential struggles. Our undergoing evil and our capacity to rejoice in creation might be linked in a particular philosophical-religious vision, but rejoicing is not the solution to an intellectual problem, any more than evil is an intellectual conundrum awaiting a theoretical solution. The question of what one can do and endure and celebrate is not a question addressed merely to our puzzle-solving or purely discursive skills. Philosophers are more than conceptual technicians.

In a marvelously subtle dialectic, Kierkegaard undermines an easy opposition between Athens and Jerusalem, between the skeptical interrogations of Socrates and a faithful wrestling with the God of Abraham, Jacob, and Isaac, or with the "offense" of Christ. An initial way to understand this dual loyalty is to imagine Socrates as disposing of false knowledge, taking away overstuffed academic and cultural pretension (including theatrical sermonizing), in order to make way for the openness of Christian faith.[3] What makes this dual loyalty possible is the fact that Christ interrogates local customs and that Socrates is a *religious* thinker concerned for the soul and informed by love who can set his own radiant example of love, courage, and devotion. This considerably narrows the opposition between Athens and Jerusalem. Socrates and Kierkegaard are *skeptical and religious*. They pair a praise of love with privileging the care of convictions integral to *a way of life*. They are suspicious of misplaced care for puzzle-solving or detached theory or stale, distracting doctrine. The living questions of love and life and death are worthy of both philosophical and religious pursuit, yet will become moribund when approached from the distant impersonality of grand theory.

Questions that are personally urgent or "existential" arise in moments of trouble. Responses to them, properly released, are modulated to the specific texture of a person's perplexity or pain. In the nature of the case, the abstract generalities of theory do not address persons as they are immersed in the concrete conditions of a specific need. Abstract theory targets a universal "everyone-hence-no-one-in-particular." Kierkegaard addresses "my dear reader." Socrates addresses individuals in their specific need, blindness, evasion, and confusion. Jesus addresses persons intimately one by one, focusing on their specific need.

Christ and Socrates begin their care of others by challenging idols of temporal or spiritual power, and providing superior objects of attraction. Socrates lets his moral-religious passion manifest as love of beauty, love as ascent toward saving truth, loyalty to friends, fearlessness in death, a conviction that the good exempts a soul from harm. This philosophical-religious vision overlaps a Christian one. Kierkegaard makes an effort in the *Postscript* to mark the dialectical differences between this Socratic and a more specifically Christian vision, but overall, he's less concerned with the gap between the Socratic and the Christian than with the gap between this pair, taken as a potentially seamless unity so far as "love on the street" is concerned, and the unconcern of Copenhagen's Christendom for anything like a philosophical-religious passion, Christian *or* Socratic.[4]

Socrates' presence as a religious thinker exerts an influence that's seamlessly attuned to a Christian calling—so intimately attuned, we might say, that in their work against Christendom, they work hand in glove. In a well-tuned couples' dance, it may make little sense to rank one partner's contribution over (or under) the other, and may make little sense to try to determine who leads and who follows. Kierkegaard was far from disinterested in impenetrable disguise. A shopkeeper can be a knight of faith, a Christian in Copenhagen might become a Socrates (Kierkegaard avows that *his* task is Socratic), and Socrates can become a Christian (Kierkegaard asserts in *Point of View* that this has happened). Seeking out differences between Socrates and Christ—creeds or doctrines or the social forms of ritual or priesthoods, say—distracts from the virtues of questioning, of reflecting, of turning over one's commitments and attunements in the solitude of inwardness, then to move out to inhabit one's life in a new way. That's a Christian task, and a Socratic one.

By all appearances, Kierkegaard never ceased Socratic questioning amidst his Christian convictions. In *The Concept of Irony,* we find Socratic intervention in Romantic ways of life; in *A Literary Review,* there's Socratic critique of "the crowd" and the press; the last pages of *Fear and Trembling* give Socrates as a model of composure before death; a conversation between the signed *Discourse* literature and the pseudonymous works has the look of a Socratic exchange.[5] Kierkegaard refuses to put Socrates outside his Christian tent. He is a filter against thoughtlessness and a paragon of those passions necessary for a fully moral and religious life.

In the last years of his writing Kierkegaard was fiercely against Christendom and against the Church, going so far as to reject, on his deathbed, its final ministrations. It's likely that in his student years his faith was in danger. And we have his striking protestation from late in his life, "I do not call myself a Christian!" even as he confessed that his task had always been Socratic. The extent to which he joined his Socratic and Christian cares is marked by his striking attestation that, despite all appearances, "[Socrates] has become a Christian!"[6] *That* transformation allowed Kierkegaard to be a Socratic who was also Christian.

Having one's reflections and life animated by both Socratic and Christian energies kept Kierkegaard honest at a proper level of existential intensity. That was his design for life: to avoid the pitfalls of merely academic exercises and to keep one's eye on the state of one's soul and on the state of our souls in congress with others. This is a Socratic-Christian allegiance to *Ethics, Love, and Faith.*

✳ ✳ ✳

This book of philosophical engagements opens new avenues of reflection not just for Kierkegaard scholars but for any concerned with ethics, love, and faith. We discover here a Kierkegaard who adopts a critical Socratic stance toward religious matters and who then shifts, like Socrates himself, to the register of poetic-religious vision. Thus Kierkegaard sidesteps a debilitating cultural "either/or" between uncritical vision and visionless critique, exhibiting what Tyler Roberts calls a "critical piety."[7] This is a critical stance that identifies decadence and even violence, and yet brings into view, as great criticism does, those things and aspects of things that call for affirmation. A critical piety toward matters of ethics, love, and faith separates the dross from the gold. No one has done more than Alastair Hannay to keep the best of Kierkegaard, and the best of Kierkegaard scholarship, alive over the past three decades through his sympathetic yet supremely intelligent and critical philosophical readings. Many of the essays included here respond to this work, and Hannay's interspersed reflections on them advance their collective impact.

The essays fall into four sets, each followed by Hannay's remarks. The first set traces Kierkegaard's themes of selfhood, personality, or character. Dreyfus and Mooney explore subjectivity, passion, personality, and the Kierkegaardian schema for selfhood. Taking a more historical approach, Kirmmse lays out the emergence of a modern view of self, the person subject to anxiety and uncertainty and to the threats of affectation and self-deception.

In the second set of essays, the theme is love, especially as Kierkegaard develops it in *Works of Love*. What do we make of a *command* to love? Are passions under our command? And what is the contrast between neighbor love (which is difficult) and loving those we're attracted to (which in comparison seems easy)? Furtak defends Kierkegaard's view that the attunements of love give a proper direction to our thinking about others and our place with them. Ferreira explores whether neighbor love must be in necessary conflict with preferential attachments of friendship and romantic love. Roberts shows that Kierkegaard's map of the ethical landscape we inhabit has little to do with fashioning a moral *theory*. Kierkegaard's discussion of Christian love is his example of philosophical reflection aimed elsewhere than theory construction.

The third set of essays contains a pair focused on Kierkegaard's themes of despair, melancholy, and depression. Marino takes *Sickness unto Death* to show the contrast between depression, a nonreligious concept, and despair, a theme that Kierkegaard develops Christianly. Cappelørn explores the subtle ways that melancholy and despair are construed in *Either/Or*. The fourth set explores tensions between the claims of faith and of philosophy, a topic we've broached above. Pattison shows that Kierkegaard's *Discourses* are a site where the critical stance of philosophy and the dogmatic stance of theology can be negotiated. Piety links the tension between faith and philosophy to Kierkegaard's method of indirection, and Conway finds that tension both buried and revealed in Kierkegaard's invention of varied narrative styles. Finally, Davenport explores the notoriously baffling account of ethics, love, and faith in Kierkegaard's masterpiece, *Fear and Trembling*. He argues that this work construes faith as eschatological trust.

Kierkegaard dares us to recognize the despair and slumber that can be our unhappy lot, so easily papered over by fashion, pride, and pretense. He hopes to maneuver us toward a view of life—and the living of it—that is at home with passion, aspiration, and full skeptical interrogation, whether these arise in ethics, faith, or love. It's not Kierkegaard's reflections alone but existence *itself* that provokes the questioning and counter-questioning and affirmations that these essays, and the accompanying reflections from Hannay, so compellingly undertake.

Part 1.
Commitment,
Personality,
and Identity

1.
Kierkegaard
on the Self

Hubert L. Dreyfus

Kierkegaard's existential thinking clearly has its roots in the *Pensées* of Blaise Pascal. Looking at the variety of cultures and religions that were becoming known at the time, Pascal concluded that human beings have no essence, but rather define themselves through their cultural practices. "Custom is our nature,"[1] he wrote. But, although the self has no nature, according to Pascal, it does have a structure. Plato already understood the self as combining two sets of factors: body and soul. On the Greek account, if both sets of factors were equally essential, the self would be in hopeless self-contradiction. It could not fulfill all its bodily, temporal needs while at the same time fulfilling its intellectual, eternal needs and so would be pulled apart by its earthly and heavenly desires.

So Plato concluded that the factors were merely *combined,* and, if one realized that only one set of factors was essential—for example, that one was an eternal soul, stuck with a temporal body and so one "died to the body"—the conflict and instability could be overcome. Thus, for the Greeks, life was a voyage from confusion to clarity and from conflict to harmony. Since the self was potentially whole and harmonious, all one had to do was to realize which factors were essential, and then live so as to satisfy one's true needs rather than one's superficial desires, and one would experience peace and fulfillment.

Pascal, however, realized that, according to Christianity, *both* sets of factors are essential, and the self is, thus, not just an unstable *combination,* but something much more upsetting, an unstable *synthesis* of two incompatible sets of factors. As Pascal put it: "What a chimera then is man! ... What a contradiction, what a prodigy! Judge of all things, imbecile worm of the earth; depositary of truth, a sink of uncertainty and error; the pride and refuse of the universe!"[2]

According to Pascal, a person's highest achievement was not to deny or overcome this contradiction—by getting rid of half the self—but to relate to one's self in such a way as to be fully alive to the tension. He noted that "we do not display greatness by going to one extreme, but in touching both extremes at once and filling all the intervening space."[3] So he held that we must take a stand on our selves in our way of life that expresses both our "greatness and our misery," avoiding both pride and despair, as Jesus did in humbly accepting that he was both God and Man. But Pascal had little to say about how we normal human beings should do this.

Søren Kierkegaard, the first person to call himself an existential thinker, took up the insights of Pascal to combat the influence of Hegel, the last philosopher to attempt to synthesize our Greek and Judeo-Christian heritage. Kierkegaard argued that Hegel did not succeed. As usual, the supposed superiority of detached reflection and the truth, universality, and eternity it allegedly revealed covered up the Christian message. So, instead of trying to understand the Judeo-Christian revelation in Greek terms, Kierkegaard highlighted the opposition. He showed that any attempt to rationalize the Christian experience resulted in claims that, to the Greeks, would have sounded absurd. According to Kierkegaard: Truth is subjectivity; the individual is higher than the universal; and eternity is only possible in time. To see why he says such outrageous things, we have to begin with Kierkegaard's elaboration of Pascal's anti-Greek definition of the self as a contradiction that has to take a stand on itself in its way of life.

Kierkegaard affirms that the self is a *synthesis* between two sets of opposed factors, not just a combination, that is, that each set is essential and requires the other. Let us now look at this claim in more detail. Here is Kierkegaard's dense definition of the self:[4]

> *Despair is a sickness of the spirit, of the self, and so can have three forms: being unconscious of the despair of having a self (inauthentic despair), desperately not wanting to be oneself, and despairingly wanting to be oneself....*
>
> The human being is spirit. But what is spirit? Spirit is the self. But what is the self? The self is a relation that relates to itself.... A human being is a synthesis of the infinite and the finite, of the temporal and the eternal, of freedom and necessity....
>
> Such a relation which relates to itself ... must either have established itself or been established by something else....
>
> The self is such a derived, constituted relation, a relation that relates to itself, and in relating to itself relates to another.... The self cannot by itself arrive at or remain in equilibrium and rest by itself, but only in relating to itself by relating to that which has established the whole relation.[5]

Ways of Futilely Attempting to Be a Self

Like all existential thinkers, Kierkegaard holds that the only test of what is the right way to live is to throw oneself into many ways of life until one discovers which way gets one out of despair. In his earlier works such as *Either/Or* Kierkegaard describes various ways of life and how they break down. In *Sickness unto Death* he lays out his conclusions, which we can summarize in schematic form as follows (see Chart 1.1):

**Illustration of Kiergekaard's
Definition of the Self**

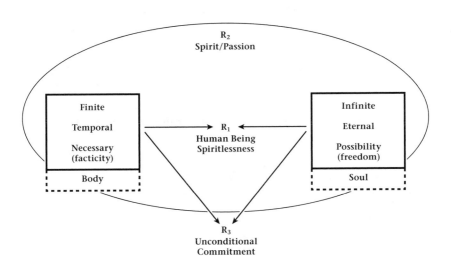

R₁—This is what Kierkegaard calls "Spiritlessness." One has a sense that the self is a contradiction that has to be faced, but one lives in what Pascal called distraction—his examples were playing tennis and sitting alone in one's room doing geometry—so that one never takes a stand in one's life as to how to get the factors together.

Kierkegaard thought that the most dangerous distraction in his time was the Public Sphere, where one could discuss events and people anonymously without ever having to take responsibility for one's views. One could debate, on the basis of principles, how the world should be run, without running the risk of testing these principles in action. This form of distraction is now consummated in talk shows, and especially chat rooms and news groups on the Internet.[6]

R_2—If a human being refuses to face the incompatible essential aspects of the self, he or she is not yet a self. To be a self, one must relate oneself to oneself in one's actions by taking a stand on both sets of factors. One must manifest that something about the self is essential by making something in one's life absolute. This existential stance can take a negative and a positive form.

Negative R_2—Kierkegaard says:

> In a relation between two things the relation is the third term in the form of a negative unity, and the two relate to the relation, and in the relation to that relation; such a relation is that between soul and body when man is regarded as soul.[7]

When the relation is a negative unity, the relation relates to itself in the Greek way: denying one of the sets of factors and acting as if only the other aspect of the self is the essential one. One can, for example, take the soul to be eternal at the expense of the body as Plato did, or do the opposite, as did Lucretius.

This would work if the self were a combination, but it is a synthesis. Thus, if one lives just for the temporal, one loses the eternal and doesn't have any continuity in his life at all, while if one tries to make the infinite and the eternal absolute, one loses the finite and the temporal. As Kierkegaard puts it, such mystical types can't bring their God-relationship to bear on a decision as to whether or not to take a walk in the park.

Positive R_2—Such selves try, by themselves, to express fully both sets of factors in their lives, but this turns out to be impossible. For example, if one makes possibility absolute and lives constantly open to new possibilities, one is in the aesthetic sphere of existence (Kierkegaard's anticipation of Nietzsche and the postmoderns) but one has no way to express the self's facticity. If one tries to make facticity absolute, one loses possibility and one is paralyzed by fatalism.[8]

Once he has worked through all the stands the self can take on itself and has shown how each leads to despair, Kierkegaard claims to have shown that "the self cannot by itself arrive at or remain in equilibrium and rest."[9] His

Christian view is that the self does not have the truth in it; it is a contradiction that does not have in itself the resources to live a stable and meaningful life. And, according to Kierkegaard, everyone who has not managed to perform the impossible task of getting his or her self together in a stable, meaningful life is in despair.

A person might well think that this is a preposterous claim, since I, at least, am not in despair. One may feel that one is having a great time enjoying all one's possibilities, or living a fulfilling life taking care of one's family, or that one's life is worth living because one is working to eliminate suffering, and so forth. In general, one may feel sure that one is fulfilling one's capacities and one's life is working out fine. Kierkegaard would say, however, that you might think you are living a life worth living, but in fact you are in despair.

What right does he have to say this? His answer is in *Sickness unto Death*:

> Despair differs dialectically from what one usually calls sickness, because it is a sickness of the spirit. And this dialectical aspect, properly understood, brings further thousands under the category of despair. If at any time a physician is convinced that so and so is in good health, and then later that person becomes ill, then the physician may well be right about his having been well at the time but now being sick. Not so with despair. Once despair appears, what is apparent is that the person was in despair. In fact, it's never possible at any time to decide anything about a person who is not saved through having been in despair. For when whatever causes a person to despair occurs, it is immediately evident that he has been in despair his whole life.[10]

Kierkegaard is pointing out that despair is not like sadness, regret, disappointment, depression, etc. Rather, unlike these downers, despair exhibits what Kierkegaard calls "the dialectic of eternity." If you are sad, you know that it is temporary. Even if something so terrible happens to you that you feel that you were happy once but that whatever has happened makes it impossible for you ever to be happy again, that is certainly misery, but it is not despair. Despair is the feeling that your life isn't working and, given the kind of person you are, it is impossible for things to work for you; that a life worth living is, in your case, literally impossible.

That means that once a person experiences despair—"it will be evidence that his [previous] success was an illusion"[11]—that is, all that person's past joys *must have been* self-deceptions. So Kierkegaard concludes that, even though you now feel that things are going well for you, you must right now be in despair and not know it. Given the contradictory nature of the self, all of us, with the exception of those who have faced despair and been healed, must right now be in despair.[12]

The Self in Equilibrium and Out of Despair

Only when the self "in relating to itself relates to something else,"[13] Kierkegaard contends, can it get the two sets of factors into a positive relation. Only then is each set of factors defined in such a way as to support rather than be in conflict with the other. But how is this possible?

Whether you can get the factors together or whether they form a contradiction depends on how you define them. Or, to put it another way, the Greeks found that, if you define the factors from the point of view of detachment, you can't get them together. Kierkegaard tries to show that only if you define the factors in terms of a total involvement that gives you your identity as an individual can you arrive at a positive synthesis.

To illustrate what is at stake in having an identity, Kierkegaard draws on the Chivalric Romances. The example, on which he says "everything turns," is the case of "A young lad [who] falls in love with a princess, [so that] the whole content of his life lies in this love."[14] And Kierkegaard adds in a footnote that "any other interest whatever in which an individual concentrates the whole of life's reality"[15] would do as well.

Kierkegaard had been looking for just this sort of unconditional commitment. When he was twenty-two years old he wrote in his journal: "What I really lack is to be clear in my mind *what I am to do,* not what I am to know. . . . The thing is to understand myself, to see what God really wishes *me* to do; the thing is to find a *truth* which is true *for me, . . . for which I can live and die.*"[16] As he put it in his *Concluding Unscientific Postscript,* "Truth is subjectivity."[17]

The lad who loves the princess relates himself to himself by way of his relation to the princess. Thanks to it, he knows who he is and what is relevant and important in his world. Any such unconditional commitment to some specific individual, cause, or vocation, whereby a person gets an identity and a sense of reality, would do to make the point Kierkegaard is trying to make. In such a case, a person becomes an individual defined by his or her relation to the object of his or her unconditional commitment. The lad is the lover of the princess, Martin Luther King, Jr., is the one who will bring justice to the American blacks, Steve Jobs identifies himself with Apple Inc., etc.

According to Kierkegaard, if and only if you let yourself be drawn into a defining commitment, can you achieve that which, while you were in despair, looked impossible, viz., that the two sets of factors reinforce each other, so that the more you manifest one the more you manifest the other. By responding to the call of such an unconditional commitment and thereby getting an identity, a person becomes what Kierkegaard, following the Bible, calls "a new creation."[18]

The Necessary and the Possible

We have seen that, when you have a defining commitment, your identity becomes as necessary as a definition. But, although your identity is fixed, it does not dictate an inflexible way of acting as if it were a rigid compulsion, infatuation, or obsession. That would not be an expression of freedom. Kierkegaard calls anyone who can sustain the risk of an unconditional commitment and let themselves be more and more involved a "Knight of Faith." Kierkegaard says the Knight is free to "forget the whole thing," but in so doing the Knight would "contradict himself," since it is "a contradiction to forget the whole of one's life content and still be the same."[19]

In anything less than total loss and subsequent world collapse, one has to be able to adapt to even the most radical changes in the defining object. All such adaptive changes will, of course, be changes *in* the world but not changes *of* the world. Kierkegaard calls this "freedom" because, even though the central concern in one's life is fixed, one is free to adapt to all sorts of possible situations in all sorts of ways.

There is, however, an even more radical kind of freedom: the freedom to change one's world, that is, to change one's identity. To be born again *and again*. Although Kierkegaard does not say so in so many words, once we see that eternity can begin in time, we can see that, not only can eternity *begin* at a moment of time (the *Augenblick*), eternity can *change* in time. In Kierkegaard's terms, Abraham has faith that if he sacrifices Isaac "God could give him a new Isaac."[20] This can happen because God is "that everything is possible"[21] and that means even the inconceivable is possible. On Kierkegaard's view, one can change worlds only by being totally involved in one, deepening one's commitment, taking all the risks involved, until it breaks down and becomes impossible. As in Thomas Kuhn's *Structure of Scientific Revolutions*, revolutions depend on prior unconditional commitment to a paradigm.[22]

Kierkegaard concludes from his examination of all types of despairing ways of trying to relate the factors that the only sphere of existence that can give equal weight to both sets of factors is a religion based on an infinite passion for something finite. Kierkegaard claims that Christianity is such a paradoxical religion: "The paradoxical edification [of Christianity] corresponds . . . to the determination of God in time as the individual man. If such be the case, the individual is related to something outside himself."[23]

But, given the logic of Kierkegaard's position, it follows that the object of such a defining relation does not have to be the God-man. Indeed, in the *Postscript* Kierkegaard says, "Subjectively reflection is directed to the question whether the individual is related to something *in such a manner* that his relationship is in truth a God relationship."[24] And even more clearly that "it is the passion of the infinite that is the decisive factor and not its content, for its content is precisely itself."[25]

The Temporal and the Eternal

For one to live fully in time, some moment must be absolutely important and make other moments significant relative to it. The moment when one is transformed by getting an identity is obviously such a moment. Kierkegaard, drawing on the biblical saying that we shall be changed in the twinkling of an eye, calls this moment the *Augenblick* (*Øieblikket*). After the transformation, other moments also become significant since one's unconditional commitment must be expressed in one's day-to-day activity.

But the eternal is also expressed in one's life. Not the disinterested, abstract eternity of Plato, but the passionately involved eternity that Kierkegaard calls "eternity in time." Normally, the significance of events in one's life is subject to retroactive reinterpretation,[26] but, in an unconditional commitment that defines the self, one's identity is as eternal as a definition. The lad, who is a Knight of Faith, will henceforth always be the lover of the princess. Further events will be interpreted in the light of the content given the self in the *Augenblick*, not vice versa.

The way a commitment can produce a privileged moment is not something that can be understood by disinterested thought. Kierkegaard says: "A concrete eternity within the existing individual is the maximum degree of passion. . . . The proposition inaccessible to thought is that one can become eternal although one was not such."[27] That is, if you are unconditionally committed to a particular person or cause, that will be your identity forever (for every moment of your life). The paradoxical fact is that "only in existing do I become eternal."[28] But this does not make me any less temporal. "The existing individual *in time* . . . comes into relation with the eternal *in time*."[29]

The Finite and the Infinite

Kierkegaard calls an unconditional commitment an infinite passion for something finite. But just what makes an infinite passion count as infinite? It can't be just a very strong feeling; rather, it must in some sense transcend the finite. For Kierkegaard, an infinite passion can legitimately be called *infinite* because it opens up a *world*. Not only *what actually exists* gets its meaning from its connection with my defining passion; anything that could *possibly* come into my experience would get its meaning for me from my defining commitment. As we saw earlier, according to Kierkegaard, one's commitment defines one's reality.

Of course, the object of my infinite passion is something *finite*. We are interested in the smallest particularities of our beloved. But any such finite being is vulnerable, and yet the meaning of one's life depends on it. This makes a defining commitment very risky. It would certainly be safer to define one's life in terms of some sort of theoretical quest or in terms of some abstract idea—say, the eventual triumph of the proletariat—but that is not concrete enough to satisfy the need to make the finite absolutely significant. So it follows, as Kierkegaard says, "without risk there is no faith."[30]

Kierkegaard holds that, given the risk, to let yourself be more and more involved with something finite, you need to live in a kind of absurdity. As he puts it: "Every moment to see the sword hanging over the loved one's head and yet find, not repose in the pain of resignation, but joy on the strength of the absurd—that is wonderful. The one who does that, he is great, the only great one."[31] Such an individual, whom Kierkegaard calls a Knight of Faith, can do this because he lives in the assurance that "God is the fact that everything is possible, and that everything is possible is God."[32]

In sum, when you have a defining commitment, the finite object of your commitment is infinitely important, that is, the object of your passion is both something particular and world-defining as well. Indeed, it is the condition for anything showing up as meaningful. But since such a finite commitment is always risky, and so security is impossible, one can sustain one's infinite passion only if one has faith that even the impossible is possible.

The Teleological Suspension of the Ethical

Now we can see why Kierkegaard claims that, unless the self relates itself to "something else" with a total commitment, it is in despair, but that, if it has an absolute commitment, it will be able to get the two sets of factors together in such a way that they reinforce each other, and so be in bliss. But the idea that making an unconditional commitment is the highest thing a human being can do raises a serious problem.

Abraham had an unconditional commitment to some absolute we can call God, and his absolute commitment to that absolute required that he kill his son, Isaac. His anguish is not simply that he loves his son; it's that, if he kills Isaac, he would be putting himself as an individual with his own relation to the absolute above the ethical. But ethical principles are universal: that is, they are binding on everyone everywhere, and they require that no one make an exception of him- or herself. Still, according to Kierkegaard, the fact that Jews and Christians consider Abraham the father of the faith shows that the Judeo-Christian tradition has, from the start, implicitly held that the individual is higher than the universal.

The ethical is absolutely important because it allows us to make sense of what we do. Only if we all share a public moral vocabulary that tells us what is right and what is wrong, worthy and unworthy, can we justify our actions to ourselves and to others. Nowadays, however, we no longer believe with Socrates, Plato, and Kant that there is just one rational shared moral vocabulary. Kierkegaard understands and accepts this. "Universal" need not mean for everyone for all times, but it can mean whatever standards are accepted by whatever group we respect. In any case, a shared morality is essential for us to recognize and resist our selfish impulses while taking on our social responsibilities, and explaining our actions to others and ourselves.

Kierkegaard contends that one has to get over what he calls "so-called subjectivity"—one's superstitions, obsessions, compulsions, prejudices, and the like—and he agrees with Socrates that critical thinking and a respect for the ethical enables one to do this. Kierkegaard is, thus, the first and last existential philosopher to see something worth saving in the philosophical tradition of critical rationality. Recent existential thinkers such as Heidegger and Sartre hold that the ethical is just the voice of conformism. Kierkegaard, on the contrary, holds that being ethical, while not our highest end or *telos,* nonetheless enables people to get over being blinded and driven by their accidental particularity and so enables them to make commitments that give coherence and meaning to their lives. Kierkegaard thus is able to appreciate one of the principal achievements of Greek philosophy and, in this case, have the best of both worlds.

But in the end the Greek and Judeo-Christian worlds collide. Philosophers have always held that to leave the universal and act as a particular is selfish and immoral. Kierkegaard agrees that people have always been tempted to make an exception of themselves, but he points out that philosophers can't distinguish such unethical acts from the unconditional commitments of the faithful like Abraham: "Faith's paradox is this, that the single individual is higher than the universal, that the single individual . . . determines his relation to the universal through this relation to the absolute, not his relation to the absolute through his relation to the universal."[33]

In short, our philosophical categories have no way to distinguish unconditional commitment from selfishness. And, indeed, from the ethical point of view, in the shared public language in which we understand ourselves and others, Abraham is a criminal. If he tries to *understand* what he is doing as he gets ready to kill Isaac, he can only say to himself that he is a murderer. Yet, paradoxically, he feels he is doing his highest duty.

Criteria for Judging the Worth of Ways of Acting

Philosophers would say so much the worse for faith since it seems that someone going against the ethical like Abraham might well be driven by a compulsion like the child molester in Fritz Lang's *M,* or be tempted to kill their son by insanity brought on by too much cortisone and reading too much Kierkegaard as is the character played by James Mason in *Bigger than Life* (Nicholas Ray, 1956), or be just plain crazy like Jack Nicholson in Stanley Kubrick's *The Shin-*

ing (1980). Or, in real life, a dangerous psychopath like Charles Manson, or a fanatic like Hitler. How can one tell such dangerous criminals from Knights of Faith suspending the ethical? Granted that there can't be any public criteria for recognizing a Knight of Faith, Kierkegaard suggests that there nonetheless *are* criteria for "distinguishing the paradox from a temptation."[34]

There are at least three negative "criteria" and one positive one.[35]

(1) Knights of Faith can't be driven to their action like Peter Lore in *M*, who claims convincingly that he abhors killing children but that he can't help himself; they must be free. Remember, Kierkegaard says, "Abraham can refrain at any moment, he can repent the whole thing as a temptation."[36]

(2) Knights of Faith must respect the ethical. They must have subjected their impulses to critical reflection. In Kierkegaard's colorful terms, the Knight of Faith is not a "vagrant genius."[37] He can't just say, "I'm a superior person, and so I don't have to respect the ethical" as does Raskolnikov in Dostoyevsky's *Crime and Punishment,* or Charles Manson, as described in Vincent Bugliosi's *Helter Skelter.* The same would apply to Hitler if he took himself to be a charismatic leader above the ethical.

(3) But Knights of Faith can't justify themselves on the basis of some new universal principle either. This rules out people who invent their own ethical. Kierkegaard says, "The true Knight of Faith is always [in] isolation; the false knight is sectarian."[38] Hitler would again be disqualified if he justified genocide by arguing that science showed that Jews were subhuman.

One positive criterion follows from all the above. Individuals who respect the ethical and yet feel that their unconditioned commitment requires them freely to go against it feel, paradoxically, that what they are doing is the most despicable thing they could possibly do yet also the best thing they have ever done. From an everyday ethical point of view all suspenders of the ethical are crazy. As Kierkegaard says: "[Abraham] knows that higher up there winds a lonely path, narrow and steep; he knows it is terrible to be born in solitude outside the universal, to walk without meeting a single traveler. . . . Humanly speaking he is insane and cannot make himself understood to anyone."[39] The result, Kierkegaard says, is a "constant tension."[40] Indeed, where Knights of Faith are concerned, "distress and anguish are the only justification conceivable."[41]

To see that this dramatic talk of the anguish of suspending the ethical is not just psychological science fiction, we need an example. Consider a homosexual "lad" in Denmark in 1850 who loved a "prince" rather than a "princess." The ethical at that time would consider this defining commitment terribly immoral. And so would the lover himself. Given the ethics of the time, he could only think of his love as perverted, unnatural, depraved, and disgusting. For him the ethical would be a temptation for, if he does not go straight, he would have to live with the anguished and paradoxical sense that his love is the best thing he ever did, while being at the same time the worst.

Kierkegaard was the first to see that we in the West live in a conflicted culture permeated by two contradictory understandings of the world and of who we are. The Greeks disclosed the universal ethical, and we respect it as our highest goal because it enables us to make sense of our lives. But the Judeo-Christian experience opened up the possibility of a calling that required that an individual go against the ethical. We can't give up the ethical and still *make sense* of what we are doing, but we can't give up our unconditional commitment and still have a *fully meaningful life*. These two demands are absolutely opposed. This situation is not to be deplored, however. Only a conflicted culture like ours, that respects the ethical and yet believes that people can be transformed into individuals, can be truly historical, that is, can radically change its understanding of what it means to be a human being.

Conclusion

Now we can see why Kierkegaard claims that, unless the self relates itself to something else with an unconditional commitment, it is in despair. Only if it has an unconditional commitment will the self be able to get the two sets of factors together in such a way that they will reinforce each other, and so be in bliss. Kierkegaard says rather obscurely: "This is the formula that describes the state of the self when despair is completely eradicated: in relating to itself and in wanting to be itself, the self is grounded transparently in the power that established it."[42]

Grounded transparently means acting in such a way that what gives you your identity comes through in everything you do. But what is the power (lowercase) that established the self? I used to think it was whatever finite and temporal object of infinite passion created you as a new being by giving you your identity. But that would only be the power that established your identity, not the power that established the three sets of contradictory factors to which your identity is the solution. What, then, is the power that established the whole relation?

The "power" doesn't seem to be an ontotheological God since the word is in lowercase and Kierkegaard doesn't say that the power *created* the relation. But Kierkegaard does say that one could not despair "unless the synthesis were originally in the right relationship from the hand of God."[43] How are we to cash out this metaphor, especially if we remember that "God is the fact that everything is possible"—not an entity at all.

I think we have to say that "the fact that everything is possible" makes possible, indeed is incarnate in, the contradictory God-man. He is the paradoxical Paradigm who saves from despair all sinners—those who have tried to take a stand on themselves by themselves, either by relating only to themselves or by relating to an infinite, absolute, and eternal God (Religiousness A). The God-man saves them by calling them to make an unconditional commitment to Himself—"God in time as an individual human being."[44]

The claim that God *established* the factors has to mean, then, that by making it possible for people to have a defining commitment—in the first instance to Him—and so be reborn, Jesus revealed that both sets of factors are equally essential and can (and must) be brought into equilibrium. This is the truth about the essential nature of the self that went undiscovered until Jesus revealed it. In this way he established the Christian understanding of the self, in which we now live. His is the call that demands "the decision . . . in existence"[45] that we cannot reject without despair.

So, on this reading, "to be grounded transparently in the power that established it" would mean that the saved Christian, first, relates himself to himself by manifesting in all aspects of his life that both sets of factors are essential—by, that is, relating to someone or something finite with an infinite passion and so becoming eternal in time. Whatever constituted the self as the individual self by giving it its identity, thereby making it "a new being" and healing it of despair—that "something" would be its Savior. And, second, all such lives are grounded in Jesus, the God-man, the paradigm—the power who first made radical transformation of the person and of the world possible.

2.
Affectation, or the Invention of the Self: A Modern Disorder

Bruce G. Kirmmse

Introduction: Affectation Is Part of Modernity

"Despite the fact that I certainly see in it the expression of significant intellectual strengths, I nevertheless cannot deny that it makes a generally unpleasant impression on me, particularly because of two things, both of which I detest: verbosity and affectation."[1] This was the judgment uttered by Hans Christian Ørsted, then Rector of the University of Copenhagen, on Kierkegaard's dissertation *On the Concept of Irony.*

Anyone who has read much Kierkegaard is certainly well acquainted with his "verbosity," which was both his besetting sin and an indispensable part of his style. But what was Kierkegaard's relationship to "affectation?"

The problem of affectation was in the air, so to speak. During the opening decades of the nineteenth century it was a hot topic for investigation. Affectation meant falsity, a dissimulation in which one simultaneously deceives both others and oneself by putting on a merely *assumed* self. Affectation, the assumption of a "false" self, is a peculiarly *modern* concept, and preoccupation with the dangers of affectation reveals a fear of something that became possible only after the breakup of traditional, late-medieval society in which individual roles had come preassigned, a society in which there was, as it were, no "self." The self—which is in fact the invention of the self—had yet to be invented. Those societies which modernized[2] first were the earliest to experience the fear of affectation. In the Italian Renaissance, the breakdown of the medieval "Great Chain of Being," in which every existing thing had a preordained place and role, was noted by Pico [Giovanni Pico della Mirandola, 1463–1494], who celebrated man as "a creature of indeterminate nature . . . as though the maker and molder of thyself."[3] And already at this early date, Pico left the door of human autonomy ajar and susceptible of dual interpretation when he wrote, a propos of the human race: "Who would not admire this our chameleon?"[4] In Elizabethan times, just a few decades after Pico, "affectation" first made its way into the English language, first as a verb: to "affect" or "affectate" the appearance of something one is not. The fear of affectation became more widespread in the seventeenth century, notably in France, where fear (and ridicule) of affectation became a principal theme in Molière's dramas depicting the bourgeois pretention of being a *gentilhomme*. Preoccupation with (and fear of) affectation can be found in Danish letters as early as the comedies of Holberg, who is often called the Danish Molière. In any event, by the mid-eighteenth century the problems and perils presented by the possibility of putting on a new self were widely acknowledged in the European world. At first, of course, the peculiar freedom to "affect" a self was open only to those inhabiting the uppermost echelons of the bourgeoisie.

Eighteenth-century Europe was a society of estates, albeit one that was rapidly unraveling. By the early nineteeenth century, with the cumulative effect of the growing market economy, the Enlightenment, the French Revolution, and the wars of Napoleon (who was widely, if misleadingly, portrayed as a social upstart, a Corsican corporal), the entire sympathetic/antipathetic problem-complex around "affectation" became an obsession.[5] In a way, the modern novel itself— that is, the French novel—precisely because it was something "novel," can be said to be *about* affectation and the search for the will-o'-the-wisp called authenticity. This certainly is the principal theme for the two greatest French novelists of the nineteenth (and any other) century, for what else are the characters of Julien Sorel (in Stendhal's *Le Rouge et le Noir*), Madame Bovary (in Flaubert's novel of the same name), and Frédéric Moreau (in Flaubert's *L'Éducation sentimentale*) but extended meditations on affectation and the (im)possibility of escaping from it? Indeed, in his novel *Le Rouge et le Noir,* which significantly bears the subtitle "*Chronique du XIXe siècle*," Stendhal's hero Julien Sorel finally finds rest (and as Sorel puts it "rest is the right word" for it)[6] by refusing to seek clemency and going quite cheerfully to his execution, where, finally, "everything took place simply and properly, without the slightest affectation on his part."[7] Similar literary phenomena characterized the rest of the nineteenth century and on into the twentieth. Like a comet, the plasticity of the sympathetic/antipathetic feelings that constituted the affectation-complex pushed ahead of itself an entire nebula of "dandies," ranging from the prototypical Johnny Walker/*New Yorker* figure Beau Brummell,[8] to Baudelaire (who made dandyism into one of his major theoretical categories), to our own Boy George, Elton John, and Madonna. Parallel with its negative twin, the phenomenon of the dandy, the obsession with avoiding affectation and cultivating authenticity—with "being oneself"—runs right through the nineteenth century: think of Whitman's self-obsession and Nietzsche's sibyllic prescription for the avoidance of affectation, "Become what you are." And by the early twentieth century, we were all invited to join Joyce amid the deafening clangor of the "smithy" of his soul—and our own.

Poul Martin Møller: Kierkegaard's Guide to Affectation

As we will see, Søren Kierkegaard was no stranger to the problem-complex represented by affectation. Among other things, he had been introduced to it in quite detailed fashion by the one teacher who, for him, towered above all others, Poul Martin Møller (1794–1838), whose posthumously published works contain the very interesting preparatory materials for an extended (though never completed) essay, "On Affectation." In his late twenties, disappointed in love and at loose ends, Møller signed on as a ship's chaplain on a Danish merchant vessel bound for China and other points in the Far East. During his two-year voyage (1819–1821) Møller began composing a series of aphorisms or "random thoughts" (*Strøtanker*), a custom he retained after his return to Denmark and until shortly before his untimely death at the age of forty-three. Early on, Møller had conceived a serious interest in Hegel's philosophy, but, as reflected by his penchant for short articles, reviews, discursive essays, aphorisms, drafts, and fragments, Møller was neither professionally not temperamentally suited to do systematic philosophy, and he ultimately joined the ranks of the Danish philosophers—including Frederik Sibbern, one of Kierkegaard's other principal teachers; Rasmus Nielsen, who for a period was regarded as Kierkegaard's principal disciple; H. L. Martensen, Kierkegaard's former tutor who became his prime ecclesiastical target; A. P. Adler, an interesting psychological-theological case who provided much grist for Kierkegaard's mill; and Kierkegaard himself—who can be said to have passed through a Hegelian "phase."

One of the recurrent themes in Møller's aphorisms was the problem of *affectation,* and in 1837 Møller began to compose his essay "On Affectation," in part by gathering together the various aphorisms on the subject that had appeared in his three collections of aphorisms, in part by writing what appears to be a general introduction to the entire topic. The essay was never finished, but the draft as it stands takes up twenty-six pages of Møller's *Posthumous Papers*[9] and gives a reasonably coherent idea of Møller's thoughts on the subject.

Toward the beginning of "On Affectation" Møller indicates that his purpose is "to review affectation as it appears most commonly, both in human life generally and *especially in these times.*"[10] Thus, like Stendhal and others during the period, Møller was particularly interested in affectation as a *modern* phenomenon. As he puts it later in the essay, "In the state of nature, everyone lived separate from others, and since he was not disturbed by many people, he developed an obstinate personality. Nowadays, by means of abstraction, people form a universally valid self, a social ideal without edges, an ideal without individuality."[11] Thus, according to Møller, affectation is of particular interest "in these times," and the danger that affectation presents "*nowadays*" is that individuals will round themselves off into sociable ciphers.

Before investigating the specific form of falsity constituted by affectation, Møller sets forth his notion of the various gradations of "truth," that is, "personal truth."[12] At the lowest level, a person who "unfeignedly follows his natural desires" has what Møller calls "a kind of truth." The next-highest level is occupied by the sort of person who has "attained virtue (in the sense of the term employed by antiquity), so that even while still taking the content of his actions from his natural instincts, he has nonetheless achieved sufficient mastery over them to observe a certain moderation in satisfying them." Finally, Møller attributes "a still higher level of personal truth" to the life of the person "who determines all his intentions by means of pure rational autonomy."[13]

Next, Møller provides his definition of affectation:

> To the extent, then, that the human being's pure self-definition is the will that has been sanctified by religiosity, it will act in complete harmony with the entire world of Reason. It is what it is and cannot attain any higher truth. But this truth is nothing other than morality, and all deviation from it is immorality. Affectation is certainly one sort of this untruth, but we must define more precisely the position it occupies in the larger scheme.
>
> To the extent that a human being has affectation in its life, it does not define itself with complete moral freedom; its actions do not originate from its true self, which is its free, moral will. The will is determined by one or another merely natural aim, which induces it to present itself as an alien person or to take on a false role, not the role assigned to it by life.
>
> Thus, first of all, the essence of affectation is that it is a falsehood. But not every falsehood is affectation. Someone who is clearly conscious of lying or dissembling takes upon himself the guilt of lying and dissembling, [but] in so doing does not manifest any affectation. In saying this, we by no means say that affectation is any lesser a vice than clearly conscious dissimulation. In what follows, it will become clear that while one degree of affectation presupposes less immorality than does calculated dissimulation, another degree of it displays a greater degree of immorality. Affectation is thus not unalloyed falsehood; rather, it always contains an element of self-deception, for it is a part of the very concept of affectation that a person is striving to be what he cannot be. But he cannot strive in this way without for at least a moment imagining that he can be it. Yet by the same token, it is equally impossible to label as affectation an absolutely unintentional self-deception which is totally devoid of falsehood. Thus the two component parts mentioned here—falsehood and self-deception—are always found in connection with [affectation].[14]

Møller then proceeds to a tripartite examination of "the degrees of affectation according to their greater or lesser connection to a subject's [i.e., a human person's] *character*."[15] The lowest and least serious degree of affectation is what Møller labels "*momentary affectation*," a generally harmless and typically youthful sort of affectation in which a person identifies himself or herself too completely with someone with whom he or she wishes to be in agreement, even though they in fact are not in agreement. This momentary affectation is a lesser offense than the genuine lie, and it is often a learning experience for the person involved, who will in the future be on guard against elements that "are not part of his or her being."[16]

Møller appends an interesting aside to his description of this most innocent form of affectation. So far is this youthful, "momentary" sort of affectation from being truly harmful, that a person who has never experienced it, a person who, from the very beginning of his development, has never been the least bit affected, even in the innocent manner of wanting to be in complete agreement with a friend, may certainly

> by nature possess a very uniquely pronounced individual personality. But it is another question whether this person thus possesses the most fortunate sort of nature. His talent for preserving his individuality unadulterated and free of extraneous ingredients could also be rooted in an egoistic tendency to encapsulate himself solely within the sphere of his own thoughts and in a lack of ability to open his mind to outside influences. The person who, in his interactions with others, is incapable of giving himself to them in such a way that he for a moment becomes one with them, entirely abandoning himself and losing himself in a different sphere of consciousness—such a person is certainly able to use his reserve in such a manner as to preserve himself from being overwhelmed by any intellectual-spiritual [aandelig] power; but the individuality that can only be rescued in that manner always becomes one-sided and impoverished. Like physical growth, intellectual-spiritual [aande-lig] completeness can only be promoted when the individual regularly merges itself into something other than itself, apparently sacrificing itself, in order to return home to itself, enriched.[17]

Thus Møller does not utterly reject every sort of affectation. Far from it. Indeed, at one point he even notes aphoristically that "Some self-deception is necessary, for it constitutes life."[18] And at another point—again, apparently referring to this first, mild form of affectation—Møller notes that "as odd as it might sound at first blush, dread of affectation can be pushed so far that it results in an abnormal mental state. This dread calls forth a misunderstood clinging to one's abstract identity with oneself."[19]

After discussing the relatively harmless, "momentary" form of affectation, Møller turns to its second, more intense form, "permanent affectation":

> A higher degree of affectation is present in the person who has made a habit of a particular sort of false statement because he imagines that he has certain opinions, interests, or proclivities because, for one or another extraneous reason, he *wishes* to them. . . . Here, the possibility of self-deception depends on the logical consistency with which the assumed role is pursued, but the center which supports this universe of appearances is extraneous to the subject himself. In moral respects, this second degree of affectation is not a whit less culpable than the fully conscious lie or dissimulation, for the reason it is not brought to full consciousness is merely that the person concerned does

not *want* to bring it to consciousness. Attention is directed to this because an entirely incorrect notion concerning this has become current: Many people believe that self-deception contains its own sufficient justification, or at least an excuse—even for outright wickedness. The erroneousness of this view becomes obvious when it is pursued to some of its unavoidable consequences. For according to this view it would of course follow that a person would be able to push his falsehood so far that it became honesty, and that a person who lies for so long that he himself comes to believe his own made-up stories would become a better person when he reached that level, because his lies had been changed into self-deceptions. . . . In this second degree of affectation, a person incorporates within himself a false element and distorts his personality so that the personality's utterances are not connected with its real self. To the extent that it thus has a double interior—one that is real, which is repressed, and one that is apparent, which is supposed to be accepted by itself and by others—with respect to the latter, in the end, the personality leads only a sham life.[20]

Møller then proceeds to describe *"changeable affectation,"* which is "the third and worst degree of affectation":

This is when a human being's character does not possess one or another pretended trait, when he has not habituated himself to one particular sort of affectation, but is skilled in affectation generally, so that affectation takes one specific form after another. In accordance with its greater or lesser degree of development, this wickedness approaches a greater or lesser degree of total untruthfulness in one's personal life. If a person could reach the culmination point [of this sort of affectation], there would be no abiding center to his thinking or willing, but at every instant of his life he would be forming a temporary personality, only to abolish it at the next instant. Most of these people would probably be like the sorts of animals who change their colors according to their surrounding, and thus be the passive products of their situations. But since this is only one of affectation's forms, its course could not be calculated in accordance with the simple rule that it would resemble its surroundings—because affectation can also manifest itself in an attempt to depict the peculiar, the unusual. No one can push things to the point of such a total lie in his inner life, but if someone could, it would be moral suicide, by which he would have utterly annihilated himself as an integral figure in the moral world.[21]

In an aphoristic remark a few pages later, Møller appears to give us another glimpse of this utterly demonic, borderline type of affected person: "The people who are utterly disintegrated, whose lives are nothing but mimicry, sometimes have so rich a nature that they could portray an assumed character with such power that the individuals who actually possess this character could scarcely carry it off more powerfully."[22] Similarly, at another point Møller sings the praises of the human personality, when it is realized "in accordance with its idea"—but then he again raises the specter of the most terrifying possibility of all, utter perdition, the person who has *become* his affectation:

Every personality, when it is realized in accordance with its idea, is something infinitely glorious. But on the other hand when someone lets it [the personality] get overwhelmed by extraneous considerations, one falls short of one's destiny. What is perhaps even more dangerous to morality than the conscious lie is untruth mixed with self-deception, whereby a human being amalgamates the false self with the real. If one seriously intends to do so, one can put aside a fully conscious lie, but one can grow into a false self and become unable to wrest oneself free. One transforms oneself into a moral changeling.[23]

Møller even produces a couple of aphoristic remarks on affectation that almost seem as if they could have been directed at Kierkegaard himself, though of course they were not. (Yet perhaps we should remember Møller's insistence that affectation was particularly characteristic of "these times"—and as Kierkegaard himself well knew, he was in this respect, as in so many others, a child of his times.) Here, in any event, is Møller on affectation: "It is a perennially recurrent affectation to conceal one's diligence at one's work";[24] and "Affectation can arise from one's imagining that one is working for an idea, thereby *gaining for oneself greater self-esteem*."[25]

Intermezzo

The problem of affectation is thus not a simple one. It is not simply the question of avoiding inauthenticity and choosing authenticity. As we have seen, Møller insisted that *some* degree of affectation was not only normal, but *necessary*. Indeed, the inability to become someone else for a while—"the incapacity of giving oneself to other people in such a way that one for a moment becomes one with them, entirely abandoning oneself and losing oneself in a different sphere of consciousness"—may be "rooted in an egoistic tendency to encapsulate oneself solely within the sphere of one's own thoughts." And as we have also seen, Møller amplifies this point by emphasizing that the "dread of affectation can be pushed so far that it results in an abnormal mental state," namely, "a misunderstood clinging to one's abstract identity with oneself." Thus, while affectation is both the sign and the curse of the times, "some self-deception is necessary, for it constitutes life," and the phobic avoidance of affectation can itself summon up the very dangerous condition of *solipsistic encapsulation*.

The problem of affectation *is* a problem because modernity seems to require that we choose who we are. The choice cannot be avoided, but how does one choose one's "real" self? How does one even *recognize* one's "real" self? What if the very conditions of "choice" make *any* decision a form of "affectation?" This is the form in which the dilemma was faced by the nineteenth century, the century in which the fascination with affectation was democratized so that it addressed itself to a much broader public than the Molièrian pantaloon- and knee-breeches-wearing bourgeois elites of earlier times. This was the form in which the affectation dilemma confronted Søren Kierkegaard and many others of his time.

In sum, what must be borne in mind is that the problem of affectation—of pretending to someone you are not—is real because it is part of a larger and equally real development that had been under way since the Renaissance (when it became a problem for the very few) to the early nineteenth century (when it became a problem for the many). This development meant the replacement of a recognition system based on social and genealogical identity with one based on *self*-identity. And by Kierkegaard's time the problem of being one's "real" self had become the problem of *recognizing* one's own real self when one sees it.

Søren Kierkegaard's Battle with Affectation

It is not irrelevant that Kierkegaard's father, Michael Pedersen Kierkegaard (1756–1838), a somewhat out-of-place member of the Copenhagen mercantile patriciate, was in fact a jumped-up shepherd boy from Jutland. Michael Pedersen Kierkegaard was the first in his family to *choose* his children's full names. Up to the generation of Michael Pedersen Kierkegaard's grandfather, Christen Jespersen (ca. 1676–1749), peasants simply had their given names and their patronymic. Christen Jespersen (Christen, the son of Jesper) had two sons, Peder and Anders, both of them "Christensens," that is, sons of Christen, just as Christen had been the son of Jesper. But Christen Jespersen's sons were to have different "last" names because of their differing inheritances. *Peder* Christensen had inherited the larger farm, a farm originally owned by (or leased from) the church, hence a "Kierkegaard." *Anders* Christensen had inherited a smaller, fenced-in portion of land, a "Gade." These geographical terms became for the first time part of a *name*, a family designation that would henceforth be an inheritable marker of identity. Kierkegaard's grandfather, Peder Christensen Kierkegaard, thus jettisoned this vestige of the faceless patronymic churning that constituted the medieval naming system. "First" (or "Christian") names had long been the prerogative of parents to choose for their children, and by the innovation of his father's generation, Michael Pedersen and his children also had a "last" name, namely, "Kierkegaard" (though at some point this had been modified from "Kirkegaard" to the more distinctive spelling "Kierkegaard"). But now, with Michael Pedersen Kierkegaard's generation, the patronymic itself (all those "-sen" and "-datter" middle names) was to go. Søren ought to have been Søren Michaelsen Kierkegaard, but No, the modern, urban preoccupation with *choosing* identity induced Søren's parents to chose a modern-style middle name, "Aabye," after a distant relative and business connection. Thus, during the generations immediately preceding Søren's birth, the Kierkegaard family was literally making a name for itself.

There can be no question that Kierkegaard had a lifelong involvement with the problem of affectation. We have seen that in the early nineteenth century affectation was very much on the agenda. As noted, Kierkegaard was close to Poul Martin Møller, who seems to have served not only as a teacher but also as a mentor. In his recollections of Kierkegaard, Hans Brøchner tells us that Kierkegaard "often mentioned Poul Møller and always with the most profound devotion."[26] And in a journal entry entitled "The Extraordinary," which dates from near the end of his life, Kierkegaard mentions the signal importance to him of an admonition from Møller: "I recall the words of the dying Poul Møller, which he often related to me while he lived, and which, if my memory is not mistaken . . . , he enjoined Sibbern to repeat to me again and again: 'You are so polemical through and through, that it is quite frightful.' Oh, despite having been so polemical through and through, even in my youth: Christianity is still almost too polemical for me."[27] Despite a paucity of direct testimony, Kierkegaard appears to have discussed a number of important matters with Møller; this is attested to in Kierkegaard's journals,[28] where he alludes to an "interesting discussion" with Møller that took place on June 30, 1837, apparently regarding the relation between irony and humor as a parallel to the relation between Socrates and Christianity. There is no record of Kierkegaard having specifically discussed affectation with Møller, but it is difficult to imagine that they would not have done so, and in any event, Møller's thoughts on affectation were available to Kierkegaard in his *Posthumous Papers* (1st ed., 1839–1843), which Kierkegaard purchased as soon as they became available.

The theme of affectation abounds in Kierkegaard's writings. For the purposes of the present investigation, we will confine ourselves to a few specific loci that afford us a reasonably clear overview of his engagement with the concept: *A Literary Review, Concluding Unscientific Postscript*, writings connected with the so-called "attack on Christendom," the *Two Ethical-Religious Essays* that emerged from his preoccupation with Pastor Adler, and *The Sickness unto Death*.

In *A Literary Review*, Kierkegaard, like Møller, singles out "affectation" as typifying the times, symptomatic of the superficiality of "the present age":

> The age of revolution is essentially passionate. Therefore it is essentially *cultivated*. The elasticity of the inner being is indeed the measure of essential cultivation. A serving girl who is essentially in love is essentially cultivated. A man of the common people who has an essential and passionate commitment to an important decision is essentially cultivated. A superficial and fragmentary set of manners based upon an inner emptiness; a colorful display of swaggering weeds instead of the humble bowing of the blessed grain; the artificial beating time in a dance that lacks festiveness; the elaborate decoration of the binding of a book that is vacuous in other respects—this is mere form and affectation.[29]

Toward the beginning of *Concluding Unscientific Postscript*, in his ridicule of "the proofs" advanced by "the centuries" and purporting to demonstrate "the truth of Christianity," Kierkegaard again alludes to affectation as a sure sign of shallowness:

> It is not God's fault that habit, and routine, and lack of passion, and affectation, and chatter with the person next door and with the person across the street gradually come to corrupt most people, so that they become thoughtless—basing their eternal happiness first on one thing, then on another, and then on yet a third thing—not noticing that the secret is that their talk of eternal happiness is affectation precisely because it is devoid of passion.[30]

Here Kierkegaard—both in his own name and as Climacus—takes the position that that which is without passion is affectation. On the other hand, during his "attack on Christendom" Kierkegaard points out that the opponents of his "passionate" Christianity have advanced precisely the opposite argument, that passion and subjectivity are in fact signs of affectation. In *Judge for Yourself!* Kierkegaard has a representative of common sense, of reasonableness, say the following with respect to radical Christianity: "This is not true nobility, but is precious and affected, an exaggeration."[31] And in issue number 8 of his *Moment*, Kierkegaard points out that his opponents, "the docents" (sometimes translated as "assistant professors"), insist that Christianity must be taught "objectively." Kierkegaard's "docents" charge that it is impossible to teach Christianity subjectively, "because the subjective is sickliness, affectation."[32] Once again, while Kierkegaard himself maintained that affectation is the *absence* of passion or subjectivity, he has his opponents charge that affectation is marked by the *presence* of such passion or subjectivity.

Who is affected, then—Kierkegaard? or his opponents? Poul Møller of course insisted that in the present age, at any rate, everyone is—or at least ought to be—at least somewhat affected, and that the attempt to avoid affectation altogether can have dire consequences. In any event, affectation appears to be a labile, or as Kierkegaard might call it, a "dialectical" concept. And nowhere does the complexity of this concept become clearer than in Kierkegaard's investigation of the problem of "authority" in "On The Difference between a Genius and an Apostle," one of the *Two Minor Ethical-Religious Essays* written in conjunction with Kierkegaard's treatment of the difficult case of Pastor Adler:

> This, however, is the way things stand. Doubt and unbelief, which make faith futile, have, among other things, also made people embarrassed to obey, to submit to authority. This rebelliousness worms its way into the thinking even of the better sort of people, who are perhaps unaware of it—and then all this confusion (which deep down is treason) about profundity and the profound and about the miraculous-wonderfulness one can glimpse, etc. Thus if we were to take one, specific term to describe Christian religious discourse, as

it is heard and read nowadays, we would have to say that it is *affected*. Usually, when we speak of a pastor's affectation, we are perhaps thinking of the way he decks himself out and pretties himself up; or that he speaks sweetly, in lush, languorous tones; or that he wrinkles his brow and rolls his "R's" Norwegian-style;[33] or that he strains himself, striking vigorous poses and making leaps of revival, etc. But all these things are of minor importance, even if one could always wish that they did not exist. But what is corrupting is when the thinking behind the sermonic discourse is affected; when a sermon comes by its orthodoxy by accentuating the wrong thing; when it basically calls upon us to believe in Christ, preaching faith in Him on the basis of something that absolutely cannot be the object of faith. If a son were to say, "I obey my father not because he is my father but because he is a genius, or because his commands are always profound and brilliant," this filial obedience is affected. The son accentuates something utterly wrong; he accentuates the brilliance, the profundity of a *command,* while those categories are of course a matter of indifference with respect to a command. The son wants to obey by virtue of the father's profundity and brilliance, and it is precisely by virtue of these things that he cannot *obey* him because his critical stance with respect to the question of whether the command is profound and brilliant undermines his obedience. And thus it is also affectation when there is so much talk about appropriating Christianity and believing in Christ because of the profoundness and profundity of the doctrine. If he is to speak entirely properly when he cites the words of Christ, a pastor must speak as follows: "These words are from Someone to whom, according to his Own words, all power in Heaven and on earth has been given. Now, dear listener, you yourselves must consider whether or not you will submit to this authority, accept and believe these words—or not. But if you will not, then for the sake of God in Heaven do not go and accept the words because they are brilliant or profound or miraculously wonderful, because that is mockery of God, that is the wish to criticize God." When the dominant note of authority, the specifically paradoxical dominant note of authority, has been sounded, everything has been qualitatively transformed; then that sort of appropriation—which in other circumstances is permissible or desirable—is crime and presumptuousness.[34]

Here, as early as 1847, Kierkegaard equates affectation with a failure to accede to "authority," but even at the end, during his attack on the Church in 1854–1855, Kierkegaard was consistently unwilling to invoke the category of authority against his opponents. (As we will see toward the conclusion of the present essay, Kierkegaard was compelled to develop another, less absolute, category to serve him in his struggles.) In his essay "On The Difference between a Genius and an Apostle" Kierkegaard further claims that the failure to recognize "authority" is typical of the way Christianity is preached "nowadays," and in this reference to "nowadays" he is consciously or unconsciously echoing a number of P. M. Møller's "random thoughts."[35]

The quasi-comical Grundtvig, long a figure of ridicule for Kierkegaard, as he was for Heiberg, P. M. Møller, Martensen, and Mynster (just to name a few), is of course the target here, but he is not the *main* target. The main target would seem to be the Christianity of Mynster and Martensen, whose method of mediating the Gospel seemed to sidestep sounding the obligating ("dominant") note of *authority*. (Interestingly, in one of the "random thoughts" written during his trip to China, Møller had noted that "a pastor's authority as a teacher is easily asserted when speaking from the pulpit but is difficult to put in practice in everyday speech.")[36] Yet who has the authority to say that he or she has "authority?" Perhaps no one, and certainly not Søren Kierkegaard. And if an entire age is "affected," if *all* are affected, how can any particular person—least of all, Søren Kierkegaard—dare point the accusing finger of affectation at someone else?

By the time Kierkegaard composed *The Sickness unto Death* it had become clear to him that this affectation itself, for all its falsity, is an infallible, if indirect, indicator of the status of the *real* self. The relationship between affectation and despair emerges distinctly at a number of points in *Sickness*, particularly in the section entitled "The Universality of This Sickness (Despair)":

> Of course, one can affect being in despair, and one can erroneously confuse despair, a category of spirit, with all sorts of transitory dejection and gloom which then disappear without having come to despair. Nonetheless, the person who specializes in the soul regards this, too, as a form of despair— because precisely this affectation is despair. He sees quite well that this dejection, etc. is not very significant—but precisely this fact, the fact that it is not very significant, is despair.[37]

> Therefore, the common view that despair is a rarity, is as far as possible from the truth—on the contrary, it is quite universal. It is far as possible from the truth that the common view is correct when it assumes that everyone who does not believe or feel himself to be in despair is not in despair, and that only that person is in despair who says he is. On the contrary, the person who without affectation says that he is in despair is, in fact, a little bit—one dialectical category—closer to being healed than all those who do not regard themselves as being in despair.[38]

Despair is in fact "entirely dialectical," and thus "there is no *immediate* form of spiritual health."[39] Just as everyone is *affected*, so is every person *in despair*, whether or not he or she is conscious of it, and "so far is ignorance from abolishing despair or making it into non-despair that, on the contrary, it can be the most dangerous form of despair."[40] For "the prize of infinity is never won except via despair,"[41] and in order "to reach the truth one must go through every negativity."[42] Therefore "it is the greatest misfortune never to have had it [this illness, despair]—a true stroke of divine good fortune to have it, even if it is the most dangerous of all illnesses if one does not want to be healed from it."[43] Kierkegaard labels the simplest, most fundamental form of despair "spiritlessness." What responsibility does the spiritless individual have for his own spiritlessness, even though he is ignorant of it? To be ignorant of one's own despair is just one more act of despair. We *make ourselves* ignorant, or as Kierkegaard puts it, our ignorance is a "*produced* ignorance" [*frembragt Uvidenhed*].[44] As we have already seen, here Kierkegaard's notion of spiritlessness forms a direct parallel with Møller's treatment of "permanent affectation," where Møller writes: "In moral respects, this second degree of affectation is not a whit less culpable than the fully conscious lie or dissimulation, for the reason it is not brought to full consciousness is merely that the person concerned does not *want* to bring it to consciousness."[45] As Kierkegaard notes in *The Sickness unto Death*, "the will," the specific category of Christianity, comes into play here, making people responsible even for their own "forgetting."[46] And, just as we make ourselves ignorant, no one is born spiritless: "Is it something that *happens* to a person? No. It is the person's own fault. No one is born spiritless."[47] And, as Kierkegaard had read in his edition of Møller's *Posthumous Works,* an affected person risks becoming "a false self" who is "unable to wrest himself free": "One transforms oneself into a moral changeling."[48]

Thus, to *affect* despair is indeed to be in despair, even though it is merely an *affectation*. On the other hand, to declare oneself—"*without affectation*"—to be in despair is also to be in despair, but this latter person is nonetheless closer (by "one dialectical category") to being healed than the person who does not believe he or she is in despair—for such a person is merely *affecting* to be healthy. Thus affectation, like despair, is dialectical. Affectation is what Kierkegaard might call a "negative determination of spirit." Everyone has it. As Kierkegaard would have learned from Møller, those who refuse to admit their own affectedness or who flee from it in "dread" are worse off than those who acknowledge it and are thus in a better position to go beyond it. And as with despair, everyone is in a position to know with certainty that he or she is himself or herself affected. But how can we know whether *another person* is affected, whether that person, regardless of how he or she appears, is authentic or inauthentic? Who can be a "Knower of Hearts?" Who has the right to judge others—in particular, those who call themselves Christians and leaders of the Church—and conclude that they are merely "affected?" As the mid-1840s wore on into the 1850s, Kierkegaard certainly implied this more and clearly with respect to his ecclesiastical opponents—Grundtvig, of course (though he was primarily a figure of fun), but especially Martensen and, worst of all, Mynster. But did this not require that Kierkegaard invoke "*authority*," the very category he had declined to invoke against Adler?

Perhaps the answer to this question emerges from yet another of Kierkegaard's examinations of affectation, this time in a journal entry from 1854 entitled "The Depravity of the Age":

> It is fundamentally nothing but affectation and hypocrisy when people in our age say, "As long as my character is not attacked, I fear no other attack, nor do I concern myself very much about it."
> The matter is quite simple. Assuming it is not a criminal case of libel that would damage one's good name and reputation in such a way that one is hampered in one's occupation or in the enjoyment of life, an attack on one's

character—for example, if it is said that a person changes his opinions, is lacking in character, exploits his position for his own advantage, etc.—means nothing whatever. Because that is how we all are. In our age, attacks of this sort have no more significance than if, in a penal colony, one person were to say to another, "Well, you, of course, are a convict."

The depravity of the times consists precisely in the fact that such attacks no longer mean anything—that the human race in its despair has abandoned everything higher.

Next, the depravity of the times consists of the hypocritical affectation that one actually attributes any importance to these attacks.

No, the times are so demoralized and wretched that really and truly, the only attack that is feared is ridicule—except that in this case things are reversed, so that precisely because one fears it one says, "It's nothing."

Oh, I indeed saw truly and made the right choice when I singled out ridicule as the real sign of dissolution in Denmark and (as a high-level police officer) voluntarily chose to subject myself to it.[49]

Thus Kierkegaard's reply to the "depravity of the age" that expresses itself in "affectation" is the reestablishment of "*character*," a concept that has been debased but that is the proper antidote to affectation and hypocrisy—and that does not require that Kierkegaard invoke what he fears he does not possess, namely, "authority."

In conclusion, the contention of the present essay is that as Kierkegaard approached the attack on Christendom his historical-conceptual universe looked something like this:

1. In *ancient* times one's relation to oneself and the truth was marked by *heteronomy*. One could be spoken to directly by God and be entrusted with a mission, thus becoming a prophet or an apostle who had *authority*. The greatest opportunity and the greatest danger was *possession*, either divine or demonic. In a sense, one was a passive participant in the role of *being chosen*.

2. In *modern* times one's relation to oneself and the truth is marked by *autonomy*. Authority is out of the question, and the ever-present problem is that of *affectation*. Since heteronomy has been replaced by autonomy, the greatest danger is no longer that of divine or demonic possession, but of productive or crippling (encapsulating) *obsession* (which, it is true, Kierkegaard sometimes speaks of as demonic possession, though scarcely in any literal sense). And because the disappearance of the Creator God means that one can no longer view oneself as chosen, there is an abiding temptation to *create oneself* [*at skabe sig*], which, in Danish, once again means "to be affected" or "to put on an act."

3. *Kierkegaard's response to modern times* was not to attempt to turn the clock back to heteronomy, authority, and so on, but to attempt to find a middle term between absolute heteronomy and absolute autonomy in the concept of *character*. As Kierkegaard well knew, "character" derived from the Greek *charassein*, to engrave. Thus, one's self is not absolutely determined by the Deity. Nor, on the other hand, is one absolutely free to create oneself. Rather, one is

engraved, or carved with a certain "character," and it is one's task in life to live up to that character or to live *into* it [*at træde i Characteer*]. When it became Kierkegaard's task to attack Bishop Mynster, he did so not by invoking "authority" but by insisting that Bishop Mynster's preaching of Christianity "was not in character, that outside of the quiet hours [i.e., church services] he was not in character, not even in the character of his sermons."[50] One cannot create oneself, but one can "*choose oneself*," yet one cannot choose just anything, lest one be affected. To choose properly one must choose to realize, in one way or another, one's *character.*

Kierkegaard learned from Poul Martin Møller that the times were awash in affectation and that no one was or could be immune from it. His ultimate response to the affectation of his times and to Møller's challenge—"You are so polemical through and through, that it is quite frightful"—was not to invoke "authority" or to call for a return to the absolute heteronomy of antiquity, but to call for the conditional autonomy he termed "character."

3.
Postscript Ethics: Putting Personality on Stage

Edward F. Mooney

In his recent biography, Alastair Hannay characterizes *Concluding Unscientific Postscript* as "an itinerary for personality."[1] Kierkegaard himself says of *Postscript* that "*what is new is that . . . here we have personality.*"[2] Personality is a moral status one works to attain. This is true as well of subjectivity. Each demarcates an ideal that calls on me to respond in a way that truly recognizes what I am and can be. In this way, subjectivity and personality are *moral* concepts or ideals.

In its classical sense, moral philosophy addresses the question how one should live. It takes persons to be answerable to norms and to be proper objects of our praise and blame. Persons inherit pictures of what life should or could be, and respond to these in attitudes of attraction or distain. They take a stance toward values, toward the virtues and vices enclosed in portraits of a life's unfolding.[3] One might defiantly *reject* the thought that value makes demands that we must answer. But such a move toward nihilism or despair is itself a normative response, a response that evaluates value. In this light, the ethics of Judge Wilhelm in *Either/Or II,* or the tangle of ethics that Johannes *de silentio* describes in *Fear and Trembling* are contrasting *moral* orientations. And a Christian stance becomes a moral stance, a stance toward value bequeathed and toward the donor of that value.

By taking *Postscript* subjectivity as a moral ideal, I depart from the view that Kierkegaardian subjectivity must be either a Cartesian state of consciousness or a special place from which one can know. We have instead an ideal, a moral status to interpret, revise, and realize. *Postscript*'s theme of subjectivity maps out and embodies the drama of *realizing personality*.

There are three angles from which we can view this unfolding drama. First, we can watch personality become realized in the text as it models aspects of what human life can be. Various characters or figures—Socrates, the subjective thinker, the assistant professor, the declaiming parson—personify moral themes. This allows us to resonate with ideas in the way we resonate with figures on a stage. Second, we can take in the fact that *Postscript* subjectivity or personality makes existential demands on its readers. The text shows us aspects of personality and urges us to embrace some and disavow others. Third, we can step back to extract from this itinerary for personality a rough set of conditions that constitute the possibility and fulfillment of personality. This is to entertain and assess a set of philosophical claims *about* personality.

To begin to see how *Postscript* works, let's trace the subtle process that puts personality on stage.

Part 1

Seeing Titles as Tableaux

Is *Postscript* a treatise? It has an impressive table of contents, a seven-page spread of chapters, parts, divisions, appendices, and numerous subdivisions. But Climacus is a humorist.[4] The look of sober organization might be tongue-in-cheek.

Consider the title: Alastair Hannay's fresh translation (found in his Kierkegaard *Biography*) sparkles and makes us think: *Concluding Unscholarly Addendum to Philosophical Crumbs*.[5] Here we have scaffolding for a theatrical tableau. "*Unscholarly Addendum*" sounds quite close to "inconsequential afterthoughts." "*Crumbs*" sounds inconsequential, too. Are these *mere* crumbs? Picture them as remains falling from the table of a royal impresario, who with dramatic flourish turns them into fodder for an acquisitive mind. But why should scholars read unscholarly afterthoughts, or dive after crumbs? Well, they might be magically transformed into something nourishing. Alternatively, we might read the title retrospectively: what we *took* to be the nourishing promise of a treatise turns out to be *mere crumbs*.

The subtitle, "*A Mimic-Pathetic-Dialectic Compilation—An Existential Contribution*," is equally unsettling if we expect a treatise. Mimicry, or miming, suggests theater or the stage, a place where feeling, emotion, or mood (that is, pathos, passion) can unfold, and unfold contrapuntally (that is, dialectically). Johannes Climacus might be the impresario directing this "mimic-pathetic-dialectic compilation" staged as comedy, tragedy, satire, or farce. This complex "compilation" is also "*An Existential Contribution*." We can picture the contribution of an actor delivering up the living flesh and blood and spirit of the character assigned. That would be an existential sacrifice of one's talent, skill, and dedication toward the fulfillment of a scripted personality.

Perhaps we have a lesson to take offstage, as well. Taking in the full impact of a theatrical performance of another's personality is not yet the realization of our *own* personality. Reading (or watching) *Postscript*'s drama is no substitute for attentively living out the detail of our *own* seeds of personality or character. *Postscript* in hand, we initially expected the outlines of a philosophical position. Now the text begins to take on the aspect of a drama of personality. As Kierkegaard puts it, "*what is new is that . . . here* [in *Postscript*] *we have* [not a doctrine or a thesis but] *personality.*"[6]

Mixing Genres

"*Here we have personality*"—or "*character,*" or even "*a master virtue, subjectivity.*"[7] How can *Postscript* deliver these? Well, we have characters with names like "the subjective thinker," "the docent or assistant prof," "the speculative philosopher." Climacus pens out a part for himself, too: smoking his cigar in Deer Park, or watching an old man grieve in Assistens Cemetery, or enjoying the role of raconteur.[8]

Getting Climacus in view (as personality) is like getting Hamlet or Faust in view. Hannay suggests that *Postscript* can be seen as a continuation of the "Faust project" that preoccupied Kierkegaard in his student days. Martensen published *his* recasting first; dejected, Kierkegaard set his aside. In the old version, Faust sells his soul to get knowledge. In the revived *Postscript* version, Faust-Climacus sells off objective knowledge to *get* a soul—to realize personality or subjectivity.[9]

To be on a Faustian quest is to explore what Climacus calls the "existential categories" of thought, passion, imagination, personal relation, and suffering.[10] A Faustian drama would depict the living personality that emerges in the artful interplay of these categories. The premise is that "science," or disciplinary academic research, or listening to the crowd or the media can't tell me how thought, passion, relationship, or imagination are to get embedded in *my* life.

To gain his soul, Climacus-Faust refuses to pledge full allegiance to the pursuit of propositional, doctrinal, or detached knowledge. Climacus knows that formal philosophy can be quixotic, tilting at windmills. Chasing Climacus through *Postscript* can be like chasing Quixote across the arid Spanish plain.

Postscript paragraphs spin out as prologues and soliloquies; as episodes of comic relief and jokes; as moments of grief and recognition; as parodies and parables; as meditations on melancholy, truth, and joy. And since what we have is an *itinerary* for personality, there is something like a series of rest stops or platforms, each of which functions as a stage for the particular personality-realizations that are appropriate to that stage.

Six Strands of Subjectivity

You might think at this point that I've neglected what's central to *Postscript*. It can be read quite easily, you might say, as a treatise on subjective truth or subjectivity.[11] Well, if a drama is in progress, its characters do have something to say. *What* Climacus says is every bit as important as the *how* of his delivery, his concern for his enactment of a dramatic role.

The *how*, as I've said, is performed on relatively stable platforms: the stage of scholarly distraction, the ethical subjectivity of Socrates, the subjectivity of guilt consciousness and of Christian consciousness. These rest stops or platforms give us a sense of *what* a *Postscript* drama might have to say about Socrates or scholars. But rather than start down that familiar road, exploring stages on life's way, I want to look at what I called above the conditions for there being personality or subjectivity.

Unraveling these constituent strands of personality reinforces our negative case: *Postscript* subjectivity is *not* whim, eccentricity, or arbitrary taste; *not* a philosopher's pure consciousness (the sort of world-deprived autonomous subject that Heidegger and others seek to undermine); and *not* primarily an epistemological concept. Rather than exploring the ingredients of worthy *knowing,* subjectivity asks us to explore and take on features of worthy *living.*

As part of *Postscript's* positive case, I'm asked, among other things, to

- *Live out a complex relational pattern of deep personal concern.* Life should be more than an arena for trivial distractions, one-upmanship, say, opinion mongering, or the puffery of market success
- *Inhabit the ethico-religious stage of existence or character.* Life should transcend the shallow "objective" stage of scholarship, aesthetic voyeurism, or passionless urban life of "see and be seen"[12]
- *Exercise practical moral agency where responsibility is paramount.* Life should not be reduced to world-observing or theoretical knowing[13]
- *Show an adverbial "how," a style in which I go about my tasks.* Persons are not just an objective "what," say, what one has learned or acquired or what status one has attained; action has a manner or style
- *Exercise self-avowal.* Take up something as my own project or commitment. Persons are gifted with more than a capacity for self-observation, or for action
- *Cultivate an imagination and faith-wrought proportion of aesthetic, ethical, and dialectical virtues (Bildung).*[14] Persons can counter pulls toward fragmentation and disintegration, bringing themselves up, letting themselves be built up.

This sixfold breakdown of the ingredients of subjectivity really amounts to six features of the broad demand that the ideal of subjectivity makes on us. Working to meet these conditions or demands is traveling the road to personality. In the second half of this chapter I want to explore the natural interweaving of these strands of character or personality through several central *Postscript* passages. I'll do this under four headings: first, *Lessing's view of subjectivity;* second, *subjectivity and objective knowledge;* third, *subjectivity as acknowledgment and answerability;* and last, *subjectivity as aesthetic/ethical/dialectical capacity.*

Part 2

Lessing and Subjectivity

Did Lessing make a deathbed confession, as Jacobi averred, that he was a "Spinozist"—not a proper Christian? Strictly speaking, by his own standards, anything Lessing confessed ought to be *irrelevant* to Jacobi and to the German cultured elite poised to listen in. Far from being a scandal or a cause célèbre, Lessing's convictions shouldn't make another's conviction swing one way or another. So his reported confession is—or ought to be—superfluous, a curiosity, a diversion from one's *own* ethical or religious vocation. Note that, at the close of *Postscript*, Climacus characterizes his massive effort as "superfluous." With regard to *my* existential work, it's a long diversion. And Kierkegaard revokes any authority to specify its meaning.

A general disquisition on religion can't be existentially successful. We long for an all-purpose road map that any number of reasonable people could follow in their drive to invest themselves religiously. But that's impossible. A road map is useless if I have no idea *where I am* or *where I want to go, or what my interests are.*

Road maps can't give me my immediate existential orientation. They can't tell me where in particular I am or what I have to invest. They can't tell me which direction I face or where I want to go. Without such primal, passionate orientation, I can't know which map to consult, or which sector of it to peruse. What it means to *me* to be the person I am, to know where I stand and the direction I face is something forged, as Stephen Dedaelus has it, in the smithy of my soul. For it to happen, concern, responsibility, and the capacity to claim a path as mine must be in place.

Objective Gaps and Subjectivity

Leaving Lessing behind, Climacus turns to subjectivity and objectivity as ways to truth. Misguided critics often assume that Kierkegaardian subjectivity must be a kind of last-ditch epistemological recourse, a bulwark, a fallback position to call on when cognitive answers are missing. But *Postscript* subjectivity is a task, a *moral* goal to realize, and so the truth it seeks to realize is *not* a truth of objectivity. There is nothing in this commitment to a moral goal that banishes or *undervalues* objectivity.

Subjectivity becomes an apt and even urgent orientation, a master strength or virtue, because our needs as persons far exceed our cognitive needs. *We need much more in life than cognitive success.* God has perfect cognitive success, as Climacus might say, yet even He exhibits thorough subjectivity.

If a scientist or scholar or news reporter is subjective or biased in producing her results, this marks an epistemological vice. But humans can—and must—

exhibit a *different* sort of subjectivity, a virtue not of knowing but of *living*, a matter not of facts but of *becoming*, not of consciousness but of *agency, inwardness,* and *"personality."* The several strands of personality tallied above—self-avowal, responsibility, style, agency, concern—amount to an anatomy of the truths, the strengths, the underlying constituents of subjectivity and personality.

Epistemology considers standards, like coherence and respect for fact, to which candidates for objective truth must respond as they compete for the honorific title "Knowledge."[15] Candidates for subjective truth, on the other hand—say, a heartfelt vow or confession—aspire to embody and express one's very self or soul, to deliver one's fullest personhood or personality.

Objectivity demands that as participants in a community of knowers, *we* respond to a collective demand to clean up the common *store of fact or theory,* and bring our personal beliefs or opinions as close to the thriving common norm as possible. Subjectivity, on the other hand, demands that on my own *I* clean up my individual *standing* as a *person,* a task that can be undertaken apart from concern for common norms, and when conceived religiously, undertaken under the eye of the unknown, of the wholly other, or of a watchful God.

A biblical God exhibits subjective truth (alongside his perfect objective knowledge) insofar as He exhibits truth in agency and love, at the least; devotion, in character and responsiveness, in responsibility and concern. Persons (divine or otherwise) have capacities to know, but also to love and appreciate, to judge and create, and to exhibit personality as self-avowal: "I am what I am"; "I will be what I will be."

A life restricted to objective uptakes of the world would be less than human. A human agent might value objectivity, but that means aiming to *cultivate* an objectivity, striving to *realize* it, which means being reasonably subjective.

Of necessity, objectivity will be pursued within the confines of a life that will contain much else—dressing, eating, collaborating with colleagues, and catching the bus—tasks each of which requires agency, some responsibility, some concern for things other than cognitive success. Without the goods of personality, an ardent objectivist has no life that settles in as her *own.* She lacks a personal attunement or orientation to and in the world. She lacks a personality or character she can *call*—and that will *be*—her own.[16]

Subjectivity as Acknowledgment and Answerability

What spins by me objectively as just another path that anyone in general might find attractive is transformed as subjectivity engages and I recognize or acknowledge *this* path or response *as mine* and vow I'll *answer* for it.

Descartes located the essence of a human self in its capacity to *know* itself transparently. Kant pictured an *"I think"* as the elusive self-relation that makes a thinking thing a self. Climacus could take the essential self-relation to be not an *"I know"* or *"I think,"* but an *"I acknowledge . . . as mine"* or *"I will answer for . . ."* This brings out what's essential in making an "existential contribution."[17]

Existential *acknowledgment* and *answerability* must accompany any part of what I feel or do or think insofar as I am operating, then and there, as a *moral self*.

As well as developing third-person disquisitions *about* existential contributions, Climacus *makes* one. We find this in his attestations of vocation, as in his famous Deer Park resolution: "I decided it was my task to make things difficult"; we find it as he plays out his project in attacks on the complacent "speculative thinker." And we find it as Climacus passes the baton back to Kierkegaard, who then avows responsibility for what he *has* done and disavows what he hasn't, which happens in his "final deposition" (or "First and Last Explanation").[18]

This demand for acknowledgment and answerability is a Socratic, ethical demand. It's a demand for an accounting of one's life. This does not mean producing a factual account, a comprehensive C.V., as it were. One enters a deposition, standing up for the way things seem and are, as before a judge, a court, or an ideal that calls one *to* account. It's a promise that one is truthful in delivering one's account and a promise to stand by it. Socratic acknowledgment and answerability are caught as they are deposed at his trial in testimony before the Athenian people. What we call self-knowledge is not self-observation or self-theorizing but related to the strands of subjectivity we called concern, responsibility, and self-avowal. It's the capacity to acknowledge and answer for what *has been* one's life, and so to avow, under assessment and on balance, what one's life *now is;* and so in that light, to avow, once more, what it *will be.*[19]

One bears witness because one is concerned for the course of one's life, and concerned to account for it to others (or to Another). One finds oneself responsible even if one cannot name or focus the source of whatever it is that puts one's life in question. We find ourselves as humans under the burden of an answerability broader and deeper than the demands of civic or legal accountability. Aesthetic, personal, and religious standards measure the accomplishments and failings of one's life, the quality of engagement with friends, with art, with civic institutions, with family, with natural or urban landscapes, with faith (or lack thereof).

Finding ourselves answerable is finding ourselves under the eye of measures or ideals that claim us, that place us in a space that calls for reasons and actions that elaborate and answer. Living under the gaze of such ideals is the welcome/unwelcome burden of having a life I can call my own.

✳ ✳ ✳

At first I worked to establish *theater* as a natural frame for *Postscript.* The live onstage performance shows *how* the serious analysis should be delivered. Then I turned to see *what* was delivered: I suggested that it was a set of demands that constitutes the ideal of subjectivity, an ideal that gets worked out in central *Postscript* passages. In ending, I return to Climacus and theater. Climacus appears as an impresario, a critic of the text he runs by us, a kibitzer. But his presence is not just clowning.

Subjectivity as Aesthetic/Ethical/Dialectical Capacity

Here is a powerful characterization of "the subjective thinker" that brings together aspects of subjectivity that we've canvassed above. It fills out the idea of subjectivity as artistic style and as *Bildung*, the cultivation of an imagination and faith-wrought proportion of aesthetic, ethical, and dialectical virtues.

> *The subjective thinker's form [. . .] is his style. . . . His form must first and last be related to existence, and in this regard he must have at his disposal the poetic, the ethical, the dialectical, and the religious.*[20]
>
> *The subjective thinker is not a scientist-scholar; he is an artist. To exist is an art. The subjective thinker is aesthetic enough for his life to have aesthetic content, ethical enough to regulate it, dialectical enough in thinking to control it.*[21]

Is Climacus a subjective thinker? If we suspect that the answer is Yes, then Climacus is related "first and last to existence," and "has at his disposal the poetic, the ethical, the dialectical, and the religious."

Hannay notes that *Kierkegaard*'s ghost hovers spookily around the pseudonymous texts.[22] Surely we find *Climacus* hovering ghostlike over *Postscript*, constantly appearing, interrupting things, refusing to let the argument or exposition speak for itself.

Here are telltale signs of an author playing ghostly hide-and-seek: (1) Pseudonymity calls attention to the eccentric writer present and not present in the pseudonym. (2) Extravagant titles call attention to the show-off inventing them. (3) An extravagant (and lopsided) table of contents exposes an author flaunting his capacity to perform outrageously. (4) Mammoth footnotes call attention to an author unable to bring a stop to his interventions, even after the galleys are returned from the printer. (5) An interlude is brashly inserted that discusses a shadow author's previously published works (and we know the shadow is just another shape Kierkegaard assumes); Climacus shows us *what* the shadow author has done, what his thoughts *about* it are; and we see him put himself there before us *doing* the show-and-tell. (6) Stylistic virtuosity is a sort of self-advertising; the writer showcases an extravagant variety of styles: dialectical exercises, comic skits, parables, melodramatic scenes set in graveyards and public parks. (7) In a finale to the book, the author makes a double run on stage to comment on the play we've seen and to bracket, or retract, its "message." (8) Unnumbered final pages draw attention to the composer behind the scenes (or, more accurately, to the composer who can't *stay* discreetly out of view); he's shown plainly in the act of adding an extra unpaginated postscript to the preceding appendix-addendum to the *Postscript*.

Climacus is like a comic who doesn't just *tell* the funny story, but constantly reminds you that *he's telling* it, and that nothing would be happening if *he* weren't happening. He writes *about* the topics of acknowledgment and answerability, and shows us his *own* striving to acknowledge and answer for his words—hovering over them poised to assimilate them, to alter or reject them, and hence to make an existential contribution that will be his deposition.

He painstakingly makes and remakes a place for himself within his exposition. If he wrote only *about* personality's contribution, then we could pass off what he says as just another piece of interesting theory, a thesis. But in striving to make his words his own, striving to make the liveliness of the words the liveliness of his life-as-author, Climacus shows—as theater shows—the existential contribution itself.

4.
Kierkegaard on Commitment, Personality, and Identity

Alastair Hannay

These comments group around Bert Dreyfus's powerful analysis of selfhood. Dreyfus's skill in putting together clear-headed and topical accounts of texts widely considered inaccessible is enviable and legendary. Any doubts Dreyfus's readers may entertain about whether the authors of these texts would feel at home in his renderings are balanced by the way they throw fresh light on current issues. As with Dreyfus's Heidegger, spokesman for "the primacy of practice" and a radically anti-representationalist account of action, so too with Kierkegaard, the first thinker to "call his own thinking existential." The adjective appears in the *Postscript*'s subtitle, but while I don't recall it ever being used by Kierkegaard to define his own thinking, it sounds a compelling note, and we might certainly call it that.

It seems there are two broadly different ways of reading Kierkegaard, one as a radical revisionist (so to speak) within a tradition he did not leave, and the other in terms of all that he can be seen to have contributed to breaking with that tradition. On the first of these, Kierkegaard belongs with Hegel and Marx, and a host of fellow travelers, appropriately labeled "dialectical" thinkers, whose terms of reference are unambiguously modernist. For these, reality reveals itself most cogently and truthfully in the form of opposites, or "contradictions," whose resolution it is then the task of such a thinker to propose and formulate in the form of a single truth. For Hegel such resolutions occurred in our understanding as it converged ideally on a vision of absolute knowledge as reason. For Marx the tensions were to be found in the working arrangements of society, and the corresponding resolutions required political action on the part of those (collectivities) best placed to bring them about. The oppositions that Kierkegaard brought to mind concern dilemmas faced by individuals in their confrontation with life, independently of the political situation, although, perhaps as even Kierkegaard himself might have stressed, they become salient only under certain social and cultural conditions.

On this traditionalist reading, in campaigning in his final years under the banner "Christianity within Christendom," Kierkegaard the modernist would be proposing a replacement for the Hegelian absolute. The truth of Christianity would be another (kind of) single truth upon which all understandings converge. The philosophical radicalism in this would consist in the insistence that from our inescapably existential point of view the polar opposites that metaphysics sought to bring together are ineluctably separated and can only, and must, be brought together in a unity we bring to our actions, one that has no possible precedent in the realm of thought. Existence (*Tilværelse,* a Danish equivalent of *Dasein,* sometimes translated as "determinate existence"), limited as it is in ways later adumbrated by Heidegger, its satisfactions if any (repairing the breach), must depend on the God-man and on the existing individual's appropriation/imitation of what, to the faithful, the temporal narrative of the man-God reveals about eternal truth.

The second way of reading accepts what might be called Kierkegaard's *Daseinanalyse,* if only as a rough although prescient anticipation of Heidegger's more professional version, and sees it best represented in the oppositional schema of *Sickness,* as in Bert Dreyfus's chart. But it sees this as a matrix in which alternative projects of fulfillment, or if you like, alternative cancellations of human deficits, can be developed. Where Kierkegaard (on any straightforward reading) applied it to just one culturally specific form of fulfillment, namely, the "bliss" granted by Christianity to Christians—and in doing so may be said to have retained at least the essentials of what Caputo recently called the "reassuring framework of a classical Aristotelico-Hegelian metaphysics of infinity"[1]—others apply it to a wider range of human deficits having the same formal position as Kierkegaard's "despair" but with the project consistently outside that (in Kierkegaard's hands not so obviously) reassuring framework. Michael Theunissen has argued that, with some correction though without losing anything essential, Kierkegaard's analysis can be rescued from the seeming parochiality of its "religious premiss."[2]

Dreyfus, too, lifts Kierkegaard out of a culturally parochial concern with Christian truth. But he assumes this is possible without alteration to the text. Dreyfus reads Kierkegaard as concerned with "modern nihilism," and the solution that Kierkegaard offers to this is unconditional commitment, a commitment taken to be "defining." What commitment defines is personal identity, and the deficit/fulfillment project becomes one of first lacking and then securing this identity. In his essay Dreyfus, as he notes, modifies his earlier position. Formerly he took it that anything in time could form the basis of such a defining commitment. Now, however, he recognizes that this is an inadequate account of that basis. If, as he claims, the formula for success in securing identity is "get[ting] the two sets of factors together in such a way that they will reinforce each other," then there must be (and in accordance with *Sickness*'s version of the formula) reference to a "power" responsible for the structure in which the project of selfhood arises.

A way of reading Dreyfus here is to see him as admitting that unless this latter condition is met, to say that the infinite and finite are brought into a mutually reinforcing relation by unconditional commitment is merely a fancy way of saying the commitment is made unconditionally. That keeps us clear of the metaphysics of infinity but at the same time leaves out something that the text treats as vital. Contrary to what one might now expect, however unexpectedly, Dreyfus is not reintroducing the full-blown infinite. Basing himself on the text's formulation, God is introduced not in a traditional way but in the non-ontotheological form of "the fact that everything is possible." Nor is Dreyfus here reserving personal identity for the "saved Christian," though the wording at the end of his essay seems at first to suggest that. There are two sides to unconditional commitment. One side enables the object of Christian belief to serve as an example for a wider audience. On the one hand, there is (as before) the requirement that one be related with 'infinite' passion to something or someone—and, again as before, this is all that "becoming eternal in time" amounts to, to which we might again object that it is simply a fancy way of saying the commitment is made unconditionally. But now there is, on the other hand, the requirement that one see this something, or someone, to which, or to whom, one is unconditionally committed as a kind of token of the God-man type. On this very interesting account, a "savior" is whatever or whoever a person relates to with infinite passion, with the God-man serving a double role: that of a "paradigm" for all such identity-provided newborns, and that of a (or the) point in time that has revealed for humankind the possibility of being thus reborn.

Dreyfus's is a powerful reading based on an unusually rich alloy of texts. Kierkegaard scholars would hesitate to introduce the God-man into a reading of a text (*Sickness*) where the notion never explicitly occurs; nor would they so cheerfully wed the doctrine of the stages to the theory of the synthesis (nor so robustly ignore matters of pseudonymity). So although to many students of Kierkegaard Dreyfus's many-saviors view will appear wonderfully liberating, to others, including myself, it will seem plainly wrong. Showing how and why it is wrong is, however, no easy matter, and in his characteristically eclectic way Dreyfus has assembled an impressive case. Note, for instance, those three references to *Postscript* in justification of the claim that "the object of . . . a defining relation does not have to be the God-man." I have pointed out on previous occasions where I differ from Dreyfus on these matters[3] and will spare readers the details here. I would like, however, to focus on one main difference, since it allows me to outline the special features of Dreyfus's notion of Kierkegaardian despair and to show where it differs from my own.

Dreyfus talks of the commitment "in the first instance" to God as one for those who "have tried to take a stand on themselves by themselves, either by relating only to themselves or by relating to an infinite, absolute, and eternal God." I take "have tried" to imply here "have not succeeded," the despair then being consequent upon failure to commitment in either of these ways. Not being in despair is to succeed in committing oneself to something or someone in time, though in the light of the paradigm offered by Jesus as the God-man.

Note the use of the term "despairing" in Dreyfus's sentence beginning "Kierkegaard concludes from his examination of all types of despairing ways to try to relate the factors. . . ." A despairing way, it seems, is one that won't work, whether the person trying to relate the factors knows this or not. This adverbial use of the notion of despair is, on my reading, quite inappropriate to what the text tells us, namely, that it is the attempts themselves that are cases of despair, not the fact or sense that the attempts will fail and that this is why they should be said to be undertaken in despair. On my reading neither "despairingly" nor (least of all) "desperately" (the other of Dreyfus's modifications of the translation) has any place in the translation of Kierkegaard's text. *Fortvivlet* means "in despair," and "despair" is the condition of one who has given up hope, the hope of the "eternal bliss" offered by Christianity. Its strongest form ("the highest intensification of sin," as it says on the last page of *Sickness*) is to say that Christianity is a pack of lies. At the other end, in its weakest form, it is a semi-aware reluctance to approach the project at all. Anti-Climacian despair is a range of dispositions between these extremes, ways of life, even whole cultures (like that of what Kierkegaard castigates as 'Christendom' [*Christenheden*]), by means of which individuals separately and en masse deny themselves the route to Christian fulfillment. Kierkegaard's despair is not a hopelessness that occurs when you fail in the attempt; it is the condition in which no genuine attempt is made at all.[4]

Nor is it quite right to say that the project is that of securing a personal identity. The terms in which the guiding spirits in Kierkegaard's society were inclined to see the task of self-realization were that of the "person," personhood being a philosophically well-established notion (see below), and the problem facing society that of retaining it under conditions in which it was becoming increasingly difficult to bring together the factors required for personhood. Interesting here, given the parallel Dreyfus offers with Pascal, is Kierkegaard's own positive reference to Pascal's view that to know the divine involves a transformation of the person. As Kierkegaard puts it: "one must become a different person in order to know the divine," adding that this is "completely forgotten in our time." Ethical transformation is considered "superfluous . . . to say nothing of religious transformation."[5]

Some useful clues to what might be termed the problematic of personhood are provided by Kirmmse's essay on affectation. Note, however, that Kirmmse calls affectation a "modern" disorder. The background he provides for the phenomenon and for subsequent critical interest in it might encourage us to think that the problem facing people was indeed, as Dreyfus has said, modern ni-hilism, and that what they therefore lacked and sought was personal identity. Indeed, in a society where "there was . . . no 'self'," you might expect the task of acquiring one to be a first priority, not least in the minds of those respon-sible people concerned for their society's welfare. But, lacking selves, the lay members of the society, too, would no doubt be feeling the pinch in some ways, among them no doubt ways that would be contributing to that concern. But if Kierkegaard's mentor, Poul Martin Møller, can be taken as representative, this was not how the concerned actually saw it. To them, what the situation demonstrated was the need to work toward a "personal truth," a truth that a "self-less" age had lost sight of, or perhaps one that it was now at last able in its selfless state clearly to identify. It was in any case due to the assumption of this truth that they could talk of affectation. Affectation is being untrue to one's self, to one's true self. This brings it close to Kierkegaardian despair. Indeed, certain forms of would-be despair ("all sorts of passing dejection or distraction") are described by Anti-Climacus as "affectation," the fact that they have no real sig-nificance being the true despair of those who affect these.[6] As Kierkegaard says in one place, affectation is "lying to oneself about oneself" (*Tillyvelse*).[7] That is not an easy thing to do, or to get away with. In fact, self-deception in any form, however subtle or complex, assuming it actually occurs, can never be brought off completely. In this respect, then, affectation follows Kierkegaardian despair exactly. A modern malady, yes, but also, as the humane Møller suggests, af-fectation is also a way of avoiding too rigid a possession of the true self. It can therefore have its liberating uses. But despair in all its forms, according to the far less humane Anti-Climacus, is the vain attempt to be rid of the true self, and in the worst case a (self-refuting?) denial that there is such a thing.

The notion of 'personhood' is pursued by Ed Mooney in light of a comment of mine based on a remark by Kierkegaard in his journals. To the complaint that people had thought of him as defending a cause and had "translated ev-erything into the objective, and . . . tried to find a new doctrine in the work," Kierkegaard replied that they had failed to see that "here we have personality."[8] As always I enjoy accompanying Mooney on his exploratory trips through and beyond Kierkegaard, and especially so when, it seems to me, we may have "gone further." I am not certain whether or from what point that may be the case here, but just to indicate why such a thought may nevertheless be harbored on this occasion, I will add a supplement to Kirmmse's sketch of the background, say-ing a little more about this notion of personality (*Personlighed*, cf. the German *Persönlichkeit*).

Naturally, the notion of personality here has nothing to do with the media concept of celebrity, nor even with that of force of character, as the word once naturally implied. It refers to something more general and less flashy, though also to more than just the legal notion of a locus of civil and other rights. It was in fact a notion in terms of which influential thinkers understood the concept of

God. Those who wanted to ascribe the notion of personality to God were critics of Hegel but some of them still sufficiently Hegelian to be collected under the banner of the Hegelian Right. Like Kierkegaard, they tended to regard Hegel's philosophy as pantheistic and accordingly to have dissolved the conception they needed, or wanted to retrieve, of a personal God, a primal entity that stood for and formed a divine image of individual existence.[9] Kierkegaard refers early on to one of these critics of Hegel, Immanuel Hermann Fichte (1797–1879), son of the older and better-known Fichte. The reference is to a work published in 1834 (mentioned in a lecture series Kierkegaard was attending)[10] and entitled "Die Idee der Persönlichkeit und der individuellen Fortdauer" (The Idea of Personality and Individual Subsistence).[11] For these thinkers (unlike Hegel's view where, at least as they saw it, the world proceeds from God's head as a process of logic and conceptual auto-generation), God had actually to be a personality and the world his free creation. The younger Fichte's books, practically all of which Kierkegaard acquired, were dedicated almost exclusively to the task of developing and proving his view that a conscious personal being must be recognized as the basis for all world phenomena. To quote the younger Fichte himself: "The highest thought that truly solves the problem of the world is that of a primal subject, or absolute personality, transparent to itself in its ideal as well as in its real infinity," and "[t]he creation and preservation of the world that make world reality, consists solely in uninterruptedly and fully consciously following the will of God, in such a way as to be only consciousness and will, but both in higher union, therefore only person, or being that in the most eminent sense."[12]

That Kierkegaard's Christian believer becomes a person by combining consciousness and will in this way is something we might well allow, but the same can hardly be said of *Postscript*'s God. Will and consciousness in some sense, no doubt, but not person. To be a person you must at least exist and thus be subject to time. Consistently with his own principles, Climacus says that God does not exist, he is eternal. He doesn't think either, but creates.[13] If, as we might suppose, there must be at least enough personhood in God for there to be love, since God loves humankind and shows this by sending us his son, here, too, Climacus is consistent. His references to love do not extend to God's love, and the idea of God's love is left to what is implied in the thought of the incarnation as God's gift. God, then, at least in Climacus—in contrast to the tone and expression of the Discourses—is almost entirely impersonal or perhaps apersonal. For Climacus, who is examining what it takes to become a Christian, personhood as an ideal, or personality, must come in some other way, and that is by way of the incarnation. As *Postscript* says, "[t]he object of faith is God's reality in existence as a particular individual, the fact that God has existed as an individual human being."[14] So the personality of God is encapsulated in the God-man.

It is easy to see the theoretical advantage of the God-man concept in a view like the younger Fichte's, where to avoid pantheism there must be a God that is both personality and transcendent. If God is not here but infinite, and yet sense is to be made of a drive toward a personhood that has divine authority, the God-man offers a personality-project in which God is nevertheless revealed in a way that can form a task for individuals, the task of moving themselves in the direction of the example of Jesus. Here, then, contrary to Dreyfus, for whom the God-man is a sort of guarantor for self-made identities whose significance is, in a quite general way, to rise above the grip of a universal ethics, we have an example of an actual way of life presented as a pattern to be imitated. On this reading, the God-man is a paradigm not in the Kuhnian sense, as Dreyfus implies, as a new way of thinking that makes way for personal projects and what moral philosophers now call agent-centered prerogatives, but in the sense of a model way of addressing the world that we should constantly bear in mind as an ideal to which whatever projects we choose must defer.

Given this, there is still much to be said for treating *Postscript* as an itinerary to personality, though it might also be described as a kind of negative prolegomenon. Many including myself have suggested that *Postscript* describes a journey like Hegel's in the *Phenomenology* but in reverse; proceeding not to absolute knowledge but to total ignorance, in order to clear the way for the cognitive position and personal posture proper to faith, that of the individual unaided by any authority. Kierkegaard's innovation in the matter of personality is to have said that it is only from here and in this frame of mind that the personality project can be approached in a way that can secure its fulfillment. *Postscript* prepares us for that faith through which alone the ideal of personality is available to us. The itinerary is not a blueprint; it does not guide you to personality, only to a better idea of where to begin and of how to and how not to proceed. *Postscript* provides no recipe for my or your personal fulfillment, by indirect communication or some such. How could there be a recipe if our fulfillments are to be individually our own? At best it provides a kind of general frame in which the project of personality and its relation to truth are outlined in terms that leave readers to develop their own individually best versions of truth as revealed in the example of the God-man.

So, once again, what secures our identities is not whatever thing or person we decide unconditionally to devote our lives to; it is the belief that, whatever we do, doing it in the right spirit is a way of fulfilling the younger Fichte's idea that we are (or can be) "within" God even when God is outside it all, the anti-pantheistic move (cf. *Postscript*'s "Nature, the totality of created things is the work of God [and] yet God is not there").[15] But where the younger Fichte's conception that we are within God is basically idealist—we *are* within God whatever—Religiousness B bursts the idealist bubble. For all we *know*, we may be outside God. To come within, a two-steps-in-one transformation of the person is required. First, we must freely accept the paradoxical idea of the God-man, and then we have to accept the further paradoxical accompaniment that God appeared as the lowest instead of the highest. From then on we are bound to the project of comporting ourselves accordingly. The first step provides an identity; whatever task or tasks we commit ourselves to in life, we are at the outset no longer "lost." The second tells us that, whatever achievements we may become identified with in the world, it is the way we tackle our tasks that matters, not what impact we have on the world.

All this, if the interpretation is admitted, can be a stumbling block to those who find the religious "premiss" to Kierkegaard's writings confining but at the same time want, like Dreyfus, to recognize his originality. Consider those who, again like Dreyfus, see what is original in Kierkegaard his bringing on stage the conflicts now discussed under the heading of agent-centered prerogatives. Whatever they make of his writings, and unlike Dreyfus, many philosophers have found it hard to take Kierkegaard the author seriously, some would be quite happy to take Kierkegaard himself as a paradigm, as one who personifies the important but contested ethical principle that identity-conferring personal projects need not be overridden by calculations as to what is best for human-kind, in the way received moral theory has generally assumed. There is surely something to be said for using the biography in this way. On the other hand it leaves out what Kierkegaard himself says about exceptions to the universal. Dreyfus does better, he applauds Kierkegaard for introducing the God-man as a paradigm, if not, as I have argued, in the way Kierkegaard intends. For Kierkegaard what is important is not that personal projects be in defiance of accepted expectations, though they may often be so, but rather that, even when they are, they are motivated by faith. The sheer need to find an identity would not suffice.

Part 2.
Natural and
Commanded Love

5.
Love and the Discipline of Philosophy

Rick Anthony Furtak

In this chapter I'm going to take my lead from two essays by Alastair Hannay that have been reprinted as the first two chapters of his recent collection *Kierkegaard and Philosophy*. The earlier of the two was originally called "Kierkegaard's Philosophy of Mind," and the latter first appeared as "Kierkegaard and What We Mean by 'Philosophy.'"[1] Accordingly, I will first say a few things about the importance of taking a humanistic approach to the study of mental phenomena, and then I will proceed to discuss the philosophical significance of Kierkegaard's writing style. The logical relation between these two topics ought to become clear as I go, if it is not already obvious to a reader familiar with Kierkegaard's work. Whether or not he would have wanted us to remember him as a philosopher, Kierkegaard can be seen as making what Hannay calls "contributions to a 'thickened' philosophy that takes fuller account of the ways in which we find ourselves in a world and of our ways of responding to these."[2] Not only do his writings address some of the central problems of philosophy, but they also challenge us to reevaluate our standard ways of approaching these problems. If contemporary philosophers hesitate to view Kierkegaard's work as pertinent to their concerns, this is just another sign that the discipline of philosophy, as it currently exists, is in need of a Kierkegaardian thickening if it is to survive in a form that is worthy of its own name.

Part 1—Kierkegaard and the Philosophy of Mind

There is a lot of talk in philosophy of mind about the "hard problem" of consciousness, or "the problem of *experience*."[3] Within this context, Thomas Nagel has famously argued that the "subjective character of experience" is not adequately captured by scientific explanations that assume that we obtain "a more accurate view of the real nature of things" only as we "move in the direction of greater objectivity."[4] Regarding certain objects of inquiry, it makes sense to eliminate personal bias and to rely upon highly restricted techniques of measurement. But when we are trying to understand love and other varieties of meaningful human experience, this is a dubious move: by abstracting away from the viewpoint of a specific person, we may lose touch with the phenomena we are ostensibly talking about. Nagel is concerned about this tendency to adopt what he calls *the view from nowhere,* since "there are things about the world . . . that cannot be adequately understood from a maximally objective standpoint"—for instance, "the pursuit of objectivity with respect to value runs the risk of leaving value behind altogether."[5]

Of course, the unacknowledged source of this distinction between the outer and the inner is Kierkegaard, whose insistence upon the validity of the first-person perspective "goes against the grain of most recent philosophy of mind."[6] But even those Anglophone philosophers who have taken an interest in "the view from within" have generally failed to recognize that they could benefit from a serious engagement with Kierkegaard's writings. Nevertheless, as the field of consciousness studies continues to expand its horizons, it is likely to find itself moving in this direction sooner or later. Kierkegaard shows us why *objectivity,* so often conflated with *accuracy* or *rationality,* might sometimes be a misguided ideal; and he helps us to understand how it is that love can provide us with a kind of insight that isn't available from the vantage point of dispassionate cognition. Even if it were possible to ascend to a God's-eye point of view on human experience, we would find it impossible to breathe in that atmosphere: the sort of thing that it matters for us to know is visible only from the vantage point of a person who is engaged in the business of living on earth.[7]

It ought to go without saying that this business is an unscientific one. If it were the case that research in the natural sciences could make any discoveries that would clarify mental or spiritual life, Kierkegaard writes, then "I'd be the first to get my hands on a microscope."[8] His aim is not to disparage biology or physics, but to point out that the sort of thing he cares about as a moral psychologist does not yield to scientific investigation. The target of his criticism in this journal entry from 1846 is the tendency to speak as if such things as promises do not *really* exist, since they cannot be seen through a microscope, nor can they be weighed or measured like a stone or a potato. Quine is neither the first nor the last philosopher to argue that "[w]hatever can be known can be known by means of science alone,"[9] and this positivistic assumption is tacitly shared by the intellectual culture of our time, influencing even the most well-intentioned members of the popular media. A striking illustration of the prevailing scientism is provided by John Dupré, a philosopher of science who describes an educational television program that he happened to stumble upon:

The official topic of the episode was Love. In between images of chemical clouds bubbling out of glands and diffusing through the body, the program traced the effects of hormones on sexual differentiation *in utero* and in puberty. Distinguished scientists reported the exciting and sometimes surprising results of our recent ability to measure the levels of hormones in bodies, and correlations between these levels and the emotional states of the subjects were noted. As different behavioral tendencies were shown to develop in males and females, evolutionists informed us about the functions these might have served for our Stone Age ancestors. Reaching the official topic of love, we were taught to distinguish its various phases—infatuation, obsession, companionship—and their hormonal correlates. Magnetic Resonance Imaging of obsessed lovers revealed similarities between their brain activities and those of the mentally disturbed, providing, apparently, scientific evidence that love is indeed a form of madness. Later, we learned that whether male [rodents] remained faithful to their partners or indulged in untrammelled promiscuity depended on the presence of specific hormones, and we were invited to speculate as to whether similar mechanisms might operate in humans. And so on. Although much of this work was admitted to be at a somewhat speculative stage, the scientists involved expressed no reservations about the possibility that love might turn out to be caused by, or just to be—such ontological subtleties were not addressed—a sequence of hormonal surges. . . . This programme illustrates the hold on our culture of what I call scientism, an exaggerated and often distorted conception of what science can be expected to do or explain for us. One aspect of scientism is the idea that any question that can be answered at all can best be answered by science. This, in turn, is very often combined with a quite narrow conception of what it is for an answer, or a method of investigation, to be scientific. . . . Everywhere this implies a restriction of the powers of the human mind; but nowhere is this restriction more disastrous than in the mind's attempts to answer questions about itself.[10]

Even in the philosophy of mind and in ethical philosophy, we hear plenty of doubt as to whether beliefs and pains are real, or whether aesthetic and moral values such as beauty and honesty are *actually* just as nonexistent as unicorns and phlogiston.[11] If you want to understand love, according to those who believe that philosophy ought to be "hard" and not "soft," then you must ask the leading behavioral scientists of the day. You are likely to hear them speculate about the arrival of a "completed neuroscience" that will somehow explain away the phenomenon and tell us what is *really* going on. Then we will have no more talk of promises, holidays, reputations, misunderstandings, and threatening gestures; since none of these things can be quantitatively weighed or measured, the positivist argues, they must be unreal.[12] As one philosopher of this stripe remarks, in the midst of a discussion of conscious awareness, "there may be no such thing as awareness."[13] This is equivalent to a philosopher going to the ballet and then concluding, in the name of a naturalized aesthetics, that there is actually no such thing as gracefulness (or lack thereof, for that matter). If beauty does not show up in our scientific account of the world, according to this way of thinking, then it must lie in the eye of the beholder; and the idea that we experience meaning in life can only be dismissed as a myth about the existence of some obscure substance that no physical instrument is able to detect.

According to this hard-nosed naturalistic way of thinking, it is hard to see how there can be such a thing as (for example) matrimony: if there were, then "people would have to be bound to one another in marriage, and everything we see . . . goes to suggest that the only way that people can be bound to one another is *with ropes*."[14] But when we speak of meaning or value or significance, we are not referring to something that could be put in a jar, like peanut butter. Rather, we are focusing upon a relational property of objects viewed in a certain light, by a subject who is emotionally involved in the world that he or she is experiencing. Our emotions provide us with a valuable mode of awareness, since they call our attention to the salient features of things, making whatever matters to us stand out in sharp relief. If I am annoyed, then something must be annoying me; and I cannot sincerely claim to be afraid of you unless I see you as frightening for some reason. We cannot even identify these emotions without using intentional language that makes reference to the external world: no study of what is going on inside my skull could distinguish, for instance, my unrequited love for Cordelia from every other possible state of mind.[15] An MRI scan may be able to indicate a general pattern of agitation, but it cannot explain what has made me upset: in order to distinguish what emotional response I am undergoing, one must look at the whole situation and give an account of what is going on between mind and world.

In a certain sense, things would be easier for us if we could inhabit the view from nowhere rather than an emotional point of view: our vulnerability to emotions is a direct consequence of our passionate engagement with a world that we did not create and do not control. The ancient Stoic avoids the risk of emotion by cultivating an impersonal perspective, proclaiming that "the lofty mind always remains calm, at rest in a tranquil haven."[16] And there is no better way to guarantee tranquility of mind than to view human existence as devoid of meaning or value, rejecting every appearance of significance until life has been reduced to absurdity. We will not be moved by the beauty of a purple robe if we see it as "nothing but" a piece of sheep's wool dyed with the blood of a shellfish, nor will we be troubled by human affairs if we see them as "nothing but" a worthless and disgusting progression from sperm to ashes.[17] When objects make a claim upon us by appearing meaningful, the Stoics tell us that we must break them up into their constituent parts, strip them bare, and destroy the myth that they are of any significance.[18] The goal of this revaluation of values, according to Marcus Aurelius, is to end up viewing things "scientifically"; what he means by this is something like looking through a microscope at whatever is most precious in life so that, under closer scrutiny, it does not appear to be so impressive after all.

This project is certainly liberating, but it ought to remind us of Kierke-gaard's remark that "the way to make life easy is to make it meaningless."[19] We should not represent as scientific rigor what is nothing other than moral insensitivity, and yet our quest for objectivity can lead us to doubt whether the world really is the way that it appears to be from the perspective of an emotional person. It is a remarkable feature of human beings that "we are creatures to whom things matter," as Frankfurt points out, but it ought to seem no less remarkable that the world matters to us as it does.[20] Emotions arise from our caring engagement with reality, and they reveal as much about that "objective" reality as they do about our own subjectivity. When we are fully disengaged from our surroundings, everything seems empty and absurd—but this is a departure from our ordinary emotional mode of being. The stoical withdrawal from contingent experience into abstract detachment is a kind of perversion: in trying to isolate mind from world, we forget that our consciousness has no content except in relation to its environment.[21] And it is possible, as Nagel says, to reach "a standpoint so removed from the perspective of human life that all we can do is to observe."[22] For his part, Kierkegaard remarks that something has gone wrong when the *participants* in a specific activity "have judiciously transformed themselves into a crowd of *spectators*."[23] When we strive for an "objective" vantage point, we find ourselves alienated from a world that no longer provokes any emotional response, since its significance is simply lost on us.

By virtue of what do we find ourselves inhabiting a significant world, seeing things from a perspective quite unlike the view from nowhere? In a word, Kierkegaard's answer is: *love.* "Love," he writes, "is the source of all things and . . . the deepest ground of spiritual life."[24] His descriptive account of love as the source of emotional life is integrated with a normative reflection on what it means to be a loving (or "caring")[25] person. To see things with loving eyes is to embrace their concrete particularity in the most favorable light, appreciating them for being exactly what they are; to love (or to care for) someone is to take an unselfish interest in his or her interests, without asking for anything in return.[26] Because "what one sees depends upon how one sees," Kierkegaard argues that the world is experienced as meaningful only if we view it with a charitable disposition.[27] Love is what illuminates the human world, enabling us to perceive the distinctive significance of things, and thereby providing us with focus and orientation in a life that is worth living. We might say that love bonds us to what is beyond us, creating between self and world the "engagements in which we find ourselves."[28]

Our lifeworld is one in which ordinary things are weighted with significance: a corpse is revolting, a living room soothing. At a glance we see the police officer's anger, even though we may fail to notice the color of his eyes. Objects are not merely inert bulky structures; they "lure and threaten us, support and obstruct us, sustain and debilitate us, direct us and calm us."[29] In short, experience is routinely permeated with meaning; however, the axiologically salient features of reality would be perceived as neutral facts by anyone other than a loving subject—that is, if they were perceived at all. Love, in other words, "is not solely a warm approval of what is already present": it is what enables things to show up and be noticed in the first place.[30] A passage from Dostoevsky's "Dream of a Ridiculous Man" suggests that a person who drifted through life in a state of complete indifference would be profoundly out of touch with the world:

> I realized that it *would not matter* whether the world existed or whether there was nothing at all anywhere. I began to intuit and sense with all my being, that *there was nothing around me*. At first I was inclined to think that in the past there had been a great deal, but later on I divined that formerly too there had been nothing, it had merely seemed otherwise for some reason. I gradually became convinced that there would be nothing in the future either. It was then that I suddenly stopped being angry at other people and almost ceased to notice them. Indeed this became apparent even in the most trivial matters: for example, I would bump into people as I was walking along the street.[31]

Except for a bit of Cartesian certainty about his own existence, this narrator has lost the world in his apathetic detachment: as far as he is concerned, even the people he bumps into on the street might as well not exist. What he conspicuously lacks is the emotional disposition that is required in order to be able to perceive the significance of things. Now, to an unloving or skeptical observer, it will never be obvious that anything *deserves* to be loved.[32] But this statement is analogous to Locke's claim that the red color of porphyry is not *really* in the object, but is only an illusory appearance—because, as he famously argues, we cannot see its color in the dark![33] What it is for something to be red, of course, is for it to appear red, when suitably illuminated, to anyone with eyes to see.[34] Just as colors cannot be seen in the dark, values cannot be seen in the absence of the required emotional receptivity. In this sense, our capacity for viewing things in the best possible light has something in common with color vision. Objects can be experienced as meaningful (or colorful) only if we perceive them under favorable conditions and in the appropriate way.

"If you yourself have never been in love," Kierkegaard argues, then "you do not know whether anyone has ever been loved in this world, although you do know how many have affirmed that they have loved": it is only "if you yourself have loved" that you know what it is like to experience the world in this way.[35] Likewise, he adds, "[t]he blind person cannot know color differences; he must be content that others have assured him that they do exist and that they are thus and so."[36] In order to understand this comparison, we should take into account the fact that the person who is *not* blind does not spawn the world of light and color out of his own mind, but must be constituted in a certain way in order to perceive what is visible. What is visible, such as the red color of the rose, is certainly "out there" in the world, but it would be nonsensical to ascribe this property to the object as viewed from nowhere. What it means to say that the rose is visible and colored is that these appearances are there "to be met with in the object's relation to the subject," to borrow a phrase from the *Critique of Pure Reason*.[37] Extending this point into the domain of emotional perception (where Kant would not follow us), we could say that when an object is "met with on the path of care, it is experienced as meaningful."[38] As Heidegger also realizes, it is not merely an incidental fact about us that we are loving or caring beings—rather, it is a foundational condition of life as we know it. The features of the world that we perceive as loving subjects are no less real for being undiscoverable by any scientific investigation; we have no more reason to doubt the reality of what love reveals to us than to be skeptical about the material existence of the red rose.

This is why, according to Kierkegaard, our conception of rationality needs to be drastically redefined: "to love and to know are essentially synonymous," he contends, "and just as to love signifies that the other becomes manifest, so it naturally means that one becomes manifest himself."[39] Following up on this idea (although, like Heidegger, failing to acknowledge its source), Jean-Luc Marion writes that love "opens up knowledge of the other as such."[40] It is a virtue to be truly in love, but simply to call it a virtue is to risk missing the moral-psychological point: without love, we would not be able to lead a life that is recognizably human. If love is a category through which we perceive the world, then we must reconsider what it would mean to see things as they really are. It is an untenable prejudice to believe that reality is more accurately perceived without emotion, or that existence can be clarified from a stripped-down, value-free, "scientific" viewpoint. Although I am outside of you, I can see you either as living flesh or as dead meat.[41] The former way of seeing is the caring awareness that an executioner must omit; the latter might be defended as more "rational" or "objective" by a scientific observer. But what we perceive when we occupy an emotional point of view is nothing other than the concrete particularity of the world, seen by an appreciative participant. Defining his criteria for a state of knowledge that would put the human mind in touch with the world, Kierkegaard writes: "an objectivity which takes shape in a corresponding subjectivity, that is the goal."[42]

Elsewhere, he adds that all understanding basically depends upon "how one is disposed toward something."[43] When we size things up from a skeptical perspective, we find no shortage of reasons for complaining about our circumstances; by virtue of love, however, we may be able to overcome this habit of distrust. The person who loves finds that the world is charged with a significance that could not be appreciated by a differently constituted observer. At the same time, he develops a kind of unscientific cognition "that displays how the world is *seen*, known by *this* self, and moved by *these* emotions."[44] This mode of knowing has its own validity according to premises quite unlike those that lead many philosophers to prefer the view from nowhere: ultimately, there is no reason to assume that the world is *not* just as meaningful as it appears to a loving subject. This way of seeing can therefore be described as a dispositional prerequisite for the recognition of value in the world. Although it would be unrealistic to expect that *everyone* could be convinced that a life on such terms is worth living, we should at least be able to agree that the flight to scientific objectivity does not always lead us closer to the truth. If we still insist upon developing a "science of the mind," then we ought to approach the topic in such a way that our *scientia* (in the classical sense) can take the form of a humanistic "understanding."[45]

Part 2—Literature and the Art of Philosophy

Be that as it may, the language of philosophical argument is not commonly influenced by this humanistic ideal: our picture of how philosophy ought to be written is much more likely to have been shaped by the legacy of scientistic positivism. Since this is not the best idiom in which to give an account of the significant mind-world relations that are the fabric of moral life, our standard vocabulary can actually limit our understanding. One way of describing the challenge posed by Kierkegaard's writings to those of us who practice philosophy is that they force us to reconsider the pictures that hold us captive, and that define our attitude toward the conceptual issues that concern us. Operating with the wrong picture of how philosophy ought to be written could prevent us from saying anything at all about the person—and this, as Hannay points out, is "a deficiency serious enough to make comedy when philosophy claims to speak to our personal needs."[46] Following Stanley Cavell, Hannay suggests that we view Kierkegaard's religious sphere of existence as a Wittgensteinian form of life, with a distinctive grammar that provides us with a way of seeing the world and of interpreting our own experience.[47] The world of the person who believes in a God of love is not the same as the world of the reductive positivist who seeks to naturalize all mental phenomena, so we should not be surprised to find them talking past one another:

> Religious solutions to human misery are often seen as makeshifts awaiting genuine amelioration through some beneficial adjustment in the conditions of life. But it is also possible to look at it the other way around. One may always, of course, give psychological and sociological explanations of why people like Kierkegaard have such needs. But one may also choose to side with Kierkegaard, to see things as he does, and say, "This is how it really is."[48]

What ought to move us to accept or to reject Kierkegaard's ideas is not primarily their dogmatic content, but whether or not we find that they offer us "a persuasive or adequate depiction of the human condition."[49] One of his goals, then, is to move his readers to reflect upon their own presuppositions, and to realize that different internally coherent ways of experiencing reality are available, each with its own language. But in order to create a space in which a person might change her basic way of seeing the world, it is necessary to get her to reconsider the most familiar terms of her self-understanding, either directly or indirectly. This goes some way toward explaining why Kierkegaard's works are written in such an unusual variety of styles, and why he rejected the philosophical dialect of his contemporaries with a polemic that, as Hannay notes, would be just as relevant in the present day.[50]

Most of those who are known as "philosophers" in the Western tradition are authors of one kind or another, and the rare exception of a nonliterary figure such as Socrates is remembered as a philosopher largely because he was admired and memorialized by a very good writer. And yet few people involved in the discipline of philosophy seem to think of themselves as authors, even when they have in fact written many books. David Hume claimed that his *Treatise of Human Nature* was composed just after he had resolved to devote himself to "the improvement of my talents in literature";[51] however, this notion of philosophical writing as a literary art has remained largely foreign to the treatise writers of the English-speaking world. For the most part, Anglophone philosophers would prefer to think of themselves as "conceptual engineers," or something of the sort, rather than as writers. In this climate, it is worth turning to the assaults on philosophy that literary authors have been making since Philip Sidney's "Defense of Poesy" to see if they might be identifying problems that the philosophers cannot afford to ignore. For instance, in an essay entitled "Why the Novel Matters," D. H. Lawrence complains that the "damned philosophers" like to "talk about infinity, and the pure spirit which knows all things"[52]—whereas, "if you pick up a novel," he says, you immediately recognize the inability of such abstract and purified writing to capture the practical knowledge that we rely upon in the context of embodied life. Now, to a positivist, Lawrence can only be seen as an irrationalist gratuitously threatening to bring sensuous material into the realm of calculation.[53] But this bias is based upon the notion that philosophical thought is, and ought only to be, abstracted from any human vantage point, like any other "hard" science. Once we realize that the terms "hard" and "soft" are no more useful for describing philosophers than for classifying novelists, we are in a position to rethink the common belief that philosophical writing should be closer in style to the scientific article than to the literary narrative.

Take emotional perception, for example. Each time I am emotionally affected in one way or another, I experience what a phenomenologist would call a modification of my subjectivity. Therefore, my own perspective must be central to any characterization of what is happening: a language in which "all significant questions become general" will not be able to do justice to this particular event.[54] Already we can see the problem with philosophical argument that takes place in an "abstract realm, without characters, without situations," as if the path of abstraction will always lead to truth.[55] If it hopes to illuminate the human condition, philosophy must speak from *within* concrete existence rather than launching into the sort of objective reflection in which the thinker forgets himself, speaking a merely abstract language "which explains nothing and understands nothing," and dissolving all of existence into "utterly indifferent talk about Persia, China," and so on.[56] Vague generalizations about world history may have their place, but they are hideously unable to address the complexities faced by the individual who loves and suffers. In order to be attuned to this predicament, Kierkegaard suggests, the philosopher requires a different kind of sensitivity and a vocabulary that is appropriate for his subject matter: "Nothing is easier for any reasonably literate person than to give, for instance, a kind of survey of the art of Chinese, Indian, Persian, ancient, and romantic drama . . . on the other hand, nothing is more difficult than to examine and elucidate a single dramatic performance by an actor or an actress."[57]

Something is wrong with philosophical writing that supposedly has to do with moral situations, but which is so dead to the properties of objects in the world, so descriptively inept, that it cannot say what it is that makes anything honest, graceful, ugly, or shocking, or why we ought to apply one of these evaluative terms rather than another in a given situation. Yet as frustrating as it is to hear a positivist declare that axiological terms add nothing to the factual content of a statement,[58] there is something equally objectionable about philosophical writing that cleverly invents a neologism and then declares that this bit of jargon *du jour* is neither a concept nor a word but the nonoriginal origin of all differences.[59] Whether analytic or continental in their orientation, philosophers get into trouble when they insist upon speaking an alienating technical vocabulary: when their words are unrelated to ordinary language, their readers may be left with the impression that nothing other than theory is at stake, or that what they are reading does not pertain to human existence. As if he were foreseeing both kinds of bad writing, Kierkegaard states that when philosophy invents its own peculiar terminology (rather than "appropriating the given"), it "usually ends in silence" or in the "personal isolation of jargonish nonsense."[60]

What mode of expression could avoid the literary deficiencies of both Ayer's and Derrida's writings? To begin with, it would have to be one that allows us to come to terms with the predicament of a situated human being, rather than abstracting the human being away from his or her connections with the world.[61] And the philosophical treatise is not the literary genre best suited to explore *what it is like* to respond to the salient features of a particular situation—such as the blush on a person's cheek or the dreamlike atmosphere of evening.[62] It is much more likely to be in the novel or the poem that one finds a record of everything that appears significant from the vantage point of an emotional person. Opposing the philosophical notion that "the task is to become more and more objective, to divest oneself of his subjectivity," the poets (according to

Kierkegaard) claim that it is a rare achievement to give voice to one's own experience as a loving subject.[63] From the reader's point of view, an engagement with literary works of art helps to guard against moral insensibility by exercising our imaginative awareness of what it is like to be someone other than ourselves,[64] and by calling our attention to morally relevant qualities in the world. As noble as it is to think of myself as a citizen in the kingdom of ends, I will be nothing but an insensitive bus passenger in a real city if I fail to notice that someone is standing uncomfortably and that there are no more seats.[65] The obtuseness that I display by not being attuned to this situation is a moral shortcoming that can be averted through the cultivation of sympathetic imagination: or, in other words, passionate understanding. "Accurate, clear, decisive, impassioned understanding is of great importance," Kierkegaard says, since "it facilitates action."[66] Moral agency relies upon the mode of perception in which we recognize the significance of contingent particularity. If novels and poems are uniquely able to help us refine our moral and emotional perception, then they ought to be recognized as contributions to our philosophical knowledge.

Iris Murdoch has observed that "[w]e differ not only because we select different objects out of the same world but because we see different worlds," and she also argues that fine-grained changes in our way of seeing are most adequately examined not in philosophical texts but in literary works.[67] The lyrical delineation of a slight change of heart, or the narration of an ambiguous situation in which the moral of the story is *not* clear, enables us to explore intricate and difficult issues as they might arise in the context of our own experience.[68] Among the Greeks that Kierkegaard held in such high esteem, philosophical and literary writings were not sharply distinguished, and both were expected to help a person understand the significance of an experience such as falling in love. When Alcibiades (in Plato's *Symposium*) is asked to speak about love, he gives "no definitions or explanations of the nature of anything, but just a story of a particular passion for a particular contingent individual."[69] Likewise, when Johannes de Silentio sets out to introduce the category of "infinite resignation," he does not offer an abstract account of this state of consciousness and its place in world history, nor does he give us a list of necessary and sufficient conditions expressed in pseudo-scientific language imported from set theory: he simply tells the story of one "young lad" who falls in love with a princess.[70] This mode of exposition is appropriate to its subject matter because—as Plato must have realized—some truths about love are inescapably particular, and can be illustrated only in concrete and poetic language. Warning philosophers not to shy away from such raw material, Martha Nussbaum notes that "it is of such incongruous juxtapositions, such intimate perceptions and failures of perception, that real-life love, and philosophy if it is to tell the truth about love, are made."[71] Unless contemporary philosophers are not even up to the task of adding "footnotes to Plato" on this particular theme, we must go beyond making the vague observation that literature "seems to have something important to do with our lives,"[72] and begin to engage more seriously with literary texts and the all-too-human phenomena they bring to our attention.

As he occasionally tells us and continually shows us, Kierkegaard is not accidentally writing in a literary style from which the content of his work can be safely abstracted. It is frequently clear that his meaning would not survive a paraphrase—especially one in which terms that have a particular significance are replaced with more general language. A resistance to paraphrase is often cited as the distinguishing feature of poetic texts,[73] and it is true that some devices in Kierkegaard's writings resist being captured by any translation that does not manage to re-create the style of the original. Roger Poole believes that English translators have not captured the alliteration in *The Concept of Anxiety*,[74] but in other cases this poetic effect does seem to have been well conveyed by Kierkegaard's translators: for instance, "Where does love come from, where does it have its origin and its source, where is the place from which it has its abode from which it flows?"[75] This passage, from early in *Works of Love,* is followed by a number of ontological claims, all of which are written in a language rich with vivid imagery.

> [J]ust as the sun's rays invite a person to behold the glory of the world by their help but warningly punish the presumptuous one with blindness when he wants to turn around in order, inquisitively and brazenly, to discover the origin of the light . . . in the same way it is love's desire and wish that its secret source and its hidden life in the innermost being may remain a secret, that no one inquisitively and brazenly will force his way in disturbingly in order to see that which he cannot see anyway without forfeiting, because of his curiosity, the joy and blessing of it. . . . Love's hidden life is in the innermost being, unfathomable, and then in turn is in an unfathomable connectedness with all existence. Just as the quiet lake originates deep down in the hidden springs no eye has seen, so also does a person's love originate even more deeply in God's love.[76]

Here Kierkegaard's poetic metaphors are not merely ornamental: it would undermine the point of the whole passage if he were to speak in the dead, flat language of logical positivism or the behavioral sciences, or in the fashionable jargon that dominates much of continental philosophy. Likewise, the sequence of poetic snapshots of Abraham and Isaac in the opening "Attunement" (or "Exordium") to *Fear and Trembling* have all the intensity, and the cryptic suggestiveness, of the best lyric poems: every time we revisit them, we find something we have not seen before. Although theories of linguistic meaning normally don't say very much about those aspects of an utterance that are not captured by an indirect quotation, these examples ought to give us pause the next time we are tempted to imagine that the soul of a text can be harmlessly separated from its flesh.

Of course, the philosopher is not the only kind of author whose words can either succeed or fail to do justice to the world of human experience, and even a work filled with conceptual argument can demonstrate an evident awareness of what it is to be a living, breathing individual who is interested in the matter at hand.[77] Perhaps the best philosophical writing succeeds at performing the kind of abstraction that stays within sight of the reality from which it has abstracted. But this is just to say that philosophy succeeds at illuminating existence from within only insofar as it is animated by an acute literary imagination. Kierkegaard would presumably agree that "the philosopher must go to school with the poets in order to learn the use of language, and must use it in their way: as a means of exploring one's own mind, and bringing to light what is obscure and doubtful in it."[78] His bizarre variety of writings give us reason to believe that philosophy will be impoverished as long as it lacks a poetic sensibility. The question of how to go on in light of this realization is one that must be faced by every one of us who cares about both Kierkegaard *and* philosophy.

6.
Kierkegaard and Ethical Theory

Robert C. Roberts

Introduction

Anyone who happens to read both Kierkegaard's writings and the works of moral philosophers from the last hundred years or so is bound to be struck by the great difference in character of these two bodies of literature. One might well read *Works of Love* or *Practice in Christianity* or *Upbuilding Discourses in Various Spirits* as a source of personal moral strengthening, as part of daily spiritual exercises. Indeed, Kierkegaard intended these works for just such use. The reader who chose David Gauthier's *Morals by Agreement* or Michael Slote's *Morals from Motives* for the same purpose would be sorely disappointed—or, if he somehow persisted in the endeavor, might actually suffer damage to his moral constitution.

Yet Kierkegaard is often treated as in some sense a philosopher, and one whose thought is highly relevant to ethics; were it not relevant to ethics, it would lack the upbuilding potential that he carefully puts into it. So the thought occurs—and this is the one I want to explore in this chapter—that while Kierkegaard is doing moral philosophy in some sense, he is doing something interestingly different from what professional philosophers of ethics do, philosophers whom Kierkegaard might well have lumped with "the professors" (for the vast majority of them are such). Sometime in the middle or later period of modern philosophy, philosophers of ethics began to speak of "moral theory," though the thing itself was being done before it was named. Today, the word 'theory' dots the pages of moral philosophers, and they quite happily think of their main business as constructing theories. In this chapter I am going to try out the idea that the word 'theory' provides a nice key to the difference—or at any rate an important part of the difference—between what Kierkegaard is doing in his writings and what the professors are doing. My thesis is that Kierkegaard does not have a theory in the sense that ethics professors are supposed to, and that what he is doing in his writings is better thought of as a conceptual exploration, within a given moral tradition (Christianity), that expresses, seeks, and seeks to engender *wisdom*. Theory and wisdom, then, will both be conceptual activities, and they will have some overlapping properties. Otherwise, how could they both be philosophical and about ethics? But they will also be deeply different, and that difference will account for our sense of difference as we read the two kinds of writing.

In the next section I will try to get clear on what an ethical theory is, and will look particularly at a couple of proposals of a "virtue theory" of ethics, because Kierkegaard does quite often write about virtues—love, faith, hope, patience, gratitude, humility, courage, and the like—and because on my understanding of how he is seeking wisdom, and seeking to promote it, he does so largely by exploring such virtue-concepts.[1] Then, since a peculiarity of the ethical thought that we find in *Works of Love*[2] is the emphasis that Kierkegaard places on the fact that Christian love is commanded, I will consider the possibility that he has, in some sense, a divine command theory. To get a clear contemporary example of a divine command theory before us, I will look at the one that Robert Adams proposes in *Finite and Infinite Goods*. We will see that Adams's procedure deviates pretty significantly from paradigm cases of moral theorizing, but is still recognizable (and intended) as such. Finally, I will turn to *Works of Love* to compare what Kierkegaard does there with what Adams does, and will argue that Kierkegaard's discussions of divine commands in that work are better regarded as embodying wisdom than as proposing a divine command theory. I will try to characterize what I take to be the connection, in Kierkegaard's agenda, between his comments about the divine command and the concept of love.

Ethical Theories

Early modern philosophy is preoccupied with finding common ground beneath disagreements, ground so solid and so obviously so to everybody that it can sustain a superstructure of knowledge about which everyone who stands on it can agree. The superstructure is somehow attached to the ground by equally incontrovertible fasteners (say, of logic or mathematics). Some say that behind this preoccupation with securing agreement was horror at the wars of the Reformation, which were made possible by the breakup of the medieval consensus regarding God, morality, and the meaning of life.[3] If only we could find incontrovertible ground on which all people of good will could base their beliefs, then such deadly conflicts would be stopped at their sources, thought such thinkers as René Descartes and John Locke.

The classical ethical theories were products of this preoccupation. For Kant, the ground of all moral obligations was pure practical reason, expressed in the formulas of the categorical imperative. Being reason (*pure* practical reason, no less!), the ground was to be completely solid and incontrovertible, and all that was needed to secure agreement was to derive all the other imperatives of morality from this one, perfectly secure principle. The early utilitarians, perhaps not feeling quite secure on the Kantian ground, offered an alternative "groundwork," namely, quantified pleasure. Who could deny that happiness, thought of in this simple way, was what everybody wanted? And who could deny the principle, *the more the better*? So all we need, to get agreement about controversial moral questions, is to calculate the amount of overall happiness that each alternative is likely to afford. In a similar way, social contract theories took harmonious social interaction, with its obvious desirability, to be a solid ground from which all genuine ethical values could be derived. These theories, far from resolving the disagreements, were themselves disagreed about, and by now we have become pretty cynical about the prospect of any single theory succeeding as a means of securing agreement. In many college ethics classes that center on these moral theories, the professor's de facto educational accomplishment is just the opposite of the authors' original intention: he or she induces a kind of skepticism by presenting morality as *needing* a foundation of the kind the theories posit, and by showing that none of the candidates can bear the load.

But despite our realism about prospects for the foundationalist program in ethics, philosophers continue to model ethical inquiry on these theories. If we look at recent writings on the virtues—say, Michael Slote's *Morals from Motives*[4] and Rosalind Hursthouse's *On Virtue Ethics*[5] and many papers on virtue that have appeared in professional journals in recent years—we note frequent recurrence of words like 'derive,' 'derivative,' 'depend on,' 'subordinate,' 'define in terms of,' 'construct out of,' 'based,' 'grounded,' 'grounding,' 'independent,' 'conceptually prior,' 'supreme,' 'fundamental,' 'foundation,' and the like in connection with moral concepts. That is, we find authors preoccupied with *ordering* moral concepts in such a way that some of them are subordinated to or derived from other concepts or some single other concept so that some one or small number of moral concepts become the source, the ground, the foundation, the base, of the others. This ordering will also be an order of justification. The foundational concept presumably does not need justifying, or is self-justifying, and it is what justifies the other concepts. This ordering is also an order of explanation. The foundational concept does not need explaining or is self-explanatory, and the other concepts are explained by reference to it. Ethical theories then differ according to which concept or concepts provide the foundation, and which ones are derivative. They will also differ as to how the derivations work and which concepts are closer to the foundation and which more distant from it.

The various virtue-theories are *virtue*-theories because they give the concept of virtue the conceptual priority that Hobbes gave to social contract and Kant to practical reason and Bentham to pleasure.

Michael Slote's recent book is a particularly clear example. His project is to defend an "agent-based approach to virtue ethics" that "treats the moral or ethical status of acts as entirely derivative from independent and fundamental aretaic (as opposed to deontic) ethical characterizations of motives, character-traits, or individuals" (p. 5). Slote's proposed moral theory accounts for the moral status of acts (good or bad, right or wrong) by deriving it "entirely" from aretaic construals of motives, etc. Thus if we wish to know whether a particular action is a good one, we will try to ascertain the agent's motive in performing it. If his motive was virtuous, then the action was good, and if his motive was vicious, the action was bad; and presumably the same for the states of affairs generated by the action. So if I give a beggar $10 out of a morally indifferent motive such as a desire to lighten my billfold a bit, my action is morally indifferent; and if I do so out of a virtuous motive, such as compassion for the beggar, my action is good; and if I perform the action out of a vicious desire to embarrass my walking companions, my action is bad. And this is the *whole* story about the moral goodness or badness of the action, on the sort of theory that Slote is promoting. These moral qualities of the acts do not derive at all from the social consequences of the acts—say, the benefit or harm I do to the beggar or the damage I do to my relationship with my walking companions—nor do the acts have an "independent" moral value. Furthermore, the moral status of the motives of compassion or cruelty is not derived from any ethical concepts at all. It is "independent [of other moral concepts] and fundamental." This arrangement of the concepts is artificial and paradoxical, but has the merit of bringing a simplifying order to the conceptual array, an order, furthermore, that is *secured* at a certain point. The whole idea of a base or foundation is that of something that needs no securing or deriving, something that will stand fast by itself and give orientation and steadiness to the whole. And Slote's theory is an example of *virtue*-ethics because of the place the virtue concepts occupy in the conceptual system: they form the base or foundation.

Slote's thought is a particularly clear example of this understanding of moral theory, but we find many examples in the literature. Gary Watson says that an ethics of virtue is "a set of abstract theses about how certain concepts are best fitted together for the purposes of understanding morality . . . [in which] the concept of virtue is in some way theoretically dominant." "An ethics of virtue is . . . the . . . general claim that action appraisal is derivative from the appraisal of character."[6] Linda Zagzebski says that her favored type of moral theory "makes the concept of a right act derivative from the concept of a virtue or some inner state of a person that is a component of virtue" and that "pure virtue theorists deny that virtue is an excellence because it is a means to some external good."[7]

Robert Louden's critique of virtue ethics assumes that it's a theory analogous to deontology and utilitarianism, thus characterized by "conceptual reduction-ism."[8] We see this pattern in Rosalind Hursthouse's comment that "according to virtue ethics—and this book—what is wrong with lying, when it is wrong, is not that it is unjust (because it violates someone's 'right to the truth' or their 'right to be treated with respect') but that it is *dishonest,* and dishonesty is a vice."[9] Note the exclusions. (But isn't injustice as much a vice as dishonesty?) Later in the book she affirms vegetarianism "on the grounds that (1) temper-ance (with respect to the pleasures of food) is a virtue, and (2) for most of 'us,' eating meat is intemperate (greedy, self-indulgent)" (p. 227). But her theory is not a virtue ethics in the strict sense of Watson and Slote, since it makes human nature even more fundamental than the virtues (see chapters 9–11).[10] My point is just that the standard way of doing business in ethical philosophy these days is to play the game of deriving moral concepts from some more "fundamental" concept—or if need be, from some small set of concepts. That is what philoso-phers these days call moral theory. Given that these philosophers do not have the kind of ethical hope for their theories that the earlier modern philosophers had for theirs, it is hard to see why they persist in this enterprise, unless it is just that they are in the grip of a cultural professional habit: *if you are a philosopher, this is what you do.* If that is their "thinking," it is a far cry indeed from the missionary mentality of Kierkegaard.

Virtue theories in ethics are even more implausible than their classical modern predecessors, and I shall not waste time showing that Kierkegaard is not a virtue ethicist in this sense. In the next section I will try to formulate, in an abstract and textually unsupported way, what I think Kierkegaard does do with ethical and spiritual concepts as he executes his program of reintroducing Christianity to Christendom.

Kierkegaard's Wisdom

In *Works of Love* Kierkegaard expounds the concept of Christian love in a wide variety of its facets; indeed, the book looks like an attempt to be virtually com-prehensive. On the reading that I shall propose, Kierkegaard's dialectical-poetic activity in *Works of Love* is like a microscopic travelogue charting the surface, as well as the transparent depths, as plumbed from various vantage points, of a beautiful diamond. That multifaceted jewel is of course the concept of Christian love. We can think of each aspect of the concept as like a structured facet whose shape and angle are determined by the neighboring facets, with the character of the whole jewel constituted of all the facets taken together. Kierkegaard explores the diamond from each of many vantage points on its surface, but also often compares it with other, different, gems or semiprecious stones that differ from it in their contours; for example, he compares and contrasts it with the concepts of pagan friendship and romantic (erotic) love.

We might say that the "definition" (that is, the well-defined shape) of this concept of love is determined by the biblical (and to some extent later) Christian tradition, and that the philosopher's task, as Kierkegaard pursues it, is to chart that definition, to bring it to light in all the fine complexity of its aspects and their interrelations. Any concept is determined, in its character or shape or definition, by its situation with respect to other concepts internal to the system of concepts to which it belongs; so these placements are what I am likening to facets. Some examples of facets of the concept of Christian love are its relationships to the concepts of **neighbor, God, action** ("work"), **requital,** the **needs of the lover, duty, conscience,** and **divine command.** Kierkegaard specifies the relations between Christian love and human **inclinations,** both **natural** and **second-natural.** He explores love's relations with **freedom, self-sufficiency,** and **independence.** He looks at the **perceptual** implications of love—what the loving person "sees" (for example, the "**inner glory**" of the neighbor) and does not "see" (for example, **distinctions of rank and value** among human beings). He explores the relation of love to several **emotions: envy, joy, peace.** We might say that each of *these* concepts is itself a diamond, with respect to which the other concepts in the moral outlook are *its* facets; so that when we examine one concept philosophically, we treat the other concepts as facets of it, but each of these other facets may in its turn be treated as the diamond, and the other concepts in the outlook become *its* facets. The concept of romantic love is a different concept of love because it does not have the same orientation to duty, neighbor, God, and conscience as the Christian concept.

Kierkegaard's aim in all this is not to order the concepts into a hierarchical, derivational system and to solve the puzzles that inevitably arise from such a misguided enterprise. His idea is that this kind of poetic-dialectical activity can actually foster Christian love in a suitably receptive reader by fostering an understanding that is also an "inspiration"; and this is his aim in writing. To someone who is looking for theories in the classical modern style, the fact that there are indeed dependency relations among the concepts in an ethical outlook, and that Kierkegaard is tracing these, can seem to encourage this interpretation. But if Kierkegaard had a divine command theory in the modern sense, then he would be trying to show how all (or possibly just some, depending on the theory's scope) of these ethical concepts are grounded in divine commands; the concept of a divine command would somehow be the foundation of this system of ethical concepts. Or alternatively, if he had a virtue theory, he would try to ground all the other concepts in the concept of a virtue (or perhaps in the concept of some particular virtue, such as love).

Wisdom, as I mean to attribute it to Kierkegaard, is a kind of understanding. It is the opposite of the orientation that Kierkegaard thought many of his contemporaries had to the Christian concepts; for he thought that the Christian concepts had become so woefully confused that one could think one was living as a Christian while in fact one was living in entirely different categories.[11] We may distinguish understanding as an epistemic good from other goods such as justified true belief (roughly, true belief that is somehow well formed in the subject) and acquaintance (an immediate sensory, quasi-sensory, or rational impression of the thing known).[12] Understanding is a disposition to grasp the connections among things—explanatory connections, conceptual connections, logical connections. A person who knows how all the parts of an internal combustion engine interact in the functioning of the engine understands the engine. A person who can specify (or at least follow) the patterns of implication and nonimplication and contradiction in Hegel's *Phenomenology of Spirit* understands the book. A person who can anticipate what his friend will say or do in a variety of situations, and explain why the friend does one thing in one situation and another in another, understands his friend. And a person who can make all the conceptual connections that Kierkegaard makes in *Works of Love* regarding the concept of Christian love understands the concept of Christian love.

But this last sentence is not quite right, and its shortfall from adequacy distinguishes wisdom, as I wish to attribute it to Kierkegaard, from mere understanding. *Merely* conceptual analysis of Christian love would not achieve Kierkegaard's missionary purpose, which is to promote Christianity. Kierkegaard writes in such a way that the reader will not only understand *what* Christian love is, but will also appreciate it and will be moved to exemplify it himself. In *Concluding Unscientific Postscript* Johannes Climacus speaks of Christianity as *pathetic*-dialectical, and Kierkegaard calls himself a poet-dialectician. By this they mean to point out that Christianity is a life-view and way of living that is structured by concepts, by a discourse with a distinctive "logical" or "dialectical" character, but that what is to be structured is a person's "pathos"—one's concerns and interests and emotions and consequently one's actions as arising out of these motivational components. In traditional language, the Christian "dialectic" is a dialectic of the heart. This means that purely conceptual analysis, such as is typical of some philosophical writing, is not adequate for ethics. The language of ethics, as a practical discipline, must be such as not only to articulate the special logic of the ethical concepts, but also to speak to the heart, to articulate the *pathos,* to *move* the thinker, speaker, reader or hearer. But in that case we could also say that a merely conceptual understanding of Christian concepts falls short of being an understanding of them. Or perhaps we could say that it is *some* kind of understanding of them, but not a Christian understanding. I think that the "poetic" character of Kierkegaard's work is an effort to promote a "pathetic" understanding, one that is more adequate to the subject matter, namely, in the present context, the Christian concept of love. Only this understanding that involves the heart will count as what I am calling wisdom. Kierkegaard does not use the word 'wisdom' very much, but it seems to me a useful term for distinguishing what he is promoting from a merely "academic" or detached intellectual understanding of the Christian concepts.

A Divine Command Theory

Before we go on to consider the function of the concept of a divine command in *Works of Love,* let us look at a contemporary divine command theory. Few would deny that Robert M. Adams is the leading contemporary exponent of a divine command theory of ethics. To satisfy the model of a "pure" moral theory as expounded in the second section of this chapter, a divine command theory of morality would state that divine commands explain "moral properties in general" or "the nature of all values."[13] Just as utilitarianism attempts to explain the goodness of all actions, the obligatoriness of all actions, the goodness of all virtues, and the goodness of all social arrangements, by reference to their ability to effectuate the greatest happiness of the greatest number of beings capable of having happiness, and just as Kant's deontology wishes to explain both the goodness and the obligatoriness of all actions and virtues and social arrangements by reference to the categorical imperative, so a pure divine command theory would explain the goodness of all good actions, the goodness of all good states of affairs, all virtues, and all obligation whatsoever by reference to God's commands. Thus, on this theory, if I am obliged to tell the truth in certain circumstances, it is because God has commanded that I do so; if it is good for people to be happy and bad for people to be unhappy, it is ultimately because God has commanded that people should be happy; if justice is a virtue, it must be because God has commanded people to be just; and so forth. Furthermore, divine commands will be the only ultimate explanation of these moral properties. For example, we do not have to assume that the God who issues the commands is good; because the only way he could get to be good on this theory is by being subject to a divine command to be as he is, and so the command comes before any goodness or any other moral property that something can have.

Such would be a "pure" divine command theory of ethics. Adams's theory is not a pure divine command theory. He means to explain only part of the moral domain by reference to divine commands, namely, obligation. That means that he can assume that the God who issues the commands is good. A cruel, hateful, malicious God would not, by his commands, bring about our moral obligations. As Adams says, his theory of obligation presupposes a theory of the good.

So Adams is not saying that divine commands are the foundation of all ethical values. This makes his theory a "mixed" one, one that is less reductive and mono-derivative and thus one that is more like the wisdom model of ethical philosophy that I am attributing to Kierkegaard. Furthermore, on Adams's understanding the reference to God essential to divine command theory restricts it to certain moral outlooks. He says, "I believe that a theory according to which moral obligation is constituted by divine commands . . . is the best theory on the subject *for theists*" (p. 249, italics added). Thus he acknowledges another restriction on the theory, namely, that it can be accepted only by people who believe in (a certain kind of) God. This also sets it apart from the standard theories, which try to put in the foundations only what any rational person would accept. One of the points essential to the original idea of a modern ethical theory was that the theory should be acceptable across worldviews, so to speak, and not restricted to a certain community or kind of community.

Adams begins with what he takes to be our generic concept of moral obligation, and his theory is a conceptual explanation of that concept. The explanation points out the basis of that concept in other concepts. In his particular theory, the concept of a command of God is the other, more basic concept in terms of which the concept of moral obligation is explained.

The concept of moral obligation has a "role" among the practices of morality, and this role has certain "features" (p. 252). That is, we expect the concept of moral obligation to do certain things for us. Adams's argument consists in showing that if we think of our moral obligations as deriving from God's commands, the concept of moral obligation does these things for us very well, perhaps better than if we think of moral obligations as deriving from elsewhere, say, practical reason or the conventions of society. The features or functions of the concept of obligation that Adams discusses are

1. To supply us with *reasons* for satisfying our obligations
2. To be *objective* and not merely a matter of taste or convention
3. To *agree with our pre-theoretical beliefs* about our obligations
4. To *supply us with information* about the content of our obligations
5. To be a *basis for guilt* in case we violate our obligations.

I will comment on just 3 and 4, since they are especially relevant to our comparison of ethical theory with what Kierkegaard is doing in *Works of Love*.

3. Adams holds that divine commands should agree in "large measure" (p. 256) with our pre-theoretical beliefs about our obligations. In the abstract, divine commands do not seem more likely than other possible sources of obligation to agree with our pre-theoretical beliefs about obligation. In fact, depending on what you think about God, and what you think about humans' aptitude to judge morally without divine aid, it seems plausible to expect that God's commands might be significantly at variance with what human beings on their own would think their obligations to be. We will see in the next section of this chapter that on Kierkegaard's analysis, the Christian virtue of love, the love commanded in the central divine command, is radically at odds with ordinary human intuitions about our obligations.

Adams's enterprise has different ambitions from the paradigm ethical theories of early modern moral philosophy, which attempted to offer foundations that could be agreed to by everybody and that therefore could be expected to resolve substantive disagreements among people coming from different moral outlooks. The program was to homogenize morality for the sake of peace. Adams does not expect his proposed foundation to garner assent outside of theistic communities. And yet, here in this otherwise arbitrary requirement that divine commands conform in large measure with secular intuitions about our obligations, Adams seems to express something like the spirit of early modern moral theory.

4. Since divine commands are by definition communicated, they satisfy the desideratum, for a theory of obligation, that "facts of moral obligation should *play a part in our coming to recognize* actions as right and wrong" (p. 257, italics original). This advantage seems to be slightly in tension with the previously listed one. If Kierkegaard is right that the divine Law is shockingly different from what the world would expect, then it is clear that divine commands are significantly informative. But if Adams is right that divine commands agree and should agree in large measure with secular moral intuitions, then they would seem to be less significantly informative.

Adams enters into a debate with Mark Murphy that may afford insight into the nature of moral theories. Murphy thinks that the ground of obligation is not God's commands, but God's will, and that the command that communicates God's will to us is at most a necessary "*validating condition* of obligation" (p. 262, italics original); though he seems to think that it may not even be that—maybe we can be obliged by God's will without any communication at all of that will to us. Adams thinks we couldn't be obliged to do God's will if God didn't let us know what it is. But what Murphy mainly wants to affirm is that "the *grounds,* or 'cause, or source [of obligation],' could still be in the divine will" (ibid., italics original), and Adams responds, "I am more than willing to affirm it too, in an important sense, inasmuch as divine commands, as voluntary acts, must necessarily have their grounds or cause or source in the divine will" (ibid.). And Adams points out the difference between wanting somebody to do something and wanting that person to be obliged to do that thing; and that the function of a command is often to bring it about that the person becomes obliged to do that thing. It seems to me that Adams wins the debate about whether, in addition to God's will as the ground of obligations, God's command is also necessary.

I have proposed a conception of moral philosophy according to which it is a sort of conceptual exploration rather than a monistic hierarchizing of concepts in which a single concept is privileged as the conceptual source of all the other concepts. We have seen that Adams's "divine command theory" does not quite fit the conception of moral theory that we found in some of the virtue ethicists discussed in the second section of this chapter, for various reasons including the fact that he does not pretend to derive *all* other moral concepts from that of a divine command, but only the concept of obligation. But now Murphy comes along and proposes a "divine will theory" of obligation, suggesting that it is *not* divine commands, but the divine *will*, that is the ground of obligations. And this becomes a big debate, carried on in a professional journal[14] and a university press book. If we take the approach that I am ascribing to Kierkegaard, I think we will be inclined to think, What's the big deal? If you're a Christian, then you believe in God's commands, and you think they create obligations; but you also believe in God's will and believe that God wouldn't command what he doesn't will (at least for the most part) and that if he wants you to be under obligation to do something, surely he'll let you know. So we are inclined to say that divine commands and divine will are *both* on the Christian map, and the important thing philosophically is just to place them correctly so that people will understand how Christian morality works. Both God's commands and his will are important grounds of our obligations, in interlocking ways that we can specify. So the debate, which gives the impression that a great deal is at stake here, is really a lot of wind whipped up by a conceptual confusion inherited from modern moral philosophy. Murphy believes in divine commands and believes that they are very important for obligation; and Adams ends his discussion of Murphy with the rather mild-mannered comment "What I mean to insist on is just that the divine will must be communicated in order to impose obligations. As long as that is true, I don't see why we should not interpret obligation in terms of divine commands; I also don't see why we should not regard the commands as at least *part* of the grounds of the obligations" (p. 262, italics original). If a "divine command theory" requires only saying that God's commands are *part* of the grounds of our obligations, then a divine command theory *is* a divine will theory; and since the divine will is an expression of the divine nature, they are also a divine nature theory (Adams holds that only a good God could create our obligations by his commands); and since humans couldn't be under obligations if we didn't have a nature that makes us subject to divine commands (rabbits presumably don't have obligations), this must also be a human nature theory of obligation; and since people in different social roles have different obligations in virtue of the divine commands (mothers have different duties than children), this must be also a social role theory of obligation; and since it takes a certain amount of moral maturity to be genuinely obedient to God's commands, this will also be a virtue theory of obligation; etc. All of these ethical elements are necessary *parts* of the picture of obligation, grounds if you will, on which the concept of obligation sits—or better, other (supporting) nodes in the web to which the Christian concept of obligation belongs. My point is that the tendency to call these positions "theories," and thus to think of them as rival explanations, is a throwback to the days when people really believed that some one ethical concept might play the role of grounding all the others. The word 'theory' seems to be a major factor in making Murphy and Adams think that something big is at stake here; if they adopted Kierkegaard's approach, their work would more effectively clarify and communicate how the Christian conceptual scheme works.

Of course, the Christian conceptual scheme really does disagree with secular explanations of obligation, and this may not be clear to everybody. And it is the business of philosophers to clarify such disagreements. Often this is what Kierkegaard is up to, say, in the middle section of *Works of Love* III, A where he shows how different the secular conception of law and love is from the Christian one, or in *Philosophical Fragments* where Johannes Climacus shows how different the relation between Christ and his disciples is from the relation between any ordinary teacher and his. But here the point is not to offer rival explanations ("theories") of what really is the same thing (law, love, the teacher-pupil relation) but to show how what goes by a single word ('law,' 'love,' 'the teacher-pupil relation') is *not* the same thing. It is to display the rivalry (and of course some overlap as well) between rival conceptual schemes.

Virtue and Divine Command in Works of Love

We have seen that Adams's "divine command theory of obligation" diverges sharply from the structure of the classical modern moral theories. It does not pretend to offer the foundation of all moral concepts, even within a particular moral outlook; it no longer aspires to universal appeal but accepts a communitarian parochialism; it has even mitigated the claim that its favored concept is the sole foundation of the aspect of parochial morality that it does claim to be a foundation for (now it is just *part* of the foundation of theistic obligation). The many qualifications threaten to deprive this "theory" of its status as such. However, Adams still thinks of his account as a theory of moral obligation, and we have seen that his account still serves an ideal of theory inherited from early modern moral philosophy. Reminiscently of the concern for universal appeal, he still wants his theory to accord with deontic judgments not under the control of the Christian (or any specifically theistic) moral framework; and he still wants the favored concept (divine command) to have some privilege of status vis-à-vis the grounded concept (obligation). In Kierkegaard's *Works of Love* we see a robust and purposeful kind of moral discourse that is genuinely philosophical, but weaned from the modern inheritance and directed to a different purpose.

The concept of a divine command is prominent in deliberations II and III of *Works of Love*, which constitute about a third of the book; and the entire book is about the concept of love, one of the classical theological virtues of the Christian tradition. But Kierkegaard gives neither of these concepts a function even remotely resembling the one they might be given in a moral theory. The aim of Kierkegaard's conceptual exploration is not to secure the foundation of morality, but to facilitate the development of Christian wisdom in his reader, wisdom about love in the Christian tradition; and this wisdom is a "reflection" of love itself. Such inculcation of wisdom is part of Kierkegaard's larger project of "reintroducing Christianity to Christendom,"[15] which is the loving reflective project of awakening his reader to Christian existence, of which the Christian virtues are a dominating aspect. The character of the commandment lends to the concept of Christian love several of the features that set it apart from other concepts of love. The clarification of these conceptual connections and distinctive features is not to give grounding for a general concept of obligation, but to foster understanding of a very distinctive concept of love. Nor does the concept of love in *Works of Love* function in anything like the way concepts of virtue function in the writings of Michael Slote or Rosalind Hursthouse. Kierkegaard does not aim to make love (or more broadly, the concept of a virtue) the basic concept in a system of ethical concepts, as though the system was the *telos* of the thought; the clarification of the concept of love is itself the aim of his deliberations, with the further aim that the reader's mind and heart should be transformed with the aid of this clarification. Because he aims to facilitate the inculcation of wisdom in the reader, Kierkegaard's discussions of moral concepts are always highly psychological, giving careful attention to motivational and epistemic conditions—either ones that are required for proper moral functioning or ones that constitute barriers to such functioning. And because wisdom is a disposition of the heart, Kierkegaard's discourse has a mood of seriousness and personal exhortation that is foreign to moral theory.

Moral theories aim at universal accessibility and universal appeal. An obvious way in which *Works of Love* diverges intentionally from this ideal is in Kierkegaard's characterization of it as "Christian deliberations." The book announces its parochial character by being a set of expositions of New Testament texts, and throughout we find references to what Christianity teaches, the miracle of Christianity, true Christian inwardness, the essentially Christian, the difference between Christian love and pagan loves, etc. This feature is nowhere more evident than in deliberation III, B, "Love Is a Matter of Conscience," where a casual count of the references to Christianity and its distinctiveness with respect to conscience and love in these eighteen pages yielded eighty-seven. In *Works of Love* the concept of conscience functions as one more of the conceptual loci for the analysis of the concept of Christian love, one of the facets of the diamond that is love, and III, B is an exploration of love with respect to that facet. The analysis belongs in Deliberation III because of the relation that conscience bears to law (law creates duty, sensitivity to duty is conscience), despite the fact that law is hardly mentioned in III, B. The concept of conscience is prominent in some moral theories (though not usually as the foundation), but in moral theories it is typically taken to be a generically human power of moral discernment/motivation. In contrast, Kierkegaard does not regard the content of conscience—what it actually enjoins—as innate. The Christian concept of love is distinct because Christianity makes love a matter of conscience, and the kind of love that the Christian conscience keeps in mind is the one that is uniquely revealed in Christianity. To say that one loves as a matter of conscience is to say (1) that one loves with a sense of individual responsibility to God; (2) that one's ultimate reason for loving is nothing special about the one who is loved; and (3) that one's ultimate reason for loving is that God wills it, or that God is love. Thus, conscience is a disposition of obedience to God as he is identified in Christianity.

I want to discuss two themes that stand in "dialectical" relation to one another in Kierkegaard's discussion of Christian love and the divine command in *Works of Love*. Both themes are about the issue of continuity or lack thereof between pagan conceptions of love and Christian love. The divine command *both* creates a radical discontinuity between pagan and Christian love *and* resolves several inadequacies of pagan love, thus offering a fulfillment of human aspirations for it. I want to think about what bearing Kierkegaard's stress on these two themes has on the question of his relation to ethical theory.

We have seen that one of the marks that modern moral philosophy has left on Robert Adams's divine command theory is the requirement that the basis of obligation should agree with our pre-theoretical beliefs about our obligations. The requirement is there because a theory is supposed to have universal appeal and is supposed to specify the foundation of a generic morality. The concept of a divine command is supposed to satisfy this desideratum, and I remarked that whether a divine command agrees with our pretheoretical beliefs about our obligations depends on what we think God has commanded. Kierkegaard flies directly in the face of this desideratum of moral theory by going out of his way to impress on his reader that the Christian love commandment is radically discontinuous with ordinary human intuitions about what our duty is.

A distinguishing mark of the Christian concept of love is that love is *commanded,* and thus made into a *duty.* This is an "apparent contradiction." The idea of this kind of love "did not arise in any human heart." The appearance of contradiction is due to the pagan supposition that love is a "play of feelings, drives, inclinations, and passions, in short, [a] play of the powers of immediacy" (pp. 24–25). Since the pagan views this play of immediate feelings as beautiful and something to be celebrated, a stroke of good luck in the one who experiences it, it appears to the pagan that by commanding love and commanding that one love the neighbor (who in the pagan's eyes certainly lacks glory and specialness) Christianity degrades love into something pedestrian and unworthy and common. So the pagan has two objections to love as a duty: (1) the object of duty is nothing special, but the object of love is and ought to be; (2) anything that's a duty is not spontaneous, but love is or ought to be spontaneous.

But in our day, says Kierkegaard, the language of Christian love has been degraded into something ordinary, so that in Christendom the shock of love's being commanded, the unnaturalness of the idea, the sense of wonder at com-

manded love, has been lost. The shock of offense in the pagan confronting commanded love should have a counterpart shock of gratitude in the Christian who
reflects about the love commandment. Not to be passionately grateful for the
revelation of Christian love is to lack Christian love (pp. 26–27). Thus this gratitude, this impression of Christianity's glorious originality, is a criterion, a mark
of love. The conceptual clarification that dispels the illusion that commanded
love is something ordinary is part of Kierkegaard's program of reintroducing
love (the virtue, not just the idea of love) into Christendom. It is part of a missionary program of education.

In the middle of III, A are several pages in which Kierkegaard discusses the
logical or conceptual relations between, on the one hand, the Christian understanding of the Law and of the love that it requires, and on the other, what he
calls "worldly wisdom." He uses some very strong vocabulary to characterize
this relationship: These two outlooks "disagree about what the law is, and this
disagreement is an infinite difference." Worldly wisdom lacks "a true idea of
what it is to love oneself" and thus lacks a true idea of what it is to love another
as one loves oneself. "[I]f God and the relationship with God have been omitted," as worldly wisdom omits them, "then this, in the Christian sense, has not
been love but a mutually enchanting defraudation of love" (pp. 106–107). To
someone who understands love only in the worldly sense, "Christianity, which
certainly is the protector of love, will not hesitate to lead him out in the horror
of a collision such as no poet dreams of or has ventured to portray." This horror,
that the Christian may "out of love and in love . . . hate the beloved," is a "madness, humanly speaking." It expresses "the infinite difference of Christian truth
between what the one [worldly wisdom] and the other [the Christian thinker]
understand by love" (pp. 108–109):

> [T]he world before the time of Christianity never saw that in loving there was
> the possibility of a collision between two conceptions between which there
> was a difference of eternity, between the divine conception and the merely
> human conception. But if there is such a collision, then, in the divine sense, it
> is indeed love to hold fast to the true conception, eternity's conception, to love
> by virtue of it, whereas the person or persons loved must regard this as hate
> if they have the merely human conception. . . . According to a purely human
> understanding, this collision can never happen, because according to a purely
> human understanding the basic idea of what love is must essentially be held
> in common. Only according to the Christian understanding is the collision
> possible, since it is the collision between the essentially Christian and the
> merely human. (pp. 109, 113)

This infinite difference between the loves is made by the fact that to love
another in the Christian sense is to will for him, and to effect for him as far as
one can, a right relation to God, where this relation is itself conceived as one
that may set the beloved at loggerheads with the world; whereas according to

the merely human conception of love, to love another is to will for him, and to effect for him as far as one can, what the other wants, in some shallower or deeper sense, but in a sense that the other can recognize from his own point of view. The chief and only perfect example of love in the Christian conception is that of Jesus Christ, who indeed was hated for his love. Even the disciples were so deeply mired in the worldly conception of love that they failed to understand Jesus' love and responded only with love on the worldly model. Peter, for example, tries in good will to divert Jesus from the cross, and to Jesus it is as though Peter hates him: Get behind me, Satan. To the world, it hardly looks like love, for Christ not only to let himself be sacrificed, but to put his disciples in the position to be similarly sacrificed for love of God and their human fellows.

So far, Kierkegaard's treatment of the divine command seems very far from aiming to satisfy the typical concerns of moral theory. His conceptual remarks about the connection between the divine command and the virtue of love do show that the divine command is one of the bases for the distinctive Christian virtue. But this is hardly a theory of the virtue in the usual sense, since Kierkegaard makes no effort to show that the divine command is the unique or privileged base for the other concept. And he is very explicit that he is expounding one moral tradition, namely, Christianity; he is not trying to give a general account of love. Indeed, the whole drift of the discussions I have expounded so far is to show how different—even shockingly, repellingly different—the Christian virtue is from its pagan counterparts. And the purpose of this is clearly his missionary intention of reawakening an awareness of what Christian existence is like—what its requirements and blessings are—and thus, if possible, fostering Christian love itself in himself and his readers.

But the second theme I want to consider, a theme that stands in dialectical tension with the discontinuity theme that we have been considering, may offer a bit of encouragement to those who wish to see Kierkegaard as a kind of moral theorist. On pp. 114–118 Kierkegaard discusses the secular tendency (which may be traced to a perverse understanding of Christianity) to want radical liberation for human beings—liberation from all bonds, "also beneficial ones" (114). The most profoundly beneficial bond for human beings is to obey God. But, to quote Scripture, when one ceases to think of God as one to be absolutely obeyed, one is "without God in the world" (115) (it is as though one has the *word* 'God' but has lost hold of the *concept*). This passage, which is smack in the middle of one that is strongly anti-apologetic or even incommensurabilist, can be construed as an apologetic for divine authority. The apologetic takes the following form: If one gives up on divine authority in one's life, one becomes vulnerable to "the vortex." What is the vortex?

Kierkegaard's idea is that human freedom is necessarily a relative notion: one is free *for this*, free *from that*. The 'this' and the 'that' are essential to the concept of freedom. The idea of being free for anything, or free from everything—

the freedom dreamt of by some French philosophers of the last century—makes no sense. The result of it can only be, for an existing human being, disorientation, skepticism, an inability to act—despair. This is what Kierkegaard here calls "the vortex." The image is of a destructive whirlpool, which is all motion and with nothing fixed. Because of the human destructiveness of such radical disorientation, the point is to "stop it" by finding a fixed point. Imagine being caught in a vortex. One is rotating helplessly with the water, moving ever closer to the deadly center where one will be completely lost. The trick is for somebody to throw you a rope that is tied to a fixed point on the land, or for you to grasp a root or a rock so as to stop your movement toward destruction. And according to Kierkegaard, the only thing capable of stopping the vortex is the individual's relationship to God, whose will/Law/authority is a fixed point that sets a limit to human freedom and allows freedom *for this,* or freedom *from that,* to make sense. The concept of the vortex comes up also in Kierkegaard's *On My Work as an Author,*[16] and there it is connected with another image, namely, that of someone sewing without knotting the thread. When sewing, unless one somehow stops the thread from pulling through—stops it *on the back end*[17]—one does not manage to *sew,* but only "goes through the motions." Again, what is needed is a fixed point. Of course, not everyone appreciates the need for the authority of God; Kierkegaard's point is made from a Christian perspective and may well be opaque to people (like the French philosophers) who do not share his viewpoint. But then again, some life-circumstance might put even them in a position to appreciate the point. This would be a context for conversion.

Earlier in *Works of Love,* on pp. 29–43, Kierkegaard points out similar psychological-conceptual continuities more directly in connection with the concept of love. He notes that people who love one another with intense friendship or romantic love tend to find a kind of eternity in their love. They *feel* that this is forever, and yet they also feel vulnerable to the ravages of time. They feel that their love is secure, and yet they strive to secure their love. They do this by swearing fidelity to one another. But if they are fixed in this immediacy, they can find nothing higher to swear by than their love, and so, rather comically, they swear fidelity in their love by the love in which they are swearing to be faithful. This is a bit like Wittgenstein's man who buys a second copy of the newspaper to verify his first. Thus the spontaneous love contains a demand that spontaneous love cannot satisfy. It needs to be secured by something outside it, something that is not temporal but really eternal. Kierkegaard says that spontaneous love has the eternal in itself "in the sense of the beautiful imagination" (p. 31), but this is an essentially false and thus unsatisfying eternal.

Spontaneous love will find the fulfillment of its inner teleology only if it is transformed into a duty. Duty has the eternal character that spontaneous love is yearning for: it doesn't change from one moment to another, or from one year to another, and it has its source in God. So if in my love for my beloved I am made anxious by the thought that my love for her may change, I can find consolation in the thought that continuing to love her is my sacred *duty*. That stands fast, is completely reliable, and does not depend on my passing feelings. Thus romantic love or friendship is completed in commanded Christian love. Duty gives love what Kierkegaard calls "enduring continuance" (p. 32). The anxiety that lives in the heart of romantic love that has not been transformed by duty is often veiled and unconscious, and is manifest in the lovers' strong inclination to test one another's love. "The lover and the poet think that this urge to test love is precisely an expression of how certain it is. But is this really so? . . . But when it is a duty to love, then no test is needed and . . . love is higher than any test" (p. 33).

Love as duty secures love against change into hate. If A loves B with spontaneous love, and B does not return A's love, then A's love may turn into hate. That is, if because of her love for B, A continues to want B to love her, and B frustrates this desire by not responding, then B can begin to look like an enemy to A. But if A's spontaneous love of B has been transformed into a duty, then B's return of love is no longer a condition of A's love (no longer a demand), and so A's love cannot turn into hate. *Love as duty secures love against change into jealousy.* Romantic love demands reciprocation. Therefore A is interested in whether B loves her. But this interest (which can be more or less quiet or understated or serene) can become anxious and preoccupied. Then A becomes very attentive to B's responses, always checking them with the question "Does he love me?" "Does he love me as much as I love him?" Thus love has changed to jealousy. But if A's love has been transformed into a duty, then her chief preoccupation is whether she is loving B, not whether B is loving her, and jealousy does not arise. *Love as duty secures love against change into indifference.* Romantic love is a kind of spontaneous enthusiasm, of which its subject is a more or less passive recipient. But just as one "falls" in love, and in a certain sense does not take charge but it just happens to one, it is equally possible that one equally passively falls *out* of love, losing one's passion, becoming indifferent and lukewarm. But to accept that love is a duty is to conceive it as something one *undertakes*, the very opposite of the "habit" that one "falls" into or out of.

People who are in love are sometimes cast into what we might call *emotional despair*. Emotional despair is felt despair: A loves B and yearns "with all her heart" to be loved by B; but she sees that there is no hope of it. The phrase "with all her heart" suggests that the worth of her life, her very identity, is tied up with the beloved and can be satisfied only by his return of love. The feeling of this hopeless frustration of her passion is emotional despair. Suicide is the paradigm action of despair. Kierkegaard distinguishes emotional despair from what we might call *character despair*. Character despair is a formation of the heart such that, in some circumstances, the individual *would be* cast into emotional despair. A is in character despair if she loves B in such a way that, *were*

B to abandon her and she *were* to see clearly that the abandonment was definitive, she would be cast into emotional despair. Obviously, A can be in character
despair while being quite "happy." As long as B loves her in return, she does not
feel her despair; nevertheless, according to Kierkegaard, she is in despair.

The only cure for character despair is investment of one's heart in the eternal: "Despair is to lack the eternal; despair is not to have undergone the change
of eternity through duty's *shall*" (pp. 40–41). If A's relationship to B, whether
happy or unhappy love, is that she does not merely love him with spontaneous erotic love, but is responding to God's command that she love B, then her
identity and the worth of her life are not found in B's response to her, but in
her relationship with the giver of the command. Her love for B is frustrated,
all right, and perhaps definitively, but not *ultimately,* not desperately. So God's
command to love is consoling in a deep and thoroughgoing way, whereas com-
forts to the effect that "maybe B will come around" or "you'll find another
lover" are counsels of despair. "The love that has undergone eternity's change
by becoming duty is not exempted from misfortune, but it is saved from despair,
in fortune and misfortune equally saved from despair" (p. 42).

So Kierkegaard not only stresses how discontinuous Christian, commanded
love is from the pagan loves; he also shows in many ways how Christian love
fulfills demands that lie hidden in the pagan loves. Does this last theme show
that Kierkegaard has an interest in moral theory after all? It might be taken
to show that the divine command is the ground of romantic love and friendship, insofar as these are healthy and complete (a divine command theory?). It
might be taken to show that pagan love presupposes Christian love (a virtue
theory?). But to argue this way would be not only to forget that the concept
of commanded love is, in Kierkegaard's view, a product of divine revelation
(a starting point that is very eccentric relative to the thrust of modern moral
theory, which is not supposed to appeal to anything not accessible to unaided
human insight), but also to forget the dialectical character of Kierkegaard's
thought. Neither the divine command nor the virtue that it enjoins has the kind
of hierarchical privilege in Kierkegaard's thought (or in Christian ethics more
generally) that it would need to have to function as the base of a moral theory.
Instead, the picture of moral concepts suggested by Kierkegaard's writings—
pseudonymous and signed—is that of an array that has a jewel-like hardness
of mutually supporting complexity, inviting, as the only right philosophical
response, a multidirectional, dialectical exploration of the kind that is exemplified in Kierkegaard's many books, both pseudonymous and signed. The two
themes in *Works of Love* that I have just highlighted are aspects of this complicated and variegated response. Kierkegaard is just as interested in protecting
Christianity against the domestication and syncretism that tend to flow from
undialectical apologetics as he is in appealing to people's pre-Christian interests
as a point of departure for interesting them in Christianity.

But it is not just the logical character (so to speak) of the Christian concepts that requires one who would promote Christian wisdom to write something very different from moral theory. I have noted that Kierkegaard's literary work is *pathetic*-dialectical or *poetic*-dialectic—speaking to the fact that wisdom is an intellectual state that is at the same time a disposition of the heart. In the Introduction to *The Concept of Dread,* Vigilius Haufniensis comments on how concepts have their own native mood, which must be preserved in any discourse expressing the concepts, if the integrity of the concepts is to be safeguarded:

> The fact that science, fully as much as poetry and art, assumes a mood both on the part of the producer and on the part of the recipient, that an error in modulation is just as disturbing as an error in exposition of thought, has been entirely forgotten in our age, when people have altogether forgotten the nature of inwardness and appropriation in their joy over all the glory they believed they possessed, or through cupidity have lost it, like the dog which preferred the shadow. However, every error begets its own enemy. An error of thought has outside of it as its enemy, dialectics; the absence of mood or its falsification has outside of it its enemy, the comical.[18]

The mood proper to ethical discourse (one of the "sciences" in Kierkegaard's vocabulary) is that of Kierkegaard's *Works of Love* and other ethical writings. It is a mood of personal address, expressing that a proper response to hearing the concepts expounded is self-examination, passionate appropriation, and action. Any "ethical" discourse in which this is not the mood is a confusion of the concepts, no matter how accurate it may be from a purely logical point of view. Even if David Gauthier's *Morals by Agreement* or Michael Slote's *Morals from Motives* did not make the purely conceptual mistakes that they make, they would be travesties of ethics by Kierkegaard's lights. Such travesty appears to be endemic to moral theory, even when it tries to be Christian (though one must admit gradations here; the mood of Kant's ethical writings is quite different from that of Gauthier and Slote, despite the fact that they are ethical theory). Haufniensis points out that people who falsify concepts by getting the mood wrong suffer the revenge of making themselves comical. But it is as rare in our day as it was in Kierkegaard's that such activity should actually evoke laughter. The problem is that almost nobody has the rightly attuned sense of humor.

Conclusion

The collective experience of moral philosophers in the modern period, during which repeated efforts have been made to contrive an adequate moral theory, suggests that the thing can't be done. The reason would seem to be that moral concepts do not behave in the way they would have to behave for a moral theory to be contrivable. For one thing, moral concepts, no matter what tradition they belong to, do not seem to be monistically orderable; for another, they seem to come in irreducibly distinct moral traditions. Like the old foundationalist metaphor, the metaphor of a multifaceted diamond that I have commended for a moral concept and its relations to other moral concepts suggests structure. It suggests dependency relations (no facet is an island; every facet is systematically related to the other facets making up the diamond). But it very much eschews the unidirectional derivation characteristic of the moral theories, and consequently the picture of moral concepts that they presuppose. Moral philosophy becomes a dialectical exploratory and descriptive conceptual activity rather than a project of securing foundations.

As we look back on the history of failure in the moral theory enterprise, we may be pleased to see one major moral thinker of the modern period who seems never to have been so much as tempted by it, who nevertheless produced a rich and deep body of moral philosophy. Søren Kierkegaard has been largely neglected by moral philosophers, who have preferred to exploit the resources of much shallower thinkers such as Thomas Hobbes and Immanuel Kant and the utilitarians, because by comparison Kierkegaard did not seem to be doing real moral philosophy. But if what was thought to be real moral philosophy turns out to have been a wild goose chase, Kierkegaard may become more interesting. Were philosophers to follow his model, their work would consist in clarification of ethical concepts within one or another given tradition, with virtue-concepts perhaps at the center of their interest, the mood of the discourse would be ethical seriousness, and the *telos* of clarification would be to deepen moral self-understanding, to enhance understanding of moral concepts in such a way as to enhance the quality of moral living—in a word, to facilitate growth in wisdom.

7.
"The Problematic Agapeistic Ideal— Again"

M. Jamie Ferreira

Kierkegaard studies has much for which to be grateful to Alastair Hannay, not least of all his superb translations, his recent biography (2001), his co-editorship with Marino of the *Cambridge Companion to Kierkegaard,* and the volume on *Kierkegaard* in the "Arguments of the Philosophers" series. The latter, an early work (1982), marked the definitive inclusion of Kierkegaard in the philosophical canon, and what Hannay calls its "logical sequel," *Kierkegaard and Philosophy,* has recently appeared (2003). Hannay's concerns in the first work are reiterated and developed in these later essays, and I want to focus on one of those concerns—namely, love. I want to focus on Hannay's early discussion of "Love of One's Neighbour," rather than the later essay, because Hannay's specific way of exploring the problem there seems to me to be a particularly fruitful resource for shedding light on a persistent and widespread criticism made of Kierkegaard's valuations of love in *Works of Love.*[1]

The Charge: Moral Reprehensibility of Preferential Love?

In a discussion of "Love of One's Neighbour," Hannay reports that Kierkegaard's model of the "good will" found in "Purity of Heart" raises a question "about the content of the properly ethical frame of mind"—namely, "what fills the heart purged of self-regard, freed from the lure of inducement?"[2] Kierkegaard's mature Christian ethic *Works of Love* offers 'neighbour-love' or agape as the answer, but, according to Hannay, such an agapeistic model is "problematic."[3] One problem is that of making sense of commanded or "dutiful love," and Hannay suggests that Kierkegaard does not directly attempt to *argue* that the paradox is only apparent. A second problem is that of the evaluation of erotic love and friendship implied in the valorization of the agapeistic ideal: Hannay writes that "the arguments of *Works of Love* are directed mainly at showing that any form of love other than Christian love (neighbour-love) has no moral value, because it is self-love,"[4] and the problem is whether there are any satisfying arguments (either in Kierkegaard's work or available to Kierkegaard) for such a negative evaluation of non-neighbor-love.

Now, the claim that non-neighbor-love has "no moral value" is equivalent to the claim that only neighbor-love has "moral value." But this might merely mean that non-neighbor-love is amoral—that is, not within the realm of moral judgment. And this is in line with Hannay's suggestion that, on Kantian and Kierkegaardian terms, instinctive responses like erotic desire and feelings of attraction and sympathy are not willed and therefore cannot be subject to moral judgment. But Hannay suggests that Kierkegaard is committed to a much stronger claim—namely, not only that "all discriminating love is non-moral" and all "natural love lacks positive moral value,"[5] but that preferential love is morally negative, that "all natural affection involves culpable self-interest in one form or another."[6] According to Hannay, Kierkegaard's view that non-neighbor-love "has no moral value, because it is self love" entails the claim that "preferential love" is "negative" love of self, and Hannay suggests that in order to justify this claim "one would have to show why the self-regard bound up with expressions of interest of any kind becomes in this special case morally reprehensible."[7] The claim for which justification is sought is repeatedly the claim that "preferential love lacks positive moral value."[8] The shift in the formulation of the problem is striking—from non-neighbor-love to preferential love, and from non-moral to morally reprehensible.[9] Hannay commits Kierkegaard to the strongest version of the claim and then tries valiantly to see whether there could be any plausible argument for it.

To repeat, the phrases 'lacks moral value' and 'non-moral' are ambiguous—they can mean either amoral (outside the realm of moral assessment because not willed), or they can mean morally neutral (capable of being either morally good or morally bad as a contingent matter of fact), or they can mean immoral (necessarily morally bad). Hannay's formulations make it a question of the last—he asks why Kierkegaard claims that preferential loves are necessarily morally reprehensible. Looking for evidence that would support Kierkegaard's claim, Hannay proceeds to develop an elaborate set of potential arguments and counter-arguments, laced with objections and counter-objections. Hannay seems sincere in his attempt to discover plausible reasons within or available to Kierkegaard for drawing such a negative conclusion, but the question is why Hannay sees the conclusion as so negative to begin with. As I see it, the very radicalness of Hannay's description of Kierkegaard's position provides a valuable occasion for clarifying the whole issue of the status of preferential love in *Works of Love*.

At first glance Hannay's attempt to see whether Kierkegaard has a good argument for believing that the self-interest or self-regard involved in preferential caring is "morally reprehensible selfishness"[10] is quite shocking. The provocativeness of the suggestion that Kierkegaard believes something that relies on or requires an argument for the *moral reprehensibility* of preferential love leads anyone with sympathy for the ethic in *Works of Love,* like myself, to bristle. Why does Hannay insist on saddling Kierkegaard with such a radical claim? After all, Kierkegaard explicitly says that "erotic love and earthly love are the joy of life," adding later that "erotic love is undeniably life's most beautiful happiness and friendship the greatest temporal good."[11] Moreover, Kierkegaard affirms that there is no hierarchy in love—there is "only one kind of love."[12]

Perhaps Kierkegaard's judgments—which appear to preclude any negative evaluation of preferential love as such—are dismissed because both Hannay and critics conclude that Kierkegaard, despite his best intentions, is nevertheless committed to a negative evaluation of preferential love in virtue of other claims he makes. That is, perhaps the positive things Kierkegaard says about preferential love are inconsistent with deeper commitments he holds. So it is my job to see if any of Kierkegaard's commitments entail that preferences necessarily militate against genuine love—to see if preferential/discriminating love can be anything but morally reprehensible.

Hannay's formulation of the problem—namely, that all forms of love other than Christian neighbor-love are, for Kierkegaard, "forms of selfishness"[13]— seems to be another version of the common criticism that Kierkegaard devalues preferential love. But it need not be seen this way. That is, I want to argue that there is an important sense in which it is, strictly speaking, true that that all non-neighbor-love is morally selfish, but it is a mistake to see this as implying that preferential loves are morally selfish. In other words, I agree with Hannay about neighbor-love, but I disagree with him concerning preferential loves. In fact, I shall argue that Kierkegaard has an argument that preferential loves are not necessarily morally reprehensible. Interestingly, it was precisely Hannay's exploration that prompted me to find and formulate a response that I hope can finally silence a wrongheaded criticism of Kierkegaard's ethic.

Clarifications and Counter-Indications

Relationships vs. Feelings

Are there no examples of genuine but discriminating love? Is Kierkegaard committed to finding marital love, parental love, and friendship morally reprehensible? The conclusion is so counter-intuitive that one is forced to recognize a significant ambiguity in the term 'preferential love.' Is 'preferential love' meant to refer to a spontaneous inclination or to a *relationship*? Insofar as preferential love means anything more than a psycho-physiological response, it does not exist in a vacuum. If spontaneous feelings of erotic attraction or personal preference were experienced in a vacuum in which relation to another person was absolutely precluded (if I were alone on a desert island, or the last person on earth, looking at a picture of someone who aroused such feelings in me), such feelings would not be susceptible to moral evaluations. But in our real lives such feelings are not found in the abstract. They are only found in relations to others in which I have to make some choices about how to contextualize those feelings. Any real-life experience of preference or attraction will take place in a context in which the preferred or attractive one is also the subject of a choice on our part—either to treat or not treat that person simply as an object (an instrumental means) for our pleasure or utility. That choice is subject to moral appraisal. So if anything is going to be subject to moral appraisal it will be the preferential relationship. There is no middle ground between morally good and morally bad in cases of *relationships* since we are always faced with a choice, and that choice has repercussions both for the individual we prefer and for others we do not prefer.

Certainly Kierkegaard takes great pains in *Works of Love* to show that acting on our preferences can lead to selfishness—the whole point of the second deliberation is to show precisely the possibility that we can be selfishly blind to someone's needs because we are erotically obsessed with someone else, as well as the possibility that we can be selfishly blind to the very person with whom we are erotically obsessed. So there is no doubt that preferences can lead to selfish behavior. It is important to Kierkegaard to show that even when we feel attracted to people, either erotically or in terms of friendship, we can hurt them, and that the ways in which we can be selfish are quite subtle and varied; he is adept at showing that the commandment bids me avoid even the subtle ways of trying to control another, to make her an affirmation of *my* distinctiveness.

So the question is how to read the phrase "preferential love." If preferential inclination exists in a relationship to another alongside the willed treatment of the other as a sex object, or a mere means and not an end, then such preferential love is immoral, morally selfish. (Hannay calls this "opportunistic" rather than merely self-regarding.[14]) So, insofar as a preferential bond excludes the preferred other as an equal worthy of respect, it is morally bad. If preferential love, on the other hand, exists in a context in which the other is treated with respect, as an end and not merely a means, then preferential love is not morally selfish. Moreover, insofar as a preferential bond excludes others as neighbors, it is morally bad; but if a preferential bond exists in a context in which others are not deliberately excluded, it is not morally bad.[15]

That we preferentially love someone does not guarantee that we will not be selfish with respect to that person, or others. But are there reasons for thinking that preferences *necessarily* lead to selfish behavior/relationships? Or more pointedly, are there reasons for thinking that *Kierkegaard* thinks preferences *necessarily* lead to selfish behavior/relationships?

Counter-Indications to the Necessity of Selfishness

There are several indications that Kierkegaard does not think preferences are necessarily morally negative. In order to take at face value his claim that "erotic love is undeniably life's most beautiful happiness and friendship the greatest temporal good" we need only highlight his repeated contrast between "proper self-love" (WL, 18) and "selfish self-love" (WL, 23, 53, 151). He speaks of the need to love oneself "in the right way" (WL, 22) and the need to teach some people to love themselves more than they do (WL, 23). He refers several times to self-love "in a selfish sense" (WL, 21, 56). The obvious implication of such a contrast is that not all self-love is selfish.

In other words, Kierkegaard conceives of a love that is unselfish even while it is by definition self-regarding. Hannay notes that there is a "morally neutral self-regard" that is constitutive of any action—without such self-regard we could not act at all.[16] But in addition to this purely neutral self-regard, there is another way of understanding self-regard or self-love as not necessarily selfish, and here Kierkegaard is in the good company of Aristotle and Aquinas. In the *Nichomachean Ethics,* Aristotle affirms that "friendship is based on self-love"— indeed, a "friend is another self"—since "in loving a friend men love what is good for themselves."[17] "The good man should be a lover of self" because a good man's being is seen by him to be desirable because it is seen by him to be good; self-love is proper in so far as it is directed to 'the good.'[18] Aquinas too concedes the legitimate self-interestedness of friendship and the propriety of such self-love.[19] In other words, both Aristotle and Aquinas support Kierkegaard in his judgment that there is a "proper self-love."

This means that we need to read Kierkegaard's comments about "self-love" in context, and often there will be an implicit 'selfish' modifying it. For example, we can read his comments about "the selfishness in self-love" (WL, 21) or "the selfishness in preferential love" (WL, 44) as referring to improper self-love, self-love "in a selfish sense," as contrasted with "proper self-love," rather than as characterizing self-love as such. In the context of his claim that Christianity's "misgivings about erotic love and friendship" concern preferential love that expresses "selfishness" (WL, 52–53),[20] we can read his remark that "self-love is reprehensible" (WL, 57) as referring to selfish self-love, not self-love as such. Here he follows Aristotle in thinking that in general the term "self-love" (or "love of self") "takes its meaning from the prevailing type of self-love, which is a bad one."[21]

The conclusion I draw is that Kierkegaard does not think self-love is necessarily selfish.[22] Hannay, on the contrary, does not take Kierkegaard's affirmations about the goodness of erotic love and friendship at face value. Rather, he says that Kierkegaard is committed to the view that the self-love involved in preferential relations necessarily "morally invalidates a concern" for the other[23] and that Kierkegaard therefore needs an argument to justify this conclusion. Hannay reconstructs one argument: From the premises that (P1) All natural love (in practice) is preferential (behavior) and (P2) All preferential behavior is self-regarding (self-love), one can conclude that (Concl) All natural love is self-regarding (self-love). But at most, Hannay rightly judges, this shows that natural love is self-love without showing that self-love is bad. So the putative argument fails. To show that instinctive preferential love is self-love in a negative sense one has to show that it is necessarily selfish. What reason does Hannay offer for thinking that Kierkegaard, despite his affirmation of erotic love and friendship and despite his contrast between selfish self-love and proper self-love, sees the self-love involved in preferential love as necessarily selfish?

Hannay's Search for Kierkegaard's Argument

By way of a preliminary, it should be noted that although Hannay suggests that he is considering possible arguments for the "non-morality" of natural love,[24] it is clear that he is looking for arguments that natural love is immoral (i.e., that it "morally invalidates" concern for the other). We can find, he says, moral badness entering into preferential relationship from three sides—one, the side in which my self-regard is exclusively for me; another, the side where my attention to the preferred other fails to hold the preferred other as also a neighbor; and a third, where my attention to the preferred other leads me to exclude other others as neighbors. Hannay rightly concludes that such examples of selfishness from any of these do not show the necessity of selfishness.

Examples of selfishness can only show that preferences can sometimes lead us to fail to appreciate the preferred one sufficiently (i.e., nonselfishly), and that preferences can sometimes lead us to fail to appreciate others in need. But these are possibilities, rather than logically entailed by the experience of preference. They do not constitute an argument for the claim that preference entails moral selfishness. The failure to find such an argument in Kierkegaard's text might lead one to conclude that Kierkegaard is unjustified in his claim that preference entails moral selfishness. However, that failure might lead instead to questioning whether in fact Kierkegaard is committed to such a claim, after all. The fact that Kierkegaard has no good argument for a particular claim might be reason for us to reconsider our attribution of that claim to him. Hannay, however, is in no doubt about Kierkegaard's claim about the moral reprehensibility of preferential relations, and so continues to look for an argument for it.

The Argument from Demand for Exclusiveness

Hannay's candidate for a plausible argument is that something characteristic of or intrinsic to preference is "incompatible" with unselfish love for another.

He writes: "if we examine the conditions in which preference operates we will see that they place crucial restrictions on the loving concern one person may have for another, *even* when that other is genuinely addressed *as* another self."[25] Hannay examines two possible restrictions that preference places on love. He suggests that one is "a kind of restriction on the other self *qua* lovable which might be said to involve an incomplete address to the self" precisely because "It addresses a self that is one that can only have this good done to it by the addresser personally." The second restriction Hannay suggests concerns the other's own possibilities of self-development: "By pressing his preference, the preferential lover is, in fact, denying developmental autonomy to the other self." Acknowledging that "perhaps they are two aspects of the same restriction," he suggests that here "we may see a hint of what we have been looking for: a basis in fact and ordinary judgment for Kierkegaard's apparently abstract and arbitrary assumption that a good will is one purged of self-interest. If acts of love are what the good amounts to in practice, and love is a concern for the good of others, then strictly speaking the *demand* that this good come from a preferred source is not just a superfluous condition, but an incompatible one."[26] In the course of later attempts to offer "partially remedial comments," Hannay suggests that one "aspect of selfishness in an emotional tie" is "the failure to acknowledge the other (or others) *in* that tie in the sense of being willing to 'let the other be' if that other required that;[27] this seems to be another version of his earlier suggestion.

In other words, Hannay finds one plausible argument based on a "demand," intrinsic to preference, for exclusivity of donation to the other—that is, that we be the provider of the other's good. Let's examine this restriction more carefully. It might be, Hannay says, that the attempt to cultivate a relation based on preference demands that one insist on being the person who provides benevolence and beneficence to the preferred other. This means that it might be that the attempt to cultivate a relation based on preference demands that I insist on being the benefactor *even if* I think the other would be better off if I were not the one trying to bestow a good or further their well-being. But note that what Hannay succeeds here in showing is only that there is a particular interest that genuine love must be free of—namely, a particular selfish "demand." Hannay does not show that Kierkegaard believes that such a demand is intrinsic to preference. Unless this is shown, there is no plausible Kierkegaardian argument for the necessary moral reprehensibility of preferential loves.

Before arguing that Kierkegaard does not believe such a demand is intrinsic to preference, I want to consider for a moment what might be at stake for Hannay in his assumption that preference entails such a "demand." Hannay is trying to arrive at what constitutes genuine love, paradigmatic love, and he is right that more is involved in the notion of preferential love than simply wanting the good of the other because it is the good of the other. The question is whether preferential love also implies an exclusiveness that is either not good for the one loved or for others. Certainly, preferential attraction does seem to involve my own *desire* to be the one who is beneficent, the source of the other's good. Moreover, preferential attraction, whether erotic or not, inclines one to want to be with the person, to enjoy time with them, to enjoy intimacy with them.

But there is a difference between a "demand" and a "desire." Of course I *desire* to be the source of the other's good, to be the one who makes the other happy by providing what is good for him or her because they want it. I want to be important to the other's happiness—I want her or his happiness to be because of me. It would be strange if I did not. But my desire need not be a demand placed on the other, something I insist on, a condition for the expression of my love. I cannot help but want to be the other's happiness, want to be loved by those I love. But I may want something without making it a demand or a requirement. Hannay assumes that, for Kierkegaard, preferential inclination implies a demand that we be the one who does the good for the other. On the contrary, I propose that we have reason to think that Kierkegaard himself clearly saw this distinction between desire and demand. Let me explain.

Nondemanding Desire

It is true that Kierkegaard suggests that one test of genuine caring is that I would be "willing" to give up the other for the other's good (WL, 273, 274). He elsewhere speaks of our willingness to give up a "claim" on "the happiness of erotic love and friendship" (WL, 90). The demand of love is that we must be *willing* to forego the fulfillment of our desire in the context of a relationship in which fulfillment of this desire is harmful to the beloved. It is indeed possible that I might refuse to give up the other even if I thought it would be for the other's own good, but nowhere does Kierkegaard suggest that I could not do so; nowhere does he suggest that genuine caring is incompatible with preference. Kierkegaard does think such love is in fact humanly possible—his love for Regine might be said to be an example in which preferential love remains in play even while he took himself out of the specific relationship that would harm Regine. In other words, Kierkegaard does not see *demand* for exclusivity as intrinsic to preferential love. That demand cannot be used to justify a claim that Kierkegaard thinks that preference is morally reprehensible. It is entirely possible that I could enjoy a relationship based on preference without ever actually being selfish, as long as I would in principle be willing to let another be the source of my preferred one's good if it were indeed better for my preferred one that this should happen.

How do we know that for Kierkegaard paradigmatic love does necessarily include desire (for intimacy, to be the source of the loved one's joy), that it is not indifferent? Consider the first and most important of Kierkegaard's commitments—namely, to the claim that "God is love [*Kjerlighed*]." What is paradigmatic of love? God, and God's love is the model for our love (*Kjerlighed*) of others. Now, there are certain ways in which we cannot imitate God's love— for example, "God loved us first," but we cannot ever love "first." We are already loved, so we cannot love God first, nor can we be said to love others except through this God-given love (*Kjerlighed*). So, apart from loving first (which we cannot do), what can we learn about genuine love from God? We learn that God wants to be loved and that God desires intimacy with us. Kierkegaard writes in a late journal entry that "God loves—and God wants to be loved. These two in equilibrium make true Christianity."[28] Moreover, God in Christ canonizes this desire, for, according to Kierkegaard, "our Lord Jesus Christ, even he humanly felt this need to love and be loved by an individual human being" (WL, 155). Christ's "craving to hear" that Peter loved him "more than these" is paradigmatic of human love: "to love humanly is to love an individual human being and to wish to be that individual human being's best beloved" (WL, 155, 156).

If preference implies that we want to be loved by the one we love, or be considered a friend by the one we consider a friend, or that we desire intimacy with either beloved or friend, or that we want to be the source of the other's good, this does not seem in Kierkegaard's eyes to entail something morally negative. So Kierkegaard does not hold that the exclusivity *demand* is intrinsic to preference, and he does not hold that wanting to be loved and desiring intimacy entail selfishness. Let me suggest that Kierkegaard even has an argument to the effect that preference is not necessarily morally selfish.

Preservation of Neighbor-Love

The crucial premise in Kierkegaard's argument is that neighbor-love can be *preserved* in erotic love and friendship: he expressly affirms this possibility as our goal—"in erotic love and friendship, preserve love for the neighbor" (WL, 62).[29] The argument goes like this: (1) Neighbor-love can be preserved in erotic love and friendship. (2) Anything that preserves neighbor-love cannot be morally reprehensible. (Concl) Erotic love and friendship are not necessarily morally reprehensible. I am, in effect, reading Hannay against himself when I argue as follows: (A) There is one plausible argument for claiming moral reprehensibility of preference—that is, the argument based on a demand for exclusivity that Hannay reconstructs. (B) But Kierkegaard does not put forth such an argument—because Kierkegaard thinks that neighbor-love can be preserved in a preferential relation. (C) So we have no reason to think that Kierkegaard claims the moral reprehensibility of preference.

Kierkegaard's claim that neighbor-love can be preserved in erotic love and friendship means that the question is no longer 'what are we doing in preferential love?' or 'what are we doing in nonpreferential love?' The question becomes: what are we doing when we *preserve* nonpreferential love *in* preferential love?

Two things should be noted about the claim that neighbor-love can be preserved in erotic love and friendship. First, we are not speaking about the situation in which we feel no preferential attraction or inclination for the other. That raises quite different questions: with what resources we can approach someone who is not preferred; why is that worth being called love? This is what is at stake for those who are concerned that neighbor-love ceases to be recognizably love and amounts to merely indifferent benevolence. Rather, the situation of which we are speaking is one in which we do experience a preferential attraction or inclination. Here the question is: how we can preserve neighbor-love "*in* erotic love and friendship." This is what is at stake for those worried about any potential devaluation of erotic love or friendship. In the end, these may be aspects of the same issue, but I will begin by addressing the latter—the concern that a valorization of neighbor-love devalues preferential love. I want to analyze what we are doing when we love our preferred one as a neighbor: to do that I have to consider what we do when we love anyone as a neighbor, and then I have to consider how the special relation is affected by neighbor-love. I want to argue that given Kierkegaard's commitment to the preservation of neighbor-love in erotic love and friendship, the special character of special relations is not undermined by or at odds with the love commandment.

Conscience—the Distinctive Character of Neighbor-Love

For Kierkegaard, Christian love is the "foundation of every expression of the particular [love]" (WL, 141). One can assume then that it does not, in principle, ask for the sacrifice of particular love. But what is this "foundation"—what does it mean to love someone "as a neighbor" or, equivalently, to be a "neighbor" to someone? In a variety of deliberations in *Works of Love* Kierkegaard describes the commanded love of neighbor as one in which we affirm the other's distinctiveness, help the other to be independent, forgive and seek reconciliation[30]—all because we acknowledge the other as equal in created "kinship."[31] Loving the other's distinctiveness, for example, is explained by Kierkegaard by contrast with the domineering and controlling attitudes that do not respect the other as an equal before God.

The radical change involved in neighbor-love is the change of making love, even erotic love and friendship, a "matter of conscience" (WL, 140). Because every person "belongs first and foremost to God before he belongs to any relationship," every person, regardless of the particularities of the relationship, must "consult with God"—this consultation is a consultation with conscience since "to relate to God is precisely to have conscience" (WL, 143). Kierkegaard makes no bones about the reason for this: "The reason for its being a question of conscience is that a human being in his erotic love belongs first and foremost to God" (WL, 143). The idea that we (and our spouse, child, or friend) "belong to God" is what the doctrine of Creation means. For this reason, erotic love and friendship are not excluded from the commanded Christian change in all love—namely, to make love a matter of conscience.

I suggest that this necessary reference to conscience is how we should understand Kierkegaard's claim that preferential love is "dethroned" (WL, 45). Conscience has the throne. But how does neighbor-love, the reference to conscience, affect preferential relationships? The standard of conscience is the standard of reference to the judgment of the God who created us "out of nothing," but the "glad message" of love's "delight" (WL, 150) must always be held in tension with the rigorous message of love's conscientiousness. In other words, since "erotic love and earthly love are the joy of life" (WL, 150), the "delight" must not be destroyed.

Delight—the Distinctive Character of Preference

Does the acknowledgment of the other as equal, as "kin" before God, militate against any preference I might feel for them? Does it militate against love's "delight"? It may be telling that Kierkegaard does not say that we are allowed to preserve erotic love in neighbor-love, but rather that we are obliged to preserve neighbor-love *in erotic love*. The erotic love must be maintained as erotic love if this injunction is to make any sense.[32] If we are to maintain the particular love at whose foundation is neighbor-love, it will have to be the case that the *character* of my response is a function of the person's distinctive relation to me.

How do we know that Kierkegaard is committed to our maintaining what is distinctive about erotic love? He tells us so explicitly. Supporting his claim that "erotic love is undeniably life's most beautiful happiness and friendship the greatest temporal good," he tells us that as husband and wife we inhabit a particular kind of relationship: "that she is your wife is then a more precise specification of your particular relationship to each other" (WL, 141). This more "precise specification" will make a difference—"the wife and friend are not loved in the same way, nor the friend and the neighbor."

That "the wife and friend are not loved in the same way, nor the friend and the neighbor"[33] means that the relationship will be carried out in ways that differ from another relationship to someone to whom one does not have particular conjugal or familial ties. In each case my response will express itself differently—my knowledge of the needs of the other (which is increased by my intimacy with her), my ability to help, and the legitimate expectations of others regarding my role-responsibility: all these play a part in determining exactly what kind of response is appropriate.[34] Kierkegaard does not require that I respond to my wife or friend without the intimacy and affection that distinctively grounds my special relation to them. He insists that it is a "misunderstanding" to think that "in Christianity the beloved and the friend are loved faithfully and tenderly in quite a different way than in paganism" (WL, 53)—this suggests that special relations make a difference. He repeats this positively: "love the beloved faithfully and tenderly, but let love for the neighbor be the sanctifying element in your union's covenant with God" (WL, 62). Moreover, Kierkegaard recognizes "the good fortune" (WL, 51), the "earthly good" (WL, 144) of being loved and favored as well as of having people to love and favor, and all of this is just what one would expect given his appreciation of how one's response is *claimed* by another: "your friend, your beloved, your child, or whoever is an object of your love has a claim upon an expression of [your love]," and not to express it would be "withholding from someone what you owe him" (WL, 12).

When Kierkegaard writes that "Christianity has nothing against the husband's loving his wife in particular, but he must never love her in particular *in such a way that she is an exception to being the neighbor that every human being is*" (WL, 141–142, my emphasis), his point is about preserving neighbor-love in marital love. I take this to be Kierkegaard's way of reminding us that we can no more take advantage of our wife, because she is our wife, than of another neighbor. We cannot make a sex object out of our wife or husband; we cannot emotionally or physically abuse them, we cannot take them for granted—because however intimate and specific the relationship is, each remains a neighbor, an equal before God.

In sum, this ethic, as a Christian ethic, is not out to change external expressions of our love: "a wife has her most intimate relationship, humanly speaking, with her husband" (WL, 151–152), and this ethic is not out to challenge that intimacy. Christianity makes a change *within* erotic love and friendship, but not by preventing them from being erotic love and friendship. Christianity sanctifies marriage, but not by requiring the couple to behave as if they were not married. In the discourse "Purity of Heart Is to Will One Thing," Kierkegaard makes this even clearer: the discourse "does not ask if she [your wife] really is the delight of your eyes and the desire of your heart; it wishes that for you."[35] Christianity, he says, "does not concern itself much with working out in detail the different ways in which this fundamental universal love can manifest itself," because the commandment "allows all this [our 'drives and inclinations' and 'natural relations'] to remain in force" (WL, 143–144). The distinctive external expressions of preferential love are not to be excluded by neighbor-love. When he claims that the commandment will "teach erotic love and friendship genuine love" (WL, 62) he takes it for granted that they will continue to be distinguishable as erotic love and friendship. Erotic love and friendship are maintained even when they are ennobled by neighbor-love's criterion of conscience. The process is, he says, one of "transforming" erotic love and friendship (W, 112), not of annihilating or canceling or disembodying them.

The old criticism that Kierkegaard is blind to the richness possible to erotic love and friendship has been renewed recently. In an article entitled "Kierkegaard and Loves That Blossom," D. Z. Phillips raises many of the same questions raised by Hannay: Phillips asks whether neighbor-love is a higher form of love than other loves, whether preferential loves are necessarily selfish.[36] Phillips attributes such views to Kierkegaard when he charges that "Kierkegaard often discusses the different loves as though they are engaged in a battle for exclusive rights to the human soul," and Phillips rejects the idea that we must "pose the question of the relation of Christian love to other loves in this exclusive way? . . . the Kierkegaardian 'either-or,' an all-or-nothing affair?"[37]

Phillips turns Kierkegaard's emphasis on the limits of such loves (they are loves that die) on its head—focusing on Kierkegaard's alternative description of them as "loves that blossom," Phillips wants us to appreciate the preciousness of such loves. Phillips suggests that "Kierkegaard argues that the nature of eternal love can be found, not in these [loves that blossom], but in the Christian love of the neighbour." He asks: "Are his reasons for saying this justifiable, or can the love of God be said to be mediated, in a distinctive way, through the experience of loves that blossom?"[38]

Phillips suggests that Kierkegaard "caricatures erotic love as the desire to possess," confusing "seduction" with "love"; he suggests that Kierkegaard caricatures friendship by neglecting "the 'giving' and 'receiving' which are constitute of growth in friendship."[39] Phillips highlights the richness of such loves—for example, "the individual character of the loves of Romeo and Juliet . . . depends precisely on the growth and development in their love," and the way that "jealousies are transcended in the development and blossoming of love."[40] But I would argue that Kierkegaard does not, as Phillips charges, neglect the way love "grows," deepens, becomes faithful. These dimensions of richness are precisely what Kierkegaard sees as the dimensions that go beyond preferential inclination as such, thereby enriching or ennobling preferential relationships. The richness of friendship and erotic love to which Phillips points already includes more than mere preference or inclination. Inclination made faithful and devoted, affection that sacrifices for the other—these are already preserving "neighbor-love."[41] These are ways of respecting the alterity, the dignity, and the equality of another, even when our preferences or inclinations wane or otherwise alter.

Proper Self-Love and Tragedy

Two further comments need to be made regarding the charge that Kierkegaard's valorization of neighbor-love devalues preferential love. First, it is true that Kierkegaard qualifies his claim that "erotic love is undeniably life's most beautiful happiness and friendship the greatest temporal good!" (WL, 267) with the addition that "Erotic love and friendship *as such* are only enhanced and augmented self-love." But this addition is not something unique to him. Here he is agreeing, as I noted earlier, with the likes of Aristotle and Aquinas that loves based on inclination or preference (as erotic loves and friendships are) are ways of being 'for oneself,' of loving what is good for me. To say that they are enhanced self-love is not a disparagement of erotic love and friendship, but rather a way of revealing how human beings properly need to love and be loved, a need Kierkegaard calls a "craving," and that is exemplified by Jesus Christ himself in his earthly life.

Second, it is, indeed, a tragic fact that the intimacy, the sharing, the growth we experience in erotic loves and friendships cannot continue forever. Kierkegaard's claim that erotic love and friendship are life's greatest treasures implies that we are lucky to find friends and lovers, as well as that it is appropriate to mourn when we lose them. And Kierkegaard acknowledges just this when he says that Christian love is "not exempted from misfortune" (WL, 42), and that we do not have "the right to become insensitive to life's pain" (WL, 43). Preferential loves do, as he says, blossom and sadly die—they end, at the very least, with the death of the lover or friend. But the realistic recognition that erotic loves and friendships do not last forever does not devalue them—it is just those loves that blossom and die that are called life's joys. Neighbor-love is not meant by Kierkegaard to be a way of avoiding the inherent tragedy of our temporality and mortality. It misses the mark then to say, as Phillips does, that "the problems that arise in loves that blossom do not come, in my examples, from failure to see the other as a neighbour. Hence, invoking that love is no answer to them."[42] Phillips is right—sometimes the problems in our love relationships are not our fault and could not be remedied by our treating the other with greater respect. But Kierkegaard's ethic is not meant to prevent tragedy. On the other hand, there may well be cases in which the failure to honor the other as an equal is part of the problem, and invoking neighbor-love can help in that respect.

Commanded Love

Much of the preceding bears indirectly on the 'problem' of the paradox of commanded or dutiful love. Kierkegaard, as Hannay recognizes, agrees with Kant that only acts subject to the will can be appraised morally; on Kantian/ Kierkegaard's terms instinctive (not willed) responses like erotic attraction and feelings of friendship are in themselves amoral; conversely, the form of commanded moral concern cannot be love if love is a feeling or sympathy that cannot be willed. Kierkegaard, however, believes that the love that is commanded is indeed morally valuable. Accordingly, it becomes important to ask both how love of others can be morally appraised and why it is still deserving of the name 'love.'

Responsible Caring

Kierkegaard's resolution is that although it is indeed paradoxical to speak of commanded feeling (since feelings cannot be generated at will), the love of which he speaks is not a feeling or inclination. The love that is commanded is caring (*Kjerlighed*),[43] and such caring is subject to the will because it is the assumption of a responsibility to take care of another who needs care. Since the kind of love commanded is not erotic love (*Elskov*) or feelings of friendliness (*Venskab*), any conceptual paradox is only apparent.

Works of Love is a book about the love *commandment*. Inclination, affection, or preference cannot be commanded. The mark of erotic love and friendship is precisely that it is a matter of preference—that is, it is "arbitrary." On the contrary, whatever he means by "neighbor-love" *can* be commanded. What kind of love can be commanded? Responsible caring—an infinite responsibility that is never completed and that never excludes anyone.

It might be argued, as Phillips does, that a caring done 'out of duty' is less rich or valuable than a caring done out of compassion.[44] Phillips refers to the compassion that moved the Good Samaritan. But Kierkegaard too uses the example of the Good Samaritan, so he does not see duty as incompatible with compassion. Did Mother Teresa love the poor of Calcutta because of some very rare ability to want to love them, some saintly desire that drew her to them—rather than duty? I think we want to be careful here. The "sense of duty" Phillips speaks of sounds like a psychological burden, with which we give grudgingly. But I fulfill the commandment to love by compassionately loving, not by being self-righteously dutiful. Whether we like it or not, Mother Teresa did see her response to the poor as motivated by her love for God—the poor were children of God and so deserved her care. That she saw it as her duty does not mean that her care was a cold response 'out of duty.' Kierkegaard too affirms a duty to love based on kinship with others[45]—likewise, that duty can be fulfilled compassionately. A responsibility for others that does not exclude them as kin is the only love that can be commanded (and therefore the highest that can be commanded). And such commanded love is not limited to the lowest common denominator that we could offer to everyone—it may in some circumstances require us to lay down our life for the other.

Is Preferential Love Paradigmatic Love?

Why use the term "love" for our responsible caring for those for whom we feel no spontaneous affection or inclination? Precisely because *Kjerlighed,* not erotic love or friendship, is the paradigm of love. It is noteworthy that *Kjerlighed* is the immediate love by which we are loved by God and which enables us to love others—that is, Kierkegaard uses the same Danish word (*Kjerlighed*) to refer to (1) **God as love,** (2) **the love placed in us by God,** as well as (3) the **neighbor-love we are commanded to express.**[46] The love that Kierkegaard says is commanded by God is described by the same word as the love that is God (*Kjerlighed*) *prior to any specification into erotic love and nonerotic love.* The question whether nonpreferential/nondiscriminating love can be love is answered by definition.

Let me elaborate on how *Kjerlighed* is paradigmatic of love. First, it is constitutive of our nature. *Kjerlighed* is immediate in the sense that it is foundational to our being, to our createdness; it is not something we choose to have or accept. Kierkegaard repeatedly uses the strong Danish term (*Trang*) that means "craving" (WL, 10).[47] The love God places in us needs to express itself, or it will be like the plant that withers and dies because it is not allowed to follow its natural craving (WL, 11). But not only do we need to express love—we also need to be loved by others. Kierkegaard makes this point repeatedly and graphically. "How *deeply* the need of love is rooted in human nature," so that a "longing for companionship" is part of our humanness (WL, 154). We need to be loved by particular others; indeed, insofar as Christ was human, he too "felt this need to love and be loved by an individual human being," as his poignant plea to Peter reveals (Do you love me more than these?) (WL, 155).

Second, *Kjerlighed* has priority—placed in us prior to a distinction between erotic/nonerotic. The question whether the esthetic is preserved in the ethical and religious spheres is a common one. But that formulation already prejudices the discussion, putting a priority on esthetic immediacy. It assumes that erotic love or friendship is paradigmatic caring, the caring that most exhibits what caring should be; it assumes that preferential caring is paradigmatic immediacy, and then the question is how much of its immediacy can be preserved in neighbor-love.[48]

Kierkegaard, on the contrary, suggests a different approach when he formulates the goal as follows: "in erotic love and friendship, preserve love for the neighbor" (WL, 62). He reverses the question: rather than asking whether erotic love is preserved in neighbor-love, he asks us to consider whether neighbor-love is preserved in erotic love. What kind of difference does this make? Well, we are no longer prioritizing the esthetic. Kierkegaard's reversal, asking whether neighbor-love is preserved, leads us back to the priority of God's love in us, the priority of *Kjerlighed*.

Moreover, Kierkegaard insists repeatedly that there is "only one kind of love," "the spirit's love," that "can lie at the base of and be present in every other expression of love" (WL, 143, 146). Christian love is not a "higher" love, an additional love, a different "type" or "kind" of love (WL, 45, 58, 66). This means that for Kierkegaard there is no hierarchy in love.[49] The oneness of love and the impossibility of separating different "kinds" of loving is represented in the peculiarity of the Danish language that the love commandment is phrased "Du skal elske" (paralleling *Elskov*) because there is no verb form of *Kjerlighed*.

What should be at stake for those worried that *Kjerlighed* is disinterested beneficence is whether *Kjerlighed* is concrete and responsive to differences, not whether it retains the specific immediacy of erotic love and friendship. We can now formulate the relation between 'immediate' (esthetic, spontaneous) love and religious neighbor-love (*Kjerlighed*) as follows: *Kjerlighed* is expressed in erotic love and friendship in a restricted way—that is, preference limits the expression of *Kjerlighed*. The crucial divide, for Kierkegaard, is between preferential love and nonpreferential love, expressed by the Danish words *Forkjer-*

lighed and *Kjerlighed*. *Kjerlighed* is, one could say, the (linguistic) substance of *Forkjerlighed*, but in *Forkjerlighed* it is qualified—focused, directed, centered on specific others with agreeable qualities. In other words, the prefix restricts or limits the caring. There is caring (*Kjerlighed*) and there is restricted caring (*Elskov* and *Venskab*), made specific by limiting itself. Even Judge William seems to support such a view when he notes that "Obviously the real constituting element, the substance is love [*Kjerlighed*]—or, if you want to give it more specific emphasis, erotic love [*Elskov*]."[50] *Kjerlighed* is not love with concrete caring stripped away; rather, preferential modes of caring are restricted modes of immediate caring. *Kjerlighed* is immediate caring, but with the qualification that it is not actually arbitrary or exclusive; it is the second immediacy of caring, not an abstraction from it.

Conclusion

I began this essay with a claim that Hannay attributed to Kierkegaard—namely, that any love that is not neighbor-love is "morally reprehensible." I have argued above that Kierkegaard's view that neighbor-love can be *preserved* in erotic love and friendship allows that, although there is a sense in which Hannay's claim is literally true, his claim is not the same as the claim that preferential love is morally reprehensible. Kierkegaard's (reconstructed) argument is: Neighbor-love is, by definition, morally unselfish. Neighbor-love can be preserved in preferential loves. Any love that preserves neighbor-love is morally unselfish; any love that fails to preserve neighbor-love is morally selfish.

Preferential love can be sharply contrasted conceptually with nonpreferential love, yet if Kierkegaard's goal is to preserve neighbor-love in erotic love and friendship, it has to be the case that he thinks they can coincide materially. And this is just what he says: Neighbor-love should "permeate" every expression of love (WL, 112).

The permeation of all loves by neighbor-love amounts to a "transforming" (WL, 112) that shows itself by virtue of fulfilling some conditions—the other is treated as an equal, shown the respect appropriate to our kinship with each other as children of God. In the cases where we experience attraction or preference for another—whether it be erotic, parental, or friendship—the love we experience needs to be permeated or informed or transformed by neighbor-love. On the other hand, neighbor-love may sometimes exist alone—as it does when we have no preference for or attraction to the other whom we find in need, when we are in a position to help.

My analysis has distinguished certain claims from each other. First, the claim that preference is not genuine love does not entail that preference precludes genuine love; the Kierkegaardian claim is only that preference alone is not genuine love. Second, the claim that preferential loves can involve selfishness does not entail that preferential loves necessarily involve selfishness. Kierkegaard is committed to the view that we can find something recognizable as genuine love even in preferential relationships—but it is not the simple spontaneous inclination; rather, it is that inclination enobled by the caring (*Kjerlighed*) that takes responsibility both for fulfilling the needs of the other and for treating the other as an equal. The elevation or enhancement of erotic love and friendship is intended to preclude the arbitrariness and instability of preferential love. Indeed, the thrusting down of erotic love and friendship from the throne amounts to a *permeation* and *transformation* (WL, 112) that makes erotic love and friendship "more tender" and "more faithful" (WL, 44).

In sum, Kierkegaard has two main commitments that allow him to consistently claim that erotic love and friendship are valuable. First, his contrast between proper self-love and selfish self-love allows erotic love and friendship to be valuable. Second, his equation of the love (*Kjerlighed*) that is God with the love that God places in human beings in creating us and the love that is commanded of us (i.e., the unity of love) means that he reads *Kjerlighed* as prior to any distinction between selfish and unselfish, between erotic/friendship and neighbor-love: *Kjerlighed* is primary (the paradigm of love), and *Forkjerlighed* is a restriction of *Kjerlighed*.

8.
Kierkegaard on Natural and Commanded Love

Alastair Hannay

All three preceding chapters refer to *Works of Love,* the first two in the light of what that work tells us about Kierkegaard's relation to philosophy, the third in its own terms and in respect of what *Works of Love* is saying, in criticism of what, some time ago, I myself have said about that.

My remarks on Rick Furtak's essay are directed at the more general topic of the second part of his title, "the discipline of philosophy" (though we note that the second part's actual title is "the art of philosophy").

Furtak maintains that philosophy needs the kind of thickening we can see Kierkegaard's writings as contributing toward. I take it that this does not necessarily imply that what Kierkegaard gives us is actually a form of this thickened philosophy; there is still a question of whether Kierkergaard is "doing" philosophy at all rather than something else. Kierkegaard's writings are certainly thick in the sense appreciated by the better philosophers today, but are they philosophy? Furtak first presents Kierkegaard as a resource for those of us who feel short-changed by present-day positivism. The concept of love enters the picture as of concern to one of those aspects of experience significant for our grasp of our own relationship to the outside world, and one of many vital topics that escape the objectivist's net but that a mature philosophy should include.

As Furtak notes, it does appear from *Works of Love* and other texts that Kierkegaard claims a kind of primacy for love. It is primary in terms of what gives the experiencing subject's experience meaning or significance. Kierkegaard, as Furtak quotes him, says love is "the deepest ground of spiritual life," and somewhere near the same place in *Works of Love* we can read that love is the ground or basis on which to build (*opbygge*) but also both "the building and what builds."[1] That looks like a viable thesis, something anyone calling her- or himself a philosopher should be able to analyze and discuss. Furtak, a philosopher in a clear and more familiar sense than any we can apply to Kierkegaard, takes up what I assume to be a claim very like it and presents it as a defensible philosophical thesis.

Formulated in something like these words, the thesis could be plausible enough. If the notion of love in all its manifestations is sorted out a bit and those aspects of it that would fall in with the claim identified, we would be able to look to Kierkegaard to see what he can contribute in its support. One might, of course, demand rather less, merely showing what light Kierkegaard's writings on *Kjerlighed* and *Elskov* can shed on this among other areas of life neglected by positivistic philosophies. Still, the primacy of love does seem worth arguing for and at least investigating, over other aspects of emotional life that also give meaning but in other, perhaps arguably negative, ways, hate and envy being obvious instances. But we may have to be careful here. It may be a hindrance in eliciting Kierkegaard's support that what Kierkegaard means by "love" (*Kjerlighed*) is in a Christian context (the one in which *Works of Love* operates) and "problematic" in the way Jamie Ferreira's title indicates, and that its "primacy" may have to do as much with theological dogma as with what can be argued for on purely philosophical grounds. The problematic aspect of this love is that it goes beyond whatever might be said about (and for) love from a "humanistic" point of view. So what can a philosopher make of a love about which Kierkegaard might claim, in line with what Climacus has said about Christianity, that what he means by this term could never occur to anyone whose point of view is merely "*human*"?

It seems that to get through to what Kierkegaard is saying here, we need more than a thrust beyond scientistic positivism that gets us into experience and provides a philosophy able to do justice to the richness (and sometimes poverty) of a human life. Beyond thickened philosophy we need to break into the (for the philosopher) mind-boggling categories of religion, which especially in Kierkegaard make everything more difficult because they change everything around.

We may therefore wonder whether, if (as Ferreira claims) Kierkegaard really has been successfully brought into the philosophical canon, that fact is something he would have applauded. Think of all the "professors" he would have to consort with! This is not to ask, Is he, by virtue of being there, doing a good job for philosophy? Furtak's chapter amply demonstrates that the answer to that question is yes. At the very least, armed as he was with, in Furtak's words, "an acute literary sensitivity," Kierkegaard, whatever we should say he was up to, is a wonderful as well as innovative example of someone able, also in Furtak's words, to "illuminate existence from within."

Let me put the matter briefly like this. Philosophy in the century and a half since Kierkegaard died has no doubt changed. Its exemplars are no longer confined to the likes of Hegel or Sibbern. Even in his own lifetime it included Schopenhauer (who Kierkegaard appreciated) and, had he lived into old age, would also have included Nietzsche (who might have appreciated *him*). It has expanded enough to make Kierkegaard look not all that different from some thinkers included today in the canon. The question is whether by treating Kierkegaard as a philosopher we are getting all we can out of him, and again, whether we are taking from him all he himself would like to impart.

In this connection I pick up a small sentence at the end of one of Furtak's notes. It asks, "How much is our very style of writing to blame for our alienation, our sense that the human being is not at home in the world?" I think I know what he refers to in the context of philosophy. But my gut reaction to this is to think that Kierkegaard's writings, for all their ability to sensitize the reader, and indeed also by virtue of that ability, might be designed to give the reader exactly a sense of not being at home in the world, though in another way, that is to say, a sense of *not* being at home in the world in the way the reader unthinkingly assumes is the way to be at home in it. Our project today, we who can easily have a sense—when studying philosophy or teaching it—of having to leave our "views from somewhere" so as to position ourselves at a "view from nowhere," may be described as that of bringing the person back *into philosophy*. It is philosophy that has alienated itself from us. But the philosophy that has no place for us differs from the philosophy that confronted Kierkegaard. The former presents not even the illusion of including anything belonging to our views from various somewheres. But the Hegelian philosophy was able to give its students and teachers, *qua* conceptualizing creatures, a sense of their already being well on the way home.

It is by trying to say what can in principle be true for anyone that a discourse qualifies as philosophical. It is this that, for good or ill, makes a project like Heidegger's fundamental ontology more obviously philosophical than Kierkegaard's whatever-it-is-we-should-call-it. We might say, then, that a philosophy thickened enough to take us out of the view from nowhere still only aims at bringing us to a (however thickened) view from (in principle) anywhere. Kierkegaard's category of the individual is indeed a philosophical one, but at the same time it marks a boundary on which we read, "From here on you are on your own." The moral might be this: the philosopher while philosophizing need not, indeed should not, forget that he or she is an existing individual, but while philosophizing it is necessary to forget for the time being that he or she is the particular existing individual he or she is.

Most of what Roberts says seems to fit this account. His essay dots the "i"s of Furtak's by supplementing the latter's comments on what philosophy lacks and what Kierkegaard can contribute, by suggesting that the stock in trade of professorial moral philosophy (moral theory) gets in the way of such thickening, together with the claim that Kierkegaard eschews such theories but is philosophizing nonetheless.

Let me note the main points of contact, if not complete coincidence, with what I have just said in conclusion of my comments on Furtak. First, Roberts notes, convincingly on the basis of his outline of several typical versions of virtue ethics that try to derive moral concepts from some foundational concept, that this "standard way" of doing moral philosophy is "a far cry" from the "missionary mentality" of Kierkegaard. Roberts accepts that Kierkegaard is doing moral philosophy but in a way that differs from how professional philosophers do it. It differs "interestingly," and by this Roberts must mean that it points to another way of doing philosophy, one that does not consist in constructing theories in the way outlined. Turning to *Works of Love,* Roberts finds that it exemplifies such another way. He calls it "conceptual exploration." This method, very different from the "game" of derivation, is the exercise of a "disposition to grasp the connections among things." We can all readily agree with Roberts in taking this to be a philosophical way of approaching Christian love. To capture the missionary element in Kierkegaard, however, Roberts invokes another kind of understanding, which he calls "wisdom." On its own, conceptual analysis of Christian love would not accomplish the missionary aim to move the reader to "exemplify [Christian love] himself." That aim calls for structuring, not just the reader's "head," but also his "pathos."

I suggested that this is the point where Kierkegaard parts company with the philosophers but am uncertain whether Roberts thinks so too. If not, the burden is on me to point out where he does part company with them, but I am unsure that I can do that. Several reasons might be cited, however, for thinking that Kierkegaard does depart here from philosophy. One is that "pathos" is not something that philosophical discourse is equipped either to tamper with or arouse, its virtue lying elsewhere, for instance in conceptual exploration. Some would argue that the propositional form proper to philosophy cannot express pathos in any case, and if it cannot do that, how can it arouse pathos in the reader? On the other hand, if Kierkegaard's writings do contain pathos, maybe we should conclude that he is unphilosophical from the start. I must say I don't find any of these reasons convincing, and I am very reluctant to think that *Works of Love* is unphilosophical from the start

We are reminded of the age-old issue of what can motivate moral behavior. It is usually presented in the form of someone who understands what the moral thing to do is but is not disposed to do it. Things here are worse. If, as Roberts points out, what Kierkegaard's conceptual exploration fills our heads with is something "shockingly different from what the world would expect," the reader will be disinclined at the outset to believe that this is the moral thing to do. One avenue to an answer, possibly in Roberts's favor, is what Roberts himself says about the parochial, that is, less than universal, appeal of Adams's divine command theory of obligation. Kierkegaard wrote with a special public in mind, though at the time it was not parochial in any geographical sense; it was a public predisposed to be shocked in a particular direction. This public would have an initial respect for whatever was correctly called Christian love, and out of that initial respect it would, when confronted with a work able to foster a better understanding of that love, either be disposed to revise its conception of what that love amounted to or be brought to shame by its own reluctance to do so, invoking the age-old problem once more but in a way familiar enough to philosophers. The crucial thing is that the motivation to revise one's behavior on being clearer about the implications of something one is initially inclined to believe is something neither a philosophical theory nor a philosophical exploration can produce, but rather something any philosopher with a mission must presuppose.

Does Jamie Ferreira underestimate just how "shocking" *Works of Love* is? Or do we disagree on the intended impact of Kierkegaard's conceptual exploration? What Jamie finds shocking is my own attempt at finding (on Kierkegaard's behalf) a good argument for saying that the self-regard in preferential caring is always morally reprehensible. She takes me to task for not looking harder for textual support of the idea that the self-love in preferential love can be good or harmless self-love, not always (as I have said) bad self-love. And she cites a number of the passages that, if I had cited them, would seem to have made my job harder if not impossible. Here I take account of those passages, and some others, and offer an alternative way of dealing with that criticism, alternative, that is, to having to say that in terms of *Kjerlighed*, preference can sometimes be good.

Ferreira finds two commitments in Kierkegaard allowing him consistently to "claim that erotic love and friendship are valuable." One is a contrast between proper and selfish self-love (for which she sees relevant analogues in Aristotle and Aquinas), and the other is Kierkegaard's equation of God as love with the love God places in human beings in creating us and that is commanded of us. The latter love is, she says, "prior to any distinction between selfish/unselfish, between erotic/friendship and neighbour-love: *Kjerlighed* is primary (the paradigm of love) and *Forkjerlighed* is a restriction of *Kjerlighed*."

With the matter of primacy and the notion of a paradigm of love and of preferential love as a restriction on it I entirely agree. But I look at this result in a rather different way that has to do with the first point, about the distinction between proper self-love and selfish self-love.

First of all, I must offer some excuses. The book containing the chapter Ferreira comments on is one I had been commissioned (more than thirty years ago) to write in a series called the "The Arguments of the Philosophers." Rather than decline and say, No, you won't find any arguments in Kierkegaard and he doesn't like philosophy anyway, I thought it would be a pity to let the opportunity go both to learn more about Kierkegaard myself and to bring this extraordinarily significant writer within reach of the philosophers I most respected at the time. It isn't hard to detect familiar philosophical positions and assumptions in what Kierkegaard writes, and anyone reading him both carefully and widely must be impressed by the systematic nature of his writing in general and by his sure command of the concepts and the terminology of the philosophy of the time. On getting into Kierkegaardian ethics and coming upon *Works of Love*, I found there what looked to me from the start a position with very distinct parallels to Kant. In looking for the philosophy in Kierkegaard, it seemed natural to test the texts against the templates of more systematically developed positions of accredited philosophers. In some cases this is obviously anachronistic and can be dangerous. But here it would not be. In Kierkegaard's time Kant was still in the air, if principally as a target, but of interest for that reason, since Hegel was a target of Kierkegaard. If Kant and Hegel were enemies, then maybe Kierkegaard and Kant could be friends. Having in any case a soft spot for Kierkegaard, I thought I should try to see how Kierkegaard might not just measure up to Kant but possibly better him in this matter of the agapeistic ideal. Perhaps a case might be made for that ideal as one actually of love, a notion Kant found unable to apply to the Christian commandment, resorting instead to the fundamentally impersonal idea that we are bound in duty to try to like, or "love," practicing our duties to our neighbor.

As Jamie Ferreira explains, the love I thought I found in *Works of Love* was a kind of logical extension of what Shakespeare refers to in that famous sonnet (No. 116) that says "Love is not love which alters when it alteration finds." There is no want of textual support. Kierkegaard's version lies open to view in the heading "When It Is a Duty in Love to Love the Persons We See, There Is No Limit to the Love; If the Duty Is to Be Fulfilled, the Love Must Be Without Limit, It Is Unchanged Howsoever the Object Changes."[2] We can combine this with another textually well-supported notion, that of the other and the self as particulars, bare but irreducible and nonexchangeable particulars. Together, these allow us to say that, shorn of the outer garments in which peculiarity appears to us (an image actually provided in *Works of Love*), that is, of the differences and similarities that are the basis for our preferring the one over the other, love in a Christian sense can be understood as the interest one preserves through all such change, physical and even psychological, in the interest of the other self. This is at least nonpreferential and, in a not-too-strained manner of speaking, might well be called love, even without the theology that says that what is required of us here is somehow the same as the love God bestows on us in creating us. But with the theology added, the idea is of course even more telling, and it speaks of unity, the unity of humankind, in place of the formless aggregate of human attachments and relationships that is all that "love" from preference can amount to.

I assumed that Kierkegaard claimed that any condition put on nonpreferential love would be tantamount to preference and would for that reason fall short of the ideal. In support of this I looked again to Kant and *his* discussion of self-love, which is very different from those of Aristotle and Aquinas. Kant, for his own purposes, defines "self-love" as a "propensity to make ourselves in the subjective determining principles of our choice serve as the objective determining principle of the will generally."[3] Roughly, self-love is making some natural preference of our own count as a general moral principle. But then, for Kant, there is the Moral Law, our relationship to which is not to be conceived as one among these preferences; we have a notion of it but not a feeling for it, says Kant, and it is this notion that should be appealed to as the objective determining principle. However, Kant also says, and note well: "our nature as sensible beings is such that the matter of desire (objects of inclination, whether of hope or fear) first presents itself to us [perhaps the translation should be "is what presents itself to us first"?]; and our pathologically affected self, although it is in its maxims quite unfit for universal legislation, yet, just as if it constituted our entire self, strives to put its pretensions forward first, and to have them acknowledged as the first and original."[4]

Kant has said that "everything that presents itself as an object of will prior to the moral law is by that law itself, which is the supreme condition of practical reason, excluded from the determining principles of the will which we have called the unconditionally good."[5]

Transferring this to Kierkegaard, we have the idea that the Christian commandment to love is comparable to the Moral Law in Kant, though with the added benefit—as far as calling it "love" is concerned—of the theology that connects the commandment directly with God the giver of good and perfect gifts. God is right "there" so to speak, and not, as in Kantian rationalism, reconstructed in the form of a notion in our minds.

So to the matter of preferential love. *Kjerlighed* (the love commanded) in its paradigmatic form has no self-referential component beyond that required to follow the commandment. At this level, or in respect of this notion, any preference is self-love in a bad sense. All that means is that it fails to be *Christian* love. Pointing out anything as self-love in this respect is simply a way of saying it is not (in Ferreira's term) primary love. What I took *Works of Love* to be analyzing was this love, analyzing it illustratively you might say, by putting counter-examples before us, including many that will strike us as not being all that selfish, not selfish enough to count against any ordinary or generalized notion of love.

But, as Ferreira points out, *Works of Love* does also mention ordinary, everyday, preferential love: love of the beloved, friendship, and (we may add) even patriotism.[6] Let me now hazard a guess as to how she interprets the inclusion of these. Obviously they are not things Kierkegaard wants to trash; that would be monstrous and absurd. But then he must allow that they are not morally reprehensible even though they are examples of the preference he has been calling selfish and even self-love. Now, the text actually says as much; that is, it says that they are not to be trashed. It says that Christian love does not change the way we go about the relationships that we are all familiar with and are part of life itself. We might gloss this by saying that selfishness is part of the mechanism whereby any relationships and attachments come about, their necessary contextual beginning. We can extend the analogy with Kant here too. Our instinctual natural preferences come first, but then what is wrong is to make these the basis of the objective principle for our will. Substitute the commandment of love, the Christian proposal for a paradigm of love, and you get what for Kierkegaard is the basis for such an objective principle. The text is a bit peculiar here. It begins easily enough by saying that the coming of the Christian paradigm does not change all these forms of human preference: they are there, have been, and will continue to be—how otherwise would there be life? But then it immediately goes on to say that the actual coming of this paradigm "changed everything, changed all of love [*hele Kjerligheden*]."[7]

How can Kierkegaard have it both ways? Here is one possibility: all the various kinds of love come under this paradigm, which means they are all of the same kind, so that the kind can include preferential love, as Ferreira argues.

Against this, although the text says that there is only one *form* of love, as Ferreira notes, what it says is not "there is one kind of love," just that *Christianity* "knows only one kind of love," that is, "spiritual love [*Aands-Kjerlighed*]," though it then goes on to say that "this can be the basis of and present in every other expression of love."[8]

How can non-Christian loves express Christian love, and how can the latter be their basis? Here is a suggestion. The coming, by revelation, of Christian love changes all love[9] by providing a new perspective from which the possibilities of love, friendship, patriotism, that is, of love in its many and various forms and these remaining as they are or even multiplying, are seen under a unifying vision of neighbor-love. Christianity no longer sees love under merely human categories, as a "purely immediate urge, as inclination (erotic love or friendship), as feeling and inclination, with some differential addition of duty, natural condition, right, etc., or else as something to be sought after and appropriated as a worldly good,"[10] all of which (different *kinds* of love, be it noted) Christianity is not concerned with and happy to leave as it is. Christianity itself sees only "one kind," spiritual love, and sees it as the "essential" love,[11] against which, it seems we may conclude, all the kinds Christianity is not concerned with appear now in the light of a contrast in the form of an ideal, an ideal we progress toward by treating the "other" increasingly in terms of *their* possibilities, and decreasingly in terms of our personal investment in them, which is to say, more or less, in the respects in which they appeal to our preferences. It is in this way that "essential love . . . can be [their] basis."[12]

So preferential love is here to stay; it is, as Aristotle and Aquinas would agree, sometimes selfish, and in those cases bad, and in the ordinary way that we distinguish actions as selfish it is sometimes proper. But, in the light of a paradigm according to which preference is always selfish and never proper, we can discern and feel the propriety in mitigating the selfishness in our loving attachments that the ordinary distinction between selfish and self-less obscures.[13]

Part 3.
Melancholy
and Despair

9.
Despair and Depression

Gordon Marino

Kierkegaard used to complain that "the age of making distinctions is passed."[1] The age of making the distinction between despair and depression is certainly passed. Indeed, were someone today to say that he was in despair, we would almost surely think that what he really meant to say was that he was depressed. No doubt the demise of despair has something to do with the collapse of 'sacred order.'[2] It used to be that despair was considered one of the seven deadly sins, inasmuch as the despairing individual was considered to be giving up on God. Today, despair is understood to be hopelessness, hopelessness to be depression, and depression to be something that you treat, as Kierkegaard puts it, *mit Pulver and mit Pillen,*[3] that is, by throwing pills at it. Still, I have at times sensed some dissatisfaction with the present tendency to read every pang of the psyche as a symptom of an illness most frequently understood as a "chemical imbalance." Kierkegaard gave much thought to the meaning of mental anguish, and his meditations on this subject should speak to an age in which most people will, at some point in their lives, seek out professional help for psychological problems, most commonly for depression.

In this chapter I will examine Kierkegaard's thoughts on the relation between depression and despair. Kierkegaard's published writings on depression are, for the most part, written into his pseudonymous texts, *Stages on Life's Way, Repetition,* and *Either/Or.* There have been a number of commentaries[4] on the prototheories contained in these works, but scant attention has been paid to Kierkegaard's own self-observations regarding what he termed his "thorn in the flesh"[5] or depression.[6] I will focus on the introspective soundings that Kierkegaard takes in his journals, for it is, I believe, in these pages that Kierkegaard offers the most light on the difference between the night of the psyche and the night of the spirit.

From the first to the last page of his life, Kierkegaard dragged the ball and chain of his melancholy around. Like Pascal, Montaigne, and other keepers of the invisible darkness, Kierkegaard watched his depression with the eye of a naturalist, and like more modern psychological men and women, he kept copious notes on his sorrow. Through hundreds of entries there are a number of recurrent themes: for one, that he was in unspeakable and chronic mental anguish. By his own account, Kierkegaard's depression was severe enough to bring him to the razor's edge. In 1836 he made the following journal entry: "I have just returned from a party of which I was the life and soul; witticisms poured from my lips, everybody laughed and admired me—but I left, yes, the dash should be as long as the radii of the earth's orbit and wanted to shoot myself."[7]

This self-revelation hints at the theme of hiddenness, which is explicit in other journal entries. One of the fixed points in Kierkegaard's authorship is his claim that the inner and outer are incommensurable.[8] For Kierkegaard, you cannot read the liniments of a person's spiritual life off from his actions. There are hints of this anti-Hegelian precept in Kierkegaard's notes on his melancholy. Over the years he alternately gloats and moans about his ability to conceal both the fact and content of his psychological suffering: "People have continually done me indescribable wrong by continually regarding as pride that which was intended only to keep the secret of my melancholy. Obviously, I have achieved what I wanted to achieve, for hardly anyone has ever felt any sympathy for me."[9] On the basis of some experience, Kierkegaard insisted that there is nothing more painful than being misunderstood. In fact, on his reading it was the impossibility of understanding Jesus' mission here on earth that set Christ's agony apart from the pain of others who have suffered for the truth.[10] Kierkegaard can often be caught sneering at those who cannot detect the pain that he takes such pride in being able to hide, yet the journals are rife with sighs of longing for human understanding and contact.

Like later depth psychologists, Kierkegaard recognized that the ego has its ways of deflecting painful affects. He perceived that depressives try to hide from their lack of feeling by sinking their self-consciousness in the world. This defense can take the form of debauchery. In psychoanalytic circles, it is common knowledge that certain types of depressives will eroticize their lives in an effort to stave off their depression. Better to dance with libidinal desire than to feel nothing. Kierkegaard's "The Seducer's Diary"[11] shows that he recognized this defensive strategy, and his journals indicate that he saw himself as employing it in his own youth.[12]

In telling his writer's life story, Kierkegaard insists that the authorship was from the first to last a religious undertaking.[13] By his own account, it was also a radical defense against depression.[14] Kierkegaard understood his preternatural intellectual labors as an attempt to stay afloat from the preternatural depression that threatened to absorb him, much as it ultimately did his brother, who because of his depression eventually resigned as Bishop of Aalbord.

While there are lines in the pseudonymous authorship that would bring depression and despair close together,[15] there are strong indications that Kierkegaard saw a distinction between the state of depression and the activity of despair. For one, depression is a state or a mood, whereas despair is an activity that continues only so long as the individual, however half-consciously, wills that it continue. Anti-Climacus instructs us that it would be wrong to think of despair according to the medical model, that is, as a fever, as a state that you passively suffer through. If despair did not engage the will it would not be the sin that Anti-Climacus insists it is. Kierkegaard does, however, use the disease model to describe depression. Indeed, he believes that depression is something that you can, as it were, be born into or catch by contagion. Kierkegaard describes his own melancholy in just this way, as an inheritance: "An old man who himself was extremely melancholy . . . gets a son in his old age who inherits all this melancholy."[16] The identity of the heir to the throne of sorrow is transparent. In another note, Kierkegaard leaves no doubt about his view of the etiology of depression: "From the very beginning I have been in the power of a congenital mental depression. If I had been brought up in a more ordinary way—well, it stands to reason that I then would hardly have become so melancholy."[17] In contrast to depression, Kierkegaard never talks about despair as though it were something you could contract by being around too many despairing people, or inherit as a child might inherit its mother's temperament.

The Sickness unto Death makes it plain that there are forms of despair that do not involve mental anguish. Indeed, Anti-Climacus, the pseudonymous author of this lapidary text, observes that happiness is despair's greatest hiding place.[18] While the depressed individual may, *à la* Kierkegaard himself, try and succeed at appearing happy, he is not happy. A person who is in fact happy is *eo ipso* not depressed. It is not, however, unusual for a happy person to be in despair. For another point of contrast, whereas depression always involves sadness, despair is not accompanied by a unique set of emotions. A walk through the psychospiritual portrait gallery presented in *The Sickness unto Death* will suffice to show that Kierkegaard believes despair to be compatible with both the blues and feeling in the pink.

No less than Nietzsche, Kierkegaard was a virulent critic of practical wisdom. The practical wisdom of *fin de siècle* America says that it would be a contradiction for someone to assert that he was depressed but in fine spiritual fettle. Kierkegaard contradicts this piece of practical wisdom. In a journal entry from 1846 that must be reckoned the axis of this chapter, Kierkegaard records the following signature self-observation:

> I am in the profoundest sense an unhappy individuality, riveted from the beginning to one or another suffering bordering on madness, a suffering which must have its deeper basis in a misrelation between my mind and body, for (and this is the remarkable thing as well as my infinite encouragement) it has

no relation to my spirit, which on the contrary, because of the tension between my mind and body, has perhaps gained an uncommon resiliency.[19]

Clearly, the suffering to which Kierkegaard is riveted from the beginning and that he surmises to be a qualification of his particular mind-body relation is his melancholy. And yet in the above passage he seems to be claiming that this psychological disorder (depression) is not to be confused with a spiritual malady. After all, he affirms that the misrelation between his mind and body has no relation to his spirit. We have here the distinction, effaced in our own age, between a psychological and spiritual disorder. In *The Sickness unto Death* and elsewhere we are told that a human being is not a simple synthesis between mind and body. Instead, "the self is a relation which relates to itself, or that in the relation which is relating to itself."[20] The simple and automatic relation between mind and body gives rise to psychological states, but the spirit or self emerges in the way that we interpret and relate ourselves to those states. In that sense, the spirit is a kind of second-order phenomenon.

To return to the journal entry from 1846, Kierkegaard notes that it is remarkable that the misrelation between his mind and body has not affected his spirit. In other words, his depression could, in fact, have become despair. The process by which depression becomes a sickness, not of the psyche but of the *self*, is not a passive one. In the first movement of the *Sickness unto Death* Anti-Climacus sheds some light on his creator's diary and on the connection between depression and despair. Commenting on a case of depression, Kierkegaard's slightly abstracted doctor of the soul writes that the despairing depressive "sees quite clearly that this depression etc. is of no great significance—but precisely that fact, that it neither has nor acquires any great significance, is despair."[21] It is not the psychological suffering itself that is the spiritual problem (despair) but rather being oblivious to the fact that the suffering has spiritual significance. As though he had been through that cast of mind, Kierkegaard writes, "The most dreadful thing that can happen to a man is that he becomes ludicrous in the essentials, that the substance of his feelings is drivel."[22] Though there are different internal paths from depression to despair, the depressive who sees no significance in his forlorn state, that is, who regards his sadness as a kind of fever, that is, as drivel, has now developed a spiritual affliction to add to his psychological ills. Anyone who has had to trek through the inner tundra knows very well that the black sun can easily eclipse the very sense that suffering has a meaning, but it is primarily when the depressive throws up his hands and imagines that he is on some random rack that he has entered into the sin of despair.

Depression becomes despair by virtue of the way that the depressive individual relates himself to his depression. When a person who is suffering physical pain loses the ability to keep any of himself outside that pain, we say that he is in poor spirits. Likewise, when someone in agony is able to reach through the physical suffering and care about others, we say that he is in good spirits.

The individual who is physically ill and in good spirits is able to avoid having his psychological life defined by his illness. Kierkegaard's journal entry suggests that a person who is psychologically tormented has some sway in the way that he relates himself to his psychological agony. The person who collapses and defines himself in terms of his depression, or the person who finds the wrong meaning in his depression, say, that it is proof that there is no merciful God, has of his own accord, slipped into despair.

For Kierkegaard, finding meaning in your depression is in effect grasping for the spiritual significance in your psychological suffering. In the edifying coda to the *Concept of Anxiety* ("Anxiety Saving through Faith"),[23] Vigilius Haufniensis instructs us on how to sit for the spiritual instruction that only anxiety can offer. In his better days, or some would say his worse, Kierkegaard understood his depression to be a spiritual teacher. In the following jotting, Kierkegaard thanks Governance and his depression for his understanding of the category of "the single individual":

> But who am I, then? Am I some devil of a fellow who has understood this from the beginning and has had the personal capacity to maintain it in my daily life? Far from it. I have been helped. By what? By a frightful melancholic depression, a thorn in the flesh. I am a severe melancholic who has the good fortune and the virtuosity to be able to conceal it, and for that I have struggled. But Governance holds me in my depression. Meanwhile I come to a greater and greater understanding of the idea and know indescribable contentment and sheer joy but always with the aid of torment which keeps me within bounds.[24]

Kierkegaard took more advanced lessons from his depression. For a Christian, there is no higher perfection than needing God, the more intense the need the better.[25] And what, more than inexplicable suffering, can make a person turn to God for help? It is better, infinitely better, to understand feelingly how badly you need God than it is to be psychologically well adjusted relative to a community that Kierkegaard literally saw as a madhouse. Like almost all psychological states, depression, according to Kierkegaard, is dialectical—it can be reasonably taken one way or the other. On the one hand, depression has crushed the breastbone of many a person's faith. Inexplicable and crippling sorrow can be misunderstood to mean that existence is a slaughterhouse without a director. On the other, seemingly entangled in himself and feeling as though he can do nothing on his own, the depressive is especially well positioned to grasp the fact of his absolute dependence upon God.

According to Kierkegaard's self-interpretation, his depression helped him to eschew the despair of forgetting about God. Kierkegaard's identification with his father was both extensive and deep. Both the *Journals* and his posthumously published *Point of View as an Author*[26] suggest a special bond between father and son around their shared melancholy. In the same year that he published the

Sickness unto Death, Kierkegaard registers this strange debt of gratitude: "I am indebted to my father for everything from the very beginning. Melancholy as he was, when he saw me melancholy, he appealed to me: Be sure you really love Jesus."[27] While Kierkegaard was not beyond building questionable monuments to his father, this remark, made with reference to his own depression, seems to have functioned as the keystone of Kierkegaard's religious life. Kierkegaard frequently quipped that he loved and was attached to his innate sorrow or melancholy. While this kind of attachment was for him a temptation, he understood his heavy mindedness as making it virtually impossible for him to float off into the fantastic, which for a person with his mythopoeic imagination stood as no small danger. To echo his words, Kierkegaard understood his depression as keeping him "within bonds" and always mindful of God. Kierkegaard writes: "Yet it is an indescribable blessing to me that I was mentally depressed as I was. If I had been a naturally happy person and then experienced what I experienced as an author, I believe a man necessarily would have gone mad."[28]

Once again, Kierkegaard repeatedly moans that the depression that he has inherited from his physical and spiritual father has placed him outside the household of humanity, condemned to human misery. And *yet* repugnant as it rings, there is, he says, one thing that he has never prayed to God for, namely, the removal of his thorn in the flesh. Very late in his dwindling days, Kierkegaard confesses: "I dared to pray about everything, even the most foolhardy things, with the exception of one thing, release from a deep suffering that I had undergone from my earliest years but which I interpreted to be part of my relationship with God."[29]

The notion that depression could be one of God's gifts is for the present age a hard saying. At times Kierkegaard seems to specialize in hard sayings. Indeed, among Kierkegaard scholars, many of whom are quietly offended by Kierkegaard's Christianity, there is an ongoing question as how to remove the gem of wisdom from the gangue of Kierkegaard's pietistic faith. So far as the present age is concerned, what does it matter if Kierkegaard draws a distinction between despair and depression if, in fact, this distinction rests upon the assumptions of a faith that have been politely put to bed?

Or again, of what use is the distinction that Kierkegaard draws between psychological and spiritual disorders if, in fact, this distinction rests upon ontological assumptions that only the neurotic and/or half-witted are willing to make? Perhaps an edulcorated understanding of Kierkegaard's anthropology would claim that spirit has to do with the way that we relate ourselves to our immediate psychological lives as opposed to the psychological immediacy itself. To apply this bowdlerizing schema, the depressed but spiritually healthy individual understands that he is depressed, but he does not see his life as defined by his depression. For instance, one of the most harrowing symptoms of depression is that it can pull the plug on feelings that are very much connected with our sense of identity. A depressed mother may at times seem to herself to feel nothing for her child. But to follow our secularized version of Kierkegaard's distinction, depressed as she may be, she can remain free of despair by remembering that she is depressed but does not really lack the love she may cease to feel. Once again, she does not surrender her identity to her illness. For Kierkegaard, the pitfalls leading from depression to despair always involve a misinterpretation of one's depression. Most commonly, the depressive who ends up despairing does so by coming to believe that he is only passively related to his depression, that he can, as it were, do absolutely nothing about the way he feels or acts. No doubt, the melancholic individual who is also in despair would regard the belief that he has some choice over the way he relates himself to his depression as a fantasy perhaps reminiscent of old Christian fantasies. So far as he is concerned, his understanding of his depression must be a facet of his depression. Kierkegaard, however, begs to differ in that he urges us to believe that the life of the spirit is something over and above our mental/emotional lives.

For those who cannot bear the rub of Kierkegaard's invocations to faith, a secularized version of the essence of Kierkegaard's understanding of despair might amount to the idea that the depressed and despairing individual gives up on himself. Appropriately enough, the English "despair" is related to the French *desespoir,* indicating the negation of *espoir* or hope.[30] As previously noted, it used to be that despair was thought to involve actively pushing away hope relative to God, thinking, however passively or aggressively, that God could not or would not help. Instead of believing that for God all things are possible, including the possibility of healing his depression, the depressive in despair does not even try to trust that God is good and merciful and will make things right. Though he might be reluctant to acknowledge it, the despairing individual tries to murder such hopes as "God will help me through this." The author of *Sickness unto Death* is unequivocal, the belief that God is dead is itself the deepest despair,[31] and yet for a culture that may be well along in the process of talking itself out of any serious belief in a personal God, it may be more accurate to say that despair occurs when the individual makes a point of no longer having hopes in or for himself. The most common form of despair considered from this angle might well be that of the individual who has fallen into the deep sleep of firmly believing that it has become impossible for him to change to any serious degree. Someone who fits in this category might, for example, have a moment wherein he wishes that he could be a warmer and more concerned friend, but in response to the ray of that longing, the despairing individual fists his soul and reminds himself that he is just not a warm and outgoing individual and, for that matter, never will be.

The present age is one with a natural propensity for translating relational ideas such as forgiveness into individual matters. There are, for instance, many people today who act as though their real task in forgiveness is not repentance but rather learning to forgive themselves. The idea that the transition from depression to despair is really a matter, not of giving up on God, but rather of giving up on oneself would certainly be consistent with this individualistic turn. Kierkegaard would no doubt regard the suggestion of taking God out of the formula for despair as an intensely despairing way of understanding despair. As Kierkegaard would have it, the transition from depression to despair is one of making oneself, perhaps angrily, perhaps pridefully, deaf to God. And yet, so long as the depressive continues to listen for the religious significance of the perturbations of his psyche, he can avoid despair. It is not uncommon to hear depression described as "hell on earth," and yet for Kierkegaard, it is as we have seen entirely possible that a person could live in such a hell and still be in robust spiritual condition. It is, in fact, entirely possible that he saw both himself and the man he seemed to revere above all others, his father, as psychologically disturbed and yet more rather than less free of the despair that he found so pervasive in the era that he called "the present age."

10.
Spleen Essentially Canceled—yet a Little Spleen Retained

N. J. Cappelørn

Translated by

K. Brian Söderquist

In the introduction to his translation of an abridged version of *Either/Or: A Fragment of Life*,[1] Alastair Hannay discusses the appropriateness of publishing *Either/Or* in an abbreviated form and in just a single volume. He notes that Kierkegaard himself published the second edition in one single volume in 1849—in its entirety. Hannay writes: "The most obvious justification for an abridgement, therefore, is the making available once more of a portable (and readable) single-volume edition."[2] I fully appreciate his goal of creating a handy, portable, one-volume edition of this rich and, at times, disparate and fragmented work. I will not argue against it here. Nor is it the aim of this chapter to begin a general debate about the defensibility or nondefensibility of abridged works. My aim, rather, is to discuss one specific omission in Judge Wilhelm's epistolary treatise, "Equilibrium between the Aesthetic and the Ethical in the Development of the Personality" in Part Two of *Either/Or,* and to demonstrate why this omission is problematic.

Concerning the omissions from Part Two, which are said to be categorically different from those in Part One, Hannay writes: "Although conveniently contributing to the provision of a slimmer volume, the cuts here are designated primarily to bring the line of Wilhelm's argument into greater relief and thus to help it make a more immediate impact upon the reader. Whatever the purist's misgivings, the result is at least better than the far more drastic abridgement usually resorted to, patched out passages quoted out of context in textbooks."[3] With regard to the latter statement, I am in complete agreement with Hannay—for I do not consider myself a purist. But I would like to point out that just as the meaning of a text can be distorted, even marred, by being lifted out of its context and placed in a mosaic of quotations in a textbook, so also can the omission of a passage distort or diminish the significance of a text that lacks the given passage. And in my opinion, this is exactly what has happened with the omission in question in the "Equilibrium." Instead of underscoring Wilhelm's line of reasoning, the abbreviation of his thought is misleading and hinders the reader from clearly seeing the positive exit route from the apparently negative position. I will leave undecided whether this is due to a specific complexity: namely, that the philosophical-anthropological path that Wilhelm directs one to leads to an apparent theological-anthropological dead end. Instead, I will be content to argue that it is precisely this essential pathway that has been veiled and this kind of complicated thought process that has been abbreviated.

For the record, however, it must be noted that Alastair Hannay, an unfailing researcher and translator, clearly indicates where he has omitted text by adding an ellipse [. . .]. This, of course, is also the case with the omission upon which I will concentrate. And in defense of this kind of clearly indicated omission, one could always argue that the reader can simply go to the unabridged version and read the missing text. But this is hardly consistent with the expressed goal, which is "to bring the line of Wilhelm's argument into greater relief and thus to make a more immediate impact upon the reader."

The Text in Question

In order to illustrate and illuminate the implications of a lifeview that teaches that one must enjoy life and live for one's appetites—indeed, that one must live to gratify one's desires and, in the end, to enjoy oneself and one's appetites— Wilhelm includes a depiction of the gruesome and despotic Roman emperor Nero. While doing so, he entertains the idea that within an exceptionally passionate and lascivious person like Nero, a "certain good nature" can be found that "provides new proof of the immediacy which through its repression constitutes genuine melancholy."[4] In Hannay's abridged version, Wilhelm abruptly breaks off his depiction of Nero and writes to his young friend, the aesthete A:

> What, then, is melancholy? It is hysteria of the spirit. There comes a mo-
> ment in a man's life when immediacy is as though ripened and when the
> spirit demands a higher form in which it will apprehend itself as spirit. In
> its immediacy spirit coheres, as it were, with the whole of earthly life, and
> now the spirit wants to gather itself out of this dispersion, and make itself
> self-transparent; the personality wants to be conscious of itself in its eternal
> validity. If this does not happen and the movement halts and is pressed back,
> melancholy sets in. One can do much to bring it into oblivion, one can work,
> one can seize more innocent expedients than a Nero, but the melancholy re-
> mains. There is something unaccountable in melancholy. A person in sorrow
> or distress knows why he sorrows or is distressed. If you ask a melancholic
> what reason he has for his condition, what it is that weighs down on him, he
> will reply, "I don't know what it is, I can't explain it." Therein lies melancholy's

infinitude. The reply is perfectly correct, for as soon as he knows what it is, the effect is removed, whereas the grief of the griever is by no means removed by his knowing why he grieves. But melancholy is sin, really it is a sin as great as any, for it is the sin of not willing deeply and sincerely, and this is a mother to all sins. This sickness, or more properly, this sin, is extremely common in our time, and accordingly it is under this that the whole of German and French youth groan. I will not provoke you, I would treat you as considerately as possible. I gladly admit that being melancholy is in a sense not a bad sign, for as a rule only the most gifted natures are afflicted by it. . . . People whose souls have no acquaintance with melancholy are those whose souls have no presentiment of metamorphosis. These I do not concern myself with here, for I am writing only of and to you, and to you I think this explanation will be satisfactory, for you scarcely assume, as many physicians do, that melancholy is a bodily ailment, though for all that, remarkably enough, physicians cannot cure it; only the spirit can cure it, for it lies in the spirit, and when the spirit finds itself all small sorrows vanish, those reasons which in the view of some produce melancholy—that one cannot find oneself in the world, that one comes to the world both too late and too early, that one cannot find one's place in life; but the person who owns himself eternally, it is neither too early nor too late that he comes to the world, and the person who possesses himself in his eternal validity will surely find his significance in this life.[5]

Aside from the debatable English terms used for a few central concepts in the Danish text, this is an excellent translation. It grasps and conveys both the meaning and mood in Judge Wilhelm's assertions—assertions that stand as an exclamation point in *Either/Or* and as a colon for the further development of these same ideas in Kierkegaard's subsequent writings. And it is an excellent translation—aside from the omission! Admittedly, the first couple of sentences of the omitted text can easily be left out, but not the next three. Here one reads:

> As soon as this movement has occurred, the depression is essentially eliminated, although the same individual may suffer many sorrows and troubles in his life, and as far as that is concerned you know full well that I am the last person to expound the paltry commonsensical notion that it is futile to sorrow, that one should cast the sorrows away. I would be ashamed of myself if I dared to come to a sorrowing person with those words. But even the person in whose life this movement occurs most calmly and peacefully and at the right time will still always retain a little depression, but this is linked to something much deeper, to hereditary sin, and is rooted in this, that no human being can become transparent to himself.[6]

Before I continue with an interpretation of what this movement entails—a movement whichthat "essentially eliminates" what the Hongs term "depression" and what Hannay terms "melancholy" (*tungsind*)—I will dwell for a moment on a couple of issues in the text that are conditions for understanding the movement.

Melancholy or Spleen

"Melancholy" is a rendering of the Danish word *tungsind,* which corresponds to the German *Schwermut.* And if it is a cultural-linguistic fact that no English word is fully equivalent to *tungsind,* Hannay's "melancholy" is nonetheless clearly preferable to the Hongs' "depression." The latter term carries far too many connotations of a well-defined psychological illness that one could in principle treat with psychopharmacological drugs. For even though *tungsind* clearly contains emotional aspects that are experienced negatively, it is in no way a case for psychiatry. And even if it is, in its own way, a psychological phenomenon, it is nonetheless first and foremost an existential category. In this sense, "melancholy" is absolutely more fitting than "depression." I have some reservations, however, about the use of the word "melancholy." Let me explain.

In a series of four lectures delivered as a guest professor at the Søren Kierkegaard Research Centre in 1995, later published under the title *Vorentwürfe von Moderne. Antike Melancholie und die Acedia des Mittelalters,*[7] Michael Theunissen has shown convincingly that in modernity *tungsind/Schwermut* draws on a tradition that extends back to the ancient Greek concept "melancholy," which is rediscovered in the medieval concept *acedia.*

We know from Kierkegaard's journals that he was familiar with *acedia* and deliberated on its implications. In Journal EE:117, dated July 20, 1839, he writes: "What in a certain sense is called 'spleen' and what the mystics know by the designation 'the arid moments,' the Middle Ages knew as *acedia* (akedía, aridity)." And he adds, "The ancient moralists show a deep insight into human nature in regarding *tristitia* [sloth, dejection, moroseness] among the *septem vitia principalia* [seven deadly sins]."[8] Here, however, Kierkegaard uses the term "spleen," not *tungsind,* tying it to the medieval concept *acedia.* And in a purely biographical marginal note, he connects it to the expression "a quiet despair."[9]

From this journal entry, one can see that Kierkegaard's source for the medieval concept *acedia* is W. M. L. de Wette's *Lærebog i den christelige Sædelære og sammes Historie* (Textbook of Christian Moral Instruction and Its History) translated by C. E. Scharling (Copenhagen, 1835).[10] Here one finds that the Latin *acedia* and the corresponding Greek (*akedía*) have a series of interrelated meanings, first and foremost (spiritual) "sloth," "apathy," "melancholy," and "spleen," but also to be "carefree" or "careless." It is also apparent that *acedia* is an existential concept with religious dimensions. Indeed, certain medieval moral theologians used it instead of *tristitia* (sorrow, spleen/melancholy) when speaking of *septem vitia principalia,* that is, the seven cardinal or mortal sins.[11] This journal entry is in the background when Wilhelm, writing to A, says that the term "melancholy" seems perhaps too mild to A since being melancholic is currently taken to be an expression of greatness. This hardly troubles Wilhelm, however, who adds: "I subscribe to an earlier Church doctrine which counted melancholy among the cardinal sins."[12]

As noted above, it is also important to underscore that Kierkegaard uses the term "spleen," a fashionable word in the 1830s and 1840s related to the literary Byronism of the time. In *Either/Or,* when Judge Wilhelm writes in passing that he considers *tungsind* to be a sin, he ties it to "Young Germany" and "Young France." Young Germany refers to a group of German authors who in the 1830s and 1840s colored the literary and cultural debate, arguing against absolutism, church orthodoxy, moral and social dogmas, and in behalf of individualism and freedom in political and religious questions. The romantic confrontation with idealism and Biedermeier values carries with it a demand for realism and a closer relationship between literature and the political battle that followed in the wake of the June Revolution in 1830 in Paris. The Jewish-born authors Ludwig Börne and Heinrich Heine, who sought sanctuary in Paris in the 1830s, belonged for a time to this movement. In December 1835 the parliament of the German Federation decided to destroy this group of critical revolutionary writers. The group known as "Young France" included authors such as Théophile Gautier and George Sand. The German terms *Schwermut* and *Weltschmertz,* the French term *ennui,* and the English terms "Byronism" and "spleen" are all designations for the world-weariness, aestheticism, and loss of values that were common themes for European romantic writers. And it is in this group of terms that the Danish *tungsind* belongs.

In Kierkegaard's writings, then, *tungsind* must be regarded as the continuation of a long tradition that goes back to the Greek *melancholy,* through the medieval *acedia*—through reformulations, reinterpretations, refinements, and supplementations—on to the contemporary "spleen," *Schwermut,* and *ennui.* In *Either/Or* I take *tungsind*—not least because of *acedia*—to be an expression of spiritual sloth and apathy, a kind of relativism that leads to a sense of world-weariness and *tedium vitae.* The accent, however, is placed on a state of mind that considers everything to be equally valuable, and therefore equally worthless, since reality is experienced as meaningless. With this in mind, I would prefer that the Danish word *tungsind* be translated "spleen," the term I have used in the title of this chapter and that I will use below.

In "An Occasional Discourse"—the first part of *Edifying Discourses in Various Spirits* from 1847—Kierkegaard returns to "spleen" in the form of the concept of "double-mindedness" (*tvesindethed*). Here the state of being capricious or of "two minds" corresponds to a state of diversion and distraction or, perhaps better yet, to a flight toward diversion and distraction. This is due in part to a desire to numb the pain accompanying spleen, and in part to the fact that the individual does not will one thing, but wills many things at the same time—and thus, in essence, wills nothing at all, or at least nothing in particular. Opposite double-mindedness here is "simplicity" (*enfoldighed*) that is, the state of being of "one-mind" rather than of "two-minds" or "many-minds." This "many-mindedness" corresponds to the state of dis-traction or diversion, a dissolution of the unity of the will or mind such that the mind is characterized by duality or even multiplicity. The mind becomes divided or fragmented. The double-mindedness associated with spleen is related to "doubt" (*tvivl*), which means be of a divided mind.[13] Kierkegaard can therefore sharpen the concept, calling it despair (*fortvivelse;* in Danish the prefix *for* serves to amplify *tvivl* or "doubt"), just as he does when Anti-Climacus further develops the idea in *Sickness unto Death* in 1849. Spleen and despair are, in this sense, parallel existential forms of consciousness: spleen accentuates the emotional side, and despair the epistemological side.[14] In addition, Judge Wilhelm also brings spleen and despair together when he writes to A:

> Take note, then, my young friend, this life is despair; hide it from others if you will, from yourself you cannot hide it, it is despair. And yet in another sense this life is not despair. You are too frivolous to despair; and you are too melancholy [have too much spleen] not to come in contact with despair. You are like a woman giving birth and yet you are forever putting off the moment and remain constantly in pain.[15]

Spleen can be said to be an expression of a lack of will or a lack of direction. One does not will or desire one thing, one desires many things at once. This is the same thing as not willing anything definite and thus an expression of a lack of a purpose or distinct direction in life. This implies rootlessness and directionlessness, which turn out to be symptomatic of living restlessly (living *light*-mindedly [let*sindigt*] as opposed to "*heavy*-mindedly" [tung*sindigt*], as Judge Wilhelm calls it in the passage above). Spleen can thus also be said to be a psychological symptom of an existential-anthropological disharmony within a person.

If I were asked for a contemporary example corresponding to spleen, I could offer the concept of "frustration." For as far as I can tell, this is characteristic of the postmodern, fragmented, kaleidoscopic, individualistic zap-culture. One continually seeks new challenges and experiences; everything can be renegotiated—tomorrow. Somewhat paradoxically—given the individualistic tendencies of the age—frustration is precisely an expression for the failure to come to terms with oneself. The individual cannot decide what he really wants with his life and in his life, even when he *does* want to come unambiguously to terms with himself. But because he does not want to leave any possibilities behind—it could well be that better possibilities will appear tomorrow—he wants everything simultaneously, and thus, in essence, nothing at all. The individual thus loses himself in distraction, becoming scattered as he seeks refuge in diversions and events. This leads to an absorption into the manifold, the modern version of the aestheticization of existence. There could be many reasons for this dispassionate or passionless orientation toward existence. It is the postmodern correlate to the romantic feeling of a loss of values coupled with a distaste for inherited norms and dogmas and the unpleasantness associated with absolutism, fanaticism, and fundamentalism. And it is tied to a longing for the rediscovery of some fundamental values and ethical norms which carry meaning both individually and existentially.

But let us move back to Kierkegaard. In *The Book on Adler* (in the first version from 1846), one also finds spleen defined as existential dizziness. In Chapter Two, §2, he writes:

> Dizziness, as has been pointed out with physiological correctness, occurs when the eyes have no fixed point upon which to rest. Therefore one becomes dizzy by looking down from a high tower, because the gaze plunges down and finds no boundary and limitation. . . . What is dizzying is the expanse, the infinite, the unlimited, the indeterminable, and the dizziness itself is the senses' lack of restraint. . . . [T]he dialectic of dizziness contains the contradiction of wanting what one does not want, what one shrinks from, while the shrinking nevertheless only deters—temptingly.[16]

"The dizzying" here expresses a lack of focus and thus a sort of spineless vacillation. In other words, it expresses the absence of a grounded position and of an orienting grounding. It is therefore important to underscore the dialectic within dizziness: it wants what it does not want. It wants what makes it shudder because the shudder is both repellently frightening and attractively tempting. Paul gives a parallel expression in his Letter to the Romans 7:19–20: "For I do not do the good I want, but the evil I do not want is what I do. Now if I do what I do not want, it is no longer I that do it, but sin that dwells within me." With this, we approach the theological aspect of Wilhelm's anthropology. Before I go on, however, I must point out that Wilhelm, alias Kierkegaard, may declare that he is not in agreement with Paul when the latter distinguishes between the acting "I" and the sin within the "I." For in doing so, Paul ends up de-individualizing sin—perhaps against his will—since he diffuses the guilt of the acting individual.

In Alastair Hannay's translation, Judge Wilhelm writes: "But melancholy is sin, really it is a sin as great as any, for it is the sin of not willing deeply and sincerely, and this is a mother to all sins." Here, spleen is indeed characterized as sin, even a sin *instar omnium* as it is called in the Latin expression in the Danish text. I fully understand that Hannay, consistent with his goal of creating a "readable" edition of *Either/Or,* chooses to translate this expression. But the question is whether "as great as any" is a fitting term. Directly translated, the Latin expression *instar omnium* means "in place of all others" or "concerning all others," which is probably best rendered "as prototype" or par excellence.

Spleen is the prototypical sin or sin in its most fundamental form precisely because it is "the sin of not willing deeply and sincerely."

Here, another problem in the translation appears that has implications for the overall interpretation. "Sincerely" is no doubt a deft rendering of the Danish term *inderligt*. But for me, the question is whether it captures the full meaning of the word and its relation to Kierkegaard's existential concept of *inderlighed* (inwardness). The Hongs translate *inderligt* with "inwardly." This is not fully adequate, either. It is somehow too emotional and loses the active dimension. In Danish the terms *inderlighed* and *inderlig* are also tricky. They can certainly be used to express something deeply felt, and in this sense they shows traces of Pietistic influence. But as I understand it, this a questionable reduction of what Kierkegaard means. For Kierkegaard, there is an indissoluble connection between *inderlighed* and *inderliggørelse* (literally, "making inward"). I will attempt to describe the latter term more clearly to shed light on what "not willing *inderligt*" means in *Either/Or*. It can be dissected as follows: *inder-lig-gørelse*. First, it means I *make* [*gør*] something a part of my *inner* being (*indre*), for example, the good, in such a way that it is completely determinative for me. Second, I know that this something, for example, the good, has indeed been appropriated when it decisively comes to expression in my actions, in what I *do* [*gør*]. It is, then, a two-sided movement: there is appropriation and reduplication. It is important to include the active aspect here, not least in the present context where the issue at hand is the prototypical sin: not wanting to act or, more precisely, not willing to act in accordance with what human beings were created to be—by God.

I dare not suggest how this ought to be rendered in English. But I dare say that "spleen" is understood precisely as that kind of double-mindedness that makes itself known as refusal to will, a refusal to will one thing. It thus stands in contrast to the entire point in "An Occasional Discourse," namely, that "purity of heart is to will one thing." As noted above, the antithesis of double-mindedness is "simplicity" or "single-mindedness." This is characterized by willing one thing. When viewed anthropologically, it is to will "oneself in one's eternal validity"; when viewed ethically, it is to will the good; and when viewed theologically, it is to will God's will. It is from this perspective that one can understand that spleen is sin, that it is the scattered and thus paralyzed consciousness of dis-integration that cannot decide to will one thing. Accordingly Wilhelm can also speak of spleen as "hysteria of the spirit" insofar as hysteria here can mean paralysis, a paralysis of the human spirit. Spirit is so firmly in the grip of the sickness of spleen that it becomes paralyzed; it is thus lulled into slumber and made inactive. Spleen is a sickness in two senses: first, as a disharmony in the relationship of the body/mind to spirit, and second, as sin when the individual is placed before God. With this, we approach the existential-anthropological movement of spirit.

To Become Aware of One's Eternal Validity

For Kierkegaard—and this must also be considered a presupposition for Judge Wilhelm—a human being consists of a trichotomy, a three-part union of body, mind, and spirit. Or to use one of Anti-Climacus's expressions from *Sickness unto Death*, a human being is a synthesis or rather a double synthesis consisting of body and mind, but also of body/mind and spirit. Likewise, a human being is a synthesis of temporality and eternity as well as necessity and freedom. A synthesis is a composition of or the relationship between two elements. As long as there is only a single synthesis or only a dichotomy between body and mind, a human being is still bound to and restricted by an earthly life in immediacy. Or, to use an expression from "To Need God is a Human Being's Highest Perfection," the first of *Four Edifying Discourses* from 1844, it is "the first self." Kierkegaard writes:

> When a person turns and faces himself in order to understand himself, he steps as it were, in the way of that first self, halts that which was turned around in hankering for and seeking after the surrounding world that is its object, and summons it back from the eternal. In order to prompt the first self to this withdrawal, the deeper self lets the surrounding world remain what it is—remain dubious.[17]

Of course, the aim here is different from that of *Either/Or*, but the anthropological concepts "the first self" and "the deeper self" are well-suited as clarifying concepts. In this edifying discourse, "the first self" finds itself entirely within the temporal, and "the deeper self" emerges for the first time when a person becomes aware of the eternal. After this discovery, a struggle for superiority arises between "the first self" and "the deeper self."[18] It seems to me that in his own way and in his own terminology, Judge Wilhelm speaks of a similar struggle, namely, the struggle to determine to what degree the movement of spirit is allowed to happen or is held back from happening.

The idea here, then, is that "the first self" comes to a point in life where "immediacy reaches maturity, as it were," that is, where the individual matures to the point that dreaming spirit awakens. It demands a higher form of life than that of pure immediacy, where the individual is completely absorbed in earthly life, that is, is completely integrated into his generation and surroundings, is a product of environment and heredity. Kierkegaard described this initial separation process as early as the summer of 1835 in the entries from Gilleleje in *Journal AA:* "[W]hen I try to come to an understanding with myself about my life, things look different. Just as a child takes time to learn to distinguish itself from objects and for quite a while so little distinguishes itself from its surroundings that, keeping the stress on the passive side, it says things like 'me hit the horse', so too the same phenomenon repeats itself in a higher spiritual sphere."[19] Even though the aim of this entry is slightly different from that of *Either/Or*, the same fundamental existential-anthropological conditions are the object of focus: the passive first self is still an integrated part of its surroundings, not yet having become an "I." It lives re-productively or re-actively with regard to its surroundings and has not yet become a subject for its own actions. Or, to put it differently, it is not yet conscious of its deeper self. It is the beginning of this process of consciousness that Wilhelm wants to describe as a first movement of spirit, a movement which lies at a higher spiritual plane, to be sure, than a child's first separation as an "I."

The process within the first stage of the movement of spirit looks like this: from a state of dis-integration and diversion—for which spleen is an emotional-existential symptom—the spirit becomes integrated and it *forklarer sig selv i sig selv*. Hannay translates this expression: "makes itself self-transparent." And this possible rendering certainly accentuates the hopelessness of the project. For in the passage of text that was omitted, Wilhelm does indeed say "that no human being can be transparent to itself." (This is tied to hereditary sin, which I will return to later).

At forklare sig (to become transparent) or *at forklare sig i sig selv* (to make itself self-transparent) is one of Kierkegaard's favorite expressions. He is no doubt alluding to the story of Jesus' metamorphosis on the mount of trans-figuration. If I am right about this, one ought rather understand this "making transparent" as a "transfiguration" or a "metamorphosis" into a higher form or spiritual sphere, that is, a transfiguration or metamorphosis of the first self into the deeper self. In support of this interpretation, Wilhelm characterizes people whose souls have never known spleen as those who have never had the slightest inkling of a possible metamorphosis. As I see it, then, the issue at hand is a transfiguring metamorphosis of the first self into the deeper self, which cor-responds to the individual's separation from his surroundings. Or, as one reads in "To Need God is a Human Being's Highest Perfection," the deeper self calls the first self back to itself from a state of being lost in the outer. Or in Wilhelm's language, the deeper self calls the first self back from absorption in earthly life and back from the diversions sought in its surroundings.

The goal of the first stage of the movement of spirit is that the "personality" will receive its wish to be conscious of itself in its eternal validity. But this raises a few questions. First, why does Wilhelm introduce the concept of "personal-ity"? Once again, I must return to the Danish text. "Personality" is a transla-tion of *personlighed* which, I will argue, must be interpreted as *person-lighed* (literally, person-likeness) that is, resembling [*lignende*] a person. This is no doubt difficult to see and hear in English translation. But if my interpretation is correct, this means that the first self merely resembles a person, but has not yet *become* a person, has not yet become a self-conscious individual, that is, has not yet become a subject. One becomes a person only after the deeper self has gained superiority and spirit has *forklaret sig i sig selv*—has "transfigured itself from within." This is the process through which human beings become conscious of themselves in their eternal validity.

Before this movement has taken place, one cannot speak of ethics, of course, since such individuals live in pure immediacy and are therefore not conscious subjects who own their own actions. As noted above, the immediate individual acts re-productively or re-actively with regard to his fellow human beings and surroundings; he simply acts according to prejudice. In other words, the individual does not act in accordance with his own conscious evaluations and responsible judgments about what is right and what is wrong. Rather, he reproduces the already available and established judgments of others. He lives uncritically with regard to the given norms of an age and conforms to its intellectual fashions and currents. Or metaphorically expressed, the individual passes time as a pawn in a chess game in which someone or something else guides the pieces. And this is precisely what diversion is: an individual will not will anything on his own, but only as a re-action, as a re-production or a simple act of conformity. He has not yet become conscious of his freedom as a possibility.

One can ask a second question: what does Wilhelm understand by a human being's eternal validity? According to my interpretation, this expression has a double meaning. While the first meaning is obvious, the second lies buried beneath it and requires deeper insight.

The first meaning of a human being's eternal validity corresponds to the one side of the dichotomy. This consists of temporality, that is, the fact that humans beings, as temporal, are bound to time and its changes, and necessity, that is, the fact that human beings, as human, are born with a determinate genetic combination and grow up under the influence of their surroundings that are tied to heredity and environment. To become conscious of this is to choose one's inherited genetic combination and the influences of the environment as a part of one's own self, making oneself responsible for them. And along with this move, an individual also takes upon himself responsibility for the guilt that he might have incurred before he was a conscious subject for his own actions. Of course, this does not imply that he must take upon himself the guilt imputed to him by others. This means that he takes upon himself the guilt for which he is responsible and for which he is culpable. While the guilt attributed to him by others is not genuine guilt and can be ignored, the guilt that he brings about himself is genuine guilt and cannot be explained away by references to heredity or environmental influences. If the latter happens, the individual amputates his own self.

The second meaning of the human being's eternal validity corresponds to the other side of the dichotomy, namely, eternity, that is, the fact that human beings, as divine creations, have the eternal—and freedom—within them. In other words, human beings are created by God as free. And it is precisely this freedom that makes it possible for the self to "transfigure itself from within," to transform itself in a metamorphosis from the first self to the deeper self and to become conscious of itself. This double meaning of becoming conscious of oneself in one's eternal validity is also expressed when Wilhelm writes to A: "It is a grave and significant moment when one binds oneself for an eternity to an eternal power, when one receives oneself as the one whose memory no time shall efface, when in an eternal and unfailing sense one becomes aware of oneself as the person one is."[20]

At the end of the cited passage, Wilhelm returns to a discussion of the individual who has himself in his eternal validity not merely as a possibility, but rather as a possession since he has made the movement of spirit. And this is presented in conjunction with his objection to the notion that spleen is engendered by the fact "that one cannot find oneself in the world, that one comes to the world both too late and too early, that one cannot find one's place in life." And yet there is an ambivalence to his objection; for he takes the argument seriously enough to go on to argue that it is precisely this state of affairs that does not hold for the one who owns oneself eternally and possesses oneself in one's eternal validity. Such a person will surely find his meaning in life. Why? Because the individual who has made the movement of spirit has become contemporary with himself and thus a contemporary with his life. This stands in contrast to the individual who holds the movement back; this individual becomes neither contemporary with himself nor with his life. And this is due to the fact that the individual who has spleen either hesitates because he will not be himself and thus comes too late, or because he presses forward because he wills to be himself—but not by virtue of spirit but rather as copy of his own imagination or a copy of other people in his environment—and thus arrives too early. This is the reason why the individual with spleen never finds his calling and place in his God-given life. If this interpretation proves correct, one finds here, in embryo, a link to Anti-Climacus's description in *Sickness unto Death* of the two fundamental negative forms of consciousness that belong to despair: in despair because one does not will to be oneself, and in despair because one wills to be oneself.[21]

The Movement of Spirit

In the preceding section I have attempted to explain the essence of the first movement of spirit. Two important aspects of this movement, however, must be added in order to obtain a complete picture. There are still two possibilities: there is either the negative possibility where the movement is forced back, or the positive possibility where the movement is fully developed. First, then the negative.

If in the course of the process, the movement is brought to a halt and forced back, says Wilhelm, spleen sets in. Here, another piece of the puzzle falls into place. We are now closer to understanding what spleen is, namely, an emotional condition which manifests itself as a mental (psychological) symptom. This indicates that spirit is paralyzed because the first self has repressed the deeper self. When spirit is unable to take hold of itself and gather itself from a state of dis-integration, the first self falls back into an immediacy that is void of reflection and falls back into a state of fusion with the external. One continues to live in and through the external, which bars the entryway into the internal and blocks the possibility of becoming conscious of oneself.

There are no means to combat spleen, Wilhelm continues—implying that the only means are to let the movement of spirit fully unfold. And the individual cannot explain the origin of spleen because he is unaware of its deepest cause (*grund*). Here Wilhelm plays on the double meaning of the Danish word *grund:* it means "cause," that is, the cause that brings about spleen; and it means the "ground," that is, the ground in which spleen has its roots and its origin. And the fact that the individual with spleen is unable to explain (*forklare*) it (and here the Danish term *at forklare* is used in its straightforward sense, namely, "to explain") is due to the fact that spirit has been prevented from transfiguring itself through a metamorphosis of the first self such that the deeper self takes over (and here, *at forklare* is used in its metaphorical sense, namely, "to transfigure"). And here, claims Wilhelm, is precisely where the infinity of spleen lies.

This is an enigmatic assertion. For why should spleen, in and of itself, be infinite? As a matter of fact, I do not think this is how we ought to understand his claim. Rather, I think Wilhelm means that spleen is connected to infinity. According to Kierkegaard, human beings also consist of a synthesis of the infinite and the finite, of course. And as human beings allow themselves to become bound to finitude, they prevent themselves from having access to infinitude. Spleen then appears. But spleen is also related to infinity in the sense that infinity corresponds to spirit's demand for a higher form of life. In this sense, spleen is also a longing for the infinite that becomes manifest as spirit awakened. But since spirit was forced back into its sleeping chambers and becomes paralyzed, the person with spleen has only an inkling of infinity. This is tied to the fact that spleen is, in fact, sin—sin in its most fundamental form: the refusal to will deeply and inwardly which, here, is the refusal to will to become conscious of oneself in one's eternal validity. It is not sin, then, in its stronger form: to be in despair because one does not will to be oneself, a self created and posited by God—which we see developed by Anti-Climacus in *Sickness unto Death*.

Precisely because spleen is defined as sin, one finds two kinds of transfiguration, I believe. The first is a metamorphosis of the self brought about by the self; the second is a metamorphosis of the self brought about by God, which happens in and with the forgiveness of sin. This makes it possible for human beings themselves to become transparent to themselves—(this is a path back out of what I had called an apparent "dead end" in my introduction). This last point, however, regardless of how implicit it may be, lies beyond the scope of this study—and beyond Wilhelm's treatise.

Now on to the positive: the actual occurrence of the movement—(in my introduction, I called this realized movement the positive "exit route"). And at this point, we can return to the passage of text omitted from Alastair Hannay's translation. As soon as the movement has been completed, Wilhelm says, spleen is "essentially eliminated." The key word here is "essentially." This cannot mean "essence" in the substantial sense, for in the remark that follows, Wilhelm says that even in the person who has made the movement, a bit of spleen remains. To say that spleen is "essentially eliminated," then, must mean essential with regard to the first movement—and not with regard to the later, deeper movements of spirit. These deeper movements are only intimated in *Either/Or* and await further development in Kierkegaard's later authorship.

The remnant of spleen that survives in every human being, according to Wilhelm, is related to something that lies much deeper, namely, hereditary sin. It is tied to the fact that no human being is able to make himself transparent (which I called the apparent dead end in my introduction). Hereditary sin, together with the fact that one cannot make oneself transparent, are two sides of the same issue: the first is the cause, the latter the effect.

Hereditary Sin

One can see from Kierkegaard's journals and loose papers that even as a youth, Kierkegaard was occupied with the concept of hereditary sin. He struggled to arrive at an understanding of this difficult concept that played such a dominant role in theological and church history. And it is not until *The Concept of Anxiety,* published in 1844, that he arrives at his own interpretation. It is impossible to determine exactly how Wilhelm understands hereditary sin, but one could well suspect that Wilhelm—in so many ways a traditional Christian—agrees with the traditional Augustinian-Lutheran interpretation. He does not touch upon hereditary sin anywhere else in *Either/Or II*, so this is the only part of the text we have at our disposal.[22] But this section includes an important concluding phrase: hereditary sin is tied here to the notion that no human being can make himself transparent. And this might indicate that Kierkegaard here allows Wilhelm to hint at the interpretation for which Vigilius Haufniensis will later become spokesman.

Kierkegaard's preoccupation with hereditary sin as a consequence of the fall is due first and foremost to the fact that it compromises freedom. For without freedom, he argues, sin arises *by virtue of* hereditary sin and is passed on *of necessity* in hereditary sin. The implication is that human beings are not at fault. Put differently, if sin is inherited, it is necessary, and if it is necessary, it rules out individual freedom. Without freedom, there can be no individual culpability, and without culpability, there can be no individual guilt. And without guilt for which human beings are themselves culpable, there can be no individual sin. Human beings have thereby become a product. Before I examine more closely Kierkegaard's arguments against the traditional understanding of hereditary sin and his reinterpretation of it as a condition for human existence, I will take a quick look at the dogmatic history of hereditary sin.

The notion of hereditary sin—that is, the notion that sin is propagated and thereby inherited after it entered the world through the fall of Adam—is, in the historical dogmatic tradition, based on several biblical sources. First and foremost, it is based on the story of the fall in Genesis 3. Secondarily, it is based on Psalms 51:7 and Romans 5:12–14. With Augustine (354–430), the notion of hereditary sin became a dogma that holds that sin becomes efficacious in the sex act and thus in the creation of every human being. And because every human being is born in and with sin, every individual has lost the ability to do the good. Since human beings are held in bondage by sin, they cannot synergistically bring about their own salvation; salvation is totally dependent upon God's re-deeming and unmerited grace. In Augustine—and the tradition that follows— one does not find the term "hereditary sin" but rather the Latin term *peccatum originale*, translated into English as "original sin." In the Lutheran tradition, it is expressed more sharply with the German term *Erbsünde*, "hereditary sin."

The dogma of hereditary sin was passed on by the Lutheran reformers and comes to expression in the all-important Lutheran confessionary writings. One finds it in "Article 2" of *Confessio Augustana*, penned by Phillip Melanchton in Latin in 1530; in Part Two, Article 4 of *The Schmalkald Articles*, written by Luther in German; and in Part Two, Section 1.11 of the *Formula of Concord*, authored in German shortly after Luther's death in 1546. Passages from these confessionary texts are cited by Vigilius Haufniensis, in Latin, as he engages in a frontal attack on these texts in *The Concept of Anxiety*. We find this in Chapter One, §1, "Historical Intimations Regarding the Concept of Hereditary Sin."[23]

Historically and dogmatically speaking, then, Adam's sin at the fall is said to be the first sin, and with it, sin and sinfulness are said to have entered the world. The sins of all other human beings presuppose the sinfulness that is propagated and inherited throughout the generations. This Augustinian-Lutheran interpretation of hereditary sin is rejected by Vigilius Haufniensis. Instead, he posits the "first sin" or original sin (*peccatum originale*), claiming that each individual person's sin is a "first sin" in that sense that through it, sin has entered the world for that individual.

Sin is a quality that originates in a "leap" taken by each individual person, or better said, it originates in each individual person's "qualitative leap." And this "leap," which is "the fall" for each individual, happens in freedom's possibility, and not of necessity. Sinfulness, by contrast, is a quantity, an accumulation of sin that can predispose an individual toward sin, but can never be the cause of sin. Each individual is guilty of a first sin and is thus guilty of sin; sin then manifests itself in actual sins or committed sins, and becomes sinfulness. Human freedom is thus maintained and accentuated.

The question now is what happens with this freedom when sin enters into the world in the life of the individual person. The answer is that freedom is not eliminated, but it loses its way in guilt. To explain how this happens, Vigilius Haufniensis introduces the equivocal concept of anxiety. On the one hand, anxiety grasps the individual and makes him anxious. On the other hand, the individual, gripped by anxiety, becomes anxious. That anxiety is equivocally oriented in two opposite directions is clearly expressed in the following passage:

> Anxiety can be compared with dizziness. He whose eye peers down into a gaping abyss becomes dizzy. But what causes it? It is just as much his eye as the abyss. For what if he hadn't looked down? Anxiety is thus the dizziness of freedom that emerges when spirit wants to posit the synthesis and freedom peers down into its own possibility—and then grasps finitude to brace itself. In this dizziness, freedom collapses. . . . At that very moment, everything is changed. And freedom, when it again rises, sees that it is guilty. Between these two moments lies the leap, which no science has explained or can explain.[24]

The synthesis which spirit wants to posit is a composition of body and soul. But, Vigilius Haufniensis writes, a synthesis is unthinkable if these two elements are not united in a third. And this third element is spirit, human spirit that will constitute the relationship between body and soul.[25] As spirit seeks to posit the synthesis, freedom is awakened by spirit. But freedom then becomes dizzy because it looks down into its own possibility of becoming a self, a self that conducts relationships and that is responsible for how it conducts relationships.[26] It is here freedom that errs. To brace itself, it grasps finitude instead of infinitude. And this fault is its own.

Vigilius Haufniensis's use of the metaphor of the abyss and the eye that peers into it is important in order to underscore the equivocal nature of anxiety. For what brings about anxiety? The abyss or the eye? Because of the equivocalness of anxiety, the question cannot be answered. Anxiety is an intermediate term between freedom and necessity, it is "neither a category of necessity or a category of freedom; it is entangled freedom, where freedom is not free in itself but entangled not by necessity but in itself."[27] Anxiety is a foreign power that grasps an individual, but the individual, for his part, allows himself to be grasped by it—and he then grasps wrongly. In other words, the individual is *also* guilty in becoming anxious. And remains guilty. The point to be made with the equivocalness of anxiety is that the entrance of the first sin in the individual, as he freely grasps in the wrong way, happens neither of necessity nor arbitrarily. If it happened of necessity, freedom would be abrogated and sin would not be the fault of individual human beings. If it happed arbitrarily, one could imagine a human being who did not sin, and from a Christian perspective, this is impossible.

Conclusion

Back to *Either/Or*. I will here summarize Wilhelm's view. When the immediate individual wants to remain in immediacy as an arbitrary or coincidental individual and will not allow spirit to grasp itself as spirit, will not allow spirit to become conscious of and choose itself as a self in its eternal validity, spleen manifests itself. Spleen is a symptom of the hysteria of spirit in the body/mind synthesis, which implies that the individual will not walk away from his diversion so he can will one thing. Spleen is not only a sickness of spirit; it is sin. Indeed, it is sin *instar omnium,* the sin of not willing deeply and inwardly. Because what is at stake is the sin of refusing to will, it is related to a cracking and splintering of created freedom. And even if an individual undertakes this movement of spirit—gathers himself out of diversion and transfigures himself into the person he is—there is nonetheless a remnant of spleen that survives. But "this is linked to something much deeper, to hereditary sin, and is rooted in this, that no human being can become transparent to himself."

Even though this line from *Either/Or* is written prior to Vigilius Haufniensis's refutation of the traditional interpretation of hereditary sin in *The Concept of Anxiety,* I would like to suggest that when it is interpreted backwards, in light of *The Concept of Anxiety,* it appears that Wilhelm does not understand hereditary sin to be mere inherited sin, but that he takes it to be an expression for "the fall" of each individual human being. In this fall the individual human being falls out of his relationship to God as creator, and thus the connection between his spirit and God's spirit is severed at the very root or at its very ground. This is precisely the reason that the self cannot become transparent to itself and see that it is grounded in the God that has created it.

I have asserted that spleen is a phenomenon of body and mind. This seems to stand in contradiction to Wilhelm's claim that it rests in spirit, that is, in human spirit. But this is only an apparent contradiction. For spleen lies in spirit in the negative sense insofar as the origin and cause of spleen lies in the spirit that is forced back and paralyzed. And it lies in spirit in a positive sense insofar as spirit has the possibility of "essentially eliminating" spleen. The possibility of completely and totally eliminating spleen, however, has been lost because of the fall. Thus, regardless of what one does, there will always be a remnant of spleen that manifests itself as a phenomenon of the body-mind synthesis in a negative spiritual form of consciousness. Wilhelm himself offers a further argument for the notion that spleen lies in spirit but manifests itself as a mental (psychic) phenomenon when he writes: "People whose souls have no acquaintance with melancholy [spleen] are those whose souls have no presentiment of metamorphosis."[28]

Perhaps I have overinterpreted Wilhelm by bringing him too much into agreement with Vigilius Haufniensis. But I have no doubt that there is a clear connection between the Judge's short remarks on hereditary sin and the watchman of Copenhagen's refutation of the traditional interpretation of hereditary sin and his reinterpretation of it as an existential condition that is neither necessary or arbitrary. And unfortunately, it is this link or perspective that is lost when the text in question is omitted—which is the case in Hannay's abridgment and translation of *Either/Or*. Demonstrating exactly this point has been that aim of this at times critical, but unequivocal—and deeply grateful—tribute to Alastair Hannay, who, as a member of the scholarly committee, has played an essential role for the Søren Kierkegaard Research Centre during its first five years.

11.
Kierkegaard on Melancholy and Despair

Alastair Hannay

Gordon Marino more than anyone has sought to bring the ethical and moral-psychological precepts to be found in Kierkegaard's writings to bear on today's society. The most general of these, it can be claimed, is Kierkegaard's stress on not blurring important distinctions. The distinction Marino takes up is that between psychological and spiritual disorder, a distinction that Kierkegaard makes much of but is nowadays "effaced" by an age that treats what we still might want to call spiritual disorders as though they were ailments to be put right by handing ourselves over to professionals.

The distinction is traced in Kierkegaard's journal entries concerning his personal depression (Marino's term for *Tungsind*). One from 1846 Marino finds particularly relevant. It contains a notion (of spirit as a relation to the psycho-somatic compound that we are) that enters into the argument both of *The Concept of Anxiety* and of *The Sickness unto Death* and also occurs in *Postscript,* a work completed by the end of that same year. The entry says that Kierkegaard's unhappiness is due to some disharmony between soul and body but that this does not affect his spirit. This implication is that he is still in principle able to observe, grasp, and perhaps also deal with this discord. But as Marino suggests, it seems that Kierkegaard himself never gets rid of his depression. Indeed, depression in this sense is something very hard to get rid of except perhaps by procedures far more drastic than the use of powders and pills. One is stuck with one's depression, or melancholy, but in Kierkegaard's case, thanks to this spiritual dimension, we find someone able to hold it at a distance, have it as a topic, even make a career out of it. The authorship, as Marino notes, was not just "from first to last" a religious undertaking; it was also the author's way of dealing with (though not getting rid of) his depression.

Why not go further and include the religion itself? Marino mentions Peter

Christian Kierkegaard, the elder brother whose depression finally caught up with him, the former bishop ending his days as a ward of state. Might it not fairly be said that it was the elder brother's faith that actually caused his depression? That it did so by presenting him with a set of ready-made models of conduct and attitude that in the end he found he had been unable to emulate? In Søren's case the models are grabbed hold of and subjected to an acute scrutiny. Then it is not just the undertaking itself, with its opportunity to exercise and demonstrate mental and literary skills, that saves him from drowning in his depression; what puts him above it is also the picture of religion that his religious undertaking brought to light. Kierkegaard takes over religion, steals it from the hands of those who administer it. In its concisely drawn nosology of despair, *The Sickness unto Death,* which (along with *Practice*) is the culmination of the religious undertaking, consigns the whole of Denmark, if not humankind, to despair (and sin). The work, at its close, seems clearly to be nailing its indictment of Christendom on the door of the primate himself.

Marino's essay invites yet another reflection. It stresses Kierkegaard's often recorded attachment to his own melancholy. One might consider this as analogous to the way that Karl Marx's proletariat saw things as they were because under the weight of an exploitation others were unwilling or unable to detect or to describe. Kierkegaard writes as though the melancholic who seizes the opportunity to be active enjoys privileged access to truth. Being "in the power of a congenital mental depression" puts one in the best position from which to appreciate the help that God offers and, accordingly, to grasp what God's love really means. That is, so long as the hope that the knowledge that one is in despair is not lost sight of in the hopelessness that results from the distinction between depression and despair being effaced. Depression may be a state one is stuck with, but the analysis of despair shows how it is possible either to drown oneself in it or to rise above it, putting it to constructive use. One can even end up praising God that one has been given it.

Marino's other main focus is on how far a Kierkegaardian (or Anti-Climacian) account of despair can be seen to survive (in Rieff's expression) "the collapse of the sacred order." Marino suggests that Kierkegaard's age and ours both blur the distinction between a state of depression and the activity of despair, and that common to both is their treating despair, accordingly, as loss of hope instead of as something we bring upon ourselves and can in principle "will" ourselves out of. Marino proposes, first of all, that what distinguishes a secular age from Kierkegaard's time is that loss of hope means giving up on oneself rather than on God. The question is then what if anything is to count in a secular age as not giving up on oneself, the equivalent of Anti-Climacus's faith.

At a first glance the difficulty is to think of how we might cease giving up on ourselves in a way that avoids falling under Kierkegaard's second type of authentic despair (the despair of "willing/wanting/going along with" being one's own self). Marino's hopeful suggestion is that the way out of hopelessness may have to do with regaining the idea that a self can change, in particular in respect of ways of relating to others. This seems to me just right. In describing the transition from the loss of hope Kierkegaard ascribes to our own hopelessness, Marino talks of an "individualistic turn," a translation of "relational ideas" (such as forgiveness) into "individual matters." But from the examples he offers (e.g., being able to become "a warmer and more concerned friend") he might well have put the positive point in a way that reintroduces relational ideas. In taking on the self again we not only restore confidence in our ability to change (and as Marino mentions, forgive) ourselves, we do so in a way that reintroduces a regard for others (including forgiveness) and the selflessness that can find its place in relational ideas. Not only can relational ideas work against all those negatively individualistic ways of not giving up on the self that come closest to Anti-Climacian defiance, and that we too should beware of; they bring us back in spirit if not in letter to Anti-Climacus himself. Certainly, dropping God from the formula prevents a complete return. But surely even a secular age will be inclined to allow that Anti-Climacus is fundamentally right at least psychologically. Perhaps we do really need the sense of (in his terms) a power that "posits" us and to which we are beholden, even if in our own time that sense is one we can only bring ourselves to acknowledge at the cost of that part of our self-esteem that has to do with what we are able and unable to face. For instance, that there is no God.

"Depression" is a term firmly entrenched in the language of medicine. It therefore serves as a useful translation of *Tungsind* so long as we take that to refer to a condition we cannot simply snap out of and for which we would have to seek relief in modern developments of those "powders and pills" referred to by the author of *The Concept of Anxiety*. Niels Jørgen Cappelørn prefers "spleen" as a translation of *Tungsind*. The term is one Kierkegaard himself briefly mentions, in a historical setting, in a journal entry that refers to it also under the name "acedia."[1] English-language dictionaries variously render this (or "acedy") as apathy, boredom, and torpor. It is for this reason that I prefer my own translation of the word in *Either/Or*, "melancholy." However, I think that Cappelørn, whose sensitivity to the origins, sense, and feel of the key words in Kierkegaard's texts is in my experience unequaled, is right at least to question the use of "melancholy." For instance, that term does not immediately convey all that Nero paradigmatically represents in Wilhelm's text, while it is also true that in late-eighteenth-century English literature (see Alexander Pope), "spleen" did indeed have the sense of "melancholy." Yet already in the early nineteenth century (see Jane Austen) it had acquired, as its most general meaning in English, the sense of being ill-humored or temporarily depressed, a mood rather than a settled state. This is the kind of thing that Anti-Climacus says that someone with experience of souls (*den Sjelkyndige*, translated rather misleadingly by the Hongs as "physician of the soul" and which Marino renders as "doctor of the soul") would recognize as forms of despair.[2] It is also true that melancholy is a literary notion and *Either/Or* is, as an attempt to present a "fragment" of life itself, better thought of as a contribution to soul-experience. It is a pity (and perhaps not without cultural implications) that English has no equivalent of the notion that Cappelørn so well describes as a kind of heaviness in which the individual labors, not willing to pull him- or herself together into a self and into the makings of personality. The fact is that the term "spleen" possesses so many and even contradictory meanings in current English that it says nothing definite. The reason may be that "spleen" originally refers to a supposed source of a range of behavior, not to the behavior itself. That is also true of "melancholy," but the latter has the double advantage, like *Tungsind* (and the German *Schwermut*), of being an everyday term, at least in the nineteenth century, and of carrying a considerable culture-historical ballast that goes some if not all the way to picking up the features Cappelørn refers to,[3] and are captured nicely in an entry from Kierkegaard's journals: "One stands as though on the mountain of transfiguration, ready to go, but then finitude's small claims and dribbling debts to the grocer, the cobbler, the tailor get a hold on one and, in short, one stays earthbound and the change occurs not with oneself but with the mountain, which turns into a dunghill."[4] (An early account of the now familiar strategy known as sour grapes?)

Cappelørn draws critical attention to something I left out of *Either/Or* in making an abridgment of Kierkegaard's text. In explaining how the passage from which the omission is made can be read once the lines omitted are restored, he makes the enlightening suggestion that what Assessor Wilhelm says here contains a rudimentary version of *Sickness*'s two main forms of despair: not wanting to be oneself and wanting to be oneself. According to Cappelørn this is a good reason for not omitting the passage.

The lines I omitted say roughly this, that although it is something of a fashion these days to be melancholic, minds sharper than the common run will recognize that they are not just sharper but more guilty. Being sharper, they should be in a position to see that their guilt nevertheless involves no diminishing of their person even if it teaches them to bow humbly to the eternal power. Once that movement is made, calmly and in a well-timed way, the melancholy will be removed, though not the possibility of care and sorrow, and some melancholy will remain in any case, though with a deeper basis (than the one that is fashionable and whatever gloom such care and sorrow may occasion). This residue of melancholy is due to hereditary sin and what follows from it, namely, that no human being can ever be completely transparent to itself.

The reason I omitted the passage was exactly this reference to hereditary sin. As far as I could recall, Wilhelm had made no other reference to it, and to me the interpolation seemed out of character. As for the rest of what the omitted lines say, this could be gathered from parts of the passage not omitted. On the previous page, Wilhelm has already noted that melancholy has "become something big," and the choice of one's given self in its eternal validity is a theme fully dealt with some pages further on. Apart from that, I was reluctant to give (in a note) the lengthy explanation that would be needed for the kind of reader the abridgement was aimed at attracting. I note that Cappelørn admits that the interpolation on hereditary sin (a topic that, as he says, concerned Kierkegaard from his earliest youth) is a little odd and might have been held back until *The Concept of Anxiety,* plans for which had not yet been worked out at the time of writing Wilhelm's "treatise." Most interesting for me in Cappelørn's essay are his own glosses on the passage as a whole, with hereditary sin essentially added, and the very interesting light the notion of coming to oneself too late or too early throws on Anti-Climacus's two main forms of despair. This allows us to read into the supposedly less mature view expressed by Wilhelm (one that Kierkegaard himself says he had left behind even as he was penning it) the later and more mature view that Kierkegaard admitted was too strenuous for him to be able to adopt.

The omitted text says that the "more gifted people" will understand that their guilt does not diminish their *Personlighed.* The idea here is surely that the guilt in fact indicates that they are on the way to a fuller *Personlighed.* Cappelørn's suggestion that the word is better understood as a construction out of its components is useful in this context for making just that point. It is the kind of point Heidegger has taught us to make. But I would hesitate to say that it will do for a grasp of the word in general. For is it not both natural and reasonable to take it to refer to, let us say, person-is-ness and not only to person-like-ness?

I have further comments on Cappelørn's terminological remarks.

Take "transfigure" and "metamorphosis." Just as we may sometimes make too much of the common roots of certain terms (*tvivl, fortvivlelse, tvesindedhed*), with the result that we tend to lose sight of the clear distinctions they are used to make in context, so can the fact that a single word like *Forklaring* has two apparently so sharply divided meanings lead us in the opposite direction, resulting in a failure to see what they nevertheless have in common. The transfiguration of Jesus was indeed a metamorphosis. The Greek text says two things, he changed (the metamorphosis) and his face became radiant like the sun. The idea of transfiguration is the product of a "holy" alliance between those of change and inner radiance. But another and ordinary sense of *elampse* is "became clear," and that sense is surely also a member of the alliance. The transformation was one in which Jesus stood before the disciples "clarified," which is to say, with his true (divine) nature shining out. When the night is transfigured in the poem that is the source of Arnold Schoenberg's string sextet (*Verklärte Nacht*), it is something the two lovers experience as a clarification, and surely it is something of the same that Cappelørn refers to in connection with the movement of spirit that lands on itself, so to speak, at the right time, neither too late nor too early. There is certainly some case, then, for calling this movement one of clarification and for glossing this as the self making itself transparent to itself in its true being.

Finally, *Inderlighed.* This has always been a problem for English-language translators. "Inwardness" seems to point in the wrong direction, suggesting soul-searching instead of engagement; while all the "outward" words ("sincerely" and the like) seem too weak. Kierkegaard's *inderlig,* as a component of *Inderlighed,* clearly means more than we mean by an offhand "cordially," although this and "sincerely" can do service for some typical Danish uses of *inderlig.* Cappelørn's insistence on linking the term with *inderliggjørelse* is very important in this respect, giving the idea of something that has been caught hold of and taken to heart and that then forms part of that individual's heartfelt concerns. Expressions of such concern also come from the heart. Far from being a perfunctory and conventional expression *for* deeply felt attitudes or convictions, usable on occasions where nothing is being deeply felt or occurrently believed, *inderlig* can be used as a direct expression precisely *of* these. But then isn't this "in truth," as opposed to mere etiquette or affectation, what sincerity is?

Part 4.
Trust, Faith,
and Reason

12.
Philosophy and Dogma: The Testimony of an Upbuilding Discourse

George Pattison

No doubt there are things that look like fragments of philosophy in Kierkegaard, things like contributions to long-standing debates in the philosophy of religion, in epistemology, in logic, maybe even an attempt at a kind of proto-phenomenology. But there would seem to be a clear limit to the extent to which Kierkegaard as a whole can be read as a philosopher. For what made Kierkegaard tick, it would seem, was not philosophy but faith, and if there is an intellectual discipline corresponding to faith it is not philosophy but dogmatics (leaving aside—for the purposes of this chapter—whether dogmatics is to be understood in any more specific sense, for example, conservative or liberal, Reformed or Lutheran). Now philosophers can certainly have views on dogmatics, both as a discipline and in terms of its more specific contents, as they can have views and propose criticism of any other intellectual enterprise, but it would seem that there is a point at which, however philosophers may feel about it, the dogmaticians themselves have erected a barrier inscribed "on ne passe point." That point would seem to be constituted by the claim that certain dogmatic truths are not open for inspection or interpretation by the cognitive or hermeneutical capabilities of mere human beings. This gives the philosopher a choice. Either, it seems, he can shrug his shoulders and leave the dogmaticians to it, or he can dispute their claim to intellectual special pleading of this kind. Faced with such a disputatious philosopher, dogmaticians for their part also have a choice. Whilst preserving their claim to sole rights within the realms of faith, they can either agree with the philosophers that there is a real and interesting question as to where exactly to draw the line, or they can simply brush aside anything philosophers might have to say on the matter, maybe, adding a few well-chosen insults to speed the hapless philosopher on his way—insults like "Enlightenment rationalism," "Promethean defiance," or "speculative self-forgetfulness."

There is textual evidence enough to claim that Kierkegaard is a dogmatician of this last kind: that he is concerned not simply to draw a line between the respective language games of philosophy and faith, but to repel any philosophical attempts to deal with faith by judging them to be (without exception) manifestations of the human race's collective rebellion against God. We know, of course, that we need to take pseudonymity, polyphony, humor, and irony into account in every Kierkegaardian sentence that we read, but we can surely concede that the theological reviewer of *Philosophical Fragments* who read it as a straight dogmatic work had reasons for doing so. Whatever else there may be in that book, and however ironically the mercurial persona of Johannes Climacus may have handled his materials, there does seem to be a clear rejection in this work not only of the rights of philosophers but even of any claim to human knowledge as to the redemption wrought in Christ, a redemption that, it would seem, must surely be the highest interest of any human being who learns of it. Only faith, it would appear, can speak the things of faith. "Away, away, all would-be profaners of the sanctuary"—a warning with which a later pseudonym, Anti-Climacus, would prefix his meditations on Christ's words of invitation to "all those who travail and are heavy laden."

But, if that were Climacus's view, is he right? And did Kierkegaard think he was right?

There is, I suggest, clear evidence that S. Kierkegaard, the author of a number of upbuilding discourses, published in the same time period as the *Fragments* and of other remarkable products of the flowering of pseudonymous Danish writing in the early to mid-1840s, had a rather more complex view of things. Kierkegaard's view may seem to offer an olive branch to philosophy, and yet, the very gesture of reconciliation may itself conceal a new, if subtly different, distancing of faith and philosophy.

I shall examine this view in relation to one particular discourse, namely, the second of the four discourses of 1843. Like several other discourses, this takes as its text vv. 17–22 of the first chapter of the epistle of St. James, a text Kierkegaard described in 1851 as his "favorite."

My argument has three steps. First, I shall draw attention to elements in the text that seem to prepare the way for the *Fragments*. Second, I shall distinguish the two texts in terms of the theological distinction between a theology of creation and a theology of redemption and examine what this means also for our understanding of the *Fragments*. Third, I shall consider what the creation theology dimension of Kierkegaard's thought means for a philosophical approach to the *Fragments* and other texts that seem to deny all rights to the philosophical reader.

Johannes Climacus himself, as is well known, wrote a short commentary on the discourses in the *Postscript* to his *Philosophical Fragments,* in which he noted that Magister Kierkegaard had "refrained from using Christian-dogmatic definitions."[1] It is therefore remarkable that this particular discourse begins with an unmistakable résumé of the story of the Fall, closely echoing both Scripture and the Christian dogmatic tradition. Unlike his pseudonym, Vigilius Haufniensis, Kierkegaard does not venture on any unorthodox comments along the lines of being unable to attach any specific thought to the snake, nor does he indulge in the kind of speculation found in *The Concept of Anxiety* in which the author suggests that no external divine voice was involved in the word of prohibition but only language itself, speaking to and through Adam. Instead, Kierkegaard speaks shamelessly about the snake and about the voice of God, speaking to Adam. The description of the consequences of the Fall is also entirely within the tradition of Lutheran Augustinianism. The state of human beings after the Fall is described in terms of the divided self: this is not analyzed in dialectical categories, however, but in term of the man possessed of an unclean spirit in Luke 11. And so Kierkegaard comes to ask how someone who is in this situation can be "captured for the cause of freedom" through the discourse's "consideration" of "the beautiful apostolic word" "that every good and perfect gift comes from above." Of course, a Lutheran reader might have reservations about the genuinely apostolic sense of this text, and Kierkegaard's use of the adjective "beautiful" seems, in the light of later works, an odd way of recommending an apostolic work. However, such worries might be laid to rest by the citation of another evangelical word: "If you who are evil know how to give good gifts, how much more will your heavenly father give good gifts to those who ask him." Climacus is correct in saying that Kierkegaard "refrained . . . from naming Christ," but no reader would have been in doubt that these were Christ's words. Yet, in a turn of phrase that is typical of the discourses, Kierkegaard lets "the words" themselves become the speaker. "These words condescended to the concerned one with such sympathy, spoke so concernedly to the concerned one, that they lifted and strengthened him in the free-spiritedness of faith" (SKS 5 132) . In the following sentence "these words" become "the word," so that the text itself seems subtly to condense and reenact the movement of Incarnation, that is, the movement of the divine Word condescending to speak its word of hope to the sinner. Any hesitations about the transcendent basis of the words that guide the discourse are subliminally addressed and placated.

These reflections on the apostolic word lead to a comparison between a "human father's love for his child" and God's fatherly love, although Kierkegaard warns against conflating these. The word is to be understood figuratively, but "the word could take another explanation . . . the figurative expression could become even more comforting, when its actuality comes also to him [the concerned one] in order to explain the images of earthly life, the conclusion to be drawn from the word could become even more secure, when it is the opposite of how his soul would like it to be in those moments when life had turned everything upside down for him" (SKS 5 133). In other words, the divine love, though like a human father's love, is most comforting when it is most unlike what we might expect from a human father. For we have to recognize "that even the human being, who was nevertheless the most perfect of creatures, was himself evil" (SKS 5 133)—even the best human father, is, after all, a sinner and therefore incapable of giving the ultimate comfort to his sinful sons (the comfort, that is, that sin can be radically overcome by being decisively forgiven).

These reflections lead Kierkegaard on to consider various ways in which the word can be misunderstood and become the occasion for doubt. The key problem is a failure to understand its analogical nature. Our acquaintance with earthly fathers is not the basis of our faith in the Fatherhood of God, and it is not the motif of fatherhood that is decisive here, but that God gives good gifts, that is, *He* is the giver of every good and perfect gift. That this is so cannot be demonstrated by signs or wonders or by "the testimony of flesh and blood" (SKS 5 138), which are necessarily exposed to doubt. Doubt can be brought to a halt only by the word itself, when it points to 'the condition that makes it possible for him [the human being] to receive the good and perfect gifts' (SKS 5 139). This condition is the impulse to the good.[2] But, Kierkegaard says, "before this impulse awakens in a person, there must first occur a great upheaval" whereby "the individual can be what the apostle calls the first-fruits of creation." Now there can be talk of "a new order of things" in which the human being finds "nothing lying in between God and the self" and is "born by the word of truth" which is also "to be born to the word of truth" (SKS 5 139). This rebirth must be made one's own in the right way, namely, by becoming swift to listen, slow to anger, "and with meekness [to] receive the word" and "to keep watch with thanksgiving" (SKS 5 141).

Now, all of this might seem to read like a first draft of *Philosophical Fragments,* chapter 1, section B, where Climacus describes how the one who is in untruth or sin receives the condition for knowing truth from the teacher(/God), in a transformation that is characterized as "conversion," "repentance," and "rebirth." In the course of this transformation God reveals himself as its ultimate agent as "Savior," as "Redeemer," and as "Reconciler."

The following discourse in the *Eighteen Upbuilding Discourses* also addresses the text from James, and continues to develop the theme of the gift; here Kierkegaard begins to develop the problematic of the gift in a manner that anticipates the parable of the King and the Poor Maiden in the *Fragments,* and that reappears in that book's concluding acknowledgment that Climacus's project in its entirety merely reproduces what has been given, freely, to everyone, to all of humanity, in the scriptures.[3] This problematic of the gift, as subsequent philosophy has discovered, concerns the question whether gifts can be given at all, without the recipient being turned into the giver's debtor. Kierkegaard insists that the giver must be able to humble him- or herself under the gift, becoming smaller or less significant than the gift, and he warns against the "left hand" cleverly trying to manipulate what is being given with the right hand—an allusion to the Sermon on the Mount that Derrida will also invoke in discussing the gift.[4] Already in this discourse Kierkegaard points to the God-relationship as the only relationship in which this can happen in such a way that both giver and receiver retain their freedom.

Now, it might seem as if I have not chosen my texts very well. For this discourse seems, like the *Fragments,* to articulate a theology of redemption so extreme that there is little scope for a theology of creation. In this theology of redemption even the experienced need of God ("the condition") is an effect worked by divine grace, and the possibility of faith is dependent on an "upheaval" of the person's preceding condition. What seems to be being promoted is not a renewal of the old creation but a new creation entirely.

Nevertheless, there are some differences between the argument of the discourse and that of the *Fragments* that are important.

Where the *Fragments* speaks of the human being's relation to the Incarnation, the discourse on the gift speaks of the relation to God the Father, that is, to the Creator. It is also important to note Kierkegaard's emphasis in the discourse on the unconditionality and actuality of the gift. He writes, "It does not say, thus your heavenly Father knows how to give good gifts but it says that he gives good gifts" (SKS 5 136). The whole premise of the discourse's argument is not only that God can give good gifts, but that he has given them, gives them, and will continue to give them. He is God, indeed, because he gives good gifts, because he is the source and origin of the good. On the one hand, Kierkegaard emphasizes that the good is what comes "from above," that it is that in relation to which human beings are entirely dependent on God and that our capacity for the good is no purely autonomous function. The God-relationship is thus the condition, to use the vocabulary of *Fragments,* of our ceasing to be evil and coming to be able to do the good. But Kierkegaard can also say that "If you do not wish to continue in this [way of understanding things], it is because you do not wish to remain in God in whom you live and move and have your being" (SKS 5 137). The possibility of coming to be able to do good is, in other words, already present in our living, moving, and having our being in God, that is, in the life we "always already" have as creatures. To be the recipient of God's good gifts is therefore not something we shall only experience in that Promised Land to which God is leading us, but is the very condition of human existence. The condition that is given as the possibility of redemption is nothing other than the condition by which creation is maintained in being.

But in the light of the assertion that even the impulse toward the good is a gift of God, don't we return to the view that the human being can do nothing for himself and that we are entirely dependent on God, even with regard to the possibility of being a self at all?

In his *Upbuilding Discourses in Various Spirits* Kierkegaard will discuss the question concerning the imago dei, and he will clarify his view that there is no contradiction between being created in the image of God and being incapable of doing anything of ourselves. On the contrary. To be in the image of God is to exist as that place of nothingness, that reflective transparency in which God's image can express itself without distortion, in a relationship that Kierkegaard calls "adoration," for it is as one who adores and not as Lord of creation that the human being most resembles God (SKS 8 288–91). If not so explicitly, something of this can be discerned in the remark in the discourse on the good and perfect gift that the newly created human being has "nothing lying in between" himself and God, that is, that there is nothing external to that relationship that conditions its form and content. All of which, from another angle, confirms that the condition of coming into a right relation to God is not only given anew in redemption but is already given in creation, that the rebirth out of nothing in redemption is the repetition (I use the Kierkegaardian term deliberately) of the creation out of nothing "in the beginning."

Moreover, where the emphasis in the *Fragments* is on the moment that occurred once only in historical time and that can only occur once, the self-understanding that is acquired in the concern for the good to which this and other discourses point is not a once-for-all experience or understanding since it is inseparable from the process of appropriation that is especially emphasized in such discourses as "To Acquire Your Soul in Patience" and "To Preserve Your Soul in Patience." This process of self-appropriation reaches backwards as well as forwards in a person's life. The "gift" that is the subject of the discourse, is not a once-for-all gift, like the gift of Christ in the Incarnation, but it is a "gift" that is known as such in the temporally extended process of appropriation that, in different aspects, can be described as patience, expectation, and repetition as well as becoming as nothing. Faith is not just a matter of instantaneous recognition, but of lifelong relationship.

Interesting too is the emphasis in the discourse on "the good." Even if, in the moment in which a person takes hold of God's gifts, there is nothing between them and God, yet, in a way, "the good" does constitute something like a middle term. The giving of the gifts is only meaningful in a context in which the recipient, in his concern for the good, is also concerned about which gifts are indeed the good gifts and how good gifts can be given. This question concerning the good thus acts as a kind of point of contact for the awakening of the more radical question concerning God. Indeed, since God is the final meaning of "the good" (SKS 5 136, 137), to desire the good is already to desire God.

We might be seeming to hint at some kind of crypto-Thomist tendency in Kierkegaard, such that the creature's relation to God is in some measure understandable from the perspective that is already established by virtue of the relationship of being-a-creature (i.e., that there is an analogy of being between the creature as such and its Creator)—but there is, I think, a subtle difference. Where Thomas roots the analogy of being in the ontological determination of the creature as created being and of God as creating being, Kierkegaard speaks throughout of a relation of personal and temporal dependence. Kierkegaard never denies that human beings are creatures, but it is scarcely possible to think of him defining this creatureliness in terms of some essence: the human being is not an individual substance of a rational essence, but a being in dynamic and temporally charged ecstatic and open dependence on God, a dependence that first becomes actual in the individual's concern for the good. It is not solely, nor primarily in terms of our ontological status but in terms of our hyper-ontological freedom, that is, what the discourses call our "concern" and Climacus will call our "subjectivity," that we become capax dei, open to the possibility of the God-relationship.

It is, however, worth noting that Kierkegaard's difference from Thomas is something subtly different from the standard Lutheran rejection of natural theology, since he also differs significantly from Luther. As described by Kierkegaard, the crisis in which a human being becomes a question to himself is not, as for Luther, a result of the crisis of Law (i.e., the experienced impossibility of fulfilling the religious demand to be good), but arises from the human condition as such. Existence as such and not merely the religious crisis brought on by our failure to keep divine law is the matrix of the impulse toward the good in which the possibility of faith becomes manifest.

In this way the discourse on God's giving good and perfect gifts provides a theological context for the Christological argument of the Fragments, offering a theology of creation that complements and prepares for the theology of redemption that Climacus will develop. But this has implications for how we read the *Fragments*—at least if we are prepared to do Kierkegaard the justice of acquainting ourselves with the whole structure and development of his thought, and not just cherry-picking the most provocative and quotable works or sections. For within this larger view, the "high" theology of redemption found in the *Fragments*—Kierkegaard's "dogmatic" tendency—does not exclude such a theology of creation, but rather presupposes it. The rebirth of which the *Fragments* speaks, in which we are born again out of nothing, is meaningful only as and because it is the restoration or repetition of the original structure of our being, our state of "absolute dependence" on God. In the light of this, we might find ourselves wanting to talk with Sløk of a "humanistic" trait in Kierkegaard's thought. And, on this basis, we might begin to feel more optimistic about philosophy having a chance to get to grips with the inner sanctuary of Kierkegaardian faith as that comes to expression in *Fragments,* in the *Postscript's* religiousness B, and in *Training in Christianity's* "sign of contradiction."

And yet a theology of creation is still a theology. If it implies that all human beings, by virtue of the relationship of creature to Creator, are potentially open to the fulfilled God-relationship of faith, it also suggests that to understand this is only possible once one has stepped into the theological circle. A theology of creation is different from a natural theology that, at least in principle, claims to develop its case only on the basis of facts that are equally evident to all reasonable human beings. That a "theology of creation" element is built into Kierkegaard's radical theology of redemption may qualify charges of pessimism and misanthropy (and establish clear blue water between him and, e.g.,

Schopenhauer), yet the more positive evaluation of human possibilities that emerges is developed exclusively by means of reflection on the apostolic and divine words (yes: even here in this supposedly merely "immanent" "upbuilding discourse"). Kierkegaard's pseudonyms offer warning enough against any project of mediating philosophy and dogmatics, but if Kierkegaard's idea of the good doesn't offer "mediation" it does, perhaps, open possibilities for dialogue between these two mutually uncomprehending disciplines. That the possibility of the God-relationship of faith is the gift that God is always, daily giving us is not something that can be known by one who is unconcerned as to whether the gifts of being, consciousness, and volition are for his ultimate good or not. The possibility of a discourse concerning God as giver of every good and perfect gift making any kind of sense at all (or even just being of interest) already depends on good will on the part of the reader, and, qua will, that means a free and responsible choice. In this connection we must take entirely seriously the words from the preface to these four discourses, where Kierkegaard describes his ideal reader as "that person of good will, who receives the book and therewith gives it a good home, that person of good will, who, in receiving it, does for it in himself and by receiving it what the Temple chest did for the widow's mite: it sanctifies the gift, gives meaning to it, and transforms it into something great." Such a reader corresponds to the one who "with meekness receives the [divine] word" and with the one who "in his concern is not indifferent to himself and only preoccupied with the great troubles of life and existence, but as the concerned one, first and foremost concerned for his own cause, his little piece." In the possibility that belongs to every human being of being concerned about their own existence and of engaging with a good will in questioning dialogue directed toward plumbing the meaning of that concern lies also the possibility of the philosopher and theologian coming to understand each other's questions, if not each other's answers.

13.
The Dangers of Indirection: Plato, Kierkegaard, and Leo Strauss

M. G. Piety

I

Much has traditionally been made of the fact that Kierkegaard's writing style is not one that is usual to philosophers. Philosophers, though this is more true of Anglo-American philosophers than of any other group of thinkers, tend to write in a straightforward, exegetical, or axiological manner, whereas Kierkegaard's style is often closer to that of a novelist, dramatist, or poet.[1] Some have even argued that what would appear to be the eccentricity of his literary style actually disqualifies him from being considered a philosopher.[2] Kierkegaard's purportedly "literary" style does sometimes make it difficult to determine what he is trying to say. If Kierkegaard's style is too "literary," however, to satisfy the conceptual rigor required of philosophy, then there are a host of other thinkers whose names should also be stricken from the philosophical rolls.

First among this ragtag group of unclassifiable thinkers would have to be Plato. If Kierkegaard's works are notoriously difficult to interpret, then Plato's works are famously so. If some of Kierkegaard's works read like novels, all of Plato's work are in effect dramas. The reader, and more particularly the scholar, would do well to remember this. One cannot automatically assume that the characters in these dramas, not even Socrates, express Plato's views.[3] Is virtue, for example, a type of knowledge, as some Plato scholars have argued?[4] If so, why does Socrates contrast it, at the end of the *Meno*, with knowledge? Knowledge (at least in some form), he argues in that work, is a universal human possession,[5] whereas virtue, he suggests at the end of the work, is something the gods bestow on a select few.[6]

Thinkers who do not express their views directly appear to invite misinterpretation. The most conspicuous recent example of what some have charged is misinterpretation is the political philosopher Leo Strauss. Strauss did not employ the literary style characteristic of Plato and Kierkegaard, but his theory that the real message of a philosophical text is often presented indirectly has inclined some of his interpreters to the view that Strauss may have used this method of indirect communication himself.[7] This would, in any event, explain the otherwise puzzling diversity of interpretations of his thought.

There is also substantial disagreement among scholars of both Plato and Kierkegaard concerning the real substance of their thought.[8] All three thinkers, Plato, Kierkegaard, and Strauss, have been variously interpreted as defenders of democracy and as proponents of elitist totalitarianism.[9] The question, of course, is which of these interpretations are closest to the truth. Neither Plato, nor Strauss (if he engaged in esoteric communication as some have argued) left many clues that would help guide the reader to the proper understanding of their works. Kierkegaard, by contrast, who has been almost pilloried for the purported incomprehensibility of his oevre,[10] left us volumes, literally volumes, in the form of his journals and papers, to guide us to the proper interpretation.

I will argue that while the form of the works of thinkers such as Plato and Kierkegaard and Strauss may make them more difficult to interpret than the works of thinkers who employ a more direct style, this difficulty is not insurmountable. I will begin by looking at what I will argue is a particularly unfortunate interpretation of Plato's *Republic,* an interpretation that many have attributed to Strauss, but that others have argued may not be Strauss's. This interpretation, I will argue, is an example of how *not* to approach a text whose message, if it has one, is not stated directly. I will then proceed to contrast this unfortunate attempt to decipher the hidden message in a work with a more fortunate interpretation of Kierkegaard's *Concluding Unscientific Postscript.*

II

The political philosopher Leo Strauss is believed by many to be a proponent of the Platonic idea of the "noble lie" as a legitimate means of "leading the stupid masses."[11] The idea does appear in the *Republic.* It is not at all clear, however, that it is an idea Plato endorsed. Strauss appears himself to have been a proponent of indirect, or, as he calls it, "esoteric" communication. So it is not actually all that easy to tell what his views were. It's not actually all that easy to tell what Plato's views were either. Plato did not present his views in straightforward scholarly treatises in the manner of contemporary philosophers. His works are "dialogues," effectively dramas, with a recurring protagonist, Socrates, who purports to have no views of his own. Plato, on the other hand, like all great dramatists, clearly was trying to communicate important truths in his works.

The difficulty is simply, as it is with all great dramatic works, figuring out what those truths are.

Most people, at least most educated people, in our society have heard of Plato's *Republic* and know that it deals with the construction of an ideal city. That is as far as it goes, though, for most people. Among intellectuals, however, it is widely acknowledged that this purportedly ideal city becomes increasingly bizarre and unappealing to those of democratic predilections. It becomes a city ruled by propaganda and systematic deception.

Yes, the city described in Plato's magnum opus is unappealing indeed. Yet the *Republic* is not all that easy to interpret. The city described therein is referred to by Socrates early in the work as "spoiled," or "swollen and inflamed," depending on which of the contemporary English translations one consults, with luxuries. Socrates contrasts this city, where the citizens "abandon themselves to the unlimited acquisition of wealth" (373d7–9), with the city he first presents to his interlocutors as the "true," "truthful," or "healthy" city. The early part is ignored by people who like to dismiss the work as just another, albeit perhaps the earliest, fascist political treatise. It is this part of the work, however, that may hold an important key to interpreting the rest.

The *Republic* does not actually start out as a political treatise. The subject at the beginning of the work is the nature of a just person. Socrates is having dinner at the home of a friend, Polemarchus. There are quite a few other guests as well, including Plato's two brothers, Glaucon and Adeimantus. They are all there in the port district of Athens, a place known as a hotbed of democratic sentiments, to observe a new religious festival in honor of the Thracian goddess Bendis. Cephalus, Polemarchus's father and a man well advanced in age, is there, and he and Socrates quickly become absorbed in a discussion on the sort of wisdom that comes with age.

Cephalus observes that many of his friends complain of the hardships associated with old age. He asserts, however, that a person's character determines how pleasant or unpleasant are both his youth and the last days of his life. Toward the end of their lives, he goes on to argue, people begin to remember the tales told about how the unjust are made to suffer for their injustices in Hades, and they begin to fear that this will be their own fate, fear it to the extent, he continues, that "the man who finds many unjust deeds in his life often even wakes from his sleep in a fright as children do, and lives in anticipation of evil" (330e7–9).

The discussion turns to definitions of justice as it characterizes the behavior of individuals. This discussion takes up the whole of the first book of the *Republic* and part of Book Two. As so often happens in the Platonic dialogues, however, Socrates and his interlocutors are unable to arrive at a satisfactory definition of the concept they are attempting to define. Thrasymachus, a professional rhetorician and teacher of rhetoric, goes so far as to suggest that there really is no such thing as justice in the traditional sense; that contrary to popular belief, it is not a good in itself but is practiced only when it is unavoidable or only for its rewards, which are more easily gained by the appearance of justice than by the real thing.

Socrates is entreated to defend justice against such attacks and though he protests he is unequal to the task he says that he feels "it is wrong to stand idly by when I hear justice coming under attack, and not come to its defense" (368c2–3).

"The enquiry we are undertaking," asserts Socrates,

> is not a simple matter. If you ask me it requires sharp eyesight. And since we are not clever people, I think we should conduct our search in the same sort of way as we would if our eyesight were not very good, and we were told to read some small writing from a bit of a distance away, and then one of us realized that a larger copy of the same writing apparently was to be found somewhere else, on some larger surface. We would regard it as a stroke of luck, I think, to be able to read the larger letters first, and then turn our attention to the smaller ones, to see they really did say the same thing. (368c10–d9)

Thus they turn from defining a just person to defining a just city. Socrates starts by looking at what he asserts is the theoretical origin of a city. The origin of the city lies, he asserts, "in the fact that we are not, any of us, self-sufficient, we have all sorts of needs" (369b5–6). He constructs a hypothetical city that will meet people's needs. He does this step by step, starting with basic needs such as those for food, clothing and shelter, and progressing to more esoteric needs such as those for olives, wine, and exotic cheeses. The city Socrates describes comprises farmers, carpenters, weavers, cobblers, blacksmiths and "a whole lot of skilled workers of that kind" (370b6–7), cattlemen, shepherds, and other herdsmen. The city will also require merchants to secure from outside the city the things the citizens require but that they cannot themselves produce, and sailors to transport these merchants to foreign lands and hired laborers to help with the heavier sorts of physical tasks.

People can live very well in such a city, asserts Socrates. They will drink wine after their meals "wearing garlands on their heads, and singing the praises of the gods, they will live quite happily with one another. They will have no more children than they can afford, and they will avoid poverty and war" (372b6–c2).

Glaucon asserts, however, that the city is not yet finished, that the citizens would not be able to enjoy the full variety of dishes contemporary Athenians enjoy and that "[i]f they are going to eat in comfort, they should lie on couches [and] eat off tables" (372d5–e).

"I see," replied Socrates, in what could be argued is one of the most important sections of the work:

So we are not just looking at the origin of a city, apparently. We are looking at the origin of a luxurious city. Maybe that is not such a bad idea. If we look at that sort of city too, we may perhaps see the point where justice and injustice come into existence in cities. I think the true city—the healthy version, as it were—is the one we have just described but let's look also at *the swollen and inflamed city* if that is what *you* prefer. (372e3–9, emphasis added)

The rest of the *Republic* is taken up with the organization and management of this "swollen and inflamed city" where poetry and music are censored and the citizens are systematically deceived about both the origin of the city and how it is run.

This portion of the *Republic* is better known than the first part, so I won't take up space summarizing it here. It is interesting to note that although the plan had been to return to the discussion of what constitutes a just individual after having identified justice in a city, the discussion never really does return to this topic. It does turn to a consideration of what separates the philosopher, the proposed ruler of this inflamed city, from the masses, or the true philosopher from one who merely professes to be a philosopher. But these characteristics, for example, ethical virtue and a love of learning and wisdom and truth, would make the philosopher entirely unsuited to rule the city that occupies so much of the discussion in the *Republic*.

So what is the point? Is it that too much luxury threatens justice; that consumer societies such as ours are doomed to be characterized by systematic deception and manipulation of the citizens by those in power? That such deception and manipulation are "just" to the extent that they appear necessary to insure order in such a society?

Much is made of Socratic irony. It can hardly be denied that irony is one of Socrates' favorite literary devices. The difficulty is identifying precisely *where* Socrates, or Plato, is being ironical. One relatively uncontroversial instance would appear to come very early in the dialogue when Socrates asserts that he and his interlocutors are unable to arrive at a satisfactory definition of a just individual because they "are not very clever people." Not very clever? Of course they were clever people, among the cleverest people in Athens during what is considered to be the "cleverest" period of the "cleverest" culture the world has probably ever known. This reference would be so patently absurd to Plato's contemporaries that rather than subtly ironical it was undoubtedly intended by Plato to be directly humorous.[12]

But if Socrates interlocutors in the *Republic* are among the cleverest people of a clever time, why couldn't they figure out what justice was in an individual? And if they couldn't figure out what constituted a just person, what hope is there that they could figure out what constituted a just city? That is, if they couldn't read the fine print, how would they know where that same text was written larger? And indeed it appears that they *do* misjudge where it is written larger.

Socrates enlarges the script with his example of a "healthy" city, but this example was rejected in favor of the "spoiled" city. It could be argued further that the failure of the discussion to return to the original issue—that is, what constituted a just person—suggests that Plato did not think the true nature of social or political justice had been clearly identified by the end of the *Republic*.

So what is the point of the work? Is Socrates playing an elaborate joke on his interlocutors as he is wont to do in other dialogues? And if this city that has so captured the imagination of fascists throughout history was an elaborate joke, is there anything to be learned from the *Republic* as a whole?

One thing that might perhaps be learned from the *Republic* is that there is a point at which the cost of luxuries becomes too high, that a state (one should remember that the "cities" of ancient Greece were actually states) that exists primarily for the purpose of guaranteeing its citizens, or even some portion of its citizenry, a lifestyle characterized by a surfeit of material goods is doomed to become "diseased and inflamed." Of course I have stacked the deck a bit by using the term "surfeit" of goods rather than some more neutral term like "abundance." Even Glaucon acknowledges, however, that the goods he suggests introducing into the city are to satisfy people's wants rather than their needs.

Perhaps part of the message we ought to take from the *Republic* is that not everything people desire is actually good for them, and that it makes no more sense to slavishly seek to satisfy all the immediate desires of adults than it makes to slavishly endeavor to satisfy all the immediate desires of children. Perhaps part of the message we ought to take from the *Republic* is that materialistic societies inevitably become unjust or at least unappealing to those of democratic sentiments.

III

However one chooses to interpret the *Republic*, the suggestion that Plato was seriously proposing that what he explicitly identifies as a "swollen" or "inflamed" city was an ideal to strive for seems untenable. Such a suggestion could only spring from a singular lack of sympathy with the author. That observation brings us to the crux of what is often considered the problem of indirect communication—it relies, for its effectiveness, on a certain sympathy on the part of the reader.

There is a word game that illustrates this situation very nicely, called "Taboo." The game is played in teams, usually of two people, one who gives clues to the identity of a hidden word and the other who attempts to guess this identity based on these clues. What makes the game challenging is that each card on which the words are written also lists a series of "taboo" words— words that cannot be used in the clues. If, for example, the word were "marriage," the taboo words might include "wedding," "matrimony," "nuptials," "bride," and "groom." The clue giver must then find some way of communicating the identity of the hidden word without resorting to any of these taboo words. A clue for "marriage" might thus be something like: "the state where two people are joined together in perpetual union."

The clues are often quite creative and this makes the game entertaining to observe as well as to play. What becomes apparent relatively quickly is that the better one knows one's partner, the more successful will the team be. Siblings, close friends, and spouses make the best teams, people who know each other well, people who know how the other thinks. I have seen such pairs race through a stack of cards with only a word or two for each. These displays often appear astonishingly close to mind reading. Strangers, on the other hand, or people only recently acquainted, usually make wretchedly miserable teams.

What is clear is that the more sympathy one has with someone who is trying to communicate something indirectly, the more likely one will be to get it. Kierkegaard knew this. This is undoubtedly why he so often speaks of his "reader" in the singular. He appeals, just at it would appear Plato appeals, to someone reflective enough to have similar concerns.

Nowhere is the assumption of a similarity of concerns more important than in the writings of Kierkegaard's pseudonym, Johannes Climacus. Climacus's concern, in Kierkegaard's *Fragments* and *Postscript,* is not whether Christianity is true—a concern which according to thinkers such as Pascal, *everyone* ought to have, and to thinkers such as William James, everyone in the West ought to have. Climacus's concern is with how one becomes a Christian and this is an issue that will interest only those who have in some sense already committed themselves to the view that Christianity is true.

Fragments proposes that we can become Christian only by relating ourselves to the god in time—which is to say God in the instant (Øieblik)—and that this can be achieved only through faith rather than through any particular temporal position relative to the historical phenomenon of the incarnation. *Postscript* elaborates upon the point by examining the ways people have confounded this task with a problem of historical scholarship or speculative philosophy. Most of *Postscript* is devoted, however, to examining how one becomes truly "subjective."[13] That is, most of *Postscript* presents what Hannay calls "the path to personality" (300), the path away from objective thought and toward subjective reflection in the sense of the subject's reflection on his own situation in an attempt to determine his position relative to what he has committed himself, in some sense, to accepting as the truth. *Postscript* presents a reader with a desire to know himself and where he stands relative to this truth with a path of self-exploration, self-discovery, and self-understanding.

Postscript puts so much emphasis on subjectivity that it has actually been interpreted as championing a kind of subjectivism. Climacus, observes Hannay, says that for a "subjective reflection" truth is a matter of appropriation, a matter of *how* one believes something, not whether some proposition adhered to is true or not. In contrast to objective reflection, in which . . . subjectivity vanishes along with its task, in the case of subjective reflection it is subjectivity that is left over and objectivity "the vanishing factor." So it doesn't really matter whether the *what* of the belief corresponds to facts "out there." Indeed, as Climacus notoriously adds, "if only the how of [the] relationship is in the truth, the individual is in the truth even if he should happen to be related thus to untruth."[13] The highest truth available to an existing individual is "an objective uncertainty held fast in a most passionately inward appropriation."[14] (301)

"That statement," continues Hannay, "has been read as carte blanche legitimation of any zealously held point of view. But we should not forget that *Postscript* is a postscript to *Fragments*" (301). That is, the concern of *Fragments* is with how one becomes a Christian, not with how one becomes truly subjective. The point of *Postscript,* or *one* point of *Postscript,* is to show that the path to authentic subjectivity and the path to Christianity are the same, that authentic selfhood brings one before God or that as Kierkegaard explains, there is a *how*—genuine, in the sense of *passionate* subjectivity—that brings the *what*—God—along with it.

Unfortunately, *Postscript* was published pseudonymously by an author who does not claim to be Christian. This has posed such a problem for philosophers that the work has sometimes been dismissed as "nonsense."[15] *Postscript* is shot through with humor, which, when philosophers are able to recognize it as such, leads them to conclude that it cannot be making a serious point. To add to the confusion, Climacus, the pseudonymous author, Hannay observes, "recants the entire book. Indeed, in the postscript (*Tillæg*) to *Postscript* ('for an understanding with the reader') he not only 'revokes' the work but announces its 'superfluousness'" (313). It's bad enough that *Fragments* and *Postscript* were published pseudonymously, but then to have the pseudonymous author disavow any relation to their content had led some scholars to conclude that the works are nothing but an elaborate joke.[16] A parody of speculative philosophy.

Hannay asserts, however, that it makes little sense to suppose Kierkegaard would spend "eight months of what he feared might be the last years of his life preparing a party trick he might never enjoy, and an untopical jest at that, since Hegel's star had long been in the decline" (310). The book, observes Hannay, is not completely serious. "But serious enough to be saying something, and not saying it just to take it away again" (310). "The book is superfluous," he explains, "because it has no life beyond the orbit of a reader who understands where it leads, and because the life it has only begins if the reader has the right kind of interest" (313).

The right kind of interest is not in whether Christianity is true. The right kind of interest is the subject's interest in whether he is truly a Christian, which is to say that it is the subject's interest in whether he is living as he ought to be living. This is a kind of ethical interest that, when pursued consistently, gives a coherence to the subject's existence, a coherence that is part of what one could call the subject's "personality." "Personality," Hannay observes, "was a concept very much in the air, and Kierkegaard's contribution was to give it a new twist by making his controversial notion of faith the unifying factor. What *Postscript* provides is an itinerary on the path to personality" (300).

"To be or to become the single individual, to prepare oneself in the only possible way for purification and redemption, by standing alone in a God relationship—that at least," observes Hannay, "can stand as a not implausible corrective to the 'parody' reading" (312).

It is not suprising that many philosophers fail to appreciate that this is the most plausible interpretation of *Postscript*. What philosopher in his right mind is interested in perfection and redemption? These are subjective concerns, and philosophers today—if they have not always done so[17]—strive for objectivity.[18]

IV

It is not necessary, however, to have precisely the same concerns as the author of a work one is trying to interpret in order properly, or at least productively, to identify what the author is trying to say. A certain sympathy with the author's temperament—for example, an ability to recognize when he is being humorous—and concerns is all that is required. One needs, first and foremost, to employ the principle of charity—that is, to assume that the author is not a blithering idiot who contradicts himself at every turn, but an intelligent, reflective person who has come to some coherent insight about the nature of human existence that he would like to pass on to others. Second, one needs to have a particular interest in the class of concerns this insight would illuminate. If, for example, one's interests (at least conscious interests) are overwhelmingly esthetic, it is unlikely one will gain much insight into the message of a text whose message is essentially ethical.

There is no guarantee, of course, that one will succeed in understanding the message of a given text, even if one's concerns are similar to those of the author. Such similarity only makes success more probable. This situation is complicated by the fact that one can never really be certain that one's concerns are similar to those of a particular author. Strauss may have thought he and Plato were kindred spirits. The incoherencies, however, of the interpretation of Plato's *Republic* as advocating the use of noble lies, the apparent dependence of such an interpretation on the failure to recognize the irony and even humor with which the work is laden, suggest that it is not an interpretation that would appeal to someone whose sensibilities were similar to Plato's. Was this really Strauss's view of Plato? It is a widely held view. Even if this was Strauss's view of Plato, that does not necessarily mean that Strauss was himself a proponent of the use of "noble lies." Perhaps Strauss was intentionally vague on this point in order to prevent his students from simply slavishly adopting his own view. Perhaps his intention was to get his students to decide for themselves what they believed on this point.

Plato's indirection leaves it to every reader to decide for him- or herself whether he actually advocated the use of "noble lies" in the *Republic*. It leaves open as well the question of whether anyone who interprets the work in this way shares the sensibility with the Plato that would be requisite to understanding what it was he really meant to say. That does not mean, however, that there is no fact of the matter, that Plato was not saying anything in particular, that all interpretations of his works are equally good.

Plato may not have known, as he was writing the *Republic*, exactly what point or points he wanted to make in the work, just as Kierkegaard did not always know the precise significance of his own works. It is common for authors to speak of the feeling of being guided by some force greater than themselves, of being mere instruments through which the universe makes it own points. We may never have a definitive interpretation of the *Republic*, but that does not mean that some interpretations are not better than others. Even if Plato thought the human condition so miserable that swollen and inflamed cities were all we would ever have, the suggestion that he presented the city described in the *Republic* as an ideal for which to strive seems untenable.

Strauss, it has been argued, actually endeavored to be obtuse.[19] He observed that stating one's points directly could be dangerous. He argued that it had in fact been so dangerous throughout various periods of human history that an entire tradition of obscurantist writing had developed. This tradition, he believed, obscured the true, or "esoteric" message of a text beneath a more obvious "exoteric" message.[20] Strauss appears to have been an elitist who believed that the mass of humanity would be too simpleminded and unreflective to appreciate that what a particular text appeared to say may not be what the author actually intended to communicate. This would insulate the author from the recriminations of the mob if it did not like his views. That is, the views would be presented in such a way that the mob wouldn't get them.[21]

Kierkegaard has sometimes been interpreted as a kind of nineteenth-century Leo Strauss, that is, as someone who addresses his works to "my reader" in the singular, because he does not want to be understood by the multitudes. Kierkegaard may well have been an intellectual elitist. Hannay's biography makes clear, however, that Kierkegaard thinks of his reader in the singular not because he wants to be misunderstood by the masses, but because he is pessimistic about being understood by the masses. The obstacles to understanding the import of Kierkegaard's works are not ones designed to fell the dimwitted. They are ethical obstacles Kierkegaard clearly believes are built into any attempt to help others along the path to personality or to authentic subjectivity in the sense of the self that is transparent before God. We could speculate that perhaps this pessimism came on Kierkegaard as the result of personal experience or that he may have started from such a position to the extent that scripture asserts that the path, or pass, to authentic selfhood in this sense is too narrow for most people. The answer is probably a combination of both.

There is, as Hannay observes, a kind of "anti-intellectualism" in some of Kierkegaard's works. This is not because Kierkegaard, who undoubtedly was something of an intellectual elitist, had contempt for reason as such, but because as Hannay makes clear, he so often saw it masquerading as a substitute for subjectivity—the one thing necessary not merely to make it possible to become a Christian but to make the interest in becoming a Christian make any kind of sense. The reason so many scholars have been confused, alienated, and even infuriated by Kierkegaard's works is not because they are intellectually impenetrable but because they are subjectively, or ethically, demanding. A proper interpretation of the content—at least in a general sense—of Kierkegaard's works is not difficult for a reader who is not offended by the question of whether he is living as he should. Indeed, I have met many people who are not philosophers who appear to have a profound grasp and appreciation of Kierkegaard's thought. One of the chief joys, in my experience, of being a Kierkegaard scholar is seeing, every once in a while, someone's eyes light up when they hear I work on Kierkegaard. This has happened to me at dinner parties, political protests, and poetry readings. "You study Kierkegaard," people will exclaim. "Oh, I love him!" The rest of the evening will then be spent in delightful, elevating conversation with this kindred soul.[22]

These people are Kierkegaard's "individuals." They understand the works not because they are particularly intelligent (though many of them are indeed exceptionally intelligent and anyone in our culture who has even heard of Kierkegaard is at least inclined to be better educated than the average person), but because they are not offended by the suggestion that perhaps they are not living as they should be living, but actually are drawn to it as was Kierkegaard.

It is tempting to consider that Plato may have been drawn to this question as well. Why else would he have taken such pains to present otherwise clever people as apparently clueless when it came to what it meant to be just? It is clear, in any case, that he was drawn to the question of whether we were living collectively as we should, and he was certainly smart enough to see that the questions of how the individual ought to live and how people ought to live together in communities are inextricably linked. Perhaps human existence was as mysterious to Plato as it was to Kierkegaard. Certainly it was mysterious to Socrates—-a fact that Plato, his student and admirer, dutifully and carefully recorded. In any case, Plato's works carry the suggestion of what Kierkegaard would call a religious temperament to the extent that they are shot through with humor. Those who interpret Plato as a proponent of "noble lies" can do so only by ignoring the humor in the *Republic* and only on the assumption that Plato thought he had the answer to how we should live all figured out. Such people forget that the *Republic* is a dramatic work, that Plato does not even appear in it as a character. They do not approach it as one should a dramatic work—that is, with the hope of finding edification in it, but as a didactic work with the expectation of finding straightforward rules of how to order a state. Such a sensibility would appear far removed from Plato's own and thus unlikely to produce a helpful interpretation of the work.

All this is just speculation though. Plato left us little in the way of a key that would help us to unlock the mystery of his often mysterious texts. Our situation with respect to Kierkegaard is more fortunate because we have a wealth of material on which to draw in interpreting Kierkegaard's works. Hannay has availed himself amply of this material. Many scholars, including myself, have eschewed "biographical readings" of Kierkegaard. Hannay's book makes clear, however, that the aversion should not be to biographical readings as such but to the often perverse readings of Kierkegaard's works that have earlier passed for biographical ones. Hannay's reading, on the other hand, is illuminating because it gives us not merely an interpretation that makes sense of the works, but one that helps us to make sense of the man. It does not answer every question raised by the works, but no single interpretation would, because over and above the author's perhaps not fully formed intentions is the "more" of providence (or that force that through the pen fuse drives the author).

14.
Abraham's
Final Word

Daniel W. Conway

Here I am.

ABRAHAM, GENESIS 22:1

That man . . . did not know Hebrew; if he had known Hebrew, he perhaps would easily have understood the story of Abraham.

JOHANNES *DE SILENTIO, FEAR AND TREMBLING*

Introduction

Even a brief encounter with Johannes *de Silentio* confirms that he is decidedly, even comically, misnamed. Garrulous to the extreme, he is prone to lengthy disputations, didactic digressions, elliptical illustrations, and parabolic comparisons. Despite announcing on several occasions that he does not understand Abraham, he nevertheless proceeds to weave an elaborate narrative concerning the various ways in which his readers might approach the mysterious patriarch. One might naturally conclude that the misnomer of Johannes *de Silentio* constitutes a simple exercise in irony, as if the name of Kierkegaard's pseudonymous narrator were nothing more than a spoof of his gift for gab.

Yet irony alone fails to capture the complexity of Johannes's relationship to his name. First of all, we know from Johannes himself that incessant "chatter" can yield a kind of wordful silence (116).[1] If nothing of import is uttered, if passion is neither produced nor replenished nor conveyed, then speech may just as well be silence.[2] In addition to his weakness for chatter, Johannes also maintains a more literal silence on topics that one might plausibly judge to be of central importance to his discussion of Abraham. He is mostly silent, for example, about the larger context of Abraham's life, as recorded in the Book of

Genesis. While he acknowledges in passing the potential importance of events that precede and follow the journey to Mount Moriah,[3] he clearly wishes to isolate this journey, excising it from the larger narrative of Abraham's remarkable life. He consequently restricts the focus of his discussion to the story of the *Aqedah*, i.e., the binding of Isaac, which is related in Gen. 22:1–19.[4]

This restriction of focus is noteworthy in that it helps us to fix more precisely Johannes's purported interest in the *faith* of Abraham. For the most part, Johannes is not interested in what others might identify as Abraham's most impressive displays of faith: his acceptance of the covenant; his willingness to relocate under a new name and a new God; his negotiations with his God over the (admittedly few) righteous citizens of Sodom and Gomorrah; his confidence in his God to ensure the fruition of an aged couple's loving embrace; and his trust in his God to bless the pregnancy of his skeptical, laughing wife. While it is certainly possible that Johannes may mean to presuppose these (and other) precedent acts of faith, his explicit discussions of the faith of Abraham pertain nearly exclusively to the story of the *Aqedah*. When Johannes celebrates the faith of Abraham, as that which makes the patriarch *great,* he usually has in mind the faith that sustained Abraham's journey to Mount Moriah. As we shall see, in fact, he regards the faith of Abraham as the product of the second stage in a "double-movement," which originates in his resolute decision to obey the command to sacrifice Isaac. Indeed, Johannes is relatively unique among commentators in his relentless attention to Abraham's *reception* of this command. It is here that Abraham makes the "double-movement" that marks him as a "knight of faith." For Johannes, *everything* that follows Abraham's faithful reception of the first command—including, most notably, his decision to terminate the commanded sacrifice—pales by comparison.

Even with respect to the story of the *Aqedah,* however, Johannes remains conspicuously silent. For example, he is mostly silent about Isaac, blithely proceeding as if the lad related to his father as we supposedly do.[5] He is also mostly silent about Sarah and the implications of the journey for the ethical life of the family. But his most obtrusive silence pertains to the events that transpired atop Mount Moriah. Of particular interest to me in this essay is his silence with respect to Abraham's response to the angel of the Lord (Gen. 22:11). Johannes not only fails to acknowledge this response, but also assigns its rightful place— namely, as Abraham's "final word"—to another, earlier utterance. In developing his interpretation of Abraham's "final word," that is, he refuses to acknowledge the final word attributed to Abraham in Chapter 22 of Genesis.

In an attempt to respond to Johannes's silence, this essay undertakes an investigation of his avowed interest in Abraham's "final word." As it turns out, Johannes not only misidentifies Abraham's final word, focusing instead on the famous promise of divine providence, but also avoids a direct confrontation with the patriarch's genuinely final word. It is no coincidence, I propose, that Abraham's final word in Genesis 22—"Here I am"—conveys his response to the angel's salutation, especially inasmuch as this response announces the kind of moral awakening that Johannes cannot allow himself to attribute to Abraham. This practice of avoidance, I further propose, illuminates the ulterior motives that inform the "dialectical lyric" of *Fear and Trembling*. In the end, or so I maintain, Johannes recoils from the prospect of an Abraham who decided *on his own* to terminate the commanded sacrifice of Isaac. Johannes thus appears in *Fear and Trembling* as what I call a *knight of morality*—that is, as an unwitting advocate of the primacy of ethical universality.

Section I

Well along in the discussion that occupies *Problema III*, Johannes finally acknowledges the failure of his multiple attempts to devise an analogy that would further our understanding of Abraham. The bulk of *Problema III*, he thus concedes, amounts to an extended digression. Once again, however, Johannes refuses to return to silence. Having admitted that he "does not understand Abraham," he quickly adds that he "can only admire him" (112). What follows, apparently, is an expression of this admiration, an encomium, which perhaps is meant to earn for him the poetic license he grants himself upon returning to the biblical narrative. That Abraham needs no (human) admiration (120), just as he needs no eulogy, does not deter Johannes from articulating an extremely selective (and ultimately self-serving) interpretation of Genesis 22:8.

This is not to suggest, however, that Johannes's digressions and failed analogies in *Problema III* are fruitless. In measuring—and ultimately rejecting—Abraham's fit to the types of the "tragic hero" and the "aesthetic hero," Johannes prepares us to stand, finally, "face to face with the paradox" (113). To mark the occasion, he pronounces yet another momentous either/or: "Either the single individual as the single individual can stand in an absolute relation to the absolute, and consequently the ethical is not the highest, or Abraham is lost (113)." Rather than risk the loss of Abraham, Johannes elects the former alternative and resolves to account for the patriarch as "the single individual." Here we might note that Johannes gathers the momentum for his narrative not from any positive case in favor of the proffered interpretation, but from the putative unacceptability of the only proffered alternative. That Abraham stands in an "absolute relation to the absolute" is thus asserted rather than demonstrated.

This assertion subsequently obliges Johannes to maintain that Abraham did *not* speak to Sarah, Eliezer, and Isaac. In "bypass[ing] these three ethical authorities" (112), moreover, Abraham failed to meet his highest (i.e., familial) ethical obligations (112). (As we recall, the goal of *Problema III* is to determine whether or not Abraham was ethically justified in concealing his true plan from his wife, his servant, and his son.) Yet his failure to speak cannot be attributed to any of the familiar reasons or motives that might lead one to conceal one's true intentions. "Abraham remains silent," Johannes explains, but only because "he *cannot* speak" (113). Such is the paradox of his faith and the burden of the fate he shares with all other knights of faith. Central to Johannes's sketch of the knights of faith is the non-negotiable fact of their isolation from (human) others. There is simply no language in which they could possibly convey to others the particular content of their interiority and the specific nature of their religious obligations. (This also means, presumably, that there is no language in which the knight of faith can communicate to *himself* the nature of his religious obligations.) It is therefore crucial to Johannes's interpretation that the patriarch is unable to communicate with (human) others—hence his insistence that Abraham *did not* and *cannot* speak.[6]

After repeating this claim several times, however, Johannes concedes the obvious point: Abraham may have been a man of few words, but on occasion he addressed others and exchanged words with them.[7] He was especially fond of a particular word—*hineni,* or "Here I am!," which he uttered on three separate occasions in the story of the *Aqedah.* Rather than survey the words attributed to Abraham in Genesis 22, however, Johannes boldly asserts that "just one word [*kun eet Ord*] from [Abraham] has been preserved, his only reply to Isaac, ample evidence that he had not said anything before (115)."[8] The exchange he has in mind is found at Genesis 22:7–8, as Abraham and Isaac set out on foot—having left behind the servants and ass—to complete their journey to the sacrificial summit of Mount Moriah. When asked by Isaac what animal they would sacrifice for their burnt offering (Gen. 22:7), Abraham famously responded: "God will provide himself the lamb for the burnt offering, my son" (Gen. 22:8).

We will return shortly to consider this exchange in some detail. For now, two elements of Johannes's interpretation bear noting. First of all, he conspicuously refuses to concede that Abraham actually *speaks* to Isaac, adverting instead to the "final word" (or "words") recorded in Abraham's name. Johannes apparently means to distinguish here between *speaking* and *uttering words.* The former term is meant to involve "saying something," perhaps even "say[ing] that which would explain everything" (115), while the latter term is meant to involve nothing more than the inconsequential spewing of meaningless words. As he proceeds to explain, moreover, he regards *speaking* as conditional upon the "understanding" of the other to whom the speech is directed: "[Abraham] can say everything, but one thing he cannot say, and if he cannot say that—that is, say it in such a way that the other understands it—then he is not speaking" (113). This condition places the speech of Abraham under the constraint of its comprehension by its intended recipient, Isaac.[9] As we shall see, Johannes avails himself of this distinction not only to diminish the importance of the exchange recorded at Gen. 22:7–8, but also to justify the premature conclusion of his meditation on Abraham.

Second, Johannes relies on this distinction to discount every word uttered by Abraham leading up to and following his promise of divine providence.

With the exception of the promise of divine providence, whose significance Johannes soon will undertake to diminish, the words attributed to Abraham do not satisfy the threshold conditions of meaningful human speech. By silencing Abraham in this way, Johannes licenses himself to ignore the three occasions in Chapter 22 on which the patriarch uttered his favorite word: *hineni*, or "Here I Am!" This is a substantial piece of editing on Johannes's part, for, taken together, these three utterances sustain the dramatic and narrative continuity of the story of the *Aqedah*. When considered in sequence, moreover, these three utterances attest to Abraham's *responsiveness*, which is a trait that Johannes generally prefers to ignore in the patriarch. As we shall see, in fact, the Abraham who responds to the angel's salutation has matured significantly since the time of his initial response to his God.

Section II

Having acknowledged that "a final word [*sidste Ord*] by Abraham has been preserved" (118),[10] Johannes immediately endeavors to diminish the utterance in question as well as the exchange in which it takes place: "First and foremost, [Abraham] does not say anything, and in that form he says what he has to say. His response to Isaac is in the form of irony, for it is always irony when I say something and still do not say anything (118)." Earlier, we recall, Johannes suggested that Abraham's promise of divine providence involved him in "saying something," which he distinguished from "saying nothing at all." As we now learn, however, Abraham's "final word" is more complicated than we were originally led to believe. In response to Isaac's question, Abraham "says what he has to say," while still managing not to "say anything." This inventive interpretation thus allows Johannes to renew with minimal refinement his insistence that Abraham does not and cannot speak. It is the nature of irony, he thus implies, to facilitate a saying that in fact says nothing. He thus introduces irony as a means of accounting for words that appear to be, but in fact are not, understood by their intended recipients. Although Isaac thinks he understands what his father's promise is meant to convey, that is, he is in fact mistaken. As we shall see, moreover, this invocation of irony eventually positions Johannes to issue an ethical indictment of Abraham. Having initially claimed that the patriarch had no language in which he might communicate the nature of his religious obligations, he soon will claim that Abraham refused to make full use of the language available to him.

It is by no means obvious, however, that Abraham's promise of divine providence is in fact ironic, especially if Johannes understands irony as the strategic or incomplete communication of a literal truth.[11] Here three points are relevant. First of all, Abraham's promise was fulfilled: God *did* provide the animal for their burnt offering. He in fact provided *two* animals—Isaac and the ram—between which Abraham was obliged to choose. Second, the context of Abraham's promise would seem to provide ample (if indirect) insight into the nature of his relationship to his God.[12] At the very least, his promise reveals that Isaac, too, may place his trust in divine providence. Third, Isaac's response to his father's promise indicates not only that something essential has passed between them, but also that the bond between them has been burnished and renewed. We might go so far as to say that his acceptance of Abraham's promise inaugurates a second, more intimate journey, which they now make "together."[13] Having left behind their servants and ass, they are now exclusively reliant on one another (and, of course, on the God of Abraham).

Having reduced Abraham's "final word" to irony, Johannes proceeds to offer yet another reduction of the utterance in question and the promise it conveys:

> From [Abraham's response to Isaac's question] we see, as described previously, the double-movement in Abraham's soul. . . . After having made this movement [viz., the first movement, of infinite resignation], he has at every moment made the next movement, has made the movement of faith by virtue of the absurd. Thus he is not speaking an untruth, because by virtue of the absurd it is indeed possible that God could do something entirely different. (119)

Here Johannes suggests that irony is as close as the knight of faith can come to speaking in a way that can be understood by human others. According to Johannes, it is simply not possible for Abraham to *mean* to utter an untruth, for any promise can be fulfilled by and through his God. Here we should note, of course, that "not speaking an untruth" is not equivalent to "speaking the truth." Abraham's promise of divine providence may not involve him in an outright lie, but it falls well short of customary ethical standards for truth-telling. By introducing the importance of Abraham's *intentions,* that is, Johannes sets the stage for his later indictment of Abraham as duplicitous and manipulative.

Johannes's explicit reference to the "double movement" of the patriarch is nevertheless welcome. Here he finally situates the mysterious faith of Abraham in an identifiable scriptural context, which we may study in our efforts to discern the double movement it supposedly depicts. That is, we are finally in a position to test for ourselves the fit of the model that Johannes has proposed for Abraham, that of the knight of faith. Yet nothing in this scriptural passage supports Johannes's interpretation; there is no compelling evidence that either movement is on display. In fact, the scriptural passage in question would seem to militate against the interpretation that Johannes forwards, especially inasmuch as Isaac appears in this passage to accept and comprehend his father's promise. (If Isaac understood, as we have seen, then Abraham actually and non-ironically spoke. But if Abraham spoke, then he is not a knight of faith, for the knight of faith commands no access to a language with which he might communicate the nature of his religious obligations.) If we endorse Johannes's interpretation of Abraham's faith, then we must do so for reasons other than its explanatory power with respect to this particular passage.

Endorsing Johannes's interpretation would furthermore commit us to a deflationary reading of Gen. 22:8. According to Johannes, Abraham's promise has nothing to do with their plan to perform a ritual sacrifice. As a knight of faith, he might just as well have promised anything else, since everything, no matter how fabulous or counter-intuitive, could become true by virtue of the absurd. In fact, however, Abraham's promise to Isaac was in no sense absurd. Issuing it involved him in no contradictions, impossibilities, amphibolies, paradoxes, or suspensions of common sense. What Johannes neglects to mention, moreover, is that the God of Abraham actually *did* provide, as promised by Abraham on His behalf. When Abraham issued his promise to Isaac, he may not have known *how* God would provide, but simply *that* He would do so.

Johannes proceeds to offer a third reduction of Abraham's promise of divine providence: "So he does not speak an untruth, but neither does he say anything, for he is speaking in a strange tongue" (119). Like its immediate predecessor, this reduction reveals the strain placed on Johannes's interpretation by his campaign to diminish the significance of Abraham's promise of divine providence. Although Johannes does not specify what qualifies this utterance as "speaking in a strange tongue," he earlier claimed that Abraham "speaks in a divine language, he speaks in tongues" (114). We apparently are meant to understand that Abraham misaddressed Isaac, employing "divine language" in the presence of a mere mortal. Once again, however, the scriptural passage in question furnishes no evidence in support of Johannes's interpretation. If the reference to a "strange tongue" is meant to suggest that Abraham's promise was somehow incomprehensible or unintelligible to its intended recipient, then the scriptural passage actually contradicts Johannes's interpretation.

As far as we know, in fact, Isaac accepted without question Abraham's explanation at Genesis 22:8. He neither balked at resuming their journey nor challenged his father's appeal to divine providence. Having noticed, and commented upon, their failure thus far to procure a sacrificial animal, he reasonably might have protested the continuation of their journey. Alternately, he might have insisted that they secure an appropriate animal before transporting their provisions to the sacrificial summit of Mount Moriah. Especially if he had inherited from his father an inquisitive nature, Isaac might have refused the proffered explanation or demanded further clarification. But he did not. He accepted his father's explanation, and "so they went both of them together" (Gen. 22:8).

Here, it would seem, Johannes commits the fatal error of hanging his interpretation on a scriptural passage that proves intractable to his poetic wiles. If he wishes to dismiss Abraham's promise as the product of a "strange tongue," then he is obliged to account for its apparent reception by its intended recipient. Abraham's "tongue" may be "strange" to Johannes, as evidenced by his oft-avowed failure to understand the patriarch's words, but Johannes is not the intended recipient of the patriarch's promise. With respect to the exchange at Gen. 22:7–8, in fact, Johannes is nothing more than an onlooker, a voyeur, who follows the unfolding biblical drama keenly, but only from a safe distance. Johannes is apparently determined to misplace the fact that Abraham was speaking directly to Isaac, in the context of the only recorded exchange between them. As we shall see, this determination is characteristic of Johannes's general refusal to acknowledge any conversation or exchange from which he is excluded.

Section III

It is possible, of course, that Isaac failed to understand Abraham's promise of divine providence. Victimized by his father's deception, he may have been duped into agreeing to resume their journey. Rather than engage this interpretation in direct dispute, I wish simply to point out how little we know about Isaac and the content of *his* interiority. While it may be natural for readers to identify with Isaac and to sympathize with his plight, the biblical narrative does not necessarily confirm that he was a victim, much less an innocent child estranged from his inscrutable, terrifying father. In this context, it may be valuable to note how dependent Johannes is on the assumption that Isaac neither comprehends nor endorses Abraham's plan. This means, as we have seen, that Johannes must insist on Isaac's failure to understand the promise of divine providence, even though the textual evidence does not support this conclusion.

At this point in *Problema III,* Johannes's interpretation of Abraham noticeably begins to unravel.[14] The explanatory value of his guiding hypothesis—viz., that Abraham is a kind of knight of faith—decreases markedly as the story of the *Aqedah* advances toward its conclusion. And, I suspect, Johannes knows as much. Uncomfortable with the deteriorating fit of this model to the biblical narrative, Johannes has no choice, finally, but to bring *Problema III* to an artlessly premature conclusion. Rather than simply admit that his experiment has failed, however, Johannes contrives to indict Abraham on ethical grounds. While it may be the case that Abraham channels a "divine language" that is incommunicable to human others, it turns out that he *also* resorts to manipulative discourse:

> [That Abraham speaks in a strange tongue] becomes still more evident when we consider that it was Abraham himself who should sacrifice Isaac. If the task had been different ... then Abraham plainly would have been *justified* in speaking as enigmatically as he did, for then he himself could not have known what was going to happen. But given the task as assigned to Abraham, he himself has to act; consequently, he has to know in the crucial moment what

he himself will do, and consequently, he has to know that Isaac is going to be sacrificed. (119, emphasis added)

Here we note the sudden preponderance of a distinctly *ethical* language and mode of evaluation. As Johannes sheds the guise of Abraham's encomiast, he reveals himself as a crusading knight of morality. No longer detached, theatrical, coy, or rhetorical, he now recognizes ethical universality as the highest court of appeal. He carefully lays out the terms under which Abraham would have been "justified in speaking as enigmatically as he did" to Isaac, and he then encourages us to join him in concluding that these terms were not satisfied by the promise of divine providence. According to Johannes, Abraham withheld from Isaac the particulars of the intended sacrifice. He thereby hoodwinked his son, cruelly inducing in him a false sense of togetherness. Johannes thus reveals himself here as a stickler for the literal truth.[15] (As with most sticklers, moreover, he is far more eager to apply strict standards to others, allowing himself significant leeway and poetic license.) He even goes so far as to suggest what Abraham might and should have said to Isaac: "You are the one intended" (118).

While it is certainly easy to sympathize with Johannes's moral outrage, his account of Abraham's transgression remains unconvincing. First of all, he simply begs the titular question of Abraham's ethical obligations to others. Rather than demonstrate that Abraham was not ethically justified in concealing his plan, Johannes simply asserts this claim, pandering, as we have seen, to our likely sympathy with the victimized Isaac. Second, Johannes slides effortlessly from *what Abraham intended* to *what Abraham knew would transpire*. The problem with this finesse, of course, is that Abraham did not slay Isaac. It therefore makes no sense for Johannes to claim that "[Abraham] *has to know* that Isaac is going to be sacrificed" (119, emphasis added), for Abraham knew no such thing. The most that Johannes can claim here is that Abraham "had to know" that he meant to sacrifice Isaac and failed to disclose this intention to his son.

Third, supplying the particulars of the intended sacrifice would not have been sufficient to disclose the incommunicable secret that Abraham harbors. Even if Abraham had identified Isaac as the "one intended," as Johannes believes he should have done, the *why* of his faith would have remained both unsaid and unknown. Isaac might have come to know that Abraham subordinates his moral obligations to his religious obligations, but he still would not understand why Abraham does so. In fact, if Johannes means to suggest here that Abraham *deliberately* concealed the secret of his interiority, then he has actually revised his earlier characterization of the nature of Abraham's religious relationship to his God. While it may be true that Abraham concealed his intention to sacrifice Isaac, it cannot be said that he also concealed his reasons for so intending, as if some syllogism or calculus could be summoned to explain the priority he assigns to his religious obligations. If the knight of faith lacks a common language in which he might communicate to others the essence of his faith, then he is similarly unable, presumably, to communicate to *himself* the priority of his religious obligations. By virtue of this particular indictment, Johannes confirms that he has reduced Abraham's supposed religious obligation to the status of an ethical obligation, which, Johannes grimly determines, he has failed to satisfy in this case. He apparently has lost all patience with the thought-experiment of *Problema I.*

Fourth, the particulars of the intended sacrifice are not pertinent to the promise of divine providence, for God was in a position to modify them at any time (and in fact did so).[16] Had Abraham identified Isaac as the actual (as opposed to the intended) victim of the planned sacrifice, his "final word" would have been untrue.[17] What *is* pertinent is that Abraham was willing to obey his God's command to sacrifice Isaac. And although he did not say this expressly to Isaac at Gen. 22:8, we should beware of concluding that Isaac *therefore* did not know that his father was willing to sacrifice him if God so commanded. To draw this conclusion would be to repeat the signature error of Johannes's flawed meditation on Abraham—namely, to treat our own sympathetic identification with Isaac as the measure of his relationship with his father. We may wish for Abraham to have supplied Isaac with the particulars of the intended sacrifice, but we have no evidence that Isaac himself expressed (or harbored) any such wish. For all we know, in fact, Isaac may have understood perfectly well that his father was prepared to do whatever his God asked of him. As the epigraph to *Fear and Trembling* reminds us, after all, the specific content of an indirect communication between father and son may elude even those who are enlisted as its emissaries.

This reminder is timely, for it illuminates Johannes's ulterior motive in forwarding his preferred interpretations of Abraham (*qua* unethical deceiver) and Isaac (*qua* innocent victim). These interpretations are attractive to Johannes in part because they position him to pass judgment on Abraham. Here his express reason for marking Abraham's "final word" bears repeating: "But a final word by Abraham has been preserved, and insofar as I can understand the paradox, I can also understand Abraham's total presence [*totale Tilstedeværelse*] in that word (118)."[18] This passage confirms what we have come to suspect of Johannes—namely, that his interest in Abraham's "final word" has less to do with Abraham than with himself. As Johannes here admits, it is *his* understanding of Abraham that ultimately hangs in the balance.

On the face of it, this qualification is certainly fair enough. Johannes cannot be expected to defend an understanding of Abraham that outstrips his own powers of comprehension. At the same time, however, we may wonder how much Johannes has struggled to expand the horizons of his own understanding. Rather than challenge himself to comprehend the story of the *Aqedah,* Johannes instead edits this story to accommodate the limits of his understanding. While he has dared his readers to consider the possibility of a teleological suspension of the ethical, he is apparently unwilling to "go further" in his own efforts to entertain this possibility. Rather than work out his interpretation of Abraham in genuine fear and trembling, or so we may suspect, he has known all along that he can tame the unruly "paradox" and gather it into a neat, tidy bundle. Understanding Abraham, it would seem, is less important to Johannes than enjoying the experience of mastery that is involved in determining whether, and under what conditions, Abraham can be understood. The desire to contain Abraham, to master him and the paradox of his faith, thus motivates Johannes's interest in the "final word" of the patriarch. At the conclusion of *Problema* III, that is, Johannes presents himself as the measure of Abraham.[19]

This particular mode of self-presentation should give us pause, if only because Johannes has gone to such lengths to convince us that the faith of Abraham has no measure in the modern world. No poet is the equal, supposedly, of this singular heroic figure—though, as we have seen, this does not stop Johannes from auditioning vigorously for the job! That the biblical story does not end with Abraham's promise of divine providence, that Abraham speaks again, perhaps even to Isaac, is of no enduring concern to him. Here it becomes clear, in fact, that Johannes relies on the easy faith of contemporary Christian practice as a safety net, into which he may comfortably recline if the thought-experiments conducted in the *Problemata* should render him dizzy and vertiginous. But here we must ask: How seriously can Johannes possibly invest himself in these thought-experiments if he knows that at any moment he may relax into the comfort of Christian faith?

Section IV

The guise of the knight of morality,[20] which Johannes dons for supposedly rhetorical purposes in *Problema III*, turns out to be no mask at all. Despite his express fear of losing Abraham, he apparently cannot help but hold the patriarch responsible for this alleged ethical lapse. Here, whether he knows it or not, he once again registers an implicit preference for the ethical sphere of existence.[21] He does so, moreover, in such a way that reveals the allure of ethical universality, which in this case authorizes an otherwise undistinguished individual (Johannes) to stand in judgment of the great Abraham. Johannes thereby confirms what we have perhaps suspected all along—namely, that his awe and reverence before the knight of faith are mitigated by his general disapprobation for *all* suspensions of the ethical. According to Johannes, Abraham knows what he has been ordered to do, and he already knows how he will act "in the crucial moment." Otherwise, Johannes claims, "he is also very far from being Abraham, and he . . . is a man devoid of resolution who . . . for that reason always speaks in riddles" (119). Hence the need for Johannes's inventive interpretation of Abraham's "final word": Rather than reduce the patriarch to a "vacillator," a "parody of the knight of faith" (119), Johannes insists that Abraham's promise is "enigmatic" precisely because it says nothing (and in a "strange" tongue).

Let us examine more closely the either/or he presents here. If these are in fact the only two options available, then Johannes has no doubt chosen wisely. It would be far better to regard Abraham as speaking "enigmatically" than to judge him an irresolute "vacillator." Electing the latter option, as we shall see, would require Johannes to admit that the Abraham who aborts the commanded sacrifice, as recorded at Gen. 22:11, is no knight of faith, for a knight of faith would never change his mind, much less disobey his God. Here it becomes clear, moreover, that Johannes traces the greatness of Abraham to his "resolute" decision to obey the command to sacrifice Isaac. Johannes apparently means to claim that Abraham's infinite movement of resignation not only enables the second movement, that of faith, but also ensures his resoluteness for the duration of the ordeal. In that event, any doubt on his part, any change of heart experienced along the way, any alteration to (or maturation of) his relationship to his God, would smack of "vacillation," which in turn would belie his infinite movement of resignation. Inasmuch as the second movement both presupposes and builds on the first movement, an irresolute Abraham would also be a faithless Abraham.

According to Johannes, Abraham was great because he had faith. But he had faith only because he was already resolute, which Johannes understands to mean *steadfast, unyielding,* and *unchanging.* A strategic deception—not to mention a flicker of doubt, a change of heart, and a subsequent act of disobedience—would signal a lack of resolve. This is why Johannes concluded his presumptive "Eulogy" by insisting that "If Abraham had doubted as he stood there on Mount Moriah, if irresolute he had looked around . . . then . . . his return would have been a flight, his deliverance an accident, his reward disgrace, his future perhaps perdition (22)." Although the dramatic movement of the biblical narrative suggests a developmental interpretation of the story, Johannes collapses the entire ordeal into the single, defining moment in which Abraham resolved to perform the commanded sacrifice of Isaac. In this moment, Abraham became the "father of faith" and established his claim to greatness.

This may explain why *Problema III* ventures no interpretation of Abraham at the sacrificial summit of Mount Moriah, or of Abraham's response to the angel of the Lord. If Abraham had faith, and if faith constitutes itself in the double-movement that Johannes describes, then what transpired on Mount Moriah is simply irrelevant. Put somewhat differently: If what happened at the summit of Mount Moriah *is* relevant, then Abraham did not have faith and was not great. An Abraham who would disobey his God's command, for whatever reason, would be no Abraham at all. And he certainly would be no knight of faith.

Section V

Johannes's interest in preserving a resolute Abraham may help to explain why he refuses to acknowledge the final words attributed to Abraham in the story of the *Aqedah*. Later on, as Abraham draws the knife with which he intends to sacrifice Isaac (Gen. 22:10), he hears a voice, which the narrator identifies as descending from an "angel of the Lord" (Gen. 22:11). This voice calls out, "Abraham, Abraham!" (Gen. 22:11). Abraham then responds with a familiar utterance: "Here I am" (Gen. 22:11). The angel subsequently orders Abraham not to harm Isaac and to abort the commanded sacrifice (Gen. 22:12). The angel does so, moreover, by gradually assuming the first-person authority of the Lord who dispatched him. Spying a ram tangled in a nearby thicket, Abraham seizes it and presents it as a burnt offering to his God (Gen. 22:13). His final word in Chapter 22 is none other than *hineni*, the "Here I am" recorded at Gen. 22:11, which is the third and final occurrence of this defining response.

Rather than investigate this pivotal scene, Johannes steers his discussion to an unsatisfying close, hastily entering what Derrida has identified as the "evangelical" space that circumscribes the conclusion of *Problema III*.[22] Here, drawing on the Gospel of Matthew, Johannes concludes that Abraham needs no human admirers, for his God "sees in secret and recognizes distress and counts the tears and forgets nothing" (120).[23] If Abraham needs no admirers, of course, then Johannes is certainly justified in ending his encomium, which was under-motivated in any event. Indeed, Johannes ends *Problema III* by retreating to the safe harbor of the Christian Gospels.

To be sure, Johannes may have good reason to end *Problema III* as he does. He may feel, and perhaps legitimately so, that the events described in Gen. 22:9–19 have received sufficient treatment and adequate attention from other commentators. As he remarks, moreover, a preoccupation with the conclusion of the story of the *Aqedah* may distract us from the story's most essential elements: "we are curious about the result. . . . We do not want to know anything about the anxiety, the distress, the paradox. We carry on an esthetic flirtation with the result (63)." He also may feel, and perhaps legitimately so, that his express purpose in *Problema III* requires him to conclude his discussion as he does. He has conducted the thought-experiment he outlined, and he has concluded that Abraham was not ethically justified in concealing his plan from Isaac. Irony alone mitigates the immorality of the patriarch.

At the same time, however, Johannes may have other, darker reasons for steering clear of the remainder of the biblical narrative. In his "Eulogy," for example, he actually goes out of his way to divert his readers from the scene in which Abraham identifies himself to the angel. Having considered at length the immediately prior "scene," described at Gen. 22:10, where Abraham draws the knife and raises his right arm (22), Johannes abruptly announces that the biblical narrative is difficult—if not impossible—to follow beyond this point: "Anyone who looks upon this scene is paralyzed . . . [and] blinded (22)". While hyperbole is perhaps native to the genre of eulogy, this particular exaggeration faithfully reflects Johannes's wish that his readers *not* view the scene that immediately follows this one. If they were to continue any further with the biblical narrative, they might demand an explanation of why Abraham's response to the angel does not qualify as his "final word." Even more disturbing to Johannes is the possibility that they might perceive Abraham as a "vacillator."[24]

Johannes may be troubled in particular by Abraham's decision to *disobey* his God's command to sacrifice Isaac, especially insofar as this decision evinces a lack of "resolve." Although it is not customary for commentators to depict Abraham as *disobedient,*[25] this is precisely how Johannes is obliged to understand the patriarch's decision to unhand the knife and unbind his son. Other commentators are welcome to explain his termination of the sacrifice by appealing to the obvious, overriding priority of the second command. Abraham does not disobey the first command, these commentators might explain, so much as he ascertains the priority of the second command and obeys it accordingly. These commentators may proceed to insist that Abraham remains unfailingly obedient to his God, despite transferring the focus of his obedience from the first command to the second.

But Johannes does not enjoy the luxury of recourse to this familiar line of interpretation. His Abraham possesses faith "by virtue of the absurd," in open defiance of the "human calculation" that would be involved in determining the relative merit of the two commands (35). In light of his emphasis on the "resolute" Abraham, moreover, Johannes would need to explain—for *his* sake, and not merely for ours—why Abraham did not complete the commanded sacrifice. That Abraham had faith in Isaac's return is not sufficient to explain his failure to complete the sacrifice, for presumably Isaac could have been returned to him following the completion of the commanded sacrifice. If, according to Johannes, *anything* is possible for the God of Abraham, then the more impressive display of faith would have involved his cheerful anticipation of Isaac's return from the dead.[26]

It is also worth noting that the second command does not issue directly and unambiguously from the God of Abraham, but from an unseen "angel." Although the narrator of Genesis identifies the second command as issuing from an "angel of the Lord," Abraham might not have been in possession of this knowledge, much less the narrator's confidence in it. Also, the second command was issued publicly, most notably in Isaac's earshot, which marks a potentially significant deviation from the mode of address favored by his God. When God initially "put Abraham to the test," we recall, He addressed him privately and directly, making no use of intermediaries or witnesses (Gen. 22:1). As Johannes acknowledges, Abraham reasonably could have interpreted the second command as ingredient to the mysterious "test," perhaps even as an oblique incentive to expedite (rather than abort) the commanded sacrifice. For all Abraham knows, moreover, the first command remains in effect *even if* he is confident that the second command too issues from his God. It would not be out of character for the God of Abraham to issue conflicting commands. So even if Abraham *knew* that the angel spoke for his God, he could not have disobeyed the first command without becoming irresolute in the process.

That the second command contradicts the first command, thereby placing Abraham in an impossible double bind, also cannot prove decisive for Johannes, for he understands Abraham to possess faith "by virtue of the absurd." If Johannes's Abraham was not deterred by the apparent willingness of his God to renege on their founding agreement, then the issuance of a second, contradictory command should not have distracted him from his appointed task.[27] If it *did* distract him, moreover, then he was not resolute; and if he was not resolute, then he was not the Abraham whom Johannes admires.

This issue of Abraham's resolve, especially with respect to its role in securing both his faith and his greatness, is instructively addressed by Emmanuel Levinas. According to Levinas, what makes Abraham great in the story of the *Aqedah* is actually his *lack* of resolve, which enables him to respond to the victimization of his son:

> In his evocation of Abraham, [Kierkegaard] describes the encounter with God at the point where subjectivity rises to the level of the religious, that is to say, above ethics. But one could think the opposite: Abraham's attentiveness to the voice that led him back to the ethical order, in forbidding him to perform a human sacrifice, is the highest point in the drama. That he obeyed the first voice is astonishing: *that he had sufficient distance with respect to that obedience to hear the second voice—that is the essential [point].*[28]

What Levinas calls the "distance" that separated Abraham from his "obedience" is what Johannes calls the capacity to "doubt," which, according to him, would mark Abraham as a "vacillator" and cost him his claim to "greatness" (119, cf. 22). If Levinas is right, moreover, Abraham not only doubted, but also decided *on his own* to abort the commanded sacrifice. (Although the angel's salutation precedes the termination of the sacrifice, the angel's admonition follows Abraham's final words in Chapter 22: "Here I am.") And if Abraham decided on his own to abort the sacrifice, then he cannot be called "resolute." If he could disobey his God's command, for *any* reason, then he was not infinitely resigned to the loss of Isaac, which means that he was never in a position to make the (second) movement of faith. He was, in Johannes's words, a "vacillator."

The response that Johannes so studiously avoids, the final "Here I am" (Gen. 22:11), in fact announces Abraham's decision to disobey his God. In allowing himself to be interrupted by the angel's salutation, Abraham reveals what Levinas calls his *responsiveness* to the ethical claim that the angel is about to press, albeit in the form of a divine command. In responding to the angel's salutation, in announcing himself one final time in the fullness of his presence, Abraham preempts the angel's subsequent command and renders it superfluous. In responding to the angel's salutation, that is, Abraham has already suspended the commanded sacrifice of Isaac, prior to the angel's command that he do so. From this point forward, Abraham lives in a state of permanent disobedience, which is unchanged (and therefore unredeemed) by his subsequent acts of obedience. Of course, Johannes neatly avoids any consideration of this conclusion. In his "Eulogy," at the point of closest proximity to a consideration of Gen. 22:11, he asks, rhetorically, "Who strengthened Abraham's arm, who braced up his right arm so that it did not sink down powerless! (22)". While certainly of interest, these paralysis-inducing questions nevertheless serve to distract his readers from what might be regarded as the more pressing question: Who *released* his right arm and thereby terminated the sacrifice?

With the aid of Levinas, we thus see that Johannes has good reason *not* to extend *Problema III* to include an examination of the events that transpired at the sacrificial summit of Mount Moriah. Doing so would have obliged him to consider, and perhaps to admit, that the Abraham who released Isaac had either lost his faith or never possessed it in the first place. In either event, the Abraham of Gen. 22:9–19 was, on Johannes's formulation, no Abraham at all. That is, Johannes's attention to the paradox of faith simply cannot account for the Abraham who reached the sacrificial summit of Mount Moriah and disobeyed his God.

Johannes's recoil from this act of disobedience also may explain his persistence with respect to the analogy he proposes between Abraham and the deathbound Socrates, who was able to "consummate" himself "in the final moment" (117).[29] Despite declaring this analogy to be flawed, Johannes manages nonetheless to pursue it at some length:

> These brief suggestions are indeed not applicable to Abraham if one expects to be able to find by means of some analogy an appropriate final word for Abraham, but they do apply *if one perceives the necessity for Abraham to consummate himself in the final moment,* not to draw the knife silently but to have a word to say, since as the father of faith he has absolute significance oriented to the spirit. (117, emphasis added)

Why one would perceive this "necessity" is not clear, especially since doing so would commit one to the discredited view of Abraham as an "intellectual tragic hero" on the model of Socrates.[30] Yet Johannes finds this view surprisingly difficult to abandon, and it haunts him throughout the remainder of *Problema III*.

Johannes lingers over this flawed analogy, I suspect, because he needs to bring his meditation on Abraham to something resembling an appropriate close. His reconsideration of the example of Socrates provides him with the cover he needs to pull off a final sleight of hand—namely, settling (without saying so) on the discredited interpretation of Abraham's "final word" as evidence that "he consummates himself in the decisive moment" (116).[31] This unannounced interpretive decision is by no means trivial, for the remainder of *Problema III* is expressly devoted to a consideration of the "words" that enable Abraham to consummate himself and express his "total presence" (118). Despite having rejected the flawed analogy between Abraham and Socrates, Johannes pursues it nonetheless, imagining the patriarch as *something like* an intellectual tragic hero.[32] He does so, moreover, for no other reason than to conclude a meditation in which he finally takes the measure of the supposedly immeasurable Abraham. Better to shoehorn Abraham into the best (if inadequate) category available to us than to permit his terrifying faith to disturb the peace of contemporary Christendom. If Abraham is some kind of hero, after all, then Johannes may flatter himself as some kind of poet. While it may be true that "no poet can find his way to Abraham" (118), Johannes has found his way to Socrates, which, for him, is apparently close enough.

This flawed analogy is tempting to Johannes precisely because it allows him to identify Gen. 22:8 as the "moment" in which Abraham, again like Socrates, both "dies" and "triumphs over death" (117). If his Abraham is defined by the "resolute" acceptance of God's initial command, then the story of his Abraham *must* come to an end at or around Gen. 22:8. In no event should his Abraham be confused with the irresolute "vacillator" who disobeyed his God at the sacrificial summit of Mount Moriah. The symbolic "death" of Abraham, *qua* "knight of faith," thus marks the extreme to which Johannes will extend himself in his efforts to measure (and, so, to master) the patriarch. The irony, of course, is that Johannes insists on ignoring Abraham's true moment of triumph at Gen. 22:11.

Although Johannes does not admit as much, he is thus obliged to treat the story of the *Aqedah* as if it were *two* stories, featuring *two* Abrahams. The first story concerns Abraham the knight of faith, whose "final word" is recorded at Gen. 22:8. This "final word" calls to mind the "final moment" in which Socrates was able to "consummate" himself and thereby author an appropriate, if premature, gesture of farewell. The second story concerns Abraham the "vacillator," who aborts the commanded sacrifice and thereby disobeys his God. This latter story is so disconcerting to Johannes that it both inspires his ingenious interpretation of the promise of divine providence *and* impels his hasty retreat into the sanctuary of Matthew's Gospel.

Section VI

The pretext for Johannes's sudden departure from the biblical narrative may shed some light on the precise nature of his disquiet. Inasmuch as he rushes to steer the conclusion of *Problema III* into the sanctuary of the all-seeing, tear-counting, unforgetting God described in Matthew's Gospel, it may be the case that Johannes recoils from the prospect of a confrontation with *another* God, perhaps even a God who sees selectively, ignores human suffering, and forgets His past agreements. Just such a God, Johannes may have surmised, presided over the events that unfolded on the sacrificial summit of Mount Moriah. Seeing only parts of the whole, unmoved by the suffering of Isaac and Sarah, oblivious to His original promise to Abraham, the God of Genesis 22 bade Abraham to perform a horrifying "teleological suspension of the ethical."

Even more frightening to Johannes is the demand made of Abraham atop Mount Moriah: to disobey his God by choosing between two competing commands of divine provenance. The Abraham who suspends the commanded sacrifice is a (literal) heretic, reliant on nothing more substantial than his own choice, and obliged by his situation to become self-reliant. Although he will obey his God in either event, he must also take full responsibility for his attendant act of disobedience. As I have suggested, this taking of responsibility—not only for his disobedience but for the priority he thereby assigns to his ethical obligation to Isaac—is avowed in the utterance that Johannes so studiously avoids: "Here I am."

As troubled as he is by Abraham's irresolute act of disobedience, that is, Johannes is horrified by the prospect of a God who would maneuver Abraham into such a position. The moral outrage that fuels Johannes's reaction to Abraham's duplicitous promise is perhaps directed more properly at the God of Abraham, who placed his favorite in an impossible situation. The God of Genesis 22 obliged Abraham to yield his resolve and to take responsibility for his ensuing act of disobedience. It is precisely this kind of unfettered responsibility that Johannes most fears, and which impels his retreat into the security of the ethical universal. Put quite simply, Johannes wants no part of the spiritual awakening and moral growth that I have attributed to the disobedient Abraham. Rather than attend to his own development, as we have seen, he is content to mock his dispirited contemporaries, exaggerating thereby the slight superiority he enjoys over them.

This is not to suggest, of course, that Johannes is justified either in his fear of the God of Abraham, or in his preference for the God of the Christian Gospels.[33] Indeed, both his fear and his preference trade on familiar stereotypes, which express stock prejudices about Judaism and Christianity. He may need to see the God of Abraham as (comparatively) neglectful and arbitrary, but this interpretation is not positively supported by the biblical narrative. The truth of the matter is that he does not know why the God of Abraham placed his favorite in such an unusual, and frightening, position. And although Abraham himself is apparently untroubled by the fluid nature of his relationship to his God, Johannes cannot endure the asymmetry that informs this relationship. That the God of Abraham remains mysterious and unknown, refusing to reveal Himself even to His favorite, is apparently too much for Johannes to bear.

Johannes's recoil from this uncertainty may account for his reluctance to consider the role of Abraham's God in arranging the particular result that is described at Gen. 22:11–14. Especially surprising in this respect is his failure to acknowledge that Abraham's "final word," the promise of divine providence, was actually fulfilled at the sacrificial summit of Mount Moriah. The God of Abraham *did* provide, as Abraham had promised Isaac. He provided the unlucky ram, as even the faithless can glean from the letter of the scriptural passage. But the God of Abraham also provided the larger context, in which the presence of the ram became both meaningful and propitious. He provided the (eventually) helpless victim, Isaac, whose willing participation in his victimization may have triggered a moral awakening in his father. He provided the length and duration of their journey, over the course of which Abraham came to see his son as a spiritual party to the covenant. He provided the pretext for their journey, by dint of a command that Abraham would learn to disobey. He provided the drama of the narrative, by awarding a long-awaited son to the aged and supposedly barren couple, a son through whom the promise of Canaan would be fulfilled. And, finally, he provided the covenant itself, an agreement that Abraham could make only on the unstated condition that he remake himself in its image.

The God of Abraham may have come through in the end, but His first command to Abraham created an unacceptable degree of uncertainty and insecurity. The God of Abraham presides over an unappealingly chaotic cosmos, in which divine commands circulate arbitrarily and unethically. It is not enough, apparently, that the God of Abraham provided as promised. He needs to have done so in a gentler, more direct, less troubling way. For Johannes, and presumably for all knights of morality, all is not well that merely ends well.

Conclusion

Johannes succeeds in approaching the faith of Abraham, but only on the assumption that faith constitutes itself as a reason-defying paradox. As described by Johannes, this paradox obliges us to view the demands of religion and ethics as incommensurate and irreconcilable.

For much of the story of the *Aqedah,* this guiding assumption bears up surprisingly well. Johannes's appeal to the paradox of faith supports a compelling account of the greatness of Abraham, especially as this greatness is expressed in his willing reception of the command to sacrifice Isaac. In the end, however, Johannes's attention to the paradoxical nature of faith is as limiting as it is instructive. If constituted exclusively as a paradox, after all, faith forever eludes the grasp of reason and ultimately frustrates all efforts to understand Abraham. This is why Johannes retreats so regularly to the role of aspiring encomiast: The paradox of Abraham's faith may defy the understanding, but it invites our admiration. As I have suggested, however, Johannes also takes comfort in his inability to understand the faith of Abraham. As we have seen, the unavailability of Abraham frees him to locate the limitations of his own spiritual quest external to his striving. In this respect, a "monstrous paradox" perfectly fits his needs. Having brought us "face to face with the paradox" (113), he cannot "go further," and it is not his fault that he cannot.

This does not mean, however, that no distance remains to be traveled in the quest to understand the faith of Abraham. Nor does it mean that all aspiring pilgrims should similarly limit their expectations, even if Johannes is clearly invested in escorting us to this conclusion. That Johannes can go no further tells us a great deal about him, but virtually nothing about the faith of Abraham, especially as this faith is expressed in his decision to disobey the original command. At this point, in fact, Johannes's meditation on Abraham collides with the personal mythology of self-limitation that has been lurking until now in the background of his narrative. Like the unnamed pilgrim invoked in the *Exordium,* Johannes has been able to progress in his quest only because it has been limited, artificially, from the outset.[34] As it turns out, in fact, he was never in any real danger of breaking through the paradox and confronting the faith of Abraham.[35] As we are now in a position to realize, he set out on this quest, again following in the footsteps of the unnamed pilgrim, only on the condition that the faith of Abraham would remain locked forever within the paradox. He thus pursues his quest only until the faith of Abraham threatens to escape the protective shroud of the paradox, at which point he relaxes into the security of Matthew's Gospel. As we have seen, his meditation reaches this point as he considers the exchange recorded at Gen. 22 7–8, wherein he wishfully locates the "final word" of the patriarch.

In this respect, Johannes is not unlike the servants whom Abraham strands at the foot of Mount Moriah (Gen. 22:5). He may be able to accompany Abraham and Isaac on their journey, but he cannot bear to behold the events that transpired at the sacrificial summit of Mount Moriah. Excluded from the intensity of the bond that sustains father and son as they journey onward "together," Johannes can only speculate on the nature of their relationship and of the promise that cements it. Unlike the servants, though, Johannes is under no external order to desist from continuing. He effectively strands himself, seemingly in reach of the supposed goal of his quest, and for no other reason than his self-serving experience of having reached an external limit. Here too he calls to mind the unnamed pilgrim, whose imaginative journeys to Mount Moriah both end prematurely and authorize the (unearned) conclusion that "no one can understand Abraham." Just as this pilgrim returns from his imaginative journeys before ever reaching Mount Moriah, so Johannes departs from the biblical narrative before hearing Abraham's final word.

Johannes's resemblance to the unnamed pilgrim may help to explain his premature departure from the biblical narrative. Although he would never admit as much, he may need to end *Problema III* precisely as he does—viz., by misidentifying Abraham's "final word"—simply because he senses the fragility of his interpretation and the potentially disruptive consequences of extending it any further. Perhaps he has simply gone as far as possible with the limited interpretive resources at his disposal. This may be his way of giving up while saving face, of preferring a premature conclusion to a disastrous one. In fairness to Johannes, he has warned us all along that he does not understand Abraham. If we have wished not to believe him, then much of the blame rests with us.

Although he does not say so, his retreat to the shelter of Christian evangelism may be his way of acknowledging that he can lead us no further, that the events that transpire atop Mount Moriah truly lie beyond his understanding. Like Dante's Vergil, he may be a guide of genuine, but limited, assistance to struggling wayfarers. If we are to complete our pilgrimage to Mount Moriah, then we must either acquire a new guide or declare our independence from the need for guides. Regardless of which strategy we choose, we can hardly do better than to follow the lead of Abraham himself, especially as he gathers himself in his defining moment of disobedience: "Here I am."

15.
Faith as Eschatological Trust in *Fear and Trembling*

John J. Davenport

Introduction: The Problem

It is well known that Søren Kierkegaard's *Fear and Trembling*,[1] which he attributed to the pseudonym Johannes de Silentio,[2] is about the complex relation between the 'stages' of existence that he calls "the ethical" (characterized by moral duties and virtues) and *the religious* (or 'faith'). Despite much scholarly attention, deep disagreement remains about how these life-views or existential stages are distinguished and related, and in particular about how Kierkegaard understands the transition from the ethical to the religious. In *Fear and Trembling*, this is the movement from the "Knight of Infinite Resignation," who exemplifies a kind of limiting point within the ethical, to the "Knight of Faith" instantiated by Abraham in the story of the "Binding of Isaac" (which Rabbinic literature calls the *Akedah*).[3]

One reading of this transition from ethical resignation to religious faith situates it within a broader irrationalist interpretation of Kierkegaard's stages. In *After Virtue*, Alasdair MacIntyre argues that Kierkegaard's portrayal of ethical choice in *Either/Or* replaces the objective authority of moral virtues and duties with the arbitrary fiat of the individual will that simply chooses to acknowledge moral obligation.[4] MacIntyre also argues that in *Philosophical Fragments*, Kierkegaard invokes radical and ultimate choice to explain how one becomes a Christian;[5] similarly, he says that in *Fear and Trembling* Kierkegaard uses Abraham to show that faith requires a criterionless leap.[6] Thus, according to MacIntyre, Kierkegaard holds that faith is total submission to "the arbitrary fiats of a cosmic despot" who can make anything right by commanding it, even murder—a God who resembles Blake's "Nobodaddy."[7]

In response to MacIntyre, I have argued that the process of "choice" by which one moves from aesthetic to ethical orientations or ways of life consists in personal appropriation of ethical standards through identity-defining commitments that depend on already-recognized ethical ideals; the individual who "chooses" the ethical does not posit or create the authority of ethical norms. Since *Kierkegaard After MacIntyre,* few scholars still hold that *Either/Or* portrays the movement from the aesthetic to the ethical stage as an arbitrary radical choice; but proto-Sartrean readings of Kierkegaardian faith remain popular. In this essay I extend my anti-irrationalist interpretation of the ethical to Kierkegaardian faith. I hold that understanding "the religious" in all of Kierkegaard's thought depends on grasping the central idea in *Fear and Trembling,* without which the *Fragments* and the *Postscript* cannot be properly interpreted (though some think we can work *backward* from these later texts to a reading of *Fear and Trembling*).[8] However, as we will see, there are two quite different approaches to showing that the "teleological suspension of the ethical" in Silentio's *Akedah* is not simply irrational, and I will develop the alternative already outlined in Alastair Hannay's book *Kierkegaard* and Edward Mooney's classic commentary on *Fear and Trembling,*[9] as well as in his reading of *Repetition.*

In his critique of *Fear and Trembling,* MacIntyre has hardly been alone. For at least half a century since Kierkegaard got into English (as Walter Lowrie put it), undergraduates have been taught that *Fear and Trembling* presents *faith* as rejecting all natural knowledge and reason in favor of divine commands that can have any content or abrogate any ethical principle with purported universal application. The Danish existentialist, they were told, recommends total obedience to a God who demands our allegiance to his own inscrutable authority. This venerable tradition of portraying Kierkegaard as an absolute theological voluntarist is well represented by Brand Blanshard, who complains that in *Fear and Trembling,* religious obligation transcends Kantian universal judgment: it may be our duty "to trample down the affections of natural man and all his nicely calculated goods and evils."[10] In acting to sacrifice Isaac, Blanshard says, the only motive Abraham could have is "the command from on high to kill," since "every human consideration" could only provide motives not to commit such a heinous crime.[11] So Abraham "was called upon to renounce the moral for the religious."[12]

It is hard to overstate the violence done by this popular portrayal, which reduces Kierkegaardian faith to blind fanaticism.[13] The situation is not helped by some postmodern fans of *Fear and Trembling* who embrace this misreading and celebrate the alleged irrationalism of Kierkegaardian faith as an early forerunner of anti-universalist positions in contemporary alterity ethics. John Caputo, for instance, tells us that "Abraham is the father of all those who dare to raise their voice against ethics," meaning: against any *theory* of moral norms involving rational grounds and universalizability tests. So understood, Abraham is not really rejecting the kind of infinite responsibility for singular others that Levinas proposes; he is only "suspending the fine name of universality in the name of heterogeneity and incommensurability."[14] Thus Kierkegaard, or at least Silentio, is used to support a radically antitheoretical version of agapic ethics.

But the teleological suspension of the ethical in *Fear and Trembling* is not primarily about substituting an ethics of alterity, or any other ethics, for a rationalist ethics of universal norms or natural law. Both Kierkegaard's traditional knockers and his postmodern boosters misconstrue the function of divine commands in Kierkegaard's conception of religion and in Silentio's version of the *Akedah* in particular. They entirely obscure the main point of *Fear and Trembling,* which is to present the essence of "faith" as *eschatological* trust. As will become clear, I use "eschatology" here in a broad sense that abstracts from the differences among religious creeds concerning salvation, "last things," or the hereafter. Drawing on a comparative analysis of eschatological hope as the distinguishing feature of revealed religion in general,[15] my inclusive sense of eschatological hope does not 'Christianize' Abraham, nor take his significance in *Fear and Trembling* to be only an anagogical anticipation of Christian religiousness.

This is important, because contemporary Jewish commentators on the *Akedah* narrative often assume that Kierkegaard is defending the strongest kind of theological voluntarism, which they react against.[16] For example, Louis Jacobs notes Milton Steinberg's "lethal attack on the Danish thinker's interpretation of the *Akedah*," in which "Steinberg roundly declares that there is nothing in Judaism to correspond to Kierkegaard's teleological suspension of the ethical."[17] Jacobs himself argues that there are "three different attitudes" to the *Akedah* in Jewish thought: the first emphasizing the "happy ending," the second emphasizing the "original command," and the third dwelling on both these aspects.[18] He aligns the teaching of *Fear and Trembling* with the second of these three approaches:

> This view, very close to Kierkegaard's attitude, can imagine God commanding Abraham to slay his son. True, the order is revoked at the last moment, but the point has been made, nonetheless, that, in Kierkegaard's terminology, there can be, so far as the "knight of faith" is concerned, a "teleological suspension of the ethical."[19]

In this passage Jacobs clearly follows the prevailing view that the "teleological suspension" in the first *Problema* refers to *overriding* objective ethical norms for the sake of obedience to singular divine commands as the absolute telos. On this reading, obedience to God as the highest end is totally independent of the surprising reversal when God stops Abraham just as he raises the knife; this reprieve is reduced to a pleasant afterthought that plays no essential role in the structure of faith for Kierkegaard.[20]

On the contrary, I argue that Kierkegaard meant to present the *Akedah* according to the first of Jacobs's three attitudes, emphasizing that Abraham's salvation depends on Isaac being spared. In my view, Silentio's understanding of "faith" does *not* include the belief that God's commanding X makes X right, no matter what X is—a belief that is incompatible with most Jewish readings of Genesis and probably with Kierkegaard's own teaching in *Works of Love* that love must have outward expressions.[21] Rather, the telos toward which the ethical is suspended in Kierkegaardian faith is the *promised eschatological outcome* in which the highest ethical norms will be fulfilled by an Absolute power that transcends human capacities and promises to *actualize* goods otherwise accessible to human beings only as ideal forms in Platonic eternity. At the beginning of *Problema* I, Silentio clearly identifies a person's highest telos with his "eternal salvation" (54), which is an eschatological concept, and his goal is to argue that such an eschatological telos cannot be reduced to "the ethical," as Hegel's system implies.

As we will see, this eschatological reading retains an important role for divine commands. But if absolute reliance on God's eschatological promise is the essence of faith, then faith is possible only in relation to ethical ideals that are *not rejected* in favor of some other standard, but rather *preserved* within and complemented by religious hope. The argument for this interpretation begins with the eschatological element in the *Akedah* narrative. In section III, it is followed by a detailed critique of "higher-ethical" interpretations of Kierkegaardian faith, which are currently the most well-known and respected ways of answering the irrationalist charge. In section IV, the problems found in these readings are avoided by the eschatological explanation of the "teleological suspension" and the "absolute relation to the absolute." This alternative account depends on a clear understanding of "infinite resignation," on which there is even more serious confusion in recent scholarship, as explained in section V. The essay concludes with abbreviated remarks on the motivational and epistemic role of divine commands in existential faith.

The Absurd, Eschatological Possibility, and Eucatastrophe

Expectancy

In his first edifying discourse on "The Expectancy of Faith," Kierkegaard argues (in his own name) that faith as the highest good is a kind of "expectancy" employing our innate capacity to find meaning in the *future*. In particular, faith requires that we "conquer" the future.[22] But this seems impossible because "the future is everything," and in its manifoldness of open possibilities, "the future is not a particular, but the whole." Moreover, since the future borrows its meanings in part from the being who would conquer it, it cannot be conquered by her predictions, since "fear accompanies guessing, anxiety conjecture, and uneasiness [accompanies] inference."[23] Yet despite the apparent impossibility of calculating the future, "by the eternal, one can conquer the future, because the eternal is the ground of the future." It is in relation to the eternal, therefore, that faith is defined:

> What, then, is the eternal power in a human being? It is faith. What is the expectancy of faith? Victory—or, as Scripture so earnestly and so movingly teaches us, that all things must serve for good those who love God. But an expectancy of the future that expects victory—this has indeed conquered the future.[24]

Expectancy, then, is hopeful trust in a kind of "victory." In a later edifying discourse on "Patience in Expectancy," Kierkegaard clarifies that religious expectancy is not hope for this or that contingent particular fortune, but rather a lifelong trust in "the eternal, which is waiting every moment and at the end of time."[25] In short, the expectancy of faith is *eschatological,* in the broad sense of believing in the final vindication of ethical goodness by divine power and intervention. Different historical religions teach hope for different types of ultimate salvation: for example, individual escape from time via death without reincarnation (Nirvana), or a cosmic conclusion of time as a whole (returning us to a timeless/eternal state), or a final renewal and perfection of the physical cosmos itself, beginning a new temporal series.[26] In the latter forms, eschatological faith looks forward to a time when ethical ideals will be realized in the concrete reality of the created universe. In Kierkegaardian terms, we might call this a kind of synthesis of the ethical and the aesthetic, since it is imagined either as occurring in time or at the beginning of a *new time.*[27]

"Trusting expectancy" is also how Abraham's faith in God's promise is described (19). Yet in Christian, Islamic, or Norse contexts, "eschatology" is associated with last battles and final judgment, whereas God's promise to Abraham (before Isaac is born) is not that he will be judged and will enter heaven or that the world will be renewed in a cosmic apocalypse. Thus, to recognize the eschatological significance of the *Akedah,* we have to consider the diverse forms of eschatological victory taught in world religions and the general structure of eschatological hope underlying all these forms: namely, trust in the ultimate accomplishment of the Good by divine power. Kierkegaard sees that the story in Genesis fits this general pattern: God's promise to Abraham is "that in his seed all the generations of the earth would be blessed" (17). Through his son, Abraham will become the father of a great nation, which will bring knowledge of the true God to all peoples. The fulfillment of this promise begins in the miracle of Isaac's birth, and it waits in the background when God *seems* to contradict himself by commanding Abraham to sacrifice Isaac. This divine promise is the reason why

During all this time he had faith, he had faith that God would not demand Isaac of him, and yet he was willing to sacrifice him if it was demanded. He had faith by virtue of the absurd, for human calculation was out of the question. . . . He climbed the mountain, and even in the moment when the knife gleamed, he had faith—that God would not require Isaac. No doubt he was surprised at the outcome, but through a double-movement, he had attained his first condition. (35–36)

This is the most important passage in *Fear and Trembling:* it shows that Abraham's "faith" *consists in* his firm conviction that God's revealed promise will be fulfilled: even if Isaac is sacrificed, somehow he will still live and have children leading to a great nation chosen for God's plan.[28] As Silentio says, Abraham's faith does not depend on any calculation of *how* this could be; he is hardly expecting a ram to be substituted for Isaac at the last moment. Rather, even if he had killed Isaac on Mount Moriah, Abraham would still have trusted that what God promised would somehow *come true in time:* "He did not have faith that he would be blessed in a future life, but that he would be blessed here in the world. God could give him a new Isaac, could restore to life the one sacrificed. He had faith by virtue of the absurd, for all human calculation ceased long ago" (36). Because of his faith in God's original promise to him, Abraham does not believe that sacrificing Isaac on Mount Moriah will permanently end Isaac's life in this world. This clearly entails that Abraham believes he can sacrifice Isaac *without murdering him.*[29] This paradox depends on trust that God's promise is true, *even* when God's own later command mysteriously tempts him to doubt it. Silentio's efforts to distinguish Abraham from various inferior substitutes in other possible versions of the story are designed precisely to clarify this point (10–14).

The Structure of Eschatological Possibility

Kierkegaard recognizes that even though the content of Abraham's faith (the promise in which he believes) does not refer to a new life in a world to come, it performs the same eschatological function that faith in salvation beyond death does for Christians. These faiths share a compound intentional content, which has two main parts:

(a) The future state, ultimate outcome, or final end is *a victory of the good,* an actualization in finite/temporal existence of the infinite/eternal ideal; the created order of existence converges with what ethically ought to be.

Silentio calls this upshot-point "the fullness of time" (18), and the "fulfillment of faith" in the divine promise (19).[30]

(b) (1) Given various kinds of obstacles in their way, the relevant human agents can see no way of bringing about this victory by their own powers.

(2) Nevertheless, it *is* possible in an incalculable way by divine power, by 'miracle' transcending any rational prediction.[31]

Hannay grasps the negative half (b1) of this second condition in his explanation of "the absurd," which "means not 'logically impossible' but something like 'humanly impossible.'"[32] The other half (b2) is the positive content of being 'divinely possible.' This idea is emphasized throughout all Kierkegaard's later works, as in the discourses on expectancy. For example, in *Sickness unto Death*, Anti-Climacus argues that "authentic hope" is not based on human powers, but rather on the idea "that with God, everything is possible."[33] Thus the element of radical surprise, even for the faithful agent who believes that in the fullness of time, ethical victory will come true. As Anti-Climacus puts it, "unexpectedly, miraculously, divinely, help does come."[34]

Both conditions (a) and (b) are clarified in the long and justly famous analogy between Abraham and the "young lad who falls in love with a princess" (41). Although the lad's passion could be read as simply aesthetic, I read it in light of Judge William's treatment of marriage in *Either/Or II* as a social role exhibiting both proto-virtues of resolution and virtues of love. In *Fear and Trembling*, the young man's love is more than merely erotic: it becomes "the entire substance of his life" (41), a passion that he wholeheartedly endorses with all his will, his central self-defining commitment. This makes it a good analog for Abraham's parental love for Isaac, which is both a resolute volitional commitment and a fulfillment of the universal moral norm that "the father shall love the son more than himself" (57). Similarly, while God's perilous test makes it "humanly" impossible (in Hannay's sense) for Abraham to keep Isaac, society and circumstance make it "humanly" impossible for the young lad to marry his princess: "the relation is such that it cannot possibly be realized [by the agent's power], cannot possibly be translated from ideality to reality" (41). In my definition above, this translation of the ethical ideal into reality is first feature (a) of eschatological outcomes; the second feature (b) is that this ethical victory in the "fullness of time" is possible only by divine intervention. We see this in the knight of faith's response to the apparent hopelessness (by any human standard) of his romantic quest:

> [H]e says: Nevertheless I have faith that I will get her—that is, by virtue of the absurd, by virtue of the fact that for God, all things are possible. The absurd does not belong to the differences that lie within the proper domain of the understanding. It is not identical with the improbable, the unexpected, the unforeseen. The moment the knight executed the act of resignation, he was convinced of the impossibility, humanly speaking (46).

These qualifiers make clear that a special kind of possibility is at issue, a type of modality that makes direct reference to God as its sole source: thus trust in such a possibility necessarily involves a *relationship to the Absolute* that is its ground. For the knight of resignation by himself, marrying the princess remains accessible only in the "infinite" or atemporal senses of being logically possible and ethically necessary or ideal. Resignation stops with this *ersatz* state of affairs in the eternal realm, whereas the knight of faith embraces an *additional* kind of possibility, namely, that marrying the princess could *actually be accomplished* in future time through the unconjurable creative power of God. Thus possibility "by virtue of the absurd" refers precisely to (a) ethical victory in the fullness of time, (b) achievable only by divine action in fulfillment of a covenant or promise. These are the characteristics of eschatological possibility, as I defined it above. Thus "absurd" means 'possible only in the eschatological sense.' Given its direct reference to a divine truth-maker, the only basis for reliance on such an eschatological possibility is an experience accepted as *revelation.* I will call this kind of revelation, which by definition transcends any conclusion derivable from natural reason, an *eschatological promise.*

Again, I recognize that getting Isaac back may not sound like salvation, beatific visions, final judgment, or related concepts that Christians associate with "eschatology." Moreover, Kierkegaard's little fairy tale about the young lad and his princess may seem to have even less to do with the promise that *in the end,* the Kingdom will come, the world will be renewed (and for Christians, souls redeemed from sin will live again in resurrected bodies). Yet Silentio clearly states that in this tale, marrying the princess is an "absurd" possibility—the very term chosen to indicate how eschatological possibility must appear to those without faith. To understand why the young lad's hope is like eschatological trust, we have to *extend* the motif referred to by the phrase, "in the end," to any narrative turning point with the qualities (a) and (b) above. In other words, when a story ends with an ethical victory made possible only by grace, that story has an eschatological quality: it repeats the pattern that distinguishes all eschatological narratives. In this broad sense, then, mythological stories and fairy tales often have eschatological overtones.

Tolkien on Eucataſtrophe

We can illuminate this point by turning briefly to J. R. R. Tolkien, the twentieth-century author of the *Lord of the Rings,* in whom Kierkegaard would have found a kindred spirit. In his highly significant essay "On Fairy-Stories,"[35] which philosophers of religion have unfortunately ignored, Tolkien argues that among many requirements for a good fairy tale, the most important is a distinctive sort of "happy ending" that (even for adult readers who know the genre) provokes genuine surprise, unexpected joy, and a poignant sense of gratitude. The special kind of happy ending that marks genuine fairy stories is not *ressentiment*-filled revenge nor spiteful triumph, but rather a miraculous reprieve, beyond all hope, in the midst of apparent disaster. Tolkien describes this kind of happy ending as a "eucatastrophe":

Tragedy is the true form of Drama, its highest function; but the opposite is true of Fairy-stories. Since we do not appear to possess a word that expresses this opposite, I will call it *Eucatastrophe*. The *eucatastrophic* tale is the true form of fairy-tale, and its highest function.

The consolation of fairy-stories, the joy of the happy ending: or more correctly, of the good catastrophe, the sudden joyous 'turn' (for there is no true end to any fairy-tale): this joy, which is one of the things which fairy-stories can produce supremely well, is not essentially 'escapist' or 'fugitive'. In its fairy-tale or otherworld setting, it is a sudden and miraculous grace, never to be counted on to recur. It does not deny the existence of *dyscatastrophe,* of sorrow and failure: the possibility of these is necessary to the joy of deliverance; it denies (in the face of much evidence, if you will), universal final defeat, and in so far is *evangelium,* giving a fleeting glimpse of Joy, Joy beyond the walls of the world, poignant as grief.[36]

The sudden 'turning' or unexpected deliverance in a eucatastrophic happy ending suggests the working of a hidden power that makes possible an indispensable good that no human agency could bring about. Thus the eucatastrophic 'turn' in a good fairy story gets its poignance from its indirect *eschatological significance.* In a narrative like *Gawain and the Green Knight* or the *Lord of the Rings,* when Gawain is spared or Gollum falls in the fire with the One Ring, we sense the hand of the divine, although no angel appears to announce the divine will.

It is easy to see that Kierkegaard's tale of the young lad in love would count as a fairy story in Tolkien's sense if, for example, the lad were suddenly discovered to be a prince and brought to court to marry his princess. A knight of faith trusts precisely in such a eucatastrophe, by virtue of the absurd: "Nevertheless . . . I will get her" (46). Tolkien suggests that the 'turning' moment of grace in a good fairy tale is experienced as poignant because it includes a double-movement: tragic recognition of the evil and imperfection of our world is consoled in a joy that transcends the sorrow of vice and finitude. In this sense Tolkien says, "The Gospels contain a fairy-story, or a story of a larger kind which embraces the essence of all fairy-stories." For Tolkien regards the Resurrection as the paradigm of all eucatastrophes.[37] Similarly, Kierkegaard regards the Incarnation of the God-Man as the eucatastrophic fulfillment of prophecy: "Then came the fullness of time: the expected one, whom the kings from the east came to worship, was born, even though he was born in an inn and laid in a manger."[38] This birth is the fulfillment of faith for Anna, the expectant witness in whom the faith of the patriarchs is represented at the Temple.[39]

But there are two important differences between fairy tales in Tolkien's sense and religious narratives: in the latter, (1) the eucatastrophe occurs or will occur in *primary reality*—in our world—rather than in the 'subcreated' fantasy world, and (2) the eucatastrophe fulfills a promise that comes directly from God or His holy agents.[40] Thus a religious narrative has *direct* eschatological significance: the good to come in "the fullness of time" is *promised* in revelation and embraced by the faithful servant as ultimate assurance of life's meaning, the foundation of the trust that makes continued ethical striving possible without despair. In a fairy tale, the possibility of eschatological hope is only hinted indirectly in the eucatastrophe.

Just as Tolkien's definition of a fairy story applies to Silentio's tale of the young lad, my definition of an eschatological narrative (the religious analogue of a fairy story) applies to the *Akedah* as portrayed in *Fear and Trembling*. In this story of Abraham, the minor eucatastrophe of Isaac's conception and birth is followed in time by the major eucatastrophe: God sends His angel to stay Abraham's hand as he raises the knife, and then He sends the ram to replace Isaac (and along with this ram, implicitly, the message that human sacrifice is now forever forbidden). This emancipation is both a stunning vindication of ethical ideals and an astonishing reprieve—a miraculous "turn" that is completely unanticipatable by any human calculation. Isaac is spared, passed over, much as the nation he fathers is later preserved in the great Passover and the eucatastrophe at the Red Sea in Exodus. In such moments of extraordinary gratitude, we have the feeling of being touched directly by divine love, of having our deepest hopes requited by grace.[41]

Existential Faith

Thus the emancipation of Isaac, rather than the binding of Isaac, is the key to the story in Silentio's account. "Faith" in Kierkegaard's special sense can be defined as trust in an eschatological promise whose fulfillment will be an *ethical* eucatastrophe. This fits well with Kierkegaard's discourses on the expectancy of faith: the faithful agent depends on a possibility of a *new kind,* entirely different from the types of possibilities pursued in unsuccessful attempts to master the future. Likewise, in his "Eulogy on Abraham," Silentio tells us that Abraham's greatness can be measured by his *"expectancy"*: "One became great by expecting the possible, another by expecting the eternal; but he who expected the impossible became the greatest of all" (16). As we saw earlier, the "impossible" here does not mean the logically or nomically impossible, but rather that which cannot be brought about by the protagonist's agency, which is also the meaning of "the absurd." Silentio ends his eulogy by suggesting that "If Abraham had doubted as he stood there on Mount Moriah" and had been given the ram *before* he drew the knife, then his "deliverance" would have been an accident (22). He would have failed to conquer the future with the only thing that can conquer it: that is, faith in "the absurd"[42]—which in his case means that Isaac would endure to father a great nation even though he has to be sacrificed.

Thus Edward Mooney was exactly right that "Unlike the knight of resignation, the faithful knight embraces the hopeful trusting expectation that Isaac will be restored."[43] The faith of Abraham does not consist in rejecting ethics but in receiving "Isaac and the universal back."[44] In terms remarkably similar to Tolkien's, Mooney's describes this as a complex "redeeming joy" that retains within it the earlier grief of resignation.[45] The faithful agent goes through the painful loss of reliance on his own powers or "propriety claims" over the object of his devotion, yet maintains his care for the object in readiness to receive it back from God.[46] This also implies, as Hannay says, that "faith" in Kierkegaard's sense is much more than mere belief in the existence of God, of which knights of infinite resignation are also capable: faith is trust that the ethically ideal outcome "is possible even if humanly it is not possible."[47] As a kind of trust, faith is a practical rather than merely doxastic attitude; the agent does not simply assert the ideas expressed in (a) and (b) as propositions, but stakes the meaning of his life on them.

A Critique of Three Higher-Ethics Interpretations of the Teleological Suspension

As these comparisons suggest, my eschatological reading of *Fear and Trembling* clarifies and supports ideas concerning Kierkegaardian faith already proposed by others, including not only Mooney and Hannay, but also C. Stephen Evans, Ronald Green, John Lippitt, and John Whittaker, who have all critiqued irrationalist readings of *Fear and Trembling*. Hannay argues that the telos of Abraham's faith is a resolution that will restore ethically right relationships within the world of finitude: "the faith he is to prove is that, *in the end,* he will not be deprived of Isaac even if he carries out God's command to kill him."[48] Abraham's motive depends on his reliance on such a miraculous reprieve beyond mortal hope (based on human powers), a reprieve that is impossible by our agency, yet *eschatologically possible*. This is an anticipated apocalyptic turning *within history,* not merely in the next life or the cosmic end of time: for, as Hannay says, "'in the end' does not include 'in the hereafter'" for Abraham.[49] Whittaker agrees: "Kierkegaard makes it clear that Abraham's faith does not consist in the willingness to sacrifice Isaac, but in the belief that he will *somehow* get Isaac back."[50]

What distinguishes the *Akedah* from other eschatological stories is the unusual nature of the element that makes fulfillment of the divine promise absurd, or inaccessible to human power and reason. All eschatological and eucatastrophic narratives have at least one such element, which we may call *the obstacle* that the relevant human agents lack the power to overcome. This element is part of condition (a) above, and it is the reason for resignation. In fairy tales, the obstacle usually consists in some set of natural or social circumstances that place the goal out of reach. In Hindu stories, the obstacle may be the temporal world understood as *samsara* or the world of appearances. In Christianity, the primary obstacle may be *sin* or the will's inability to free itself from sin. But in the *Akedah,* the obstacle that makes it humanly impossible to keep Isaac and to save Isaac's posterity is none other than *God's own command* to sacrifice Isaac. This is why in his journals, Kierkegaard points out that the terrifying element of Abraham's predicament is "that it is not a collision between God's command and man's command, but between God's command and God's command."[51] For God also commands Abraham to love Isaac and to trust in His original promise; so demanding Isaac's life appears as an obstacle both to his human duty and to his reliance on God's promise that a holy nation of descendants will come from Isaac.

Three Versions of Higher Ethics

This special complication in Abraham's case is the root of irrationalist misreadings of *Fear and Trembling*: they focus primarily on *the obstacle* and assume that accepting or bowing to this obstacle is what Kierkegaard means by faith. Thus they take "faith" in *Problema* I to mean that Abraham puts aside his *lower* duty to Isaac (or to human laws) in order to fulfill his *higher* duty to obey God's command, which they usually assume is identical with the "Absolute Duty to God" discussed in *Problema* II (70). According to standard irrationalist readings like MacIntyre's or Blanshard's, the revealed ethical calling that trumps secular or humanistic ethics in the "teleological suspension" is what I will call "Strong Divine Command" ethics (SDC): God's *power* or status as creator is the sole ontological source of right or moral obligation. According to this kind of absolute theological voluntarism, God's commanding X is necessary and sufficient for X to be obligatory, and God can command anything (even murder).

SDC must be distinguished from two other ways of construing the "teleological suspension" as a movement from a cultural code or immanent ethics to a higher kind of obligation that transcends all custom and natural law in authority and/or metaphysical priority. These alternatives to SDC include a more nuanced agapic command ethics (ACE), which regards our highest obligations as deriving from the commands of a *loving* God,[52] and what I will call aretaic love ethics (ALE), which rejects any universal rules and allows only singular *phronetic* responses to unique situations. Like the eschatological intepretation, ACE and ALE readings try to avoid the irrationalism of SDC; but unlike the eschatological interpretation, they agree with SDC that for Kierkegaard, religious faith is primarily distinguished by a higher ethical attitude. Table 15.1 summarizes the relationship between the four main alternatives.

Readings of *Fear and Trembling*	Irrationalist	Anti-Irrationalist
Higher-ethical readings	SDC reading	ACE and ALE readings
Faith irreducible to higher ethics		Eschatological interpretation

The ACE approach has been rigorously developed in Steven Evans's argument that Kierkegaard "combines a divine command theory" of obligations with "a teleological view of human nature." On this view, Abraham has reason to obey God's commands because he trusts in "God's love and goodness."[53] "To view moral obligations as divine commands is to believe that those commands are directed towards good and loving ends, and not bad ends"; so an obedient Abraham would think that "God has a plan that will lead to a good end" even if we cannot understand it.[54] A similar ACE reading is given by Merold Westphal, who argues the teleological suspension of the ethical is only completed in the agapic ethics of "Religiousness C."[55]

The ALE approach comes in several versions, found mostly in recent continental thought. One variety is the radically anti-theoretical alterity ethics reading attributed to Caputo above. A slightly older version is found in Jerome Gellman's reading of the teleological suspension as defending a kind of proto-Sartrean individualistic ethic.[56] The mildest version, which is more plausibly attributed to Kierkegaard, is inspired by themes in the revival of virtue ethics, such as Bernard Williams's argument that moral theories focusing on impartial principles abstract from individual character and identities and give insufficient ethical weight to personal life-projects. This is Edward Mooney's aretaic conception of ethical responsiveness as including awareness of dilemmas, sensitivity to the uniqueness of individuals, and wholistic evaluation of concrete circumstances.[57] Although Mooney emphasizes the subjective dimension of personal appropriation, *phronesis,* and character, his higher ethic is hardly "subjectivist," since he follows Charles Taylor in holding that the significance of choice requires discoverable values.[58] But Mooney's aretaic ethic is also not "universalist" in *one* sense of that polyvalent term: it is not formalist or algorithmic, since it does not expect moral ideals to give us decision procedures. Mooney's existential virtue ethic is similar in many respects to the divine command versions of agapic ethics developed by Evans and Westphal.

Is Only Hegelian Ethics "Suspended"?

I emphatically agree with Mooney, Westphal, and Evans that such an agapic ethic is central to Christian religiousness as Kierkegaard understands it: it is the heart of his "second ethics." But I still hold that Kierkegaardian faith is distinguished by an element that is not found in such an agapic or aretaic ethics in itself: thus faith does not *consist* in transgressing lower or less enlightened normative systems, trumping communal mores, or challenging established human orders, for the sake of higher agapic ideals.[59] ACE and ALE higher-ethics readings of the teleological suspension are motivated by a worthy desire to distinguish Kierkegaardian religiousness from immoralism; they are also occasioned by clear references to Hegel in *Fear and Trembling,* from which they conclude that it is *only* ethics in Hegel's sense that is "suspended" or trumped in faith. The best textual basis for this reading is a passage in *Problema* I: "For if the ethical—that is social morality—is the highest, and if there is in a person no residual incommensurability in some way such that this incommensurability is not evil . . . then no categories are needed other than what Greek philosophy had" (55).

On this basis, Hannay explains that "The pattern of argument in the *problemata*" is a *modus tollens:* "If A then B; not-B, therefore not-A," where "A is intended as a statement of the Hegelian conception of ethics prevailing in Kierkegaard's time," and B would be the implication that Abraham is a murderer.[60] Westphal concurs, noting that each *Problema* begins with "the same formula, which goes like this: If such and such is the case, then Hegel is right, but then Abraham is lost." Thus if Abraham's faith is higher, then Hegel must be wrong.[61] Pace critics like MacIntyre and Blanshard, the teleological suspension does *not* imply any conflict between "my duties to God" and "my duties to my neighbor and myself"; rather, its target is Hegel.[62] Likewise, Mooney writes that the teleological suspension is a "gestalt-shift" from a lower "conventional" ethic to a transcendent ethic: "A *kind* of ethics gets dethroned while a superior, more complex sort gets installed."[63] More guardedly, Evans writes that "the conception of the ethical operative in the book is mainly Hegelian in character"; this social ethics is in tension with faith because it claims to exhaust ultimate meaning and morality.[64]

I agree that Kierkegaard is arguing that Hegel's ethics is incompatible with Abraham's faith, but that is not *only* because faith involves an agapic ethics that is higher than *Sittlichkeit* or "social morality." To show that the eschatological interpretation is more adequate, I will outline several objections to the higher-ethics readings. The objections show that the ACE and ALE readings share several problems with the SDC reading even though they deny that Kierkegaard means to recommend absolute obedience to arbitrary divine fiat.

(1) As Hannay says, Silentio's argument aims to show that "if you are a Hegelian, then you cannot talk glibly of faith as something you have fathomed and can proceed beyond."[65] But it does not follow that the ethical codes embodied in social life-forms (*Sittlichkeit*) are the only kind of "ethics" that is teleologically suspended in faith. Certainly Kierkegaard means to show that faith cannot be a *higher* stage than ethical consciousness for Hegel, since he regards rational comprehension of the universal in concrete ethical life (*Sittlichkeit*) as part of the absolute or highest stage of consciousness. But the defense of faith as a higher stage involves *more* than just the rejection of this Hegelian theory. In particular, it involves an account of how ethical motivation is *preserved* within faith, pace Hegel's view that ethics cannot be *aufgehoben* in faith. While there is an important difference between *Sittlichkeit* in Hegel's system and the agapic ideals of *Works of Love,* the difference that Kierkegaard meant to emphasize in *Fear and Trembling* is that such agapic devotion can be *combined* in faith with an eschatological trust that goes beyond agapic responsibility, while Hegelian ethical conscience cannot.

This crucial point deserves elaboration. For Kierkegaard, a "higher" stage of human existence (or way of being) always *includes* transformed versions of the lower stages that developmentally precede it: their valuable contribution remains a necessary component of the higher stage. In Kierkegaard's existential dialectic, each transition to a higher stage is *cumulative,* as in Hegel, rather than *exclusive,* as in Nietzsche.[66] For example, in *Either/Or,* the ethical includes the aesthetic in a transformed sense: forms of beauty, interest, and passion are re-figured in an ethical frame. As Evans puts it, in all Kierkegaard's later writings, "Although the distinction between the ethical and the aesthetic is consistently maintained, and the latter is never reduced to the former, the former seems to be included within the latter as an essential element."[67] Likewise, the ethical remains within faith, although faith transcends ethical knowledge and moral motivation.[68] Thus if Abraham simply fetishized God's power, then his loyalty would be an aesthetic passion not informed by any ethical ideal. As Hannay suggests,

> That would be the case if, for instance, Abraham acted as he did in order to show God that he was able to obey *any* command of God's, because, as one might say, he fancied himself as someone obedient to God, much as a would-be Mafia "family" member must prove through some horrific deed that he is prepared to do anything for the Godfather.[69]

Silentio emphasizes that "faith is no esthetic emotion but something far higher; it is not the spontaneous inclination of the heart but the paradox of existence" (47). What distinguishes the attitude of faith from the aesthetic is precisely the ethical pathos within it: so-called faith that does not dialectically retain ethical devotion within it is *aesthetic childishness* (47). Thus Abraham must still be morally motivated. As Mooney lays out in forceful detail, the knight of faith's reasons for action only leave a narrow circle of options that might responsibly be chosen; these reasons rule out many acts that are inconsistent with the precondition of "exemplary moral character."[70]

(2) Thus any higher-ethics interpretation of the telos toward which the ethical is suspended in faith arrives at a dilemma. Ethical attitudes of *some* kind clearly must persist and be refigured within faith: Kierkegaard's conception of the existential stages requires this. But these ethical attitudes retained in faith cannot be those of *Sittlichkeit,* because conventional or communal ethics is superceded in Kierkegaardian faith. Nor can the ethical element retained and transformed within faith be the higher agapic or aretaic attitudes that ACE and ALE readings *equate* with post-suspension faith. For the higher ethical ideals are not *aufgehoben* on this view: rather, they *are* the telos for the sake of which lower ethics is trumped in faith. But then, what elements of the "ethical" stage of existence persist yet are also transfigured within faith, as the logic of the stages requires? One possible answer is "infinite resignation," but why would resignation need to remain within faith, if faith is simply personal appropriation of a higher ethical life-view?

(3) Despite the admitted emphasis on establishing a dilemma for Hegelians, *Sittlichkeit* is not the only sense of "ethics" that Silentio addresses. As

Ronald Green has argued, there is evidence that he includes "Kant's notion of the ethical."[71] And while Anthony Rudd argues that Kierkegaard is focused on Hegelian role-based obligations or "the sphere of positional ethics," he also recognizes that "Abraham is as much a scandal to Kantiant *Moralität* as to Hegelian *Sittlichkeit*."[72] I agree that the ethical view presented in *Fear and Trembling,* as in *Either/Or,* is not simply Hegelian but rather "seems to combine themes from the entire rationalist tradition begun by Kant."[73] The term "universal" is also not restricted to "the concrete universal of the social order";[74] it is often used in reference to natural law and deontological norms. As Ulrich Knappe argues in detail, the portrayal of the ethical in *Fear and Trembling* is closely related to Kant's categorical imperative, and Kant's insistence that Abraham should be condemned as a murderer is imported as central to the purely ethical perspective.[75]

The "ethical" is also used for the *universality* of the love commands. For example, Silentio tells us that although individuals differ physically and psychologically, since they are "sensately and psychically qualified in immediacy," from the perspective of ethics each "has his *telos* in the universal" (54). This has much in common with the admonition in *Works of Love* that agapic love transcends all favoritism, not by formalistic indifference or "proudly turning back into itself," but by "turning itself outwards, embracing all, yet loving everyone in particular but no one in partiality."[76] Thus I endorse Earl McLane's insight that "There is implicit in . . . *Fear and Trembling* an ethic of 'agapism,' an ethic based on the Royal Law, an ethic that points forward to the *Works of Love*."[77] The obligations to love God and neighbor are invoked and interpreted in *Fear and Trembling.* When Silentio says that "In ethical terms, Abraham's relation to Isaac is quite simply this: that the father shall love the son more than himself" (57), the duty he mentions would be supported by biblical love-commandments even more clearly than by Hegel's analysis of the family in the *Philosophy of Right.*[78] In an effort to show that the knight of faith retains the same ethical will as the knight of infinite resignation, the "Preliminary Expectoration" dwells on "how Abraham loved Isaac" (31), reflecting in his own person the God who "is love" (34). *Problema* II also emphasizes that Abraham must continue to love Isaac "with his whole soul" even when he *apparently* acts against this fatherly love out of "his love for God" (74).

This suggests that agapic norms are integral to the ethics that is "suspended" in Abraham's faith, and not only to the faith that does the suspending. In raising the knife, or starting to sacrifice Isaac, Abraham appears to violate not only Hegelian *Sittlichkeit* but also the duties he would have under the religious ethic of neighbor-love. For, if our responsibility to love our neighbor has any deontic content *at all,* it must at least prohibit permanently taking innocent life.[79] This is why McLane, following Kierkegaard's journal statement that Abraham experiences a collision between *divine commands* (quoted above), concludes with perplexity that his situation might better be described as "a 'teleological suspension of the religious' by the religious."[80]

The eschatological interpretation resolves this problem by explaining how God's universal love commandments or agapic norms are not revoked or overridden by the singular command to sacrifice Isaac. The latter command constitutes the obstacle rather than the telos toward which the ethical (in all its senses) is suspended: Abraham's fulfillment of the universal obligation to love one's child is apparently *blocked* by the singular command to Abraham. This command to give Isaac back forces him to rely on an eschatological telos toward which the universal is "suspended"—a telos whose possibility depends on God's action. Thus God plays *three* formally distinct roles in the *Akedah* scenario as Kierkegaard understands it: as always, God is the ground of universal ethical norms; in faith, he is also the singular source of eschatological possibilities; and in this special case, he is even the origin of the mysterious obstacle.[81] This adds to Abraham's greatness, for he maintains faith even in the face of a numinos rather than a merely earthly obstacle to the good outcome.

V-Suspension: Violating Sittlichkeit for the Sake of Obedience to God

The three objections detailed above undermine the initial assumption of all higher-ethics views, namely, that it is only Hegelian or conventional ethics that gets "suspended." There are three further objections to SDC and ACE readings in particular. Both SDC and ACE readings hold that

> (i) Abraham must *violate* the social obligation to love Isaac in order to give highest priority to his love of God, where
> (ii) loving God consists primarily in obeying God's singular and general commandments as the highest source of moral obligation (either because of God's cosmogonic power, or because of his agapic goodness).

(4) The most powerful objection to this conception of the absolute duty, as John Lippitt notes, is the counterexample found in "the four 'sub-Abrahams' of the 'Attunement'" who are all "prepared to obey God's command" but nevertheless do not count as knights of faith.[82] What distinguishes Abraham from these imaginary figures is his trust in the ultimate fulfillment of God's promise, not his willingness to bow to divine commands—either as arbitrary expressions of absolute power, or as agapic expressions of absolute love.

(5) Moreover, if the telos toward which the ethical is "suspended" were simply the duty to *obey divine commands,* it would in principle be willable and intelligible without any reference to the "absurd" possibility at the heart of Kierkegaard's conception of religious faith. As Lippitt points out, all divine command readings ignore this key element in the story: they leave unclear "the significance of God's substituting the ram" for Isaac.[83] For example, Blanshard

writes that "the fact that at the last moment he was relieved of the need to strike is irrelevant in appraising him."[84] But why then is there so much emphasis on the eucatastrophe in *Fear and Trembling*?

This is ironically similar to the main problem with Hegelian accounts of religiousness: they give no decisive life-shaping role to eschatological possibilities. As Westphal notes, Hegel thought of the modern "social order" as the embodiment of reason: "Hegelian rationalism thus has a realized eschatology built into it."[85] But this means that eschatology (and revealed religion in general) is reduced to rational religion: a realization of the good that is deduced or comprehended by human reason or achieved by human power is *not* eschatological, in the sense defined above. Divine command readings give this crucial part of Kierkegaard's critique of Hegel no role in *Fear and Trembling*.

(6) A final reason to think that the divine command interpretations are looking in the wrong direction is that the duty to love God, as interpreted in clause (ii) above, is simply a universal duty to take His word as *law*. Hence, this explanation reduces "faith" to the willingness to put aside traditional interhuman duties for the sake of a higher but still universal obligation to follow divine commands. But Silentio spends much of *Problema* I arguing precisely that the "teleological suspension" involved in faith is *not* simply the abrogation of a lower universal norm for a higher universal principle, or the violation of lower cultural mores for the sake of ethical ideals with higher authority or significance. He runs through a list of heroes who performed actions that violated honor codes of family loyalty for the sake of higher purposes required for their nation: Agamemnon sacrificing Iphigenia, Jephethah giving up his daughter, and Brutus prosecuting his son (58). They are only heroes of resignation, not of faith, because their telos is still an *ethical* one: "the tragic hero is still within the ethical. He allows an expression of the ethical to have its *telos* in a higher expression of the ethical" (59).

Of course, it is possible to insist that the "ethical" within which these heroes remain is still only *Sittlichkeit:* they suspend *individual* conscience for the ideals of civil law. Westphal reads the tragic heroes contrasted with Abraham in *Problema* I this way: they show that Abraham's act cannot be justified by *Sittlichkeit:* "Abraham is lost (a murderer) unless the laws and customs of his people are only the penultimate norms for this life, ultimately subject to a higher law."[86] But I see no reason to accept that the examples of Agamemnon, Jephthah, and Brutus are meant solely as illustrations of *Sittlichkeit,* or that Silentio concludes from them that "the tragic hero is still within the ethical" only as Hegel understood it (59). Rather, I suggest that these figures are meant to illustrate *the general idea of infinite resignation* with a familiar kind of obstacle: tragic heroes cannot fulfill all the duties associated with their multiple roles because of an unfortunate conflict between them. Thus they resign themselves to the impossibility of fulfilling their ideal (success in all their roles) and subordinate the less weighty duty to the more overriding ethical requirement.[87] This is something that can happen within *any* moral outlook or set of universal norms, including an agapic ethic. When Silentio writes that "There is no higher expression for the ethical in Abraham's life than that the father shall love the son" (59), he is hardly trying to show that this love-duty is intelligible only as *Sittlichkeit*. Rather, he is arguing that the faith in which Abraham suspends this duty refers to something beyond *any* kind of universal norm, something entirely "outside the sphere of universal concepts and values to which ethics belongs," as Ronald Green put it.[88] Abraham is unlike these other heroes in having faith, but his infinite resignation is like theirs in this respect: given the obstacle in his situation, he lacks the power to fulfill all his duties.

In sum, I agree with Green's argument that "although *Fear and Trembling* has largely been read as a book dealing with ethics, its central problem lies elsewhere, in the realm of soteriology."[89] Green rightly objects to the idea that teleological suspension can be explained by "the role of revealed divine commands in trumping rational norms in the governance of human life."[90] For readings that make *Fear and Trembling* "an argument for some kind of divine command ethic . . . place Abraham definitionally back 'within the ethical.'"[91] If it was simply Kierkegaard's intention to defend a divine command ethic against a humanistic ethic, then it is was at least rhetorically perverse of him to express this by repeatedly *denying* "that we can in any way fit Abraham's behavior within the ethical."[92]

Anthony Rudd notes the same dilemma in considering Donnelly's and Bogen's rival explanations of *Fear and Trembling.* Donnelly takes Kierkegaard to mean that we have a direct and unconditional duty to God that relativizes all other demands, and he concludes that since this is still a kind of absolute moral duty, there really is no full teleological suspension of morality. Bogen takes the other horn, saying that since all duty is suspended in faith, faith should not itself be described as including a sense of "duty" to God.[93] Both these readings radically revise the text. Rudd concludes, more sensibly, that Silentio just does not resolve this dilemma: "if the God-relationship is simply regarded as the highest of the various goals towards which I'm striving, then the relativization of other goals does not constitute a radical break with the ethical thinking."[94] That is correct, but I suggest that Kierkegaard did not mean to enter this dilemma at all, because he did not intend the telos that is the object of faith to be understood as an intentional goal of human willing.

If the telos toward which the ethical suspended is eschatological—a victory of the good that is only possible through God's power—then it is not a telos in Aristotle's sense, that is, an end toward which we are motivated and for which we strive in action. In existential faith, the agent relates to the eschatological telos not by targeting it as the goal of action, but rather by embracing its possibility with his whole being as the condition for the ultimate significance of all his cares and projects. In other words, the agent's *volitions* remain the same: he may strive to fulfill his ethical ideal as well as particular life-projects under this ideal. Abraham, for example, continues to love Isaac and to will that Isaac live to adulthood, become a father, etc. But now the meaning of these devotions is transfigured in the new frame of faith: he accepts that successful pursuit of this good is conditional on the miraculous divine response in which he trusts absolutely.

The Absolute Relation, the Dogmatic Schema, and Existential Suspension

We have seen that if "faith" were correctly described on the SDC reading as acceptance of a *moral duty* with no rational foundations—an unconditional duty to obey arbitrary divine commands—then Kierkegaard would be subject to MacIntyre's objection (and to Plato's objection in the *Euthyphro*). ACE readings avoid this problem, but they deny any suspension of morality *as a whole*: only duties based on custom and tradition (or perhaps also natural law) are suspended for the sake of the revealed universal and singular commands. But this result conflicts with the text. Westphal is doubtless correct that for Kierkegaard, "to be religious is to have a higher allegiance than to my people and their conception of the Good," or to the "law of the land" in which I live.[95] But this "higher allegiance" cannot consist simply in a higher *ethical* attitude, as ACE interpretations imply. Thus we need a more nuanced way of understanding the crucial relationship between the following three concepts in *Fear and Trembling*:

- love of neighbor (including love of family and proper self-love),
- love of God,
- faith in God.

Faith as a Singularizing Relation to the Absolute

The relationship between these three terms is the central issue in *Problema* II. This section begins with the point that, assuming theism, universal duties can always be understood *formally* as "duties to God" without requiring a dutiful agent to have any essentially particularistic devotion to God as a personal creator, redeemer, or maker of covenants:

> The duty becomes a duty by being traced back to God, but in the duty itself I do not enter into relation to God. For example, it is a duty to love one's neighbor. It is a duty by being traced back to God, but in the duty I enter into relation not to God but to the neighbor I love. If in this connection I then say that it is my duty to love God, I am actually only pronouncing a tautology, inasmuch as "god" in a totally abstract sense here is understood as the divine—that is,

the universal. . . . God comes to be an invisible vanishing point, an impotent thought; his power is only in the ethical (68).

The eschatological interpretation explains why faith is more than such an abstract relation to ethical ideals: for faith involves direct reliance on a personal *promise* made by God-as-finisher, the content of which goes beyond ethical ideality to its actualization *in time* (a synthesis of the ethical and the aesthetic). In putting trust in such an eschatological promise, the human person is related "absolutely"—that is, directly, immediately—to God as an agent of infinite power whose promises, commands, and questions are always pervaded by numinos mystery. As Silentio puts it (in a phrasing that probably inspired Buber), the knight of faith becomes "God's confidant, the Lord's friend . . . in saying 'You' to God in heaven, whereas even the tragic hero addresses him only in the third person" (77). In other words, faith takes God as the *eschatological Thou*, as the personal source of prophecy and singular eschatological promises, whose miraculous fulfillment (as Tolkien put it) is never to be repeated. This contrasts with God as defined in natural theology by an Anselmian list of maximal properties (including perfect goodness). The Divine in the covenantal sense means more than the Divine conceived as the metaphysical and metaethical principle or foundation of being and goodness, and this revealed surplus requires an absolute response from the human agent.[96] Standing as a single individual in an absolute relation to the absolute means *loving* God as a personal maker and keeper of singular promises (120).

This duty to God *is* the duty to have faith in Him (51). When faith is defined *existentially* as absolute trust in God's eschatological promise to us as unique individuals, then our duty to love God must in turn mean *more* than simply obeying God as the metaethical Alpha or source of moral norms; it also means trusting in God as Omega, the actualizer of revealed eschatological possibilities. This is what Silentio means in claiming that faith involves a singularizing relation above all universal ethical requirements: we trust in an ultimate *fulfillment* of moral ideals that transcends our powers and that ethical normativity cannot assure us in time, which is only possible by virtue of God as Omega. In this light, let us examine the key passage in *Problema* II:

> The paradox of faith, then, is this: that the single individual is higher than the universal, that the single individual—to recall a distinction in dogmatics rather rare these days—determines his relation to the universal by his relation to the absolute, not his relation to the absolute by his relation to the universal. The paradox may also be expressed this way: that there is an absolute duty to God, for in this relationship of duty the individual relates himself as the single individual absolutely to the absolute. In this connection, to say that it is a duty to love God means something different from the above [i.e. God as universal principle], for if this duty is absolute, then the ethical is reduced to the relative. From this it does not follow that the ethical should be invalidated; rather, the ethical receives a completely different expression . . . for

example, that love to [or of] God may bring the knight of faith to give love to
the neighbor. (70)

Again, our task is to discern the right relation between our three critical
terms, and my prior arguments suggest the following points. First, that "the
individual relates himself *as the single individual* absolutely to the absolute"
means that the individual is singularized in eschatological trust, which is an
essentially particularistic attitude toward God as Thou. This singularizing relation is existential faith: the absolute duty to love God singles us out because it
includes a "duty" to *have faith* in God as the ultimate person. Thus the eschatological reading does recognize a direct duty to God, which is paradoxical: it
may apply universally to all human persons, but (as *Philosophical Fragments*
explains) to hear the promise in which we are meant to have faith is already
to have gone beyond naturally knowable universal principles (or immanent
knowledge, "recollection"). The duty to "believe" this promise transcends the
deliverances of natural reason; it is *revealed in* the eschatological promise itself.
For *what* the promise reveals is distorted if it is just speculatively entertained,
or merely "believed" in the doxastic sense of asserting a factual proposition;
rather, it demands a wholehearted volitional response. Unless it is appropriated this way, the content of the promise will seem absurd. For promises are
not purely factual statements: *how* we respond to a promise partly determines
what it means to us.

Second, this also explains why proper love of God involves an attitude that
is not required for agapic love of human beings: our agapic duty to God involves
worshiping Him as creator and having faith in Him as the final actualizer of
the promised ultimate good. Third, "the absolute" (used as a definite descriptor)
means 'the source of eschatological possibilities.' But determining one's relation
to "the absolute" (as rigid designator for God) by way of one's relation to the universal means taking God formally as the foundation of universal norms. This
attitude does *not* regard God as "the absolute" in the descriptive sense of being
the source and fulfiller of eschatological promises. In acting on the motive of
duty, I relate *qua* the universally human to God *qua* universal ground of the
Right. By contrast, in existential faith the individual "determines his relation
to the universal by his relation to the absolute": this means that his relationship
to duties of neighbor-love is in some sense (that we must explain) conditional
upon his love of God.

The Dogmatic Schema: How the Universal Depends on the Absolute

Silentio calls this the dogmatic schema of faith: it can be put in diagrammatic
form as a relation of relations:

A human person *qua* instantiation of responsible agency ⟷ God *qua* Universal
↑
A human person *qua* unique individual ⟺ God *qua* Absolute (personal).

The first universal relation (responsibility and free response to obligation) *depends* on the second absolute relation to God in some way. This second-order relation of dependence (↑) cannot be that which holds between a singular prescription or command and the single agent to whom it is addressed (as when I say to my daughter, "help clean up the table"). For if it were, then the faithful individual would love his fellow human beings *only* in obedience to a singular divine imperative that he do so, and loving God (the God-relation) would be reduced to obeying singular commands. As Ronald Green has said, this would be a "forbidding and frightening ethic,"[97] for it would imply that the human agent really has no duties that derive from his instantiating iterable conditions that figure in the antecedents of universal laws applying to all persons: all such universal imperatives would be converted into singular imperatives. But this would amount to saying that the absolute relation to God *revokes* the human agent's first relation to universal ethical ideality rather than *supporting* it, as the dogmatic schema requires.

Understanding the first relation as the agent's volitional response to moral ideals (such as loving those entrusted to her care), and the second relation as established by an eschatological promise reciprocated in trust helps explain how the first relation can be supported by the second, as the dogmatic schema asserts. If the second relation consists in existential faith—if loving God means trusting in Him as the ultimate fulfiller of His covenants and promises—then the second relation provides assurance that our striving for ethical ideals is not all for nothing, not destined to be meaningless in the final scheme of things. Our response to universal duty is upheld and refounded in existential faith because it denies "universal final defeat," as Tolkien put it.

On this reading, the second relation cannot conflict with the first. Faith cannot consist in our being willing to *violate* our duties to love other persons in order to do something inspired by trust in an eschatological promise: for, as we have seen, the content of such a promise is precisely the ultimate fulfillment *of agapic ideals*. In fact, faith in such a fulfillment cannot require us to *do* anything beyond continuing to strive for ethical perfection: what it adds is a reason to trust, against all odds or apparent evidence, that our ethical wish can come true. When decoded, then, the dogmatic schema for faith in *Problema* II means that our volitional response to the ethical, in which we work to fulfill universal agapic ideals, is supported and sustained by the trust that our efforts will not *ultimately* be in vain, that these ideals are not finally limited to an ideal meaning outside of time, that they can be realized *in the end*. In other words, we reappropriate our moral obligations in the new light of eschatological hope. Thus the suspension-relation (↑) is one of context-dependence, as when a figure is dependent for its appearance on the background in which it sits. A gestalt-shift occurs in the meaning of universal ethical ideals when they are seen against the background of existential faith: although their formal content is unchanged, their ultimate significance for human life has changed. The ethical will is *aufgehoben* in religious hope. Thus the eschatological interpretation, unlike its rivals, succeeds in explaining how the ethical is retained yet transformed in the religious stage, as the logic of the stages requires.

K-Suspension

I have argued that the "suspension" of the ethical involved in existential faith does not mean suspension in the *V-sense,* that is, violating a valid ethical norm as a means to bringing about a higher ethical goal. Nor does it mean being released from a normally valid obligation because of the practical impossibility of fulfilling it in the circumstances. This Kantian reading of the "suspension" may seem appealing because Abraham's two loves are described as being in tension (74): his love for God, who commands him to sacrifice Isaac, seems to make it impossible for Abraham to fulfill the requirements of his love for Isaac. Let us say that agent S's moral duty is "suspended" in the *K-sense* when it is practically or morally impossible for S to fulfill this particular obligation by her own initiative.[98] K-suspension then amounts to a valid exception or limit on the scope of a norm's application. But such exceptions are a normal part of any system of universal norms, *including* agapic systems. Moreover, on this proposal, "faith" would involve a K-suspension of Abraham's duty to love Isaac only because God happens to have commanded him to do what seems tantamount to "hating" Isaac (72). But, as emphasized earlier, that God's command plays the role of *obstacle* is a special feature of Abraham's case (which gives it its special horror). The nature of the obstacle obviously differs in other cases, such as the "demonic" circumstances that may disable a person from participation in ordinary human concourse and dialogue, which "has its beginning in his originally being set outside the universal by nature or by a historical circumstance" (106). Such persons are not simply exempted from moral requirements, however.[99] Existential faith is not limited to the few people who experience an apparent divine or "demonic" obstacle to fulfilling their moral obligations. So Silentio gives us no reason to think that every case of existential faith must involve a K-suspension of some ethical obligation.[100]

Nor is the text consistent with the K-suspension reading. In commenting on the difficult passage from the Gospel of Luke on "hating" one's family in order to cleave to God, Silentio insists that although the duty to God can lead one to do actions that "ethics would forbid," or that appear outwardly wrong,[101] it can never require an evil motive such as hatred of other persons. Thus "Cain and Abraham are not identical. He must love Isaac with his whole soul. Since God claims Isaac, he must, if possible, love him even more, and only then can he *sacrifice* him" (74). The point is clearly that Abraham *remains* under the requirement to love Isaac wholeheartedly, as a parent should. He is not excused from this obligation because it is impossible to love Isaac in these circumstances, as

K-suspension would imply. Rather, it is only because he must continue to love Isaac that he is faced with sacrifice and loss, and is unable on his own to pursue what he wills: namely, that Isaac live to father a holy nation. Mooney rightly emphasizes that Abraham fulfills this duty: Silentio "claims unequivocally that at no point does Abraham diminish his love," and this is why he is so ready to "welcome Isaac back."[102]

E-Suspension

This brings us back to the crucial point in the passage on the dogmatic distinction in *Problema* II: Silentio clearly emphasizes that the "duty" to love God does not "invalidate" the ethical, but rather gives it a new expression (70). As we have seen, in this paradoxical duty, loving God primarily means having faith in Him as the Absolute Person. This duty to trust the divine eschatological promise does not violate, revoke, or K-suspend Abraham's duty to love Isaac. Rather, it requires him to accept that he can save Isaac only by relying completely on God's original promise. On this reading, Abraham never abrogates his duty to love Isaac or considers himself exempted from it, even when he moves to kill Isaac: for Abraham relies absolutely on the (absurd) eschatological possibility that this will not ultimately cause Isaac's life to end, that he will turn out not to have murdered his son after all. He "suspends" his duty to Isaac only in this sense: he accepts that he can *fulfill* this duty only if the promised eschatological possibility is actualized by God. His intention toward Isaac remains loving, but he acts in a way that can be consistent with this love only if God's promise is fulfilled by a eucatastrophe. Call this Eschatological Suspension: a duty is E-suspended if and only if our will to fulfill it must rely on an eschatological possibility in which we can only have faith. Our will makes sense as an intention to fulfill our duty *in the context* of this eschatological hope: thus our relation to our duty depends on our relation to an absolutely promised eschatological telos.

Thus the suspension in *Fear and Trembling* can also be understood as "suspense" in the *narrative* sense of anxious hope and dread. The E-suspension of X is not the overriding of X when justified by higher obligations, but rather letting X's fate hang on objective uncertainty, accepting that its viability depends on something independent of our active pursuit of it, which we await in hope and awe. Thus Auerbach emphasizes that, unlike Homer's characters, Abraham is a figure of ethical depth whose story is one fraught with "overwhelming suspense."[103] But this suspense is different than the feeling leading up to the cliffhanger ending of a thriller movie, because of its ultimate significance: Abraham remembers "what God has promised him and what God has already accomplished for him—his soul is torn between desperate rebellion and hopeful expectation," as Auerbach says.[104] In Silentio's *Akedah*, existential faith operates as a gestalt-shift in which the ultimate meaning of Abraham's love depends on something beyond his will. More generally, religious suspense concerns the answer to the ultimate question: in the end, are ethical ideals just an eternal dream doomed to tragic failure, or will they be realized in new reality, in a world transformed by God?

Hannay Was Right

This account of the E-suspension of ethics supports and deepens Hannay's own interpretation of *Fear and Trembling:*

> Abraham, so long as he remains firm in his faith, would not say that he was rendering himself incapable of accomplishing the universal but that he is *reaffirming* his capacity to accomplish it—for after all, his belief . . . is that he is going to get Isaac back even when he sacrifices him. In his faith, Abraham does not think he is putting himself outside the universal; his belief is that showing God his faith means putting the possibility of his continuing to exercise his fatherly love into God's hands.[105]

This passage contains in summary form the thesis I've developed: Abraham's fatherly love is suspended in the sense that it *depends* on God fulfilling his promise. His righteousness in relation to a universal moral ideal depends on the validity of his faith, not because faith is obedience to singular divine commands, but rather because faith is trust in an eschatological victory that will fulfill the infinite requirements of the ethical. This makes sense of Hannay's claim that Abraham "reconstitute[s] the ability to serve the universal on the strength of the absurd."[106] Rather than rejecting universal norms in favor of a higher law, Abraham is "retaining or reaffirming his capacity to realize the universal."[107] Although Abraham's circumstances are special, from a point of view higher than Silentio's (e.g., Climacus's), *every* singular individual faces the limits of his imperfect will as an obstacle: anyone who accepts the reality of sin must E-suspend "the ethical," even in its highest agapic sense, in eschatological faith.

A Response to Green

In making this point about the universal need for faith, however, I am not endorsing Green's anagogical reading of the teleological suspension as primarily a figure for the overcoming of sin through grace.[108] *Fear and Trembling* certainly anticipates the treatment of these themes in the *Fragments, Postscript,* and other later pseudonymous works: the human agent who recognizes sin as an obstacle to righteousness that he cannot overcome, yet has faith that sin can be overcome by virtue of divine grace, instantiates the same *psychological structure* of existential faith for which Abraham is the paradigm illustration. Thus the "paradox of sin" and redemption contains an "analogy" to Abraham (112).[109] But unless God's command to sacrifice Isaac is *only* read anagogically as a figure for human sinfulness, the specific nature of the obstacle and thus the specific content of the eschatologically possible reprieve differ in these Jewish and Christian examples, which is precisely why Silentio repeatedly insists that sin is not the issue for Abraham (112). Thus I would also modify Whittaker's conclusion that Abraham's faith should be understood primarily as a metaphor for the faith of one "who dares to believe that he is forgiven by God."[110] The structure of existential faith is more general than Christianity or Religiousness B; it describes the subjective attitude of faithful persons in many religions, such as the Zoroastrian who trusted absolutely in perfect justice to be found in a hereafter, and Socrates' similar trust that a good man cannot really be harmed, in the end.

There are two other problems, in my view, with Green's claim that "Abraham stands for every person of faith who in believing in forgiveness accepts something which by moral standards of just desert is absurd."[111] First, as Lippitt points out, Green's analogy compares divine and human action: "just as Abraham teleologically suspends the ethical ... God can teleologically suspend his justice (read: 'the ethical') in service of a higher *telos*: his love for humanity."[112] But this is an account of divine mercy to human beings, not of *human faith* in God, which is the target of Silentio's analysis. Second, it takes the strict retributivist Law of the Torah as suspended in the Love that Christ says is the whole of the Law. But *love* of Isaac, and not merely the law that the parent shall cherish the child, is what Abraham suspends in faith—however we understand "suspension." Reconciliation achieved through accepted forgiveness is not a violation of the ideal of agapic love, but rather figures among its highest expressions. Abraham's faith involves agapic love and more: it involves trust in the miraculous possibility of Isaac's restoration.

In sum, the eschatological reading explains how soteriology can be the central theme of *Fear and Trembling,* as Green rightly insists, without implausibly adding that Christian redemption is the only kind of soteriology that Kierkegaard intended to include within his conception of existential faith. Outka is right that Green tries "to assimilate *Fear and Trembling* too unqualifiedly into the classical Pauline-Lutheran doctrine of justification through faith alone."[113] Existential faith as eschatological trust can come in other forms too. Thus Abraham's faith is not merely a figure for the Atonement, nor for divine mercy that transcends the rigorism of universal law. Even Kierkegaard's own agapic ethics is E-suspended: existential faith is trust in a revealed promise that goes beyond the content of the love-commandments to the idea that *amor vincent omnia:* love will conquer all, in the end.

The relation between our three crucial terms is now clear. Success in the task of loving our neighbors as ourselves depends on the love and support promised to us by God, and trusting ourselves to this promise is the most important part of the love we owe to God. Our duty is not only to worship God as our creator, but to have faith in the final outcome of God's creation. Thus we cannot fully love our neighbor without this personal or singular (non-iterable) relation to the divine as Absolute, as the mysterious source of eschatological promises and absurd possibilities.

Infinite Resignation as an Essential Condition of Existential Faith

We have now seen how Abraham's trust in God's promise that Isaac will live, introduced in the long "Preliminary Expectoration," provides the key to understanding both the teleological suspension of the ethical in *Problema* I and the absolute duty to God in *Problema* II. The same is true in *Problema* III for the impossibility of communicating faith in a way that makes its content rationally comprehensible (though I only discuss *Problema* III briefly in section V below).[114] It should not be imagined that because the theme of eschatological hope is developed in a section titled "Preliminary," it is left behind in the later sections. Rather, the "preliminary" section provides the frame for all three *Problemata:* they all "draw out" the same paradox that seems to make murder acceptable by giving "Isaac back to Abraham again, which no thought can grasp" (53). The various themes of the *Problemata,* such as the refutation of Hegel, are all developed as subthemes *within* the central eucatastrophic theme. In particular, the contrasts between the tragic heros of *Problema* I and Abraham are *instances* of the general distinction between the knights of faith and infinite resignation discussed in the "preliminary" section.

This implies that infinite resignation is not only a concern of the Preliminary section: its relation to faith remains crucial for understanding the aspects of faith discussed in the three *Problemata.* Yet the eschatological reading seems to be the only interpretation that adequately explains why, as Hannay writes, "There is no faith without prior resignation."[115] Rival accounts are usually unable to explain why infinite resignation remains an *ongoing* component of faith.

Cross and Lippitt

Though a full defense of this decisive point would require discussing much of the voluminous scholarship on *Fear and Trembling,* a few examples will illustrate the difficulties that non-eschatological readings encounter with infinite resignation. Now, my reading seems to be a more developed version of a view that Andrew Cross describes as follows: Abraham "believes that Isaac will remain with him, believes this 'on faith alone'" and so does not understand his act as murdering Isaac.[116] Against this, Cross argues that if Abraham really believes that he will get Isaac back, then he makes no real sacrifice, and is only "calling God's bluff, so to speak."[117] For his resignation to be real, Cross thinks that "Abraham must be interpreted as being completely convinced that Isaac will die by his hand," even though this action is wrong and the voice that commands it therefore cannot be God's![118] Cross is forced to this counter-textual conclusion because he sets up a false dichotomy, holding that either Abraham must be certain the Isaac will die permanently, or he is merely manipulating God. Since the latter disjunct is unacceptable, he opts for the former and concludes that "Abraham's faith cannot manifest itself as a belief, say, that God will not demand Isaac of him after all."[119]

Against Cross, John Lippitt has ably defended the view that Abraham does not see his act as murder. Lippitt points out that there is "no problem with imagining an Abraham who would be prepared to go through with the sacrifice if need be, but whose trust in God is such that he continues to believe that Isaac will be spared."[120] This is exactly right, since Silentio emphasizes that Abraham is not engaging in any *calculation* about how the divine promise will be fulfilled (which is why the ram is eucatastrophic). Abraham believes that God's promise will be fulfilled in some incalculable way *even if* Isaac dies by his own hand on Mount Moriah; he is not trying to trigger any divine action, as a magician might try to conjure a spirit. That Isaac will not be permanently lost is the object of faith, not knowledge; the only thing he knows for certain is that he is carrying out the sacrifice as commanded (119).

Cross is certainly right that anyone who would play a game of 'chicken' with the Absolute, betting that God will blink before the knife hits, or that he will repair the wound after the knife hits, etc., is not what Kierkegaard means by a knight of faith. But that is because bluff-callers and chicken-gamers are *manipulators* of their opponent who believe these strategies are likely to be effective means of securing their desired ends. The eschatological reading makes clear that the knight of faith does not believe that he has any such way of forcing the divine hand. However he responds to the obstacle, he does not believe that his ethical goal will be realized as a *controlled consequence* of his action; but he nevertheless believes that it will be realized miraculously. Thus he does not *intend* or act to produce this miraculous outcome. Once we distinguish between intended and expected outcomes, Cross's false dichotomy is dissolved.

Lippitt still worries that his interpretation might conflict with a passage near the end of *Problema* III suggesting that "Abraham must know that Isaac is to be sacrificed."[121] This perfect future tense paraphrase is slightly misleading, though, since all that Abraham knows is that *he* cannot save Isaac if God demands him. Lippitt's solution is to say that Abraham has resigned Isaac in the sense that "he has steeled himself for the eventuality that *if* his faith is misplaced, then he will sacrifice Isaac."[122] I agree that Abraham expects to lose Isaac forever *if* his faith is wrong,[123] but this is not what Silentio means by the movement of infinite resignation. Abraham is *not* resigned to losing Isaac forever, but rather to the practical impossibility of saving Isaac by his own effort. In Kierkegaard's sense, my *resigning an end* about which I care deeply does not entail my believing that it definitely *will not* occur (which would be inconsistent with faith that God can bring it about); rather, it means accepting that *I* cannot bring it about,[124] even with reasonably pursuable human aid or feasible enhancements to my own powers.

Cross argues that such explanations leave Abraham "with still too much to say in defense of what he is doing," and thus fail to account for the insistence in *Problema* III that the knight of faith cannot explain himself, even to other faithful believers.[125] Now this objection does have force against higher-ethics readings. The SDC approach, for example, amounts to making faith into a universal moral obligation,[126] which implies that the knight of faith should be able to explain herself (at least to anyone who thinks God's power gives Him absolute authority). But the eschatological reading says that Abraham cannot "speak" because he cannot betray God's confidence. The eschatological promise of Isaac's progeny is secret, given to him alone: "silence is also divinity's mutual understanding with the single individual" (88). Abraham's position in this respect is analogous to the heroine in Andersen's *The Wild Swans*: if she speaks, she cannot save her twelve brothers; so she cannot explain herself to her husband, and must even risk death to keep the prophecy secret. What the knight of faith believes might be intelligible to faithful persons, but then he would fail the test. Likewise, Silentio tells us that the bridegroom of Delphi could tell his bride what is happening—but not without reducing his trial to an unhappy love affair (91). The knight of faith's silence is a result of the divine promise coming to him or her "quite privately" and thus establishing "a purely private relation" (93). To share this revelation with others would be to fail to respond in the way that the promise itself demands.

Infinite Resignation and Faith: Cross, Lippitt, and Hall

These points explain how eschatological trust is compatible with infinite resignation. Because Cross holds that they are not compatible—that Abraham is not resigned unless he believes that Isaac will die and never return—he is forced to the implausible conclusion that Abraham's faith is a non-cognitive "trust" that coexists with being certain that God will disappoint him.[127] To avoid this, Lippitt follows Ronald Hall's analysis of infinite resignation as "an ever-present temptation that must be continually annulled" by faith.[128] But Hall's approach seems to *agree* with Cross that resignation is an all-things-considered conviction that the object of the agent's care (e.g. Isaac) is totally lost. Hall differs from Cross only in holding that faith is a rejection of this kind of "resignation" (which Cross would combine with a trust that almost contradicts it). Abraham's faith thus involves continually annulling "the temptation to give in to 'infinite resignation': to take heed of the evidence, lose hope and trust in God, and resign himself to the loss of Isaac."[129]

Now, certainly this kind of doubt is an ever-present temptation for existential faith; but an all-things-considered judgment that Isaac is forever lost—a judgment that faith logically must annul—would constitute *despair*. Resignation *simpliciter* must be distinguished from the complex resignation that is identified as a form of despair in *Sickness unto Death*: namely, "to be unwilling to hope in the possibility that an earthly need, a temporal cross, can come to an end."[130] This is resignation *plus* the refusal to "[h]ope in the possibility of help, especially by virtue of the absurd, that for God everything is possible."[131] Clearly this compound attitude is incompatible with existential faith; but resignation *simpliciter* has to be compatible with faith. For Silentio says plainly and repeatedly that faith *includes* the tragic/heroic movement of resignation as its necessary but not sufficient condition; resignation in this sense is essential to the very fabric of faith. Indeed, Silentio argues that without resignation, faith collapses into the "first immediacy" or aestheticism because resignation is the ethical component that the aesthetic immediacy lacks. So the right reading must explain how faith builds *cumulatively* on continuing resignation, but the explanations offered by Cross, Hall, and Lippitt all fail on this score.

The model of existential faith as eschatological trust neatly solves this problem by defining resignation as the (b) component of existential faith (see p. 201 above): the resigned agent accepts that *he* cannot bring about the ethically required end, that no accessible human powers would be enough to enable him to realize the good that he wills. For example, if Agamemnon told Iphigenia that "by human reckoning" it was possible to save her, then she could understand him, but then he "would not have made the infinite movement of resignation and thus would not be a hero" in Silentio's moral sense (115). To be resigned, Agamemnon only needs to believe wholeheartedly that Iphigenia's salvation is humanly impossible, *not* that it is impossible in all modal senses, or that it certainly will not happen. The former belief (b) by itself is consistent with both (c), the despairing conclusion that Iphigenia will be forever lost, and with the opposite belief (a) that she can be saved by the gods nevertheless.[132] The confusion we found in Cross and Hall runs through the secondary literature because faith (as the conjunction of a and b) and religious despair (c and b) are certainly incompatible, but commentators fail to see that this is only because (a) and (c) are logically inconsistent, while (b) is necessary for *both* existential faith and religious despair. Faith annuls despair, but does not annul resignation in the (b) sense. The (a) condition is thus what faith *adds* to resignation, blending tragic recognition of human limits together with a joy that comes from 'hope beyond hope.' Now there is no difficulty in understanding how "Abraham makes two movements" at once (115), without the latter annulling or contradicting the former. He wills Isaac's good with infinite resignation, yet despite the perilous obstacle, he also trusts in the absurd possibility of Isaac's growing up to have children of his own. As Whittaker puts it, "Abraham believed himself to be participating in a drama directed by God, a drama whose ultimate outcome would not be tragic."[133]

Two Types of Infinite Resignation

We have seen that infinite resignation is in itself neutral between faith and religious despair, though it is a precondition for either. In explaining this, I have focused on the negative aspect of resignation as a recognition of finitude or limits, but resignation also has a positive aspect that distinguishes it from mere quietism: it is a state of volitional commitment to good ends or ethical striving, and so its presence within existential faith implies that a kind of ethical "work" must be ongoing in faith. One does not just leave it all up to God without first making an effort to bring about the ideal good. As Lippitt says, "belief in divine grace" cannot involve self-deception or spiritual laziness.[134] The negative experience of limitation can only follow upon authentic love or devotion to something worthwhile in this world. Louis Dupré explains this point in the specifically Christian terms of Kierkegaard's later works:

> Only a failure in the innermost depths of his own person can persuasively reveal to him his true condition and put him in the proper situation for experiencing God's redemption. The failure of ethics must necessarily precede the coming of grace. In his later years, Kierkegaard became more and more convinced that Luther . . . did not attach sufficient importance to this preparation.[135]

I believe that Kierkegaard's signed religious writings support Dupré's point; his frequent emphasis on ethical works is anticipated by Silentio's insistence that "Infinite resignation is the last stage before faith, so that anyone who has not made this movement does not have faith" (46). Because it is necessary for resignation, earnest moral willing is a *precondition* of faith, even though it cannot guarantee faith, earn salvation, or control any divine response.

"Infinite resignation," then, should be understood as involving volitional dedication to a person, social role, vocation, or other valuable end that is underwritten by perfectionist ideals of exemplary virtue. This sort of spiritual ardor is the natural limit of moral heroism in the human will (and of autonomy in Kant's sense). It is an *infinite* passion in the sense that it requires the strongest kind of resolve: the agent must identify *wholeheartedly* with her end for the sake of its ethical value:[136] "the knight will then have the power to concentrate the whole substance of his life and the meaning of actuality into one single desire [or motive]. If a person lacks this focus, his soul is dissipated in multiplicity from the beginning" (42–43). Silentio requires a passion "in which the individual has concentrated the whole reality of actuality" for himself (41 note *). This is obviously related to Kierkegaard's ideal of volitional unification in his famous discourse on *The Purity of Heart* and to the discussion of "infinite passion" in *Stages on Life's Way*.[137]

This passion is resigned in the sense that the knight *retains* his commitment to his noble end as central to the meaning of his life, even though he accepts the human impossibility of achieving it in the world of time (43–44). It is this qualification that constitutes tragic heroism, for it shows that the agent's passionate devotion to his goal is motivated entirely by the eternal validity of its intrinsic value rather than by any hope for his own happiness or satisfaction. Infinite resignation purifies the will, ensuring that it wills the noble goal solely for its own sake. In the extreme pathos of infinite resignation, the ethical thus becomes heterogeneous with all "aesthetic" interests and incentives. Tragic resignation requires "a purely human courage to renounce the whole temporal realm in order to gain eternity," to see the intrinsic value of one's ideals as entirely distinct from one's "earthly happiness" (49). I agree with Mooney's explanation that this also means giving up "proprietary claim" over the object, goal or person to which she has been committed.[138] Since the resigned agent must give up any pretension of ultimate ownership or control over this end, she is purified both of self-interested motives for its pursuit, and of any narcissistic insistence on being the one who achieves it. After such resignation, her care is "selfless" and entirely consistent with faith in the goal's realization.[139]

Yet it has frequently seemed to commentators that the knight of infinite resignation does give up on his goal, or cease caring about it in some sense that is incompatible with faith. This is part of the reason why resignation is often conflated with despair, as we saw earlier. Confusion on this point is partly due to an important ambiguity in the text between two species of infinite resignation simpliciter, each of which is *neutral* between faith and despair as explained above: they can exist on their own, *or* in combination with trust in victory through absurd possibility, *or* in combination with defiant refusal to be consoled in faith. For ease of reference, I give each of these species a representative label:

Beowulfian Resignation

(i) I can no longer see any way for me to bring about (or secure a significant chance of bringing about) my good end E.

(ii) Yet I continue to value E intrinsically, and love E as an eternal ideal; I remain devoted to E as what ought to be, in principle.

(iii) I continue actively striving toward E by any just means that I can find, however futile, without hope that this will do anything to significantly increase the likelihood of E.

Thus in striving toward my goal, I still express my continuing devotion to it; I make clear what I stand for, to the end. For example, in *The Lord of the Rings*, King Théoden tells his warriors that even though they cannot defeat the armies of Mordor, "we will meet them in battle nonetheless!"[140] In this, Kierkegaard would have heard Tolkien's intended echo of the Norse Ragnarok, an eschatological narrative that emphasizes infinite resignation: the gods of Valhalla know that they will be defeated by the demons of chaos, but they "think that defeat no refutation."[141] Similarly, Socrates presses his argument to the Athenian jury, already knowing what the outcome will be. In this kind of resignation, it is clear that the hero has not given up caring about his ethical ideal, even though he believes that his efforts cannot secure it.

But there is another kind of "resignation" covered by Silentio's concept that comes closer to the ordinary meaning of this English word, which applies to the young lad in *Fear and Trembling,* and possibly also to Kierkegaard in releasing Regina:

Elegiac Resignation
(i) (same)
(ii) (same)
(iv) I disengage from actively pursuing my end E in time.
   I do nothing contrary to E's value, which I still prize,
   but I give up actively striving for E in this life.

Because this kind of resignation brackets active expression of one's continued commitment, it can sometimes lapse into sentimentalism, or what I call bad romanticism: Werther-like hand-wringing and enjoyment of one's sorrow. Kierkegaard's *Either/Or I* explores such perversions of spirit, and this is why some critics imagine that Kierkegaard's young lad has really ceased to care about his princess in giving up the pursuit of her. But this is a misinterpretation: we know from common experience that elegiac resignation can be enacted without the least diminishment of love. Think, for instance, of a person finally 'accepting' that her dearest friend has died, or that her Alzheimer-afflicted spouse's last memories are finally gone, and similar tragedies. The love for the friend or spouse remains an infinite passion to which the agent is wholeheartedly committed, but she is resigned to the reality that they lie beyond her reach. Such resignation is a state of will involving evaluative judgment: it accepts that no valuable statement is made by keeping a vigil forever at the friend's grave, or continuing to press the completely senile spouse for some neurologically impossible flicker of recollection. There is genuine heroism here also, a heroism that is *not* well symbolized by Beowulf going to duel his dragon. The will disengages from active pursuit, but the love remains. And just as it remains possible, by virtue of the absurd, for Théoden or Beowulf to win their battles,[142] it remains eschatologically possible for the friend and the spouse to be resurrected in their perfected nature. Both kinds of resignation are compatible with such existential faith, since neither in themselves entails despair. Disengaging from active pursuit of the humanly impossible end, when appropriate, is not the same as despairing *ultimately* of it (though it is compatible with that too). Resignation in either the Beowulfian or Elegiac sense presses the spirit toward a choice between despair or faith, but neither type of resignation forces or determines the agent's transition to a religious life-view.

Elegiac resignation is what I think Kierkegaard meant in describing a resigned Abraham as giving up his desire (18). Such a "tragic hero" (34) still cares wholeheartedly about Isaac: Silentio says that if he had been in Abraham's position, then in "my immense resignation" I would "have loved him with my whole soul," yet failed to love him in the way that Abraham did (35), that is, *through* loving faith in God. The young lad infinitely resigns his princess in the elegiac sense when the object of his love is transformed from a living historical woman into "an eternal form that no actuality can take away" (43). His hope is reduced to an abstraction: "in an infinite sense it was possible, that is, by relinquishing it" (47). This means that he stops trying to win her hand in marriage, but not that he stops caring about her: "he does not give up his love" (42), nor change his deepest volitional devotion to her (43). He only accepts that this purpose, which continues to define his identity, is no longer to be pursued "within time" (32). Likewise, Silentio emphasizes that the lad's "renouncing" his princess only means disengaging from the worldly pursuit of her, not diminishing his devotion. His love is "turned inward, but it is not therefore lost, nor is it forgotten" (44). This renouncing or disengaging is an act of will (45), just like the other options of continuing to pursue the goal without hope as an expressive act (Beowulfian resignation), or radically rejecting one's love (in despair). As Hannay says, in "renouncing the possibility" of achieving her highest end, "the person does not give up the wish and try to forget it. Thus resignation is not abandoning one's heart's desire."[143]

This interpretation also supports Evans's argument that the portrayal of faith in *Fear and Trembling* is consistent with Kierkegaard's later religious writings, which stress agapic ideals. Evans concludes that Silentio "highlights the ways in which a transcendent religious faith cannot be captured by the categories of a rational morality."[144] But while we cannot bring about our own salvation, *Fear and Trembling* portrays the human self as able to will the good at least enough to discover its own limits and imperfection; without this, it cannot turn to God in hope that the good it willed (however deficiently) may be perfected and fulfilled by virtue of the absurd. Without our ethical striving, eucatastrophic grace would have nothing to *meet*.[145] The faithful human agent experiences her trust as direct dependence on God, and will experience the eucatastrophe that justifies her faith as a unique moment in time when she is touched by the transcendent, upheld by the hand that created her. Such a numinous encounter is impossible for an aesthetic agent who has willed nothing with ethical seriousness, just as it cannot be experienced in joy by a resigned agent who received an eschatological promise but failed to make the movement of faith. Ethical passion must come first, before the resigned will can look toward *an answer* from God, a fulfillment of God's will in time. We could diagram this complex relation as shown in chart 15.1:

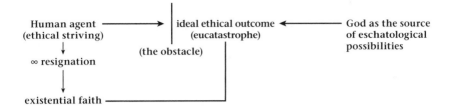

Conclusion: The Next Steps

Let me conclude by addressing two likely objections. One apparent problem with this argument that resignation as an ethical passion is a necessary yet not sufficient condition of existential faith is Silentio's admission that a sinful individual is already outside the universal, although a sinful individual can come to faith (98).[146] However, the individual is not entirely passive in the recognition of sinfulness; in fact, accepting the need for grace involves infinite resignation. Although we may give in to temptations, our higher-order will to rectitude can be pure, even though resigned to its own inadequacy without grace.[147] Thus Rumble is quite right that "sinlessness before the universal is not a prerequisite of faith,"[148] but resignation defined as a volitional state does not entail sinlessness. I have argued that we can think of sin as a different type of obstacle within the same basic structure of existential faith. But this obstacle does not imply that we are utterly incapable of any ethical effort, or we could not even come up against such an obstacle (as I argued in the previous section). As Silentio says, "sin is not the first immediacy; sin is a later immediacy," like faith, because it involves awareness of ethical responsibility that the agent cannot meet. Thus an entirely wanton aesthete could not receive the revelation of his sinfulness. Again, the cumulative relation of the existential categories implies that we cannot eliminate ethical consciousness from a religious state such as consciousness of sin. In Religiousness B, infinite resignation takes the form of the will to repentance, which becomes "the highest ethical expression" (98, note *).

Another reasonable question is whether my account denies divine commands a central role in Kierkegaardian faith. For surely Kierkegaard's later religious works show that he rejected Kantian and Hegelian theories for some kind of a divine command ethics.[149] In response, it is important to emphasize that my eschatological reading is consistent with divine commands being indispensable for human understanding of agapic ideals, and with grace playing an essential role in our capacity for moral motivation. My reading is also consistent with the idea in ACE readings that the will of a loving God is metaphysically constitutive of moral rightness, though I do not believe that this is what the "teleological suspension of the ethical" means: it is a trusting response to a divine promise concerning *actual* realization of ethical possibilities in this world (or in its end and remaking), rather than to a singular command concerning what *ought* to be. The distinctive positive thesis in the eschatological reading is that *Fear and Trembling* shows us what faith involves beyond the authority of divine commands; but as regards divine commands, its only negative thesis is that *divine power alone* is not the source of moral normativity for Kierkegaard.

Thus the eschatological reading is committed to denying that the highest ethical ideals to be actualized in eschatological victory are caused to have ethical authority by *arbitrary* divine fiat, as they are in absolute voluntarist accounts. For an eschatological outcome is defined as the miraculous realization of ethical ideals that already have authoritative content independent of the power that makes them eschatologically possible. Such turning points in time, which are the intensional objects of faith-consciousness, would be meaningless if the Good did not already have significance. Eschatological promises and their eucatastrophic fulfillment can issue from the free creative will of God only if the Good itself is not a free creation of this will, but remains ontologically prior to it, as a metaphysically necessary truth. The eschatological, properly understood, depends on the ethical for its sense or meaning, rather than the other way around.

To clarify these points, consider the distinctions between different versions of divine command ethics drawn by Avi Sagi and Daniel Statman. Moral obligation is metaphysically dependent on divine will according to the "strong dependence" thesis: "Advocates of strong dependence claim that morality cannot exist without religion, that God is both the source of morality and the exclusive basis of its validity. This means that had God commanded us to commit murder, for instance, murder would become a moral obligation."[150] On these views, then, divine commands are necessary and sufficient for moral requirement or prohibition. But Sagi and Statman usefully distinguish between the "extreme" version of strong dependence, according to which obligation depends solely on God's will as "completely free" (or arbitrary), and more moderate versions of strong dependence according to which "God's commands reflect his moral nature but are, nevertheless, the sole basis of moral obligations."[151] These are the types of divine command ethics endorsed by SDC and ACE readings respectively. Both contrast with what Sagi and Statman call the "weak dependence thesis," which holds that

> although the validity of morality is independent of God's command, morality still depends on God for its implementation. This thesis assumes that human beings, because of their flaws, can neither attain moral knowledge nor behave in moral ways unless assisted by God. . . . Human beings depend on God for the understanding and realization of morality.[152]

Sagi and Statman argue convincingly that this weak dependence view is commonly found in Jewish literature on commanded duties (*mitsvot*), according to which divine commands simply "reveal" what has "intrinsic moral value" independently of any divine free choice.[153]

In my view, Kierkegaard also accepts the weak dependence thesis, but not the strong dependence thesis, at least in its extreme voluntarist form. McLane is right that, for Kierkegaard, "God's commands flow from his nature," which *is* love, and this nature is the basis of his authority.[154] This obviously agrees with Evans and Adams (see section III above). In the signed writings of his later years, Kierkegaard accepts both that our moral duties cannot fully be known without revelation, and that we cannot fulfill them without grace.[155] Both of these claims are also central to Christianity in *Philosophical Fragments* and the *Postscript.* Yet neither of these kinds of dependence on God entail that divine fiat unlimited by prior goodness constitutes the rightness of obligations that are (partly) revealed, or whose pursuit is aided by grace. Hence, neither conflicts with my reading of *Fear and Trembling.*

In sum, my account of existential faith is fully compatible with the notion of a "second ethics" that requires revelation beyond the naturally knowable part of morality, and whose ideals are heterogeneous to wills fallen in sin. Although these topics are beyond the scope of *Fear and Trembling,* and perhaps beyond the ken of its pseudonymous author, the introduction of these themes in later works does not reject or fundamentally alter the basic structure of existential faith set forth by Silentio. For example, the distinction between religiousness A and B in the *Postscript* is primarily a difference in the kinds of eschatological possibilities envisioned in each type of faith.[156] In the future, I also hope to extend this reading to *Works of Love* and other signed works.

This will hardly be the last word. The literature on *Fear and Trembling* is as large and often as varied, rich, and creative as the literary products of Kierkegaard himself. But I hope at least to have laid finally to rest the old saw that *Fear and Trembling* teaches religious fundamentalism or absolute fideism without any place for human ethical striving. No responsible teacher can portray Kierkegaard's masterpiece as recommending a form of religious faith that constitutes total irrationalism. Trust in the hereafter, or committed hope for eschatological redemption, certainly involves subjective appropriation of promises that cannot be proven by any form of rational demonstration starting from natural sources, but it does not require rejecting all naturally knowable ethical requirements or ideals. The transition from the ethical to the religious involves a "leap" that cannot be determined by rational argument, but it is not a leap into blind fanaticism.

16.
Silence and Entering the Circle of Faith

Alastair Hannay

George Pattison's thesis is cautious. It is that there is *evidence* that Kierkegaard had a more complex view of the relation of philosophy to Christian dogmatics than that which the works assigned to Johannes Climacus leave us with. Where Climacus says, Hands off, this is religion!, the new view gives some leeway to philosophy but ends up presenting yet another way of holding faith and philosophy apart, but a "subtly different" way.

One point of interest here is that the voice usually regarded as the philosophical one in Kierkegaard's output is precisely Climacus's, while the olive branch offered here to philosophy is offered by Kierkegaard himself in the discourses. Another is that the terms Pattison uses to fill out the more abrupt "hands off faith" view are Kierkegaard's own. They are drawn from an early journal entry[1] that says, roughly speaking, that philosophers have no right to make claims to human knowledge of Christian redemption (*Forløsning*). It is implied that there must first be some inner experience, which philosophers by virtue of their terms of reference have to ignore or must presuppose. This entry was made some time before Climacus came on the scene, but when Climacus does make his appearance the 'hands-off' motif does indeed underpin his writing as well as being the implicit message of an unpublished work of his. A telling quotation from *Postscript* reads: "Dialectic [which many read as "philosophy" in some not necessarily speculative sense] is really a benevolent ministering power, which discovers and helps to find where the absolute object of worship is. . . . [I]t does not itself see the absolute, but it leads the individual as it were up to it."[2] The discovering and helping are activities that nowadays, with both the clearings of Heidegger and the ladder-climbing of Wittgenstein in our curricula, we have little difficulty in calling philosophical. Pattison, however, is asking us to see in the signed parallel works, in particular the two discourses from 1843 he cites, what he refers to as a "humanistic trait in Kierkegaard's thought." It is this that offers a hitherto unseen olive branch to philosophy. Pattison submits that "on this basis we might begin to feel more optimistic about philosophy having a chance to get to grips with the inner sanctuary of Kierkegaardian faith as that comes to expression in *Fragments*, in the *Postscript*'s religiousness B and in *Training in Christianity*."

I propose an alternative. The inner sanctuary does not come to expression in those works; it is merely referred to, sketched, formulas for preparation for it lengthily provided, and so on. Being referred to and the rest are of course ways for things to come to expression, but they are not ways of being expressed for what they are. So, secondly, I suggest, in line with Pattison, that the discourses he cites are indeed designed to bring faith to expression in the right reader, and even to edify or build the reader into becoming the right reader, and that they perform a function Climacus was not invented to perform. But I also suggest that it is problematic to focus on the theology of creation in the discourse and to say that what offers more to philosophers is the providing of this "theological context for the Christological argument of the *Fragments*." For one thing, if in the sequence of production we look backwards from *Fragments* to the discourses, the theology of creation has already been carefully presented in *Fragments* itself, in the concentrated discussion in the interlude of the transition from non-being to being through a freely acting cause. For another, it is the version there that seems designed for philosophers, even going over the edge a little in that respect (perhaps with some tongue-in-cheek), and not the corresponding material in the two discourses, whose terminology and form, however humanistic the content, offer little to the philosopher. What one might argue instead is, as just suggested, that Climacus, whether we call him a philosopher or not, speaks polemically to the philosophically literate public of the time (not least all those students who had attended Martensen's lectures and the readers of Heiberg's popularized version of Hegel), while in the discourses Kierkegaard is speaking to a public ideally unaffected by the distortions wrought by philosophy, and not really a "public," in the sense of a solid audience, as if, like Martensen, Kierkegaard wanted to gather popular support, but rather to each reader individually. Climacus's role (as the *Point of View* indicates) is that of disabusing of their beliefs those who think philosophy will explain faith, or go further than faith (though actually they are the same). *Fragments* offers a thought-experiment in which the rational-path-to-truth view of the philosopher, on which such beliefs are based, is turned upside down, or rather outside in, and the suggestion is made that words philosophers use, such as truth, have an entirely different function and meaning, one that will however only be seen to upstage or overshadow the traditional, philosophical use to someone who has come to see "the point" of it, that is, is able to receive what Climacus calls the condition.

That is how I myself would interpret George Pattison's notion of "stepping into the theological circle."

It is a rather open metaphor of course. You may think you have stepped into that circle just by reading some books, without having faith. Or you could be said to do so by thinking you know what faith is and what having it is, but not really having it, but—and here would be the crucial point—you cannot really have faith without stepping into the theological circle. There is theology there and philosophers who do not step inside cannot gainsay those who find the question of truth defined inside that circle, while philosophers who do step inside are no longer just philosophers.

On Pattison's more general points, I agree that Kierkegaard should not be read as contributing to the solution of this or that philosophical debate, unless it be the debate about where philosophy begins or ends. But in that debate, too, Kierkegaard does not write like a typical anti-philosopher, the kind Ernest Gellner chastised for keeping their well-paid positions in philosophy departments. The Kierkegaard of the discourses, the serious Kierkegaard, is central here too. It is interesting in this connection to note a passage in *Postscript* just prior to the one Pattison quotes.

Referring again to Magister Kierkegaard, and talking again of the discourses, Climacus points out that these had

> steadily kept pace with [the pseudonymous books], which to my mind was a hint that he had kept himself posted, and to me it was striking that the four most recent discourses have a carefully shaded touch of the humorous.[3] What is arrived at in immanence presumably ends in this way. Although the requirement of the ethical is affirmed, although life and existence are accentuated as a difficult course, the decision is nevertheless not placed in a paradox, and the metaphysical withdrawal [*Tilbagetagen*] through recollection into the eternal is continually possible and gives immanence a touch of humor as the infinite's revocation [*Tilbagekeldelse*] of the whole in the decisiveness of the eternity behind. The paradoxical expression of existence (that is, existing) as sin, the eternal truth as the paradox by having come into existence in time, in short, what is decisive for the Christian-religious, is not to be found in the upbuilding discourses.[4]

If something is "humanistic" because it is written from the side of immanence, then assuming what I said earlier is correct, it turns out that the philosophy in Climacus is not humanistic (and so in a deep sense not philosophy in the old sense either, however "dialectical" and philosophical in some new sense). Philosophers are dead serious, and Climacus, however serious his topic and also his project, is a humorist adopting a position in some sense *higher* than the immanentist perspective of the *Upbuilding Discourses,* but already on course away from philosophy, and in a direction that would give a reader who went in at the right coordinates the chance to benefit from the discourses. Climacus is not a Christian in the sense he gives some account of in *Postscript,* and before that in *Fragments* (where he talks of but mostly around and only indirectly of faith and sin). But he knows in "dialectical" terms ("dialectical" coming close to "philosophical" in at least one sense) what it takes and ushers the reader to what, as Climacus says in the same passage, is the final *terminus a quo,* namely humor, from which "defining" a Christian starts. The edifying/upbuilding discourses are on this side of humor, though as Climacus notes, some of them are heading in his humorous direction. Others later, the Christian discourses, are on the other side.

The thought that readers of Kierkegaard must step into the theological circle prompts other questions of the requirements Kierkegaard's reader must satisfy in order to appreciate what he wrote. The term "appreciate" is a little vague here. Even if in order to have a personal appreciation of the point of *Fragments* and *Postscript* it may be necessary to have faith, or at least some sense of the needs to which faith responds, appreciation of *that* (higher-order) fact may be all you need to grasp the point in the more hypothetical spirit characteristic of philosophers and historians of ideas. That, of course, widens the readership enormously. But then there are also considerations that work in the opposite direction. Those that Marilyn Piety brings on stage threaten to reduce that vast pool to a near-dry puddle. Her vividly drawn example of Plato's *Republic* illustrates just how the serious-minded scholar might have been misled for centuries about its author's intentions; having learned about Socratic irony we see it everywhere and thus miss clear cases of broad Socratic humor, and on the other hand, the fascism one sees in Plato's just state, instead of being a deadly serious result of applying Socratic irony, beginning from scratch as it were, could have been intended (in another ironical way) as an awful example. As I see it, and Piety seems to agree, *Postscript* has suffered the opposite fate. The widely hyped irony of the pseudonyms has led intelligent people to treat *Postscript* as a very long joke. What it is taken to say, in its jocular spirit, and to those with enough philosophy to appreciate the jest, is: This is the mess you get into when you try to approach religious truth in your way. Here, too, one fails to see the humor for the irony, though in this case the humor is not of the direct kind readable in Socrates' remark to his interlocutors (that they were not very clever people). Climacus's humor is the way to talk about the most serious things if you are not to dismiss them as absurd.

Penetrating the uncertainties of an ironical text so as to reach a position where you can appreciate the point of its pseudonymous author's humor, as identifying something beyond irony but which irony somehow helps you to locate, and, on the other, besides all that, to be able by breaking the code of the pseudonymity to reach the real author, this is asking much of the reader.

Kierkegaard's remark in the journals that *Postscript* is about personality, and that the reason why it is made to appear humorous is precisely that it is serious, must therefore seem a godsend. At one stroke it ushers us through these barriers to knowing quite well how to take the text. The reference to personality even encourages us to think that here we have a contribution to existential philosophy designed for Everyman.

But, as my remarks above in connection with Mooney indicate, for Kierkegaard and Climacus a target group of readers concerned at that time with personality would already possess some idea of having entered the theological circle. Not an adequate idea, but some idea, and this again sets limits to *Postscript*'s "public." Furthermore, since the text seems designed as much to put people off—that is, in a Socratic spirit to show up their ignorance—as to indicate the right way, we might expect its targeted reader, the appreciative reader, to be part of an even smaller group. Perhaps the best way of thinking of *Postscript*'s designed fate is as of a raft of ideas coordinated in the cause of the personality as individual, a raft cast adrift like a castaway's message in a bottle, to be picked up and read but only appreciated by those able to penetrate all those barriers on their own, without the help of Kierkegaard's audibly despairing remarks to posterity on what *Postscript* was about.

About *Fear and Trembling* Kierkegaard seems to have had none of the qualms that, judging by its last pages, he entertained in respect of *Postscript*, anxieties about finding his proper reader. He was clearly quite proud of this early work; with its "frightful pathos" it would by itself be enough to "immortalize" his name if "read" as he thought it would be and "translated into other languages."[5] The fact that it has "taken off" in the way it has would surely have delighted him. That every year something like 10,000 students in the United States alone buy copies of *Fear and Trembling* a century and a half after his death would have pleased immensely someone in whom, as the journals reveal, there was a deep appreciation of the need to appeal to creative imagination in the young.

How pleased he would have been with the ways philosophers have treated this text is another matter, one that might even be added to the innumerable issues that have been extracted from or applied to the text. Some, especially those who read the pseudonymous works as blank checks to be filled out as each reader finds it fitting and edifying to do so, see a Kierkegaardian virtue in a multiplicity of readings. That's what the text was for. But as just noted, considerable confusion is caused by the irony it supposedly contains. Doesn't the irony get in the way of any reading at all?

But how much irony is there in the text? Among some scholarly readers, and some less scholarly, there appears to be a general expectation that, whether just to provoke the reader or perhaps appeal to a humorous streak, their pseudonymous authors are out to tease. I find Dan Conway's more than scholarly reading of *Fear and Trembling* inviting this thought.

Conway detects a tease at the very start—in fact even before the start, though in order to appreciate the joke the reader must already have experienced Johannes's "extreme" chattiness. The joke is in the misnomer "Johannes de Silentio."

Just why should "Johannes de Silentio" be considered a misnomer? Why not read "de Silentio" as "concerning silence" (rather than representing it)? Recall Wittgenstein's famous remark to his publisher that his work, in the manuscript for the *Tractatus,* "consists of two parts: the one presented here plus all that I have not written," and that it is "precisely this second part" that is the "most important."[6] Wittgenstein saw himself as drawing limits to the ethical sphere "from inside." Might we not take Johannes to be drawing limits to the sayable from the sphere of what can be said? We might say that even—yet also with the prospect of some finer and significant comparisons—if for Johannes (or the purposes of his maker) ethics is included without complication within the sayable.

Is Johannes all that garrulous? Admittedly he is more talkative than the cryptic author of the *Tractatus,* but isn't it going a little far to say that *Fear and Trembling* contains "lengthy disputations, didactic digressions, elliptical illustrations, and parabolic comparisons"? How is it that I for one find *Fear and Trembling* (with *Sickness* a close competitor) the most compellingly taut of Kierkegaard's compositions? There is the brief preface clearing away unwanted interpretations of Abraham's trial; then the opening lyric of innocent but uncomprehending praise; then the positing of a distinction between the tragic hero and the knight of faith with attendant illustration; and, finally, Johannes pushing the latter in Abraham's person firmly beyond the sayable—all done neatly enough and within just over one hundred pages

And all pointing, surely, toward what on the book's terms cannot be said. Have I failed to take the full measure of this remarkable text? Is there much more to it than that? Should we look more closely at the details? Conway's example suggests we should.

If the details add to our insight into how far Johannes has to go before consigning Abraham to unintelligibility, I agree. Some philosophers think the details are what matter most. They look, as did Derrida, that most garrulous of philosophers, for those small and apparently incidental features that tend to throw another light on the most literal reading of the text, features that if highlighted may undermine and even contradict what the author appears to be saying, and perhaps even wanted to say. Conway's way with detail is not like that. It fastens on things that seem to get in the way of our understanding of how it is that Abraham escapes Johannes's understanding. Or that is how it strikes me. Not content with grasping the point of Johannes's role in the rather straightforward terms I have sketched, Conway looks in the text for things that Johannes de Silentio himself is silent about. Thus, and crucially according to Conway, Johannes is silent about Abraham's response to the angel of the Lord's telling Abraham not to lay his hand on Isaac. There are also mysteries to clear up about Johannes's revisions of the biblical narrative. Instead of accepting as Abraham's last word the sentence attributed to him in the Bible ("Here I am"), Johannes writes as though the last word were the earlier reply to his son's questioning "Father." These things provides Conway with much food for thought. His whole discussion shows great hermeneutical acuity, but as I see it the questions to which he seeks answers are at times wrongly motivated. Conway reads Johannes as though the latter's version of the narrative had to be superimposed on the biblical text and its omissions revealed as subtle or pregnant silences. I would incline instead to read the Johannes version as canonical for what Johannes wants to say within the sayable about what cannot be said, and about which he is forced by his own inquiry to be silent. Johannes says that the last word according to his own version is ironical. In saying "God himself will provide the lamb for a burn offering, my son" Abraham might as well have said nothing, since there was nothing he could say and at the same time mean in a way that Isaac would understand. But then saying nothing can also be misunderstood, so he says something, but without meaning it. What more need we say?

To say that *Fear and Trembling* contains lengthy disputations, didactic digressions, elliptical illustrations, and parabolic comparisons is itself perhaps to say something ironic. I suspect here some rhetoric on Conway's part, which, of course, is quite acceptable. But there is something misleading as well as, shall we say exaggerated, about this list, and with at least one of them I wonder if it isn't Conway who is misled, perhaps by a piece of rhetoric on Johannes's part. Conway's example of a digression is the series of failed analogies preceding Johannes's admission in the third problema that in the end he can only admire Abraham, not understand him. Why should this be a digression? The failures make ever more and ever more concretely clear precisely that point at which Abraham will not be understood. Conway writes that Johannes "concedes" that this is a "protracted digression," but if the reader sees a concession in what Johannes writes there, it may be more a matter of his style.

It is, of course, hard and probably impossible to set limits on how much can be read from this text. At some point, and just as indeterminable, it becomes unclear whether what we read out of it is not something we read into it. Can we really glean enough from Johannes's text to "chart Abraham's growth over the course of his ideal"? Or to do that must we read Johannes's text in conjunction with the biblical narrative? There are moments in Conway's discussion where Johannes sounds as if he were offering a contribution to the celebrated debate on the Aquedah. Perhaps it is not an accident that neither Johannes nor, so far as I know, Kierkegaard himself uses that term.

It is inevitable that a text at once so accessible and intractable should become a mine for scholarly delving, and that such mind-catching themes as the suspension of the ethical should attract interpretations as diverse as they have.

John Davenport cuts a refreshing and convincing swathe through most of the history of this dispute, ending up with a reading that is happily attentive to the text alone. I have one general comment to make on his discussion and several smaller ones.

The general comment picks up from Pattison's remark that we should not see Kierkegaard as contributing to the solution of particular philosophical debates. It is all too easy to place Kierkegaard's works in debates where it is far from obvious that they belong. Or if they do, then to place them there is to have them take part in disputes of a kind in which Kierkegaard would not feel at home. I don't mean to say that this should never be done. If Kierkegaard can be used to add substance and zest to these discussions, fine, but then we should always be on the look out in case what is essentially Kierkegaardian is the idea that we should not be bothered too much by discussions of this kind. Quite a lot of the fuss about *Fear and Trembling* may well be misplaced. I think that much of what Davenport discusses is of this kind, but in flexing the notion of eschatology quite a bit, as he does, he nevertheless succeeds, in his own account, in putting *Fear and Trembling* in touch with the last things, and even better, in a way we may readily think Kierkegaard intended.

The particular comments are as follows. First, there is that question of whether the Knight of Infinite Resignation can be placed "within the ethical." Davenport says he occupies "a kind of limiting point" there, which I assume we can read in conjunction with his opening remark that *Fear and Trembling* is about the relation between the ethical and the religious stages, and that this is "well known." I find that a little misleading. There are other things *Fear and Trembling* can equally be said to be about. Davenport himself says that the "main point" of the work is "to present the essence of 'faith' as . . . eschatological trust," which is not on the surface the same topic and in fact seems the better account. What the text says is that the Knight of Resignation's "stage" is the last one before faith, and that it is a necessary preliminary to faith. So why should there be anything like a preliminary to faith in what is referred to as "the ethical" in this work, which describes the ethical as a self-enclosed system, resting "immanently in itself," with nothing "outside itself"?[7] Second, I agree with Davenport's account of the *telos* toward which the ethical is suspended, as a promise that "what is only an ideal form in the moral-universal will be actualized." This seems to me both right and a way of taking what I said in reply to Jamie Ferreira about the agapeistic ideal being a paradigm. It does not mean that the variety of everyday loving relationships, even if all fail to conform with the paradigm, are immoral, but that, under the shadow of the paradigm, these relationships look less like love than we would prefer to think.

Third, Davenport notes a terminological link between *Fear and Trembling* and the first of the discourses from 1843 (the same period as *Fear and Trembling*), which Pattison also discusses. The "trusting expectancy" (Hong translation) shown by Abraham, once assured he would be the father of Isaac and the generations to come, and "Troens Forventning," which is the topic of the first of these discourses. This is interesting because the faith that is the topic of the discourse is surely closer to Abraham's attitude or state of mind before he received God's command than to the pathos-filled way he saw matters after receiving it. What the command introduces is, so to speak, another though crunching addition to what Abraham had to disbelieve even before receiving the awful command, namely, that as the years went by it was becoming less and less likely that he would have a son and thereby be the father of a great nation. I have just one slight quibble. I prefer my own translation of *Fear and Trembling*'s "trofaste forventning"[8] as "trusting [or even "loyal"] expectation" to the Hongs' "trusting expectancy," insofar as expectancy suggests a constant state of mind, even with some excitement added, while Abraham's attitude to what was promised is more like that of the trusty, or trusting, servant who believes his master and, in this case, far beyond the normal fathering age, maintains his belief about forthcoming fatherhood.

Finally, on the matter of whether the ethics that is teleologically suspended is only Hegelian or also Kantian. I think this is one of those cases where we go beyond what needs to be unraveled to catch the text's meaning. Both Kant and, strange though it may seem, also Hegel can be left out of it. As for Kant, a prima facie reason for not including Kant is the Kantianism in *Works of Love*. The more reason there is for taking *Works of Love,* and the principle of a unified ethical will, both of which belong to the religious stages, as Kantian in spirit, the less sense it makes to take the ethical that has to be suspended in *Fear and Trembling* for the religious to break through to be Kant's ethics. There is also a terminological fact. Kierkegaard's "det Almene," although usually translated as "the universal," means in a Hegelian context something less formalistic than, for example, a criterion like "universalizability" implies; something more in line with "general" and in some contexts even just what is "common." If you take a biographical perspective (not such a bad thing to do in this case) regarding the origins and motivations for Kierkegaard's works, you see that the most cogent aspect of ethics in this connection, the Abraham situation, is the reproach one receives from one's society, a reproach not based on arguments of the kind that Kant presents for ensuring goodness of the will, but on the general understanding that moral principles embodied or embedded in a given society, and not even universal between societies, are both the correct ones and also exceptionless. This is, indeed, much closer to Hegel than to Kant. But there is also a reason why it may be wrong to say that the ethics teleologically suspended is specifically Hegel's. It is the reason that Bob Roberts has given, a reason why it is wrong to say that the suspended ethics are either Kantian or Hegelian, or any other philosopher's ethics. Why should Kierkegaard have any special philosophical theory in mind at all? Was it not just that he happened to be addressing philosophically literate readers to whom Hegel's account of ethics would seem close enough to the way in which their own ethics actually worked, to the extent that it did, quite independently of the philosophers? Hegel at the time was the most influential spokesman for the form of social ethics that Abraham had to be able to find a new way of addressing. It was the very same form that Kierkegaard himself had to contend with, and which provided the motivation for his life and work.

Notes

Introduction

Epigraph from *The Moment and Late Writings, Kierkegaard's Writings* XXIII, trans. and ed. Howard V. Hong and Edna Hong (Princeton, N.J.: Princeton University Press, 1998), pp. 340–343. See also from these pages Kierkegaard's remark that "I do not call myself a Christian; I do not speak of myself as a Christian."

1. Stanley Cavell, a reader of Kierkegaard at least through the late 1950s, continues Kierkegaard's themes. He writes that I am aware of my words as mine as I abandon them, forgo owning them, as Abraham will be aware of Isaac as belonging to him as he forgoes him, relinquishes him, abandons him. His favorite comedies are of remarriage, where one gives up a marriage and gets it back, a "double movement of faith." It's also what Kierkegaard would call "repetition," giving up the world and getting it back. And it's what Kierkegaard does in 'revoking' what he says at the end of *Postscript,* say. He gives up ownership of his words there. See Cavell, *Philosophical Passages: Wittgenstein, Emerson, Austin, Derrida* (Oxford: Blackwell, 1995), p. 103.

2. Cavell writes, "the 'having' of a self is being the other to one's self, calling upon it with the words of others." "The having of a self is the very opposite of possessiveness—it is the power of receptivity; So the question becomes, on what terms will the self be received?" (*Passages,* p. 102).

3. See my *On Søren Kierkegaard: Dialogue, Polemic, Lost Intimacy and Time* (London: Ashgate, 2007). David Possen explores these themes in *Søren Kierkegaard and the Very Idea of Advance beyond Socrates* (Ph.D. diss., University of Chicago, forthcoming).

4. I defend this convergence of the Socratic and the Christian, and the downplaying of the contrast between Religiousness A and Religiousness B, in *On Søren Kierkegaard.*

5. See George Pattison, *Kierkegaard's Upbuilding Discourses: Philosophy, Literature, Theology* (New York, Routledge, 2002). Pattison argues that a unifying aim of the authorship is a Socratic pursuit of (Christian) love.

6. I discuss these striking claims in *On Søren Kierkegaard.*

7. Tyler Roberts, "Criticism as a Conduct of Gratitude: Stanley Cavell and Radical Theology" (forthcoming).

1. Kierkegaard on the Self

I want to thank Jane Rubin, who, over the many years we have taught Kierkegaard together, has helped me develop and refine the interpretation presented here.

1. Blaise Pascal, *Pascal Pensées* (New York: E. P. Dutton, 1958), p. 28, #89.

2. Ibid., p. 121, #434.

3. Ibid., p. 98, #353.

4. I'm indebted to Jane Rubin for this systematic account of the factors of the self.

5. Søren Kierkegaard, *The Sickness unto Death,* trans. Alastair Hannay, abridged and modified (London: Penguin Books, 1989), pp. 43–44.

6. See Hubert Dreyfus, *Thinking in Action: On the Internet,* ed. R. Kearney and S. Critchley, rev. ed. (New York: Routledge, 2002).

7. *Sickness unto Death,* p. 43.

8. Søren Kierkegaard, *Either/Or,* trans. Alastair Hannay (London: Penguin, 1992).

9. Ibid., p. 44.

10. *Sickness unto Death,* p. 54.

11. Ibid., p. 51.

12. The ultimate despair, Kierkegaard contends, is denying that one is in despair by denying the demand that we express the two sets of factors in our lives in a way that enables them to reinforce each other. This is not the distraction of the present age where one represses the call to be a self. Rather, someone, say, Richard Rorty, in this ultimate form of despair sees that in our religious tradition the self has, indeed, been constituted as having two sets of essential but incompatible factors, but claims that this is merely a mistaken, essentialist view that we can and should opt out of. Since the traditional Judeo-Christian understanding of the self leads people to despair, we should simply give it up and adopt a vocabulary and practices that are more useful to us now.

How can we decide who is right here, Kierkegaard or the pragmatist? I think this is a question we can only approach experientially. In *Sickness unto Death,* Kierkegaard tries to show that the Christian claim that the self is a contradiction is confirmed by a purportedly exhaustive categorization of all the ways of being a self available to us and how each fails. The only test is the test of existence.

13. Ibid.

14. Søren Kierkegaard, *Fear and Trembling,* trans. Alastair Hannay (London: Penguin, 1985), p. 70.

15. Ibid., p. 71.

16. Søren Kierkegaard, *Journals,* ed. and trans. A. Dru (London: Oxford University Press, 1951), August 1, 1835, p. 15.

17. Søren Kierkegaard, *Concluding Unscientific Postscript,* trans. D. F. Swenson and W. Lowrie (Princeton, N.J.: Princeton University Press, 1968), p. 181.

18. Ibid., p. 70.

19. *Fear and Trembling,* p. 72.

20. Ibid., p. 65.

21. *Sickness unto Death,* p. 71.

22. Søren Kierkegaard, *Training in Christianity and the Edifying Discourse Which "Accompanied" It,* trans. Walter Lowrie (Princeton, N.J.: Princeton University Press, 1967), p. 109.

23. *Postscript,* p. 498.

24. Ibid., p. 178.

25. Ibid., p. 181.

26. Sartre gives the example of a person who has an emotional crisis as an adolescent, which he interprets as a religions calling and acts on by becoming a monk. Then later, he comes to interpret the experience as just an adolescent psychotic episode, and leaves the monastery to become a businessman. But on his deathbed, he feels that his was a religious calling after all,

and repents. Sartre concludes that our past is constantly up for reinterpretation, and the final interpretation is an accidental result of what we happen to think as we die.

27. *Postscript*, p. 277.

28. Ibid., p. 506.

29. Ibid.

30. *Postscript*, p. 188.

31. *Fear and Trembling*, p. 79.

32. *Sickness unto Death*, p. 71.

33. *Fear and Trembling*, p. 97.

34. Ibid., p. 85.

35. Ibid., p. 106.

36. Ibid., p. 139.

37. Ibid., p. 103.

38. Ibid., pp. 106–107.

39. Ibid., p. 137.

40. Ibid., p. 106.

41. Ibid., p. 103.

42. *Sickness unto Death*, p. 44.

43. Ibid., p. 46.

44. *Postscript*, p. 290.

45. Søren Kierkegaard, *A Literary Review*, trans. Alastair Hannay (London: Penguin, 2001), p. 63.

2. Affectation, or the Invention of the Self

1. Bruce H. Kirmmse, *Encounters with Kierkegaard* (Princeton, N.J.: Princeton University Press, 1996), p. 32.

2. I have discussed "modernity" elsewhere, so here it will be sufficient to say that modernization involves the replacement of a relatively compact, face-to-face, rural, agricultural society with a large-scale, anonymous, urban, mercantile-industrial society. Market-determined prices and interest rates replace traditional feudal dues and guild regulations. The secret (and anonymous) ballot replaces royal, aristocratic, or ecclesiastical fiat. The anonymous voice of "public opinion" replaces deference to notables and other traditional loci of authority. And a variegated society of estates is replaced the uniformity of an atomistic-individualistic whole.

3. E. Cassirer, P. O. Kristeller, and J. H. Randall, Jr., eds., *The Renaissance Philosophy of Man* (Chicago: University of Chicago Press, 1948), pp. 224–225.

4. Ibid., p. 225.

5. Indeed, the concept of obsession itself became an obsession. Any careful reader of Kierkegaard and his contemporaries cannot fail to be struck by the number of times the concept and the terminology of "obsession" (often rendered in Franco-Danish as *fixe ide*) recurs.

6. Stendhal, *The Red and the Black*, trans. Lowell Bair (New York: Bantam Books, 1958), p. 505.

7. Ibid., p. 504. Yet only a few days before his end, Sorel had lamented that "the influence of my contemporaries still prevails. . . . Talking to myself, all alone, with death staring me in the face, I'm still a hypocrite.—O nineteenth century!" (p. 499).

There are many parallels that could be drawn between the characters in Stendhal's novel and the historical person Søren Kierkegaard. Here I will only point out that Julien Sorel's passionate and self-dramatizing mistress, the snobbish Mathilde de la Môle, who finds everything modern to be false and affected, insists that she is impressed only by utmost sincerity such as that evinced by her ancestor Boniface de la Môle, who was executed for his religious beliefs during the French civil wars of religion in the sixteenth century: "I can't think of anything which distinguishes a man except a death sentence" (p. 295). Mathilde was therefore delighted with Julien's choice of the authenticity of death—the only unequivocal escape from affectation. Kierkegaard seems to have been of the same caste of mind as Mathilde de la Môle when he commented to a friend "that from now on he was only going to read 'writings by men who have been executed'" (remark of Kierkegaard reported by C. J. Brandt; published in Kirmmse, *Encounters with Kierkegaard*, p. 59). It seems clear that this view of death—as the only definitive method of avoiding affectation—played a part in Kierkegaard's increasing fascination with martyrdom.

8. George Bryant Brummell (1778–1840), a very interesting case.

9. "Forberedelser til en Afhandling om Affectation" [Preparations for an Essay on Affection], in *Efterladte Skrifter af Poul M. Møller* [Posthumous Writings of Poul M. Møller], 3rd ed., ed. L. V. Petersen and with a biographical sketch by F. C. Olsen, 6 vols. (Copenhagen: C. A. Reitzel, 1855–56), vol. 3, pp. 163–188.

10. Ibid., vol. 3, p. 164, emphasis added.

11. Ibid., pp. 176–177.

12. All cited passages in this paragraph are from ibid., vol. 3, p. 165.

13. In an (Hegelian?) aside, set off in parentheses, Møller goes on to assert that this highest degree of "personal truth" cannot be attained "by means of merely subjective thinking," inasmuch as it requires that "the subject acknowledge that the rational order—which, without the subject's assistance, has its development within existence—is a work of the same Reason that constitutes the genuine truth of the subject's will." Møller then concludes this aside by stating, still parenthetically, that "the proof of this [is] not germane at this point" (ibid., p. 165).

14. Ibid., pp. 165–166.

15. Ibid., p. 169 (emphasis added).

16. Ibid., p. 170.

17. Ibid., pp. 169–170.

18. Ibid., p. 176.

19. Ibid., p. 181.

20. Ibid., pp. 170–172 (emphasis added).

21. Ibid., p. 172.

22. Ibid., p. 177.

23. Ibid., pp. 175–176.

24. Ibid., p. 182.

25. Ibid., p. 177 (emphasis in original).

26. Kirmmse, *Encounters with Kierkegaard*, p. 241.

27. *Søren Kierkegaards Papirer* (The Papers of Søren Kierkegaard), ed. P. A. Heiberg, V. Kuhr, and E. Torsting, 2nd enlarged ed. by N. Thulstrup, 16 vols. in 22 tomes (Copenhagen: Gyldendal, 1968–1978) (hereafter *"Pap."* followed by volume number; volume part number, if any; section letter, and entry number), XI 1 A 275 (1854). Elsewhere in the entry Kierkegaard expresses some doubt as to whether Møller had actually uttered those words to Sibbern on his deathbed, but Kierkegaard does affirm that "when he [Møller] was alive, that was his expression again and again."

28. *Pap.* II A 102.

29. *Søren Kierkegaards Samlede Værker* (The Collected Works of Søren Kierkegaard), ed. A. B. Drachmann, J. L. Heiberg, and H. O. Lange, 14 vols. (Copenhagen: Gyldendal, 1901–1906) (hereafter *"SV1"* followed by volume and page number), vol. 8, pp. 58–59.

30. *SV1*, vol. 7, p. 35.

31. *SV1*, vol. 12, p. 435.

32. *SV1*, vol. 14, p. 301.

33. A clear allusion to Grundtvig's preaching style. In his essay on affectation Møller also criticizes Grundtvig and his party as "purists [who] build a factory for domestic words which are supposed to replace other, current terms whose right to be regarded as native citizens is suspect. They save these home-made words in their piggy banks, and when they have collected enough of them they take the occasion to write about one or another trivial topic" (Møller, *op. cit.*, p. 186).

34. *SV1*, vol. 11, pp. 105–106.

35. See, e.g., P. M. Møller, *op. cit.,* vol. 3, pp. 8, 13, 15, and 33 [*Strøtanker I. 1819–1821*].
36. Ibid., p. 8.
37. *SV1,* vol. 11, p. 138.
38. *SV1,* vol. 11, p. 140.
39. Ibid., p. 139 (emphasis added).
40. Ibid., p. 157.
41. Ibid.
42. Ibid., p. 156.
43. Ibid.
44. Ibid., p. 199 (emphasis added).
45. Møller, *op. cit.,* pp. 170–72 (emphasis added).
46. Kierkegaard, *SV1,* vol. 11, p. 204.
47. Ibid., p. 212 (emphasis added).
48. Møller, *Op. cit.,* vol. 3, p. 176.
49. *Pap.* XI A, A 119 (1854).
50. *SV1,* vol. 14, p. 6.

3. *Postscript* Ethics

1. Alastair Hannay, *Kierkegaard: A Biography* (Cambridge, 2001), p. 300.

2. Papirer X 2 A 130 [436]

3. Stuart Hampshire helpfully distinguishes prohibitions, virtues, and ways of life as three strands of "the moral." This broad view of "the moral" gives a better access to "Kierkegaard's ethics" than trying to make it out to be either Hegelian or Kantian, say, or some mix.

4. *Concluding Unscientific Postscript to the Philosophical Fragments,* Vol. I, trans. Howard V. and Edna H. Hong (Princeton, N.J.: Princeton University Press, 1992). *Postscript*'s Book One, in English translations, is perhaps fifty pages; the remaining pages, numbering over five hundred, constitute Book Two. This makes the initial division crazily lopsided. Part One of Book Two presents a somewhat continuous argument through one hundred odd pages. Part Two, with various appendices, numbers roughly 440 pages, creating another lopsided division.

5. See Hannay, *Kierkegaard,* p. 315. I owe a great debt to Hannay's work, especially his appreciation of *Postscript* as the completion of a Faust project; the importance of the *Journal* revelation that in *Postscript,* "we have personality"; the neglected issue of "how long" to stay with the text; and the ghostliness of Kierkegaard's presence.

6. See Hannay, *Biography,* p. 300.

7. See Robert C. Roberts, "Existence, Emotion, and Virtue: Classical Themes in Kierkegaard," in *The Cambridge Companion to Kierkegaard,* ed. Alastair Hannay and Gordon Marion (Cambridge University Press, 1998). Roberts takes Climacus's talk of "subjective thinking" as a way of reviving the classical interest in virtue and traits of character. From the angle that Roberts presents, the maxim "truth is subjectivity" can be heard as shorthand for the following (my words): "In matters of ethical truth, what is essential is character and virtue—that is, subjectivity." Advocacy of subjective thinking is advocacy of practical wisdom (as opposed to objective thinking, which is advocacy of theoretical and observational knowledge).

8. He tells the story of a crazy fellow obsessed with proving his sanity by telling the truth and nothing but the truth, over and over: "The world is round" . . . *CUP,* p. 195.

9. Hannay, *Biography,* p. 66.

10. Kierkegaard, *CUP,* p. 357; my essay "Exemplars, Inwardness, and Belief: Kierkegaard on Indirect Communication," in *International Kierkegaard Commentary, Postscript,* ed. Robert L. Perkins (Macon, Ga.: Mercer University Press, 1999), p. 145.

11. Hannay gives a sample of the causes that claim to be *Postscript* heirs: the efforts of Husserl, Heidegger, or Sartre; the inauguration of a postmodern theology; an improved Fichtean theory of Subjectivity; an existential Christian Apologetics; a critique of the ideology and practices of "mass society"; a piece of straightforward philosophy, say, a defense of subjectivity

as conscience, commitment, perhaps a witty parody or expose of the genre of speculative philosophy, a mock-argument so cleverly constructed that only professional philosophers will get the joke. See *Biography,* p. 297.

12. Note that this division between objective and subjective stages of existence replaces the more touted threefold division of stages.

13. See Roberts, note 7, above.

14. Kierkegaard's advance on the romantics, in his conception of personality, is to shift the act of synthesis, *Bildung,* from human imagination or a human-initiated poetic or practical project, to a faith-based project dependent on other than human powers. See Alastair Hannay, *Kierkegaard and Philosophy* (Routledge, 2003), p. 23. Note that some time after Judge William, the "building-up" of personality becomes a *down-sizing* of self-importance—which might seem to be the reverse of *Bildung.* But "cultivation" remains in a paring and weeding that allows the primitivity or passion of personality to flower.

15. What Climacus calls "essential knowledge" is a kind of Socratic self-knowledge. I warn in the next section that this may be a misnomer. To know oneself or to have "essential knowledge" seems less a matter of fulfilling a cognitive pursuit than a matter of "knowing where one stands," that is, being able to avow one's commitments responsibly. "Essential knowledge," we could say, is a state of character rather than a state of cognition or knowing. It is the capacity to enter a deposition on one's own behalf.

16. This moment of taking responsibility-for-self is characterized by Paul Ricoeur as a kind of "backward promise" insofar as it's a testimony (a promise or vow) that one *has* been thus and so, as well as that one *will* be thus and so. See Anne-Christine Habbard's discussion, op. cit., p. 185f.

17. In availing myself of the image of "taking up" something as one's own, I mean not the selection of something from a static array, as if to "own" something were to lift it from the shelf, pay for it, and take it home. To make a way of being one's own is closer to taking up a theme in the improvising of a jazz ensemble, taking up with the theme or motif, and in renewing it in one's own life, showing that the rendition was not just a replication but taking up with it as one's own.

18. He's responsible for the pseudonyms, but disavows responsibility for being anything more than a "prompter."

19. See note 15, above, on "essential knowledge."

20. *CUP,* p. 357

21. *CUP,* p. 351 [Swenson's translation has ". . . dialectical enough to interpenetrate it with thought."]

22. Hannay, *Biography,* p. 152.

4. Kierkegaard on Commitment, Personality, and Identity

1. John D. Caputo, *More Radical Hermeneutics: On Not Knowing Who We Are* (Bloomington: Indiana University Press, 2000), p. 47.

2. Michael Theunissen, *Kierkegaard's Concept of Despair,* trans. Barbara Harshav and Helmut Illbruck (Princeton, N.J.: Princeton University Press, 2005). For further references see Cappelørn's essay in this volume.

3. "Kierkegaard's Present Day and Ours," ed. Mark A. Wrathall and Jeff Malpas, *Heidegger, Authenticity, and Modernity: Essays in Honor of Hubert L. Dreyfus,* Vol. 1 (Cambridge, Mass.: MIT Press, pp. 105–122), and Dreyfus's reply, pp. 321–323. See also Hubert Dreyfus and Jane Rubin, "Kierkegaard on the Nihilism of the Present Age: The Case of Commitment as Addiction," *Synthese* 98, no. 1 (January 1994), pp. 3–19, and my reply, pp. 103–106.

4. If we adopt an adverbial reading and take "fortvivlet" to mean "desperately" or "despairingly" to modify the cases *Sickness* categorizes as "despair" (not wanting to be oneself and wanting to be one's own as against one's God-given self), we get something like the following.

The former reads as "not wanting to be oneself, but realizing one has to be it all the same, trying even harder not to be oneself or clinging to the project of not being oneself even though it now seems impossible"; and the second reads as "wanting to be one's own self, while knowing one has to be the self based on God (or the "power"), and either despairingly trying even harder to be one's own self or desperately supporting the project of being one's own self in the realization one will have to let go of it." Both might be defended by appeal to the notion of the sickness unto death itself, as something that cannot be eradicated by death. The idea would be that we are forced to admit that we have to become (to put it a little glibly) our true selves, however much we try to avoid being them by not being ourselves or by trying to be our own selves. The reading may seem plausible up to a point but has at least one crucial drawback. In the text despair is discussed as a more or less deliberate and entrenched disposition to shun truth (identified in the second section of *Sickness* as sin), but the adverbial reading renders despair as no more than the frame of mind of someone who shuns truth (what more properly counts as despair) but somehow sees that it cannot be shunned. None of this is supported by the analysis of despair provided by the text. A third possibility, proposed by Michael Theunissen but with the text adjusted correspondingly (Theunissen, op. cit.), takes the first of the two forms of despair in *Sickness* (not wanting to be oneself) to be a general reluctance to be the self one happens (historically) to be, and not, as on my reading and Kierkegaard's text, as a variant of the second form, which the text describes as a kind of defiance (of Christian truth). Here, since so far there is no sinning as such, the "frame of mind" reading works (being landed despairingly with what or who one is, i.e., wanting not to be that self but sensing one can't get rid of it).

5. *Journals and Papers,* trans. Hong (Indianapolis: Indiana University Press, 1975), 3109; *Kierkegaards Papirer [Papirer],* 2nd enlarged ed. by N. Thulstrup (Copenhagen: Gyldendal, 1968–78), X3 A609 (1850); *Søren Kierkegaards Skrifter [SKS],* ed. Søren Kierkegaard Forskningscenteret (Copenhagen: Gads Forlag, 1997–), NB 21 (vol. not yet published).

6. *The Sickness unto Death,* trans. Alastair Hannay (Harmondsworth: Penguin Books, 1989), p. 54.

7. *Papirer,* VII 1 A 89.

8. *Papirer,* X 2 A 130; *Papers and Journals: A Selection,* trans. Alastair Hannay (Harmondsworth: Penguin Books, 1996), p. 436.

9. Hegel himself talks of "pure" personality (*Hegel's Science of Logic,* trans. A. V. Miller [London: George Allen & Unwin, 1969], p. 841), but in Hegel images of divinity are to be replaced by reason; pure personality is not part of a theistic notion from which an ideal of human personality can be derived; it is what the individual becomes insofar as images of God as any kind of concrete subject are replaced by absolute knowledge. Here, of course, Kierkegaard stands diametrically opposed to a Hegel who can say: "[T]he ego, as personality, is already the Idea, though in its most abstract shape" (*Hegel's Philosophy of Right,* trans. T. M. Knox [Oxford: Oxford University Press, 1967, p. 253). However, it is true to say both that Kierkegaard shared with Hegel and other philosophers, for instance, Jacobi, a belief in the importance of the concept of personality, and that, except as regards the manner of its realization, it was the same concept that they shared. One shared aspect of the concept is the "spiritual" nature of realized personality (cf. the early *From the Papers of One Still Living,* where Kierkegaard asserts that writers must first "win a personality" in order for their works to contain anything like an "immortal spirit that survives everything," a notion linked there to those of a life-view and the need for a literary work to have its own center of gravity [*SKS* 1, pp. 36–38]).

10. See *Papirer,* XII, C19, p. 74, II A 31, pp. 29–30, etc.

11. *Papirer,* X 2 A 130; *Papers and Journals: A Selection,* op. cit., p. 436.

12. "Der höchste, wahrhaft das Weltproblem lösende Gedanke die Idee des in seiner idealen wie realen Unendlichkeit sich wissenden, durchschauenden Ursubjekts oder der absoluten Persönlichkeit [ist]. . . . Die Weltschöpfung und Erhaltung, was eben die Weltwirklichkeit ausmacht, besteht lediglich in der ununterbrochenen, vom Bewusstsein durchdrungenen Willenserweisung Gottes, so dass er nur Bewusstsein und Wille, beides aber in höchster Einheit, er allein mithin Person, oder sie im eminentesten Sinne ist." The quotation, whose references I

have been unable to locate, is cited in R. Steiner, *Die Rätsel der Philosophie in ihrer Geschichte als Umriss dargestellt* (1914), in *Gesamtausgabe,* Dornach: Rudolf Steiner Verlag, 2002, p. 281 (Eng. trans., *The Riddles of Philosophy,* Spring Valley, N.Y.: Athroposophic Press, 1973, pp. 204–205).

13. *Concluding Unscientific Postscript,* trans. David F. Swenson and Walter Lowrie (Princeton, N.J.: Princeton University Press, 1941), p. 296/ *Kierkegaard's Writings,* Vol. XII, 1, trans. Howard V. Hong and Edna H. Hong (Princeton, N.J.: Princeton University Press, 1992), p. 332.

14. Ibid., p. 290/326.

15. Ibid., p. 220/246.

5. Love and the Discipline of Philosophy

1. In *Kierkegaard and Philosophy,* they appear in reverse chronological order: "Kierkegaard's Philosophy of Mind" appears as "Philosophy of Mind" on pages 24–41, while "Kierkegaard and What We Mean by 'Philosophy'" is reprinted on pages 9–23 as "Climacus among the Philosophers."

2. *Kierkegaard and Philosophy,* 3–4.

3. David Chalmers, "Facing Up to the Problem of Consciousness," 201. It is in the process of defining the "hard problem" that Chalmers cites Nagel's essay.

4. "What Is It Like to Be a Bat?" 166–167.

5. *The View from Nowhere,* 7–8, 209. Edward Mooney discusses Nagel's work in connection with Kierkegaard's writings in *Selves in Discord and Resolve,* 77–88.

6. Hannay, "Kierkegaard's Philosophy of Mind," 179 (see *Kierkegaard and Philosophy,* 39). See also *Human Consciousness,* 38–41.

7. Kierkegaard speaks of *knowing* and *breathing* as analogous more than once in his journals: see, e.g., *Pap* II A 302 & II A 524.

8. Journal entry from 1846: *Pap* VII 1 A 191. Hannay translation: *Papers and Journals,* 240.

9. "Philosophical Progress in Language Theory," 1. Explaining the faith of his fellow positivists, Carnap writes that "[w]hen we say that scientific knowledge is unlimited, we mean: *there is no question whose answer is in principle unattainable by science.*" —*The Logical Structure of the World,* 290.

10. *Human Nature and the Limits of Science,* 1–2.

11. See, e.g., Dennett, *Consciousness Explained,* 460; Paul Churchland, *Matter and Consciousness,* 44; and Mackie, *Ethics,* 15. Regarding what follows, see also Natanson, *The Erotic Bird,* 13.

12. On category mistakes involving things that can be said to "exist" in different senses, see Ryle, *The Concept of Mind,* 22–23. See also Putnam, *Representation and Reality,* 58: if a thoroughly impersonal scientific explanation would show that there are no such things as "beliefs" and "purposes," then it would also show that there are no such things as "chairs" either! (Since a chair is a seat for one person with a back, and the concept of a chair is not part of the vocabulary of physics or neuroscience.)

13. Patricia Churchland, *Neurophilosophy,* 309. Cf. Hannay, *Human Consciousness,* 51.

14. I borrow this facetious example from Paul Grice: see *The Conception of Value,* 45.

15. Putnam, *Reason, Truth, and History,* 227. See also Mulhall, *Inheritance and Originality,* 251: "Such feelings can fit or fail to fit their context, but they cannot be identified at all in the absence of the types of situation that give rise to them."

16. Seneca, *De Ira* III.6.1. For a more extensive discussion of Stoic philosophy and Kierkegaard's polemical relation to it, see my book *Wisdom in Love.*

17. Marcus Aurelius, *Meditations* VI.13 & IV.48. For a sympathetic reading of the "almost medical" scientism that can be found in Stoicism see Hadot, *Philosophy as a Way of Life,* 185–187.

18. See *Meditations* VII.29 & XI.16. Regarding what follows, see also Kierkegaard, *Pap* VII 1

A 190: "It is simple and beautiful and moving when a lover looks lovingly at the loved one, but it is most fashionable to gaze at her through opera-glasses. And the physicist uses the microscope as a dandy uses opera-glasses; only, the microscope is focused on God." My translation.

19. *Journals & Papers*, §2993 (*Pap* XI 2 A 127). For a brief account of Kierkegaard's relation to the ancient Stoic theory of emotion, see my essay "The Virtues of Authenticity," 425–427.

20. *The Importance of What We Care About*, 80. See also John McDowell, *Mind and World*, 101. Burwood and his colleagues describe McDowell's position as follows: "What is natural about us, he argues, is not exhausted by what can be captured within the domain of scientific law. It is an entirely natural fact about us that we are the kind of creatures for whom the world presents itself in meaningful and significant ways, ways which give us reasons to judge and act. Such natural facts do not require anchorage within the framework of scientific explanation." —*Philosophy of Mind*, 111. Cf. Heidegger, *Being and Time*, §29.

21. Cf. Hannay, "Kierkegaard's Philosophy of Mind," 159–160 (see *Kierkegaard and Philosophy*, 25–26). See also *Human Consciousness*, 33–34, 62–63. John Riker describes emotions as "the glue that binds the psyche and world together . . . situating us in a vast web of interdependencies." —*Human Excellence and an Ecological Conception of the Psyche*, 106.

22. *The View from Nowhere*, 209.

23. *A Literary Review*, 65.

24. *Works of Love*, 215. My translation.

25. Kierkegaard's understanding of love as a kind of *care* prompts Ferreira to read *kjerlighed* as "caring": see *Love's Grateful Striving*, 43–44.

26. Cf. Hannay, *Kierkegaard and Philosophy*, 178.

27. *Eighteen Upbuilding Discourses*, 59.

28. Ferreira, *Love's Grateful Striving*, 287. See also Kierkegaard, *Works of Love*, 12.

29. Lingis, *The Imperative*, 120–121. Some of the preceding examples are also borrowed from Lingis: see *Dangerous Emotions*, 15–17.

30. Vacek, *Love, Human and Divine*, 56. See also Marion, *God without Being*, 136: "That which is, if it does not receive love, is as if it were not."

31. In *A Gentle Creature and Other Stories*, 108.

32. *Works of Love*, 225–228. Cf. Rudd, "'Believing all Things': Kierkegaard on Knowledge, Doubt, and Love." See also Burwood et al., *Philosophy of Mind*, 164: "Moral values [according to McDowell] are real features of the world, but are detectable only to creatures like ourselves equipped to respond to them in a characteristic way."

33. *An Essay Concerning Human Understanding* (Book II, Chapter 8, §19), in *Metaphysics*, edited by Cooper, 141.

34. See McDowell, *Mind and World*, 29–33. It has been recognized since the time of Berkeley that "the arguments against the idea that things are colored in the way they seem to be also cut against the idea that they are *shaped* in the way they seem to be, *solid* in the way they seem to be, etc." —Putnam, *The Threefold Cord*, 39. The mistake of naïve realism, of empiricism which is not aware of its own presuppositions, is that "it ascribes sense-dependent or mind-dependent properties to independently existing things," as if we had any access to objects other than through our own experience. See Magee, *The Philosophy of Schopenhauer*, 74–83.

35. Kierkegaard, *Christian Discourses*, 237. Cf. Jackson, "What Mary Didn't Know."

36. *Christian Discourses*, 237. Cf. Husserl, *The Idea of Phenomenology*, 4: "The blind man who wishes to see cannot be made to see by means of scientific proofs. Physical and physiological theories about colors give no 'seeing' clarity about the meaning of color as those with eyesight have it. If, therefore, the critique of cognition is a science, as it doubtless is in the light of these considerations, a science which is to clarify all species and forms of cognition, *it can make no use of any science of the natural sort*."

37. Kant, *Critique of Pure Reason* (footnote to §70 of the B edition), in *Metaphysics*, edited by Cooper, 194. In this note from the section called "General Observations on the Transcendental Aesthetic," Kant says that illusion arises if one ascribes the redness to the rose *in itself*, without taking account of its relation to the subject.

38. *Phenomenological Interpretations of Aristotle,* 68. On the following page, Heidegger adds that "it is not the case that objects are first present as bare realities, as objects in some natural state, and that they then in the course of our experience receive the garb of a value-character, so they do not have to run around naked." Roberts makes a similar point in *Emotions,* 80.

39. Kierkegaard, *Journals & Papers,* §2299.

40. Marion, *Prolegomena to Charity,* 160. Regarding what follows, see *The Book on Adler,* 108.

41. Commenting on the view held by many cognitive scientists who fail to distinguish between "flesh" and "meat" in describing the brain, Joseph Weizenbaum says, "[w]hat this worldview does is present a picture of what it means to be a human being, which allows us to deal with human beings in a way that I think we ought not to—to kill them, for example." From an interview with Baumgartner and Payr in *Speaking Minds: Interviews with Twenty Eminent Cognitive Scientists,* 68.

42. From an 1849 journal entry: *Journals & Papers,* §6360.

43. *Journals & Papers,* §4554 (*Pap* X 2 A 355).

44. Mooney, *Selves in Discord and Resolve,* 18.

45. As is suggested by William Lyons in *Matters of the Mind,* 225. Alternatively, we could just align ourselves with Simone Weil, who argues in *The Need for Roots* that science (properly understood) ought to be defined as "the study of beauty in the world." Quoted by John Dunaway in *Simone Weil,* 97.

46. "Kierkegaard and What We Mean by 'Philosophy'," 18. Hannay employs the Wittgensteinian notion of "pictures which hold us captive" in *Human Consciousness,* 19 & 60–61. Cf. Genova, *Wittgenstein: A Way of Seeing.*

47. "Kierkegaard's Philosophy of Mind," 180–181 (see *Kierkegaard and Philosophy,* 40–41). See also Wittgenstein, *Tractatus Logico-Philosophicus* 6.43 and Cavell, *Must We Mean What We Say?*

48. Hannay, "Introduction" to the Penguin edition of *The Sickness Unto Death,* 18–19.

49. Pattison, *The Philosophy of Kierkegaard,* 165.

50. "Kierkegaard's Philosophy of Mind," 161–162 (see *Kierkegaard and Philosophy,* 26–27).

51. Hume, "My Own Life," xxxiv.

52. D. H. Lawrence, "Why the Novel Matters," in *Phoenix,* 534.

53. See Ayer's account of Lawrence's attempt to seduce Bertrand Russell into his "cult of unreason" (Ayer's words) by persuading him to be "a creature instead of a mechanical instrument." —*Bertrand Russell,* 12–13.

54. Hannay, "Kierkegaard and What We Mean By 'Philosophy'," 16–17. An example of this impoverished approach can be found in "the cartoon cut-outs that philosophers have to use as stand-ins for human beings in their scholastic attempts to fit human mentality into antecedent physicalisms."

55. Cf. Milan Kundera, *The Art of the Novel,* 29. Kathleen Dean Moore, in a philosophical and literary meditation, laments that we philosophers too often "pluck ideas out of contexts like worms out of holes," only to be left with "a sadness we can't explain and a longing for a place that feels like home." —*Holdfast,* 14. To what degree might our style of writing itself be to blame for our sense that the human being is not at home in the world?

56. Kierkegaard, *Journals & Papers,* §4536 (*Pap* V A 37). See also *Journals & Papers,* §4539 (*Pap* VI A 64).

57. *Pap* VII 1 B 101:7. Kierkegaard takes on this challenge in a short work entitled *Crisis in the Life of an Actress.*

58. Ayer, *Language, Truth, and Logic,* 107.

59. Derrida, *Margins of Philosophy,* 7.

60. *Journals & Papers,* §3281 (*Pap* III A 11). Cf. Austin, *Sense and Sensibilia,* 3: "Ordinary words are much subtler in their uses, and mark many more distinctions, than philosophers have realized; and . . . the facts of perception, as discovered by, for instance, psychologists but

also as noted by common mortals, are much more diverse and complicated than has been allowed for."

61. Cf. Johnson, *Moral Imagination*, 180. See also Kundera, *The Art of the Novel*, 6–7.

62. Climacus betrays himself as something more than a would-be treatise writer in passages of poetic rapture such as the one which begins "It was rather late, toward evening," on page 235 of the *Concluding Unscientific Postscript*.

63. *Journals & Papers*, §4537. See also Hannay, "Kierkegaard's Philosophy of Mind," 175–176 (see *Kierkegaard and Philosophy*, 36–37): "Hegel's 'path of natural consciousness' goes from private to public, from inner to outer, from individuality to a consummation of the individual in a publicity offering fulfillment in ready-made social roles. The progress is outward from 'immediacy' to the public domain in which spirit finds its own home, and in relation to which any pockets of privacy in the public fabric are wrinkles to be flattened out in further extensions of the common vision of objective truth. Kierkegaard's journey is inwards, as greater insight reveals the inability of the public world to provide for the individual's consummation, and as the role of will (or 'heart') and personal choice are revealed as the resources with which the finite agent must secure any consummation that may be in store for it." Robert Bly writes that "Eliot and Pound conceive maturity as a growth of outwardness. . . . The opposite is true of Yeats and Rilke. Rilke was more inward at thirty than at twenty; more inward at fifty than at thirty." —"A Wrong Turning in American Poetry," 22.

64. All we need to believe about a fictional situation, in order for it to have this effect on us, is that it represents some possible suffering: see Dadlez, *What's Hecuba to Him?* 88–89.

65. See Lawrence Blum, *Moral Perception and Particularity*, 34.

66. Journal entry from 1848: *Pap* IX A 365. Hannay translation: *Papers and Journals*, 338.

67. *Existentialists and Mystics*, 313–317.

68. Geoffrey Hill, when asked how he would respond to those who complain that his poetry is too difficult: "Human beings are difficult. We're difficult to ourselves, we're difficult to each other. . . . One encounters in any ordinary day far more difficulty than one confronts in the most 'intellectual' piece of work. Why is it believed that poetry, prose, painting, music should be less than we are? Why does music, why does poetry have to address us in simplified terms, when, if such simplification were applied to a description of our own inner selves, we would find it demeaning?" —"The Art of Poetry LXXX," 276–277.

69. Nussbaum, *The Fragility of Goodness*, 185.

70. See *Fear and Trembling*, 70–72.

71. *Upheavals of Thought*, 702.

72. Danto, "Philosophy As/And/Of Literature," 10. As Scruton writes, "there is, in the idiom of modern philosophy, such a poverty of emotion, such a distance from the felt experience of words and things, as to cast doubt on its competence as a vehicle for moral and aesthetic reflection." —"Modern Philosophy and the Neglect of Aesthetics," 102–103.

73. See, e.g., Cleanth Brooks, "The Heresy of Paraphrase," 241–248.

74. *Kierkegaard: The Indirect Communication*, 100–107. Poole actually says "assonance," but he means alliteration.

75. Kierkegaard, *Works of Love*, 8. In this case, the alliterative repetition in the original Danish text has been made predominantly assonant in the Hongs' translation.

76. Kierkegaard, *Works of Love*, 8–9.

77. See the discussion by "Johannes Climacus" in the *Concluding Unscientific Postscript*, 302, 314. As Sylvia Walsh notes, Climacus is also aware of the risk that poetry itself can sometimes be indifferent to existence: *Living Poetically*, 169–170.

78. R. G. Collingwood, "An Essay on Philosophical Method," in *Philosophical Style* (edited by Lang), 107. Thanks to Edward Mooney, Alastair Hannay, and all the other participants in the August 2004 conference for which this paper was initially written. Thanks also to Karin Nisenbaum and James Reid, for many valuable conversations about these topics over the past few years.

6. Kierkegaard and Ethical Theory

1. I have commented about Kierkegaard's penchant for expounding virtues in "Kierkegaard, Wittgenstein, and a Method of 'Virtue Ethics'" in Merold Westphal and Martin Matustik, eds., *Kierkegaard in Post / Modernity* (Bloomington: Indiana University Press, 1995), pp. 142–166; "Existence, Emotion, and Virtue: Classical Themes in Kierkegaard," in *Cambridge Companion to Kierkegaard,* ed. Alastair Hannay and Gordon Marino (Cambridge: Cambridge University Press, 1998), pp. 177–206; and "The Virtue of Hope in *Eighteen Upbuilding Discourses,*" in Robert L. Perkins, ed., *International Kierkegaard Commentary: Eighteen Upbuilding Discourses* (Macon, Ga.: Mercer University Press), pp. 181–203. See also "Dialectical Emotions and the Virtue of Faith" in Robert L. Perkins, ed., *International Kierkegaard Commentary: Concluding Unscientific Postscript* (Mercer, Ga.: Mercer University Press, 1997), pp. 73–93.

2. Edited and translated by Howard V. Hong and Edna H. Hong (Princeton, N.J.: Princeton University Press, 1995).

3. Nicholas Wolterstorff, *John Locke and the Ethics of Belief* (Cambridge: Cambridge University Press, 1996).

4. New York: Oxford University Press, 2001.

5. Oxford: Oxford University Press, 1999.

6. Gary Watson, "On the Primacy of Character," in Owen Flanagan and Amélie Oksenberg Rorty, eds., *Identity, Character, and Morality* (Cambridge, Mass.: MIT Press, 1990), 449–469, pp. 451, 452. Watson attributes to John Rawls the view that moral theories differ according to the direction of conceptual derivation.

7. *Virtues of the Mind: An Inquiry into the Nature of Virtue and the Ethical Foundations of Knowledge* (Cambridge: Cambridge University Press, 1996), pp. 79, 99.

8. "On Some Vices of Virtue Ethics" in Roger Crisp and Michael Slote, eds., *Virtue Ethics* (Oxford: Oxford University Press, 1997), pp. 201–216.

9. *On Virtue Ethics,* p. 6, Hursthouse's italics.

10. However, Hursthouse appears to me to be inconsistent in her advocacy of any moral theory at all. For she advocates peaceful coexistence among utilitarianism, deontology, and virtue ethics (p. 5) after, however, earlier noting that virtue ethics has now "acquired full status, recognized as a rival to deontological and utilitarian approaches" (p. 2), and she does do the characteristic theoretical thing of deriving other ethical concepts from her privileged one— virtue—*to the exclusion* of others, even if she does not make that concept foundational. On the purer, Watsonian or Slotean conception, virtue ethics could not peaceably coexist with the other theories because each theory's defining structure—its derivation of all other concepts from its foundational concept—is incompatible with each other theory's defining structure.

11. See, e.g., *Without Authority* (Princeton, N.J.: Princeton University Press, 1997), p. 93; *For Self-Examination / Judge for Yourselves* (Princeton, N.J.: Princeton University Press, 1991), p. 81; *Søren Kierkegaard's Journals and Papers* (Bloomington: Indiana University Press), §6943; *Concluding Unscientific Postscript,* vol. 1 (Princeton, N.J.: Princeton University Press, 1992), pp. 146, 363, 366; *Upbuilding Discourses in Various Spirits* (Princeton, N.J.: Princeton University Press, 1993), pp. 294–295. (All the above are translated and edited by Howard and Edna Hong.)

12. These three aspects of the concept of knowledge are sketched in Robert C. Roberts and W. Jay Wood, *Intellectual Virtues: An Essay in Regulative Epistemology* (Oxford: Oxford University Press, forthcoming), Chapter 2.

13. Robert Merrihew Adams, *Finite and Infinite Goods* (New York: Oxford University Press, 1999), pp. 250, 251.

14. See Mark Murphy, "Divine Command, Divine Will, and Moral Obligation," *Faith and Philosophy* 15 (1998), 3–27.

15. See *The Point of View,* ed. and trans. Howard V. Hong and Edna H. Hong (Princeton, N.J.: Princeton University Press, 1998), pp. 52–53, 123.

16. See *The Point of View*, ed. and trans. Howard V. Hong and Edna H. Hong (Princeton, N.J.: Princeton University Press, 1998), pp. 19–20.

17. Kierkegaard emphasizes the back end in the passage from *Letters and Documents* that the Hongs cite in footnote 151, *Works of Love*, p. 505.

18. *The Concept of Dread*, translated with introduction and notes by Walter Lowrie (Princeton, N.J.: Princeton University Press, 1957), p. 13 (footnote).

7. "The Problematic Agapeistic Ideal—Again"

1. In the later book, the essay "Proximity as Apartness" refers back to the discussion of this early chapter ("Proximity as Apartness," in *Kierkegaard and Philosophy* (London: Routledge, 2003) pp. 150–62.

2. *Kierkegaard*, in "The Arguments of the Philosophers" series, ed. Ted Honderich (London: Routledge & Kegan Paul, 1982, rev. 1991), p. 241. Further references to Hannay will be to this volume.

3. Ibid.

4. Hannay, p. 243.

5. Hannay, pp. 250, 247.

6. Hannay, p. 247.

7. Hannay, p. 245.

8. Hannay, p. 251.

9. He begins by looking for arguments for the "non-morality" of natural love but slides into assuming it is "morally reprehensible."

10. Hannay, p. 246.

11. *Works of Love*, Kierkegaard's Writings XVI, ed. Howard V. Hong and Edna H. Hong (Princeton, N.J.: Princeton University Press, 1995), pp. 150, 267. Hereafter WL.

12. WL, pp. 143, 146.

13. Hannay, p. 243.

14. Hannay, p. 244.

15. Note: Hannay himself forestalls one objection, when he notes that the inevitable physical inability to attend to all others as neighbors does not constitute a chosen exclusion of others (pp. 244–45). One cannot rightly choose to exclude another from the treatment as neighbor, but that does not automatically mean that one will be effective in including all others in such treatment. We simply are limited, and choosing to do one good thing often precludes choosing to do another good thing.

16. Hannay, pp. 245–46.

17. *Nicomachean Ethics*, IX, 4; VIII, 5.

18. *Nicomachean Ethics*, IX, 8.

19. Aquinas, *Summa Theologiae* I-II, Q. 28,1; II-II, Q. 26, 4 (also see *De Caritate*, Article 7, replies 11 and 13).

20. Kierkegaard's stipulation that "by the sensuous, the flesh, Christianity understands selfishness" directly follows his clarification that "the sensous [is] something quite different from what is simply called the sensuous nature" (WL, 52). And all this is part of his attempt to argue against the "misunderstanding" that Christianity "posited a cleft between flesh and spirit, hated erotic love as the sensuous"; indeed, Christianity is "no more scandalized by a drive human beings have indeed not given to themselves than it has wanted to forbid people to eat and drink" (WL, 52).

21. *Nicomachean Ethics*, IX, 8. Aristotle concludes section 8: "In this sense, then, as has been said, a man should be a lover of self; but in the sense in which most men are so, he ought not."

22. Although these affirmations have been pointed out (Ferreira, *Love's Grateful Striving:* A

Commentary on Kierkegaard's Works of Love [New York: Oxford, 2001], pp. 31–32, 35) and are, presumably, noted by anyone who reads the text carefully, still they do not seem to preclude or silence the outcry that continues to arise against Kierkegaard's exploration of preferential love in contrast to neighbor-love.

23. Hannay, p. 251.

24. Hannay, p. 243.

25. Hannay, p. 253.

26. Hannay, pp. 253–54, my emphasis.

27. Hannay, p. 267; the "second aspect of selfishness in an emotional tie"—that we can exclude others—simply repeats the possibility that we can be selfish.

28. *JP* 2:1446 (1854), p. 147.

29. "bevar in Elskov og Venskab Kjerlighed til Naesten" (*Samlede Vaerker,* Bind 9–10, p. 64).

30. WL, 2: IV, V, VI, VIII.

31. For his emphasis on "kinship" see WL, pp. 69, 74, 75, 85.

32. This is Kierkegaard's answer to the question posed by Phillips: "does it follow from this that nothing distinctive is lost if one meets neighbours, but never a beloved or a friend? Cannot the love of God be mediated through these special loves?" See "Kierkegaard and Loves that Blossom" in *Ethik der Liebe,* ed. Ingolf Dalferth (Tuebingen: Mohr Siebeck, 2002), p. 161.

33. Kierkegaard's contrast here between 'the friend and the neighbor" means that he uses the term "neighbor" in different ways in different contexts: it covers (1) the nonpreferred neighbor, which encompasses both those to whom we are affectively indifferent or affectively negative, and (2) the preferred neighbor, those to whom we feel affectively inclined. He uses the first sense too when he writes that neighbor has none of the perfections of the beloved, the friend, or the admired one (WL, 66).

34. For more explanation, see Ferreira, *Love's Grateful Striving,* pp. 89–94, 112–13.

35. "Purity of Heart," in UDVS, p. 129.

36. Phillips: "Kierkegaard and Loves That Blossom," see note 33 above, pp. 155–66.

37. Phillips, pp. 156, 157.

38. Ibid., p. 156. Sometimes Phillips is concerned about the conflict between neighbor-love and preferential love; at other times (and this seems a different concern) he suggests that Kierkegaard "assumes, too quickly, that other loves necessarily come between us and the love of God." (160).

39. Phillips, 157, 158.

40. Phillips, 158.

41. Phillips refers to Kierkegaard's claim that in "devoted self-love" the task is to give up the devotion (p. 159), but the kind of "devotion" Kierkegaard insists we give up is the kind which is "willful"—the kind of devotion we should show requires a willingness for the sacrifice of giving up the other if the other's good requires it.

42. Phillips, p. 165.

43. Although since there is no verb form of *Kjerlighed,* the command is phrased *Du skal elske.*

44. Phillips, p. 160.

45. Such love is not, therefore, based on an extrinsic and arbitrary and revisable command by God.

46. He writes: "God has placed love [*Kjerlighed*] in the human being" (WL, 126).

47. *En Kjerlighedens Trang; en Trang i Kjerligheden (Samlede Vaerker,* Bind 9–10, p. 8, p. 14).

48. For more detail on this, see my essay "Immediacy and Reflection in Kierkegaard's *Works of Love,*" in *Immediacy and Reflection in Kierkegaard's Thought,* ed. Cruyberghs et al., *Louvain Philosophical Studies* 17, 2003.

49. Pace Hannay's claim that "the three forms of love are ranged in ascending order or 'spiritual determination'" (*Kierkegaard,* p. 264).

50. EO, 2: 32.

8. Kierkegaard on Natural and Commanded Love

1. *Kierkegaards Samlede Værker*, 3rd ed. (SV3), Vol. 12, p. 209.

2. *SV3*, Vol. 16, p. 162, in my trans.

3. I. Kant, "Analytic of Pure Practical Reason," in T. K. Abbott (trans.), *Kant's Critique of Practical Reason and Other Essays on the Theory of Ethics* (New York/Toronto: Longmans, Green, 6th ed. 1954), p. 166.

4. Ibid., p. 166.

5. Ibid., p. 166

6. *SV3*, Vol. 12, p. 143.

7. Ibid., p. 143.

8. Ibid.

9. Ibid., p. 144.

10. Ibid., p. 144.

11. Ibid., p. 144.

12. Ibid., p. 143.

13. Cf. *The Sickness unto Death,* trans. Alastair Hannay, p. 75, where Anti-Climacus says that the distinction between being and not being in despair is as "unreliable as that which paganism and natural man makes between love and self-love, as though all this love were not really self-love."

9. Despair and Depression

This chapter first appeared in *Kierkegaard in the Present Age* (Milwaukee: Marquette University Press, 2001) and is reprinted with the kind permission of the press.

1. See the motto to Søren Kierkegaard's *Concept of Anxiety,* trans. Reidar Thomte (Princeton, N.J.: Princeton University Press, 1980), 3 (IV 274). (Note: following every Hong edition page reference is the page reference of the quote or section from the Danish 1st edition or the *Papirer*.)

2. I am here borrowing the term "sacred order" from Philip Rieff.

3. Kierkegaard, *Concept of Anxiety 121 (IV 389)*.

4. See, e.g., Vincent McCarthy's *The Phenomenology of Moods* (The Hague: Martinus Nijhoff, 1978) and Kresten Nordentoft's *Kierkegaard's Psychology,* trans. Bruce Kirmmse (Pittsburgh: University of Pittsburgh Press, 1978).

5. It is evident from Kierkegaard's *Journals and Papers* that Kierkegaard identified his thorn in the flesh with his depression. Consider 5:391 entry 6025 (VIII' A 205 n.d., 1847), 6:153 entry 6396 (X' A 322 n.d., 1849), and 6:340 entry 6659 (X³ A 310 n.d., 1850) in *Søren Kierkegaard's Journals and Papers,* ed. and trans. Howard and Edna Hong, assist. by G. Malantschuk, 7 vols. (Bloomington: Indiana University Press, 1967). Henceforth, the *Journals and Papers* will be referred to as *JP*, followed by volume number: page number and entry number. Again, consider the parenthetical following that references the quote's place in *the Papirer.*

6. Kierkegaard uses two Danish terms to refer to depression, *tungsindighed* and *melancholi.* Vincent McCarthy argues that *tungsindhed,* which could be roughly translated as heavy mindedness, has deeper and more broody connotations than *melancholi.* See McCarthy's *Phenomenology of Moods,* pp. 54–57. Abrahim Kahn disagrees, arguing that the two terms are synonymous in Kierkegaard's writings. See Kahn's "Melancholy, Irony, and Kierkegaard," *International Journal for Philosophy of Religion* 17 (1985): 67–85.

7. *JP* 5:69 entry 5141 (1 A 161 n.d., 1836).

8. For a signal example of this theme, consider the first page of Kierkegaard's most popular book, *Either/Or,* trans. Howard and Edna Hong, 2 vols. (Princeton, N.J.: Princeton University Press, 1987). The text begins, "It may be times have occurred to you, dear reader, to doubt

somewhat the accuracy of that familiar philosophical thesis that the outer is the inner and the inner is the outer" *(3 (I v))*.

9. *JP* 5:389 entry 6620 (VIII' A 179 n.d., 1847).

10. See Kierkegaard's *Practice in Christianity,* trans. Howard and Edna Hong (Princeton, N.J.: Princeton University Press, 1991), 136–137 (XII 127–128).

11. Kierkegaard, *Either/Or,* Volume 1, 301–445 (1275–412).

12. *JP* 5: 446–447 entry 6135 (VIII' A 650 n.d., 1848).

13. Søren Kierkegaard, *The Point of View,* trans. Howard and Edna Hong (Princeton, N.J.: Princeton University Press, 1998), 23 (XIII 517).

14. *JP* 5: 334–336 entry 5913 (VIP A 126 n.d., 1846), 6:475 entry 6840 (X⁵A 105 March 28, 1853).

15. Consider, e.g., the Judge's letters to 'A' in the second volume of *Either/Or.*

16. *JP* 5: 334 entry 5913 (VIP A 126 n.d., 1846).

17. JP 6: 306 entry 6603 *(X² A 619 n.d., 1850).*

18. Søren Kierkegaard, *Sickness unto Death,* trans. Alastair Hannay (London: Penguin, 1989), 55.

19. *JP* 5: 334 entry 5913 (VII' A 126 n.d., 1846).

20. Kierkegaard, *The Sickness unto Death* 43 (XI).

21. Kierkegaard, *The Sickness unto Death* 54 (XI).

22. *JP* 4: 37 entry 3894 (IV A 166 n.d., 1843–44).

23. Concerning the spiritual instruction contained in this chapter, see my essay "Anxiety in the *Concept of Anxiety,"* in The *Cambridge Companion to Kierkegaard,* ed. A. Hannay and G. Marino (London: Cambridge University Press, 1998), 308–328.

24. *JP* 6: entry 6659 (X³ A 310 n.d., 1850).

25. See Søren Kierkegaard's *Eighteen Upbuilding Discourses,* trans. Howard and Edna Hong (Princeton, N.J.: Princeton University Press, 1990), 297–326 (V 81–105).

26. Kierkegaard, The *Point of View,* 79 ff. (XIII 564 ff.).*JP* 6: 12 entry 6164 (IX A 68 n.d., 1848).

27. *JP* 6:12 entry 6164 (IX A68 n.d., 1848).

28. *JP* 6: entry 6603 (X² A619 n.d.; 1850).

29. *JP* 6: entry 6837 (X⁵ A72 n.d. 1853).

30. I am indebted for this observation to Vincent McCarthy. See his *Phenomenology of Moods,* pp. 85–86.

31. Kierkegaard, *The Sickness unto Death* 158 ff.

10. Spleen Essentially Canceled—yet a Little Spleen Retained

1. Harmondsworth: Penguin Books 1992. Alastair Hannay has also published translations of *Fear and Trembling* (1985), *The Sickness unto Death* (1989), *Papers and Journals: A Selection* (1996), and *A Literary Review* (2001), all with Penguin Books. More recently he has brought his eminent translation experience and competence to the new English translation of *Kierkegaard's Journals and Notebooks,* which is based on the new Danish scholarly edition of *Søren Kierkegaards Skrifter.* The *Journals and Notebooks* will be published by Princeton University Press in cooperation with Walter de Gruyter Verlag.

2. Op. cit., p. 3.

3. Op. cit., p. 4.

4. Op. cit., p. 499.

5. Op. cit., pp. 499–500. *Søren Kierkegaards Skrifter,* vols. 1–9 and 17–21, Copenhagen: G.E.C. Gad 1997–2004 (hereafter *SKS*); vol. 3 (1997), pp. 183–184.

6. *Either/Or. Part II,* ed. and trans. Howard V. Hong and Edna H. Hong, vol. IV in *Kierkegaard's Writings* (Princeton, N.J.: Princeton University Press, 1990), pp. 189–190. *SKS,* vol. 3 (1997), p. 184. The Hongs' translation has been slightly modified here—as well as in the title of

this essay. The Danish term *hævet* has been translated "eliminated" rather than "canceled" in order to underscore a sense of active removal.

7. Berlin and New York: Walter de Gruyter 1996.

8. *Søren Kierkegaard's Journals and Papers,* ed. and trans. Howard V. Hong and Edna H. Hong, vol. 1 (Bloomington: Indiana University Press, 1967), no. 739, p. 343. *SKS,* vol. 18 (2001), p. 44. This passage is not included in Alastair Hannay's translation of Kierkegaard's *Papers and Journals: A Selection.*

9. See "Quiet Despair" in one of the "midnight entries" in Frater Taciturnus's "Guilty-Not Guilty" in *Stages on Life's Way,* ed. and trans. Howard V. Hong and Edna H. Hong, vol. XI in *Kierkegaard's Writings,* pp. 199–200. *SKS,* vol. 6 (1999), pp. 187–188.

10. The German edition is from 1833. Kierkegaard had the Danish translation in his library. See no. 871 in the catalog of the auction of his book collection.

11. In addition, see my explanatory notes to EE:117 in *SKS,* vol. K18 (2001), pp. 67–69.

12. *Either/Or: A Fragment of Life,* op. cit., p. 498. *SKS,* vol. 3 (1997), p. 180.

13. See C. Molbech, *Dansk Ordbog,* vols. 1–2, Copenhagen 1833, catalog no. 1032; vol. 2, p. 546, Here one reads that *tvivle* comes from *tve,* which is explained on p. 544: "to, to Gange, som er to, i to Dele, dobbelt, o. s. v." [two, twice, of two parts, in two parts, doubled, etc].

14. I am here following Gregor Malantschuk's definition of spleen in his "key concepts," *Nøglebegreber i Søren Kierkegaards tænkning,* udg. af Grethe Kjær og Paul Müller (Copenhagen: C. A. Reitzel, 1993), pp. 194–195.

15. *Either/Or: A Fragment of Life,* op. cit., p. 509. *SKS,* vol. 3 (1997), p. 198.

16. See *The Book on Adler,* ed. and trans. Howard V. Hong and Edna H. Hong, vol. XXIV in *Kierkegaard's Writings* (Princeton, N.J.: Princeton University Press, 1994), pp. 287–288. *Pap* VII 2 B 235, s. 161.

17. *Eighteen Upbuilding Discourses,* ed. and trans. Howard V. Hong and Edna H. Hong, vol. V in *Kierkegaard's Writings* (Princeton, N.J.: Princeton University Press, 1990), p. 314. *SKS,* vol. 5 (1998), p. 306.

18. I am following Malantschuk's definition of the self in his "key-concepts," *Nøglebegreber i Søren Kierkegaards tænkning,* op. cit., pp. 142–143.

19. *Papers and Journals,* p. 32. In the Danish text, see *SKS,* vol. 17 (2000), pp. 24–25, Kierkegaard emphasizes '*me*' and speaks of two phenomena: first, to "skjelne sig selv fra Gjenstandene," and second, to "udsondre sig fra sine Omgivelser," which Hannay translates: to "distinguish itself from its surroundings." I believe one ought to distinguish between the two verbs *at skjelne* and *at udsondre.* The former could be rendered "to distinguish," and the latter, "to disengage" (as the Hongs do, *JP* 5:5100). Perhaps even better, one might render it "to separate" in order to emphasize the process involved in this disengaging separation.

20. *Either/Or: A Fragment of Life,* op. cit., p. 509. *SKS,* vol. 3 (1997), p. 198.

21. See Alastair Hannay "Basic Despair in *The Sickness unto Death,*" Arne Grøn, "Der Begriff Verzweiflung," and Michael Theunissen, "Für einen rationaleren Kierkegaard: Zu Einwänden von Arne Grøn und Alastair Hanny," as well as Hannay's response, "Paradigmatic Despair and the Quest for a Kierkegaardian Anthropology," in *Kierkegaard Studies: Yearbook,* ed. Niels Jørgen Cappelørn and Hermann Deuser (Berlin: Walter de Gruyter, 1996), pp. 15–32, pp. 33–60, pp. 61–90, and pp. 149–163, respectively. *Yearbook* 1996 also includes articles by Hermann Deuser, Heiko Schulz, and Niels Jørgen Cappelørn on the first part of *The Sickness unto Death.* Hermann Deuser has continued the debate with Hannay and Theunissen and further developed his position in his article "Evolutionäre Metaphysik als Theorie des menschlichen Selbst: Beiträge zum Begriff religiöser Erfahrung," in *Marburger Jahrbuch: Theologie* XVI, *Das Selbst in der Evolution* (Marburg: N. G. Elwert Verlag, 2004), pp. 45–78.

22. Just for the record, it should be noted that aesthete "A" also mentions hereditary sin a few times and maintains that it is indeed a substantial category—just as it is in Greek tragedy. With this interpretation, he expresses a vulgar understanding of hereditary sin when compared with the classical understanding within Lutheran dogmatics. But this is of course in the first part of Either/Or and falls outside a treatment of Wilhelm's understanding of hereditary sin.

23. See *The Concept of Anxiety,* ed. and trans. Reidar Thomte in collaboration with Albert B. Anderson, vol. VIII in *Kierkegaard's Writings* (Princeton, N.J.: Princeton University Press, 1994), pp. 25–29. *SKS,* vol. 4 (1997), pp. 332–336.

24. *The Concept of Anxiety,* op. cit., p. 61, translation modified. *SKS,* vol. 4, pp. 365–366.

25. *The Concept of Anxiety,* op. cit, p. 43. *SKS,* vol. 4, p. 349.

26. I am here in agreement with Arne Grøn's interpretation in his book *Begrebet angst hos Søren Kierkegaard* (Copenhagen: Gyldendal, 1993).

27. *The Concept of Anxiety,* op. cit., p. 49. *SKS,* vol. 4, p. 354.

28. *Either/Or: A Fragment of Life,* op. cit., p. 500.

11. Kierkegaard on Melancholy and Despair

1. *Søren Kierkegaards Skrifter,* ed. Søren Kierkegaard Forskningscenteret (Copenhagen: Gads Forlag, 2001), EE 117, vol. 18, p. 44.

2. Sygdommen til døden (The Sickness unto Death), SV3, Vol.15, p. 83.

3. See Wolf Lepenies, *Melancholie und Gesellschaft* (Frankfurt: Suhrkamp, 1969) (*Melancholy and Society* [Cambridge, Mass.: Harvard University Press, 1992]), and Harvie Ferguson, *Melancholy and the Critique of Modernity: Søren Kierkegaard's Religious Psychology* (London/ New York: Routledge, 1995).

4. *Papirer.* VI A 101.

12. Philosophy and Dogma

1. Here and elsewhere in this essay I am using my own translation from the latest Danish edition of Kierkegaard's works, Søren Kierkegaard Skrifter (Copenhagen: Gad, 1997–). I shall indicate references as SKS, followed by volume and page number. Here, the reference is to SKS 5 132.

2. What is said in this discourse about the impulse to the good seems to be paralleled and developed further in the first of the communion discourses that constitute the fourth part of *Christian Discourses.* This takes as its text the words spoken by Christ to his apostles as they prepare for the Last Supper: "I have heartily longed to eat this Passover with you, before I suffer." As Kierkegaard develops the theme in the discourse, what we are to learn is not simply that a "hearty longing" must precede our own reception of the sacrament, but that this longing is already a gift of God and is not so much to be assuaged as to be increased by participation in the sacrament. See SKS 10 265–75.

3. See J. Pons, *Stealing a Gift: Kierkegaard's Pseudonyms and the Bible* (New York: Fordham University Press, 2004), for an important discussion of this.

4. See J. Derrida, trans. D. Wills, *The Gift of Death* (Chicago: University of Chicago Press, 1995), especially Chapter 4.

13. The Dangers of Indirection

I would like to thank Edward Mooney and Brian J. Foley for their support of this project. I would also like to thank Julia Annas for providing me with some very helpful information concerning contemporary Plato scholarship. Robert B. Pippin commented on an earlier version of this paper when I presented it at a conference in Copenhagen in the summer of 2004. I revised the paper in light of his comments and the new version is, I believe, a significant improvement on the original version. I am thus indebted to Professor Pippin for this improvement.

1. Cf., e.g., Louis Mackey, *Kierkegaard: A Kind of Poet* (Philadelphia: University of Pennsylvania Press, 1971).

2. Cf., e.g., Mackey. For an alternative view, see Alastair Hannay, *Kierkegaard* (London/New York: Routledge, 1982), especially pp. 1–18.

3. Cf., Kierkegaard's observation in his journal that "God is like a poet. . . . But just as it is a mistake to think that what a particular character in a poem says or does represents the poet's personal opinion, so is it a mistake to assume that God consents to all that happens and how, no, he has his own view of things. But poetically he permits everything possible to come forth" (JP 2: 1445/Pap. XI² 98).

4. Cf. e.g., Hugh H. Benson, *Socratic Wisdom: The Model of Knowledge in Plato's Early Dialogues* (Oxford: Oxford University Press, 2006) and Terrence Irwin, *Plato's Ethics* (Oxford: Oxford University Press, 1995).

5. Plato, *Meno*, 81a–82a.

6. Ibid., 89d–99e.

7. Cf., e.g., Michael L. Frazer, "Esotericism Ancient and Modern," *Political Theory*, vol. 34, no. 1, February 2006, 33–61, and Shadia Drury, *Leo Strauss and the American Right* (New York: St. Martin's Press, 1997), 231.

8. Julia Annas remarked to me in an e-mail exchange dated September 5, 2006, that "I think it is fair to say that there has never been less of a consensus in over 50 years of Plato scholarship as to how Plato should be read, so that just about any view looking for unanimity among Plato scholars won't find it."

Kierkegaard scholars disagree on issues as fundamental as whether Kierkegaard was a proponent of irrationalism—cf., e.g., Alastair MacIntyre, *After Virtue* (Notre Dame, Ind.: University of Notre Dame Press, 1984) versus *Kierkegaard after MacIntyre*, ed. John Davenport and Anthony Rudd (Chicago: Open Court, 2001)—and whether his thought is marked by an acosmism that would preclude ethical obligation to others—cf., e.g., Louis Mackey, "The Loss of the World in Kierkegaard's Ethics," in Louis Mackey, *Points of View* (Tallahasse: University of Florida Press, 1986) versus M. G. Piety, "The Place of the World in Kierkegaard's Ethics," in *Kierkegaard: The Self in Society*, ed. George Pattison and Stephen Shakespeare (London: Macmillan, 1998).

9. Cf., e.g., Hannay, 428. Cf. also Catherine and Michael Zuckert, *The Truth about Leo Strauss* (Chicago: University of Chicago Press, 2006), and Drury, op. cit.

10. Cf., e.g., Theodor Adorno, *Kierkegaard: Construction of the Aesthetic* (Minneapolis: University of Minnesota Press, 1989).

11. Earl Shorris, "Ignoble Liars: Leo Strauss, George Bush and the Philosophy of Mass Deception," *Harpers*, June 2004.

12. Not unlike the *New Yorker* cartoon of a group of scientists abandoning their discussion, and the elaborate mathematical equations they scrawled across a blackboard, because they hear an ice cream truck outside. That is, we are all, no matter how clever, still human beings with human weaknesses. The weakness of some may be for sweets, whereas for others it may be an aversion to self-examination or to the moral law.

13. CUP I, 199.

14. CUP I, 203.

15. Cf., e.g., Henry E. Allison, "Christianity and Nonsense," *Kierkegaard: A Collection of Critical Essays* (New York: Doubleday [Anchor Books], 1972), pp. 289–323.

16. Cf. Harvie Ferguson, *Melancholy and the Critique of Modernity: Søren Kierkegaard's Religious Psychology* (London/New York: Routledge, 1994), 167.

17. The ancient philosophical injunction to "know oneself" would suggest that philosophers of this period were more concerned with subjectivity than are their modern counterparts.

18. Cf. Thomas Nagel, *The View from Nowhere* (Oxford: Oxford University Press, 1989).

19. Cf., e.g., Shorris, op. cit., and Drury, op. cit.

20. Cf. Leo Strauss, *Persecution and the Art of Writing* (Chicago: University of Chicago Press, 1988).

21. If Strauss did have elitist and totalitarian political views, it would be ironic if he thought he had to insulate himself from the recriminations of the mob to these views. The mob is generally very sympathetic to such views.

22. The forensic psychiatrist James Gilligan, author of many books including *Violence: Reflections on a National Epidemic* (New York: Random House, 1996), is such a Kierkegaard lover, as is the poet James Mancinelli. I met the former at a dinner party and the latter in a writing group of which I am a member.

14. Abraham's Final Word

1. All references to, and citations from, the text of *Fear and Trembling* are drawn from the Hongs' edition and translation. On occasion, however, I alter the translation, often to follow the translation suggested by Hannay.

2. I am indebted here to the excellent discussion by Fenves, especially chapter 4.

3. Within an excursus devoted to the faith of Abraham on Mount Moriah, Johannes embeds a passing reference to Sodom and Gomorrah, saying that Abraham "did not pray for himself, trying to influence the Lord; it was only when righteous punishment fell upon Sodom and Gomorrah that Abraham came forward with his prayers" (21). Following this brief paragraph, Johannes turns immediately to the story of Abraham as it is told in Chapter 22 of the Book of *Genesis*.

4. All citations from, and references to, The Hebrew Bible are drawn from *TANAKH*. All references identify the book, chapter, and verse in which the cited passage appears.

5. With the exception of the imaginative sketches in his *Exordium*, wherein he rehearses Abraham's faithless attempts to maintain Isaac's relationship with their God, Johannes is mostly silent about Abraham's relationship to Isaac. For an excellent account of Abraham receiving Isaac back again, see Mooney, chapter 6.

6. That Abraham did not speak is dubious; that he cannot speak is even more dubious. See Lippitt, p. 130.

7. See Mulhall, p. 359.

8. SKS 4, 203.

9. See Lippitt, p. 131.

10. SKS 4, 206.

11. As Lippitt observes, Abraham's alleged recourse to irony "hardly amounts to putting Abraham way beyond the reach of language" (132). Mulhall similarly insists on the "determinate indeterminacy of Abraham's words" (361–362).

12. Mackey's explanation, though faithful to Johannes's interpretation of the biblical passage, thus strikes me as overstated: "*Jehovah-jirah* tells Isaac precisely nothing; for all practical and moral purposes Abraham is silent" (220).

13. I am indebted to Bregman for his attention to this seeming redundancy in the text.

14. In a similar attempt to chart the deterioration of Johannes's meditation, Mulhall notes that Johannes's account of Abraham's words obliges him (Johannes) to deviate significantly from what appears to be his "interpretative ideal"—namely, "fidelity to the literal meaning of the Genesis narrative" (368).

15. See Lippitt, p. 196; and Mulhall, p. 365.

16. Mulhall persuasively defends an "alternative interpretation" of God's initial command to Abraham, wherein "God commanded Abraham to bring his son to Mount Moriah for the purpose of making a burnt offering of him, but did not command him to carry out the sacrifice itself" (363).

17. See Mulhall, p. 363.

18. SKS 4, 206.

19. On the importance of measure, see Mackey, pp. 208–210.

20. While I certainly agree with Lippitt that Johannes places "under scrutiny" the notion that "the ethical is the universal" (203), I would also maintain that Johannes's allegiance to this notion, whether conscious or not, also informs his discussion and occasionally deforms his argumentation.

21. My suggestion that Johannes serves, even if unwittingly, as a "knight of morality" is consistent, I take it, with Mulhall's claim that "In depriving Abraham of speech, de Silentio . . . is distorting his account of faith in a way which precisely corresponds to Hegel's distorted characterization of the ethical realm as exhaustive, as the only intelligible form, of spiritually meaningful human existence" (382).

22. Derrida, pp. 80–81.

23. Derrida closes his discussion of *Fear and Trembling* by revealing what he takes to be Kierkegaard's abiding (and ultimately limiting) allegiance to the Christian Gospels. Derrida thus observes that "As a Christian thinker, Kierkegaard ends by reinscribing the secret of Abraham within a space that seems, in its literality at least, to be evangelical. That doesn't necessarily exclude a Judaic or Islamic reading, but it is a certain evangelical text that seems to orient or dominate Kierkegaard's interpretation (80–81)."

24. I am indebted here to Kjaeldgaard's discussion of this "pregnant moment" (317–318).

25. A notable exception here is Katz, p. 27.

26. Johannes muses, "Let us go further. We let Isaac actually be sacrificed. Abraham had faith. He did not have faith that he would be blessed in a future life but that he would be blessed here in the world. God could give him a new Isaac, could restore to life the one sacrificed" (36).

27. See Lippitt, p. 171.

28. Levinas, p. 77, emphasis added. See Katz, pp. 25–27.

29. True to form, however, Johannes misidentifies Socrates' "final moment." It is not the deathbed invocation of Asclepius, as recorded in the *Phaedo,* but the post-judgment irony recorded at *Apology* 36a.

30. For related expressions of puzzlement, see Lippitt, p. 131; and Mulhall, p. 361.

31. In one of his infrequent footnotes, Johannes explains that Socrates "consummates himself in the celebrated response that he is surprised to have been condemned by a majority of three votes" (117).

32. That Johannes regards Abraham as some kind of hero, notwithstanding his recognition of the limits of this designation, is suggested throughout *Fear and Trembling,* most notably in the "Eulogy on Abraham."

33. While I agree with Mulhall that "[Johannes] wants his readers to work for their spiritual bread" (383), I would also add that Johannes does not want his readers to work *too* hard for their bread, especially if doing so might lead them to seek more nourishing sustenance elsewhere (e.g., in the Hebrew Bible) than in the Christian Gospels as they are conventionally interpreted. As a dispenser of bread, Johannes is most similar to Dostoevsky's Grand Inquisitor, who freely granted real bread (along with the illusion of freedom), asking only that his flock desist from longing for spiritual bread. Johannes would like to see his contemporaries work harder for their spiritual nourishment, but he does not want them to outwork him or work themselves out of the tradition he reluctantly represents. He thus presents the faith of Abraham not as an actual item on the spiritual menu, but as an appetizer that will whet their dulled appetites for the Christian Gospels.

34. I explore the resemblance of Johannes to the unnamed pilgrim in my essay "Seeing is Believing: Narrative Visualization in Kierkegaard's *Fear and Trembling.*"

35. See Mackey, p. 221.

15. Faith as Eschatological Trust in *Fear and Trembling*

This essay has a long history. A very early version, titled "The Absolute as Eschaton in Kierkegaard's *Fear and Trembling,*" was presented on the general program of the Eastern Division meeting of the American Philosophical Association (New York, December 29, 1995). I am indebted to criticisms made by Vanessa Rumble at this session. I would also like to express my thanks to Alastair Hannay for comments on that early version, as well as for his more recent comments on the August 2004 version delivered in Copenhagen at the Kierkegaard Research Center. My thanks go to Edward Mooney for organizing this conference in honor of Hannay, and to graduate students at Fordham who read a pseudonymous version of this essay in the spring of 2005. I'm also indebted to Merold Westphal for comments on the January 2006 version, which have helped shape this final result.

1. Søren Kierkegaard, *Fear and Trembling,* trans. Howard V. Hong and Edna H. Hong (Princeton, N.J.: Princeton University Press, 1984). All my references to this edition will be given parenthetically by page number in the main text. I omit the usual sigla "FT" since there are so many references to this one text.

2. In this essay I do not address the issue of Kierkegaard's pseudonymous authorship, although I acknowledge that responsible critics cannot just speak as if Kierkegaard himself is the author in a straightforward sense. Kierkegaard is the *writer* of *Fear and Trembling,* just as Plato is the writer of the famous dialogues in which he himself never appears and leaves all the arguing to his cast of characters. In my view, the point of the pseudonyms for Kierkegaard is virtually identical to Plato's reasons for "indirect communication" through semi-fictitious interlocutors: it is to allow his readers to form their own views without coercion by the author, and to bring worldviews to life. Each of Plato's major characters *embodies* a certain ethical or theoretical outlook. In much the same way, Kierkegaard's pseudonyms represent *points of view* on human existence that *show* us more concretely than any abstract description could *tell* us what it is like to exist in the attitudes they occupy. The primary difference from Plato is that these stages are not only levels of cognitive enlightenment but also structures of the will: they involve different attitudes and motives that arise from the agent's fundamental commitment to different kinds of ends, on the basis of different kinds of grounds or criteria for choices. To live in a given stage is actively to engage in its defining projects and to embrace or appropriate its evaluative framework. But like Plato, Kierkegaard treats his pseudonyms as persona, characters in a drama. In an obvious allusion to Plato, his pseudonyms even hold a symposium on love in *Stages on Life's Way.*

3. See Alastair Hannay, *Kierkegaard* (New York: Routledge & Kegan Paul, 1982, 1991), 347, note 69, where he presents a brief review of interpretations offered by James Bogen, John Donnelly, Bruce Russell, Louis Mackey, and Paul Dietrichson. Also see John Lippitt's very helpful summary and critique of rival interpretations in his new *Guidebook to Kierkegaard and "Fear and Trembling"* (Routledge, 2003).

4. Alasdair MacIntyre, *After Virtue,* 2nd ed. (Notre Dame, Ind.: University of Notre Dame Press, 1984), 39–44. MacIntyre has reasserted this critique in revised form in "Once More on Kierkegaard," in *Kierkegaard After MacIntyre,* ed. Davenport and Rudd (Chicago: Open Court, 2002), 339–355. I have responded in "Kierkegaard, Anxiety, and the Will," in *Kierkegaard Studies Yearbook,* vol. 6, ed. Niels Jørgen Cappelørn, Hermann Deuser, and Jon Stewart (Berlin: Walter de Gruyter, 2001): 158–181, esp. 2, and in *Will as Commitment and Resolve* (New York: Fordham University Press, 2007), ch. 10. Although I have criticized MacIntyre, I should emphasize that I also find insight and enlightenment in many aspects of MacIntyre's conception of virtues, practices, traditions, the narrative structure of personhood, historical conditionalization of responsibility, and community.

5. Ibid., 41.

6. Alasdair MacIntyre, *A Short History of Ethics* (New York: Macmillan, 1966), 217–218.

7. Ibid., 123. Also see Bruce Ballard, "MacIntyre and the Limits of Kierkegaardian Rationality," *Faith and Philosophy* 12, no. 1 (1995): 126–132.

8. See my essay "Kierkegaard's *Postscript* in Light of *Fear and Trembling:* Eschatological Faith," *Revista Portuguesa de Filosofia* 63, no. 3 (2007).

9. Edward Mooney, *Knights of Faith and Resignation: Reading Kierkegaard's Fear and Trembling* (Albany, N.Y.: SUNY Press, 1991); I am especially indebted to chs. 3 and 6.

10. Brand Blanshard, "Kierkegaard on Faith," reprinted in *Essays on Kierkegaard,* ed. Jerry H. Gill (Minneapolis: Burgess Publishing, 1969), 115.

11. Ibid., 115–116.

12. Ibid., 116.

13. Some commentators accept this reading, but argue that the irrationalist view belongs only to Johannes *de Silentio* and is not sanctioned by Kierkegaard himself. For example, see Jerry H. Gill, "Faith Is as Faith Does," in *Kierkegaard's Fear and Trembling: Critical Appraisals,* ed. Robert L. Perkins (Tuscaloosa: University of Alabama Press, 1981).

14. John D. Caputo, *Against Ethics* (Bloomington: Indiana University Press, 1993). I have tried to address these alterity readings of "faith" in my essay "What Kierkegaardian Faith Adds to Alterity Ethics: How Levinas and Derrida Miss the Eschatological Dimension," forthcoming in *Kierkegaard and Levinas: Ethics, Politics, and Religion,* ed. J. Aaron Simmons and David Wood (Bloomington: Indiana University Press, 2008). Interestingly, radical critics of ethical theory in analytic philosophy such as Bernard Williams have felt no attraction to *Fear and Trembling,* perhaps because they offer no alterity conception of transcendent responsibility to which they could relate Kierkegaardian faith.

15. See my articles "The Essence of Eschatology: A Modal Interpretation," *Ultimate Reality and Meaning* 19, no. 3 (September 1996): 206–239, and "Eschatological Ultimacy and the Best Possible Hereafter," *Ultimate Reality and Meaning* 25 (March 2002): 36–67. In these articles I explain in detail why eschatological visions of salvation in revealed religions develop only after, and in relation to, moral ideals that are distinct from the divine or sacred in its original form as cosmogonic principle or pure creative power.

16. See, for instance, Lippmann Bodoff, "The Real Test of the *Akedah:* Blind Obedience Versus Moral Choice," in *Judaism: A Quarterly Journal* 42, no. 1 (1993): 71–92. Bodoff notes that the "traditional understanding of the story" in Jewish hermeneutics did affirm that "Abraham . . . , out of fear of God, was willing to violate God's moral law against murder, to which Abraham was committed" (71). But Bodoff goes on to argue for a "midrashic view of the *Akedah,*" according to which Abraham *never intended* to kill Isaac: "It is a morality tale of Abraham's staunch defense of God's moral law against any temptation—even God's command to violate it" (73). Indeed, he adds that "A Jew is generally not required to obey what appear to be Divine commands to violate the law" (75).

17. Louis Jacobs, "The *Akedah* in Jewish Thought," in *Kierkegaard's Fear and Trembling: Critical Appraisals,* 3. The passage that Jacobs quotes from Steinberg shows how passionate his reaction to *Fear and Trembling* is: "From the Jewish viewpoint—and this is one of its highest dignities—the ethical is never suspended, not under any circumstances and not for anyone. *Especially not for God. . . .* What Kierkegaard asserts to be the glory of God is Jewishly regarded as unmitigated sacrilege. Which is indeed the true point of the *Akedah,* missed so perversely by Kierkegaard" (quoted in Jacobs, 3). Levinas would certainly agree with this sentiment.

18. Jacobs, 2–3.

19. Ibid.

20. In two new essays Merold Westphal now speaks of 'hope *and* obedience' as integral to Kierkegaardian religiousness (see "The Many Faces of Levinas as a Reader of Kierkegaard" in *Kierkegaard and Levinas,* and in *Revista Portuguesa de Filosofia* 63, no. 3 (2007). But this conjunction seems ad hoc; it leaves Abraham with two distinct attitudes whose essential relation is not explained. Moreover, it cannot explain cases of existential faith in which divine command plays no apparent role but eschatological hope is clearly present, such as Socrates' faith in perfect justice in an afterlife. Silentio speaks of a single telos toward which the ethical is "suspended," not two independent teloē.

21. On this point, see C. Stephen Evans, *Kierkegaard's Fragments and Postscript* (Amherst, Mass.: Humanity Books/Prometheus, 1999, reprint; Atlantic Highlands, N.J.: Humanities Press, 1983), 284–290. Also see Evans, *Kierkegaard's Ethic of Love* (Oxford: Oxford University Press, 2004), 314–316. Since the preset essay was largely composed before December 2004 when I got hold of Evans's book, I have not been able to discuss Evans's fine analysis in anything like the detail it deserves here. I try to address it further in "What Kierkegaardian Faith Adds to Moral Alterity," op. cit.

22. Søren Kierkegaard, *Eighteen Upbuilding Discourses,* trans. Howard V. Hong and Edna H. Hong (Princeton, N.J.: Princeton University Press, 1990), 17.

23. Ibid., 18–19. It is not hard to see that these ideas about the temporality of human ex-

istence in its concern for the future were a very important influence on Martin's Heidegger's analysis of the past, present, and future, anxiety, and being-toward-death in his *Being and Time*.

24. Ibid., 19. Kierkegaard goes on to distinguish this expectancy of faith from the aesthetic optimism of "the young person" who "expects to be victorious without a struggle" (20). Such optimism is not faith; but without optimistic ethical striving, a person cannot reach the point of realizing his inability to secure total victory, and then possibly accepting his need for divine assistance.

25. Ibid., 206.

26. In "The Essence of Eschatology: A Modal Interpretation," I distinguish four main kinds of eschatological doctrines in increasing order of complexity. The highest of them is the type of eschatological conception that looks forward to a divinely caused realization of the Good within time itself—both individually via bodily resurrection and cosmically as a trans-formation of the world in a new time. This is the form that corresponds to prophetic Judaism and Christianity.

27. See my discussion of this idea in relation to the Absolute Paradox in "Kierkegaard's *Postscript* in Light of *Fear and Trembling*."

28. Interestingly, my reading brings Kierkegaard's view of the *Akedah* close to Bodoff's argument that "Abraham never intended to kill Isaac" ("The Real Test of the *Akedah*," 81) and that Abraham's faith consists in believing that God will never allow his actions to constitute murder (84).

29. Thus I disagree with Jack Mulder's analysis in "Re-Radicalizing Kierkegaard: An Al-ternative to Religiousness C in Light of an Investigation into the Teleological Suspension of the Ethical," *Continental Philosophy Review* 35 (2002): 303–324. Mulder argues that since Abraham is willing to go through with the sacrifice, he is willing to attempt murder; and since Silentio's God demands this, he demands the "unethical" (307). By contrast, I think Silentio sees Abra-ham's faith as altering the content of his intention so that his intended act is not murder (since the concept of murder entails *permanently* ending a life within this world).

30. Kierkegaard also uses the phrase "fullness of time" for Christ's birth as the fulfillment of the promise in which messianic faith trusted for so many generations: see "Patience in Expec-tancy" in *Eighteen Upbuilding Discourses*, 207. The familiar parallel with Isaac's birth as the gift that is later apparently taken back yet finally restored obviously informs *Fear and Trembling*.

31. The relevant sense of 'miracle' here is not the strong sense of 'an event contradicting physical laws,' but the weaker one of 'an event that human agents can see no way of bringing about, or an event beyond their powers to secure,' which is therefore necessarily unpredictable and a *surprise* if it occurs.

32. Hannay, *Kierkegaard*, 74.

33. Søren Kierkegaard, *Sickness unto Death*, trans. Howard V. Hong and Edna H. Hong (Princeton, N.J.: Princeton University Press, 1980), Part One, §C(A)b ("Necessity's Despair is to Lack Possibility"), 38.

34. Ibid., 39.

35. Tolkien's lecture "On Fairy-Stories" first appeared in *Essays Presented to Charles Wil-liams*, ed. C. S. Lewis (Oxford: Oxford University Press 1947) and was reprinted in Tolkien's collection *Tree and Leaf* (London: George Allen and Unwin, 1967). I cite the final version found in *The Monsters and the Critics and Other Essays*, ed. Christopher Tolkien (London: George Allen and Unwin, 1983): 109–161.

36. Ibid., 153.

37. Ibid., 154.

38. Kierkegaard, "Patience in Expectancy," in *Eighteen Upbuilding Discourses*, 207.

39. Ibid., 208. Much of the rest of this discourse is taken up with a discussion of Anna's expectancy.

40. There remains one other crucial difference between an explicitly religious narrative and a fairy tale. Tolkien notes that "fairy-stories as a whole have three faces: the Mystical to-wards the Supernatural; the Magical towards Nature; and the Mirror of scorn and pity towards

Man. The essential face of Faërie is the middle one, the Magical" ("On Fairy-Stories," 125). By contrast, religious stories since the dawn of monotheism put less emphasis on the magical view of nature. Still, the three 'faces' of fairy-stories reflect a kind of eschatological perspective: the magical, for example, is nature seen as it will be in the new creation, when matter and spirit are fully joined. The double-attitude of scorn and pity toward men reflects existential anxiety before the *double-possibility* of damnation or salvation. And finally, in fairy stories, the divine enters only indirectly as the mystical, rather than directly as the ultimate Person, the creator, covenantal redeemer, or source of eschatological revelations.

41. Of course, Tolkien's own fantasy masterpiece is, in addition to being an epic, an attempt to evoke this eucatastrophic experience. See my essay "Happy Endings and Religious Hope: *The Lord of the Rings* as an Epic Fairy Tale," in *The Lord of the Rings and Philosophy*, ed. Greg Bassham and Eric Bronson (Chicago: Open Court, 2003): 204–218. Doubtless, Kierkegaard would have appreciated the echoes of Mount Moriah in Tolkien's story of Frodo and Sam approaching Mount Doom (though they chose to sacrifice themselves). I have often wondered whether Charles Williams, who served as philosophy editor at Oxford Press and helped Walter Lowrie and others get the first English translations of Kierkegaard published, might have talked with his good friends, Tolkien and C.S. Lewis, about *Fear and Trembling* or other works of the Danish sage. One certainly finds eucatastrophes at the end of Williams's major works of religious fantasy, such as *Descent into Hell* and *All Hallows Eve*.

42. Notice that Silentio also constantly emphasizes the *anxiety* that results from the paradoxical tension between the ethical and religious perspectives on Abraham's act (e.g., 28, 30). At this point, we might say that the anxiety that naturally attends all conjecture about the future has become absolute: unless the future is conquered by a faith that supports this paradox, then the contradiction destroys the single individual.

43. Mooney, *Knights of Faith and Resignation*, 91.

44. Ibid., 102.

45. Ibid., 57.

46. Ibid., 58–59.

47. Hannay, *Kierkegaard*, 74.

48. Ibid., 75 (my italics).

49. Ibid. However, as we have seen, the Christian "hereafter" is only one kind of eschatological end-point.

50. John Whittaker, "The Suspension of the Ethical in *Fear and Trembling*," *Kierkegaardiana* 4 (1988): 101–113, 103.

51. See Kierkegaard, *JP*, 1, #908; reprinted in the Supplement to *Fear and Trembling*, 248.

52. Robert Adams, *Finite and Infinite Goods* (Oxford: Oxford University Press, 1999), 281; Evans, *Kierkegaard's Ethic of Love*, 315. Adams adds that God must be good in the non-deontic sense and reasonable (not contradictory) for his commands to bind (283). But note that Adams does not think Kierkegaard understood divine command ethics in this way (290).

53. Evans, *Kierkegaard's Ethic of Love*, 21.

54. Ibid., 316.

55. See Merold Westphal, *Becoming a Self: A Reading of Kierkegaard's Concluding Unscientific Postscript* (West Lafayette, Ind.: Purdue University Press, 1996), 197–199; and Westphal, "Kierkegaard's Religiousness C: A Defense," *International Philosophical Quarterly* 44, no. 4 (Dec. 2004): 535–548.

56. Jerome Gellman, "Kierkegaard's *Fear and Trembling*," *Man and World* 23, no. 3 (1990): 295–304.

57. See Edward Mooney, *Knights of Faith and Resignation*, chs. 4–8 and Mooney, *Selves in Discord and Resolve* (New York: Routledge, 1996), chs. 4–6.

58. See the discussion of objectivity and subjectivity in Mooney's *Knights of Faith and Resignation*, 47, and in Mooney, "The Perils of Polarity: MacIntyre and Kierkegaard in Search of Moral Truth," in *Kierkegaard After MacIntyre*: 233–263, 252.

59. Lippitt seems to agree with me here, for he asks whether God and the absurd have dropped out of Mooney's picture in favor of a kind of virtue that makes no essential reference

to the divine (*Kierkegaard and Fear and Trembling*, 153). Yet, against Green, Lippitt agrees with Mooney that "one point of *Fear and Trembling* is to question the idea that 'the ethical is the universal'" (145).

60. Alastair Hannay, Introduction to *Fear and Trembling*, trans. Hannay (London: Penguin Books, 1985), 28–29.

61. Merold Westphal, "Kierkegaard and Hegel," in the *Cambridge Companion to Kierkegaard*, ed. Alastair Hannay and Gordon Marino (Cambridge: Cambridge University Press, 1998): 101–124, 108.

62. Ibid., 109.

63. Mooney, *Selves in Discord and Resolve*, 47.

64. C. Stephen Evans, "Faith as the *Telos* of Morality: A Reading of *Fear and Trembling*," in the *International Kierkegaard Commentary* volume on *Fear and Trembling* and *Repetition*, ed. Robert Perkins (Macon, Ga.: Mercer University Press, 1993), 16.

65. Hannay, Introduction to *Fear and Trembling*, 31.

66. For example, when Nietzsche talks about going "beyond good and evil," he means a set of attitudes that reject Judeo-Christian ethics as having a mean-spirited ulterior motive about which its adherents deceive themselves. Although we have to move *through* this set of ethical attitudes to awaken to their implicit nihilism and in rejecting this nihilism to reach the higher consciousness of the Übermensch, the good-evil distinction is like a ladder that we can eventually throw away. It is the opposite for Kierkegaard: if faith is 'beyond' morality in any sense, it is only as a (nonmereological) *addition to* morality that forms a higher *combination* or mental gestalt. This is what I mean by a cumulative surpassing.

67. Evans, "Faith as the *Telos* of Morality," 12. Such a cumulative relation is what Evans means when he argues that "the spheres or stages should be viewed . . . as having a ranking or hierarchy" (*Kierkegaard's Ethic of Love*, 51). I prefer the term "cumulative" because it more clearly connotes inclusion, as in nested concentric circles.

68. The cumulative relation of the aesthetic and the ethical is particularly evident in Kierkegaard's essay "The Aesthetic Validity of Marriage" in *Either/Or*, Vol. II. In my view, *Fear and Trembling* serves a parallel purpose: it can be regarded as a demonstration of the 'Ethical Validity of Faith.'

69. Hannay, *Kierkegaard*, 78.

70. Mooney, *Knights of Fear and Trembling*, 82–84.

71. Ronald M. Green, "Enough is Enough! *Fear and Trembling* Is *Not* about Ethics," *Journal of Religious Ethics* 21, no. 2 (1993): 191–209, 194. In addition to Kant's discussion of sin in *Religion within the Limits of Reason Alone*, I think Kierkegaard frequently has in mind Kant's account of the highest good in the *Critique of Practical Reason*, where Kant implies that eschatological perfect justice is something that *we* have a duty to pursue. This draws ultimate meaning within the scope of rational ethics, and leads to Hegel's vision of a philosophical realization of the Absolute. Part of Kierkegaard's aim is to return the eschatological end to its medieval place as the *purely revelational* element in theology, which is *beyond* our power or duty to pursue, although it confirms and requites the striving required by natural law *and* by the revealed love-commandments.

72. Anthony Rudd, *Kierkegaard and the Limits of the Ethical* (Oxford: Oxford University Press, 1993), 145.

73. Ronald Green, *Kierkegaard and Kant: The Hidden Debt* (Albany, N.Y.: SUNY Press, 1992), 89.

74. Westphal, "Kierkegaard and Hegel," 110.

75. Ulrich Knappe, *Theory and Practice in Kant and Kierkegaard*, Kierkegaard Studies Monograph Series vol. 9, ed. Niels Cappelørn (New York: Walter de Gruyter, 2004), 80–84.

76. Kierkegaard, *Works of Love*, trans. Howard V. Hong and Edna H. Hong (New York: Harper Torchbooks, 1962), 78.

77. Earl McLane, "Rereading *Fear and Trembling*," *Faith and Philosophy* 10, no. 2 (1993): 198–219, 205.

78. I was glad to discover McLane's agreement with this point (ibid., 199).

79. See Emmanuel Levinas, *Totality and Infinity* (Pittsburgh, Pa.: Duquesne University Press, 1969), 194, 198.

80. McLane, "Rereading *Fear and Trembling*," 205.

81. Kierkegaard really should have started with a simpler case before addressing this one; then he might not have been so badly misunderstood by so many readers. But Kant and Hegel's difficulties with the *Akedah* proved too tempting for him: doubtless it seemed that Abraham's case would provide the leverage to show that the System could not really accommodate religiousness. In addition, Kierkegaard may have believed that God also played all three roles in his own life, since he apparently thought of God as the source of the mysterious curse or melancholy that served as the obstacle to his marrying Regine. However, the atypical nature of this kind of obstacle has occasioned much confusion.

82. Lippitt, 145.

83. Lippitt, 147.

84. Blanshard, 116. Blanshard was even more confused when he said, "'Teleological' means 'for an end'," but "what Kierkegaard is praising here is the abandonment of all thought of ends" (116). On the contrary, Kierkegaard's knight of faith has a religious telos, although the latter is not something he believes that he can act to bring about.

85. Westphal, *Becoming a Self,* 29.

86. Westphal, "Kierkegaard and Hegel," 109.

87. This is only *one* way in which misfortune can make an agent's ethical ideal humanly impossible and force him to give up hope of fulfilling it. Thus one can be a knight of infinite resignation without being a tragic hero. But every tragic hero is also a knight of infinite resignation: the former category is a *subset* of the latter. This explains why, as Evans observes, the tragic hero and knight of resignation "appear to be different figures but de Silentio identifies them" in a couple places (*Kierkegaard's Ethic of Love,* 74 and n. 22). Note that Kierkegaard's conception of a tragic hero is also different than Hegel's, since Hegel blames the tragic hero's dilemma at least partly on his own stubborn or unyielding way or ethical one-sidedness. I am indebted to Stephen Houlgate for this point.

88. Green, "Enough is Enough!" 193.

89. Ibid., 191.

90. Ibid., 192.

91. Ibid., 198. Green also makes this argument in his insightful essay, "'Developing' *Fear and Trembling*," in the *Cambridge Companion to Kierkegaard,* 257–281, 263–267.

92. Green, "Enough Is Enough!" 193.

93. Rudd, *Kierkegaard and the Limits of the Ethical,* 148–149.

94. Ibid., 150.

95. Westphal, "Kierkegaard and Hegel," 110.

96. See Mircea Eliade, *The Myth of the Eternal Return,* trans. Willard R. Trask (Princeton, N.J.: Princeton University Press/Bollingen Foundation, 1954, 1974 paperback). With Kierkegaard in mind, Eliade writes: "Abraham's religious act inaugurates a new religious dimension: God reveals himself as personal, as a 'totally distinct' existence that ordains, bestows, demands, without any rational (i.e. general, foreseeable) justification, and for which all is possible. This new dimension renders 'faith' possible in the Judaeo-Christian sense" (110).

97. Green, "Enough Is Enough!" 198.

98. I call this the K-sense because it corresponds closely to Kant's principle that "ought implies can." Since for Kant the relevant sense of "can" in this principle includes not only that it is physically and psychologically possible to perform the required act (or omission), but also that it is *morally* possible (or can be attempted without employing evil means), Kant understands the principle to imply that we have no duty to do anything that we could perform only by violating other strict duties. (This principle is operative, for example, in limiting the scope of imperfect duties.)

99. It is obviously this kind of obstacle that Kierkegaard felt disabled him from partici-

pating in the universal ethical paradigm of marriage. Although the "universal" does seem to be used in the sense of Hegelian ethical life here, I note that relations of interhuman *love* and *discourse* in general seem to be interrupted by this kind of obstacle.

100. One could perhaps argue for a universal K-suspension on the basis of original sin, but that would be to import a specifically Christian category that plays no literal role in the account of faith given in *Fear and Trembling.*

101. Note that Kierkegaard admits that Abraham's *action* is unjust: "he is and remains a murderer" (74, and see also 53). But although outwardly it thus appears that "he hates Isaac," inwardly "He must love Isaac with his whole soul," or he lacks the goodness of will that is the sine qua non for faith (74). This gives Kierkegaard a way to interpret the meaning of the difficult saying at Luke 14:26, where Jesus characterizes the absolute duty to God as requiring that one "hate his own father and mother and wife and children" to be a disciple (72). This saying means that faith may require the apostle to act that way, while nevertheless still inwardly loving their family members.

102. Mooney, *Knights of Faith and Resignation,* 59.

103. Erich Auerbach, "The Sacrifice of Isaac," in *Modern Critical Interpretations: Genesis,* ed. Harold Bloom (Chelsea House Publishers, 1986): 11–15, 14.

104. Ibid., 15.

105. Hannay, *Kierkegaard,* 80.

106. Ibid.

107. Hannay, Introduction to *Fear and Trembling,* 26. Hannay's discussion in this Introduction was used as a basis for Chapter III in the second edition of *Kierkegaard.* Thus similar or identical passages occur in both.

108. See Green, "Enough is Enough!" 199–202, and "'Developing' *Fear and Trembling,*" 269–274. In the latter, Green writes that "Abraham and the merman are counterparts, positive and negative expressions of the same problem. Both have suspended the ethical, one by obedience and one by sin" (273). This confuses the *obstacle* with the *suspension,* according to my account: Abraham and the merman have different obstacles but both find the fulfillment of their moral purposes in suspense awaiting divine assistance.

109. It is also beyond doubt that Kierkegaard saw the eucatastrophe of Isaac's return to Abraham as prefiguring the greatest eucatastrophe of all—Christ's return from the grave— which is the beginning of the new kingdom to come, the beginning of the general resurrection in the cosmic eschaton.

110. Whittaker, "The Suspension of the Ethical in *Fear and Trembling,*" 109. Evans also comes close to endorsing the purely anagogical reading in *Kierkegaard's Ethic of Love,* 81–83.

111. Green, "Enough Is Enough!" 109.

112. Lippitt, 163.

113. Gene Outka, "God as the Subject of Unique Veneration," *Journal of Religious Ethics* 21, no. 2 (1993): 211–215, 212–213. However, I will not go so far as to say that existential faith is open to everyone (see note 132 below).

114. See my discussion of Problema III in "Kierkegaard's *Postscript* in Light of *Fear and Trembling.*"

115. Hannay, 73.

116. Andrew Cross, "*Fear and Trembling*'s Unorthodox Ideal," *Philosophical Topics* 27 no. 2 (1999): 227–253, 237. Cited in Lippitt.

117. See Andrew Cross, "Faith as Suspension of the Ethical in *Fear and Trembling,*" *Inquiry,* 46 (2003): 3–28, 18.

118. Ibid.

119. Ibid., 19. Yet Silentio attributes precisely this belief to Abraham, in almost these exact words (36). The text everywhere contradicts Cross on this crucial point: for example, the rich young man of the Gospel would have been a knight of faith if he had given away his fortune in resignation, and still believed that he would get it back by virtue of the absurd (49); Agamemnon, Jephthah, and Brutus are distinguished from the knight of faith because they lack his

belief that the agonizing loss accepted in resignation "will not happen anyway" (59); etc. Also see Whittaker, 104.

120. Lippitt, *Guidebook to Kierkegaard and "Fear and Trembling,"* 71.

121. Ibid., 72.

122. Ibid.

123. Kierkegaard must conceive Abraham as recognizing the epistemic possibility that his faith could be wrong (since faith is not knowledge), and therefore as recognizing the possibility that his killing Isaac could (in an epistemic sense) mean the permanent loss of his son.

124. As noted earlier, the modal sense of this "cannot," which is central to the concept of infinite resignation, is a complex one because it covers a large range of physical, psychological, social, moral, and even revelatory (as in Abraham's case) limits that function as obstacles to my achieving this end. The function of "cannot" is to say that these obstacle(s) are such as to be *insurmountable* by any effort of will that I could make.

125. Cross, "Faith as Suspension of the Ethical in *Fear and Trembling*," 14.

126. On this point, see Whittaker, "The Suspension of the Ethical in *Fear and Trembling*," 105–106.

127. See Lippitt's effective critique of Cross's position in his *Guidebook to Kierkegaard and "Fear and Trembling,"* pp. 72–74.

128. Ibid., 65.

129. Ibid., 75. Note that although Lippitt introduces this as Hall's view, he also seems to endorse it.

130. *Sickness unto Death,* Part One, §C(B)b ("In Despair to Will to Be Oneself: Defiance"), 70; see the note on "the dialectic of resignation" which refuses to will one aspect of one's concrete self.

131. Ibid., 71.

132. Of course, Agamemnon does not seem to have received any eschatological promise from his gods, which points out an important epistemic precondition of existential faith: there must be some (apparently) divine sign or revelation in which the agent can trust. Socrates satisfies this condition while several tragic heroes do not. I do not try to decide here whether this epistemic condition can be met by general revelation or whether it requires special communication to the unique individual, as in Abraham's case. But if there are people who do not meet the epistemic condition, then infinite resignation would be the highest heroism possible for them. In their case, a eucatastrophe *could* be embraced with without any regret or loss (again consider Gawain, who receives himself back in poignant joy), whereas an Abraham who failed to trust the divine promise he received could not likewise receive Isaac back with pure joy.

133. Whittaker, "The Suspension of the Ethical in *Fear and Trembling*," 104.

134. Lippitt, 70.

135. Louis Dupré, *Kierkegaard as Theologian,* 72. In the same vein, Dupré adds that "Before there can be any question of pardon, man must first try to fulfill the universal law imposed on him as man; otherwise, redemption will have no effect" (73).

136. In Harry Frankfurt's work, wholehearted or decisive identification means a second-order volition that is unambiguous or not in conflict with any other higher-order volitions expressing the agent's self-defining cares or commitments. I use "wholeheartedness" for the agent's relationship to the ground projects that constitute the heart of her agency, or commitments of her "highest-order will": see Davenport, "Kierkegaard, Anxiety, and the Will," 163.

137. See my discussion of infinite passion in "The Ethical and Religious Significance of Taciturnus's Letter in Kierkegaard's *Stages on Life's Way*," in the *International Kierkegaard Commentary 11: Stages on Life's Way,* ed. Robert Perkins (Macon, Ga.: Mercer University Press, November 2000): 213–244.

138. Mooney, *Knights of Faith and Resignation,* 53.

139. Ibid., 54.

140. From *The Return of the King,* directed by Peter Jackson (New Line Cinema, 2003). Theoden's statement in Tolkien's original text is slightly different, but in a similar spirit.

141. W. P. Ker, quoted in the Introduction to *Beowulf,* trans. David Wright (London: Penguin Books, 1957), 12.

142. Though both Théoden and Beowulf are only knights of infinite resignation, they *could* have added faith without giving up the infinite commitment of their resigned wills.

143. Hannay, *Kierkegaard,* 73.

144. Evans, "Faith as the *Telos* of Morality," 16.

145. Whether the human will requires a *different* kind of grace in order to strive towards moral ideals within the limits of its power is another question that does not enter into *Fear and Trembling,* but is left for later specifically Christian pseudonymous and signed works.

146. This point was suggested by Vanessa Rumble in comments on a much earlier version of this paper (see introductory note).

147. See Davenport, "Entangled Freedom: Ethical Authority, Original Sin, and Choice in Kierkegaard's *Concept of Anxiety,*" *Kierkegaardiana* 21 (2001): 131–151.

148. This quote is from Rumble's comments at the Eastern APA presentation of this paper (see introductory note).

149. Perhaps this thesis is most fully defended in Evans, *Kierkegaard's Ethic of Love.*

150. Avi Sagi and Daniel Statman, "Divine Command Morality and Jewish Tradition," in the *Journal of Religious Ethics* 23, no. 1 (1995): 39–67, 39.

151. Ibid., 40. It is not as obvious that the moderate versions of Strong Dependence are compatible with saying that any deontic state of affairs is independent of God's existing. Denying this is central to Philip Quinn's account of divine sovereignty.

152. Ibid., p.41.

153. Ibid., 44.

154. McLane, "Rereading *Fear and Trembling,*" 205. I do not try to decide here whether Kierkegaard accepts that the commands of a loving God are both sufficient *and necessary* for moral obligation, but on this topic, see Zach Manis's dissertation (Baylor University, 2006).

155. In *Works of Love,* for example, Kierkegaard seems to accept the view that agape is an infused virtue that is not possible for human beings without divine assistance.

156. See Davenport, "Kierkegaard's *Postscript* in Light of *Fear and Trembling.*"

16. Silence and Entering the Circle of Faith

1. *Papirer,* I 94 (October 1835) ("Philosophie og Christendom lade sig dog aldrig forene"). The entry is No. 13 in *Kierkegaard's Journals and Notebooks,* Vol. 1 (Princeton, N.J.: Princeton University Press, 2007), 25.

2. *Postscript,* Hong tr. p. 491, Swenson & Lowrie tr., p. 438 (*SKS*7, p. 445).

3. Published in August 1844 as *Four Edifying Discourses* (now in *Eighteen Discourses, SKS*)

4. *Postscript,* Hong tr., pp. 270–271, Swenson and Lowrie tr., pp. 242–242 (*SKS*7, pp. 245–246).

5. *Kierkegaard's Papers and Journals: A Selection,* ed. trans. Alastair Hannay (London: Penguin Books, 1996), p. 425.

6. Cf. G. H. von Wright's "Historical Introduction" to Ludwig Wittgenstein, *Prototractatus: An Early Version of Tractatus-Logico-Philosophicus* (London: Routledge & Kegan Paul, 1971), p. 16.

7. *Fear and Trembling,* trans. Alastair Hannay (Harmondsworth: Penguin Books, 1985), p. 83.

8. *SKS*4, p. 115.

Adams, Robert Merrihew. *Finite and Infinite Goods.* New York: Oxford University Press, 1999.
———. *Finite and Infinite Goods.* Oxford: Oxford University Press, 1999.
Adorno, Theodor. *Kierkegaard: Construction of the Aesthetic.* Minneapolis: University of Minnesota Press, 1989.
Allison, Henry E. "Christianity and Nonsense." In *Kierkegaard: A Collection of Critical Essays,* ed. Josiah Thompson, pp. 289–323. New York: Doubleday [Anchor Books], 1972.
Auerbach, Erich. "The Sacrifice of Isaac." In *Genesis,* ed. Harold Bloom, 11–15. New York: Chelsea House, 1986.
Austin, J. L. *Sense and Sensibilia.* Edited by G. J. Warnock. Oxford: Oxford University Press, 1962.
Ayer, A. J. *Bertrand Russell.* Chicago: University of Chicago Press, 1988.
———. *Language, Truth and Logic.* New York: Dover, 1946.
Ballard, Bruce. "MacIntyre and the Limits of Kierkegaardian Rationality." *Faith and Philosophy* 12, no. 1 (winter 1995): 126–132.
Baumgartner, Peter, and Sabine Payr. *Speaking Minds: Interviews with Twenty Eminent Cognitive Scientists.* Princeton, N.J.: Princeton University Press, 1995.
Benson, Hugh H. *Socratic Wisdom: The Model of Knowledge in Plato's Early Dialogues.* Oxford: Oxford University Press, 2006.
Blum, Lawrence A. *Moral Perception and Particularity.* Cambridge: Cambridge University Press, 1994.
Bly, Robert. "A Wrong Turning in American Poetry." In *Claims for Poetry,* ed. Donald Hall, 17–37. Ann Arbor: University of Michigan Press, 1982.
Bodoff, Lippmann. "The Real Test of the *Akedah:* Blind Obedience versus Moral Choice." *Judaism: A Quarterly Journal* 42, no. 1 (winter 1993).
Bregman, Marc. "Aqedah: Midrash as Visualization." *Journal of Textual Reasoning* II/1, Summer 2003. http://etext.lib.virginia.edu/journals/tr/volume2/number1/bregman.html.
Brooks, Cleanth. "The Heresy of Paraphrase." In *Twentieth-Century Literary Theory,* ed. Vassilis Lambropoulos and David Neal Miller, 239–253. Albany, N.Y.: SUNY Press, 1987.
Burwood, Stephen, Paul Gilbert, and Kathleen Lennon. *Philosophy of Mind.* Montreal: McGill-Queen's University Press, 1999.
Caputo, John D. *More Radical Hermeneutics: On Not Knowing Who We Are.* Bloomington: Indiana University Press, 2000.
———. *Against Ethics.* Bloomington: Indiana University Press, 1993.

Carnap, Rudolf. *The Logical Structure of the World.* Translated by R. George. Berkeley: University of California Press, 1967.

Cassirer, Ernst, and Paul Oskar Kristeller. In *The Renaissance Philosophy of Man,* ed. Ernst Cassirer, Paul Oskar Kristeller, and John Herman Randall, Jr. Chicago: University of Chicago Press, 1948.

Cavell, Stanley. *Philosophical Passages: Wittgenstein, Emerson, Austin, Derrida.* Oxford: Blackwell, 1995.

———. *Must We Mean What We Say?* Cambridge: Cambridge University Press, 1976.

Chalmers, David. "Facing Up to the Problem of Consciousness." *Journal of Consciousness Studies* 2 (1995): 200–219.

Churchland, Patricia S. *Neurophilosophy.* Cambridge, Mass.: MIT Press, 1986.

Churchland, Paul M. *Matter and Consciousness.* Cambridge, Mass.: MIT Press, 1988.

Conway, Daniel. "Seeing Is Believing: Narrative Visualization in Kierkegaard's *Fear and Trembling.*" *Journal of Textual Reasoning* II/1, Summer 2003. http://etext.lib.virginia.edu/journals/tr/volume2/number1/conway.html.

Cooper, David E., ed. *Metaphysics: The Classic Readings.* Oxford: Blackwell, 2000.

Cross, Andrew. "Faith as Suspension of the Ethical in *Fear and Trembling.*" *Inquiry* 46 (2003): 3–28.

———. "*Fear and Trembling*'s Unorthodox Ideal." *Philosophical Topics* 27, no. 2 (1999): 227–253.

Dadlez, E. M. *What's Hecuba to Him? Fictional Events and Actual Emotions.* University Park: Pennsylvania State University Press, 1997.

Danto, Arthur C. "Philosophy as/and/of Literature." *Proceedings and Addresses of the American Philosophical Association* 58 (1984): 5–20.

Davenport, John. "Entangled Freedom: Ethical Authority, Original Sin, and Choice in Kierkegaard's *Concept of Anxiety.*" *Kierkegaardiana* 21 (2001): 131–151.

———. "Eschatological Ultimacy and the Best Possible Hereafter." *Ultimate Reality and Meaning* 25 (March 2002): 36–67.

———. "The Essence of Eschatology: A Modal Interpretation." *Ultimate Reality and Meaning* 19, no. 3 (September 1996): 206–239.

———. "The Ethical and Religious Significance of Taciturnus's Letter in Kierkegaard's *Stages on Life's Way.*" In the *International Kierkegaard Commentary 11: Stages on Life's Way,* ed. Robert Perkins, pp. 213–244. Macon, Ga.: Mercer University Press, 2000.

———. "Happy Endings and Religious Hope: *The Lord of the Rings* as an Epic Fairy Tale." In *The Lord of the Rings and Philosophy,* ed. Gregory Bassham and Eric Bronson, pp. 204–218. Chicago: Open Court, 2003.

———. "Kierkegaard, Anxiety, and the Will." *Kierkegaard Studies Yearbook* 6 (fall 2001): 158–181.

———. "What Kierkegaardian Faith Adds to Alterity Ethics: How Levinas and Derrida Miss the Eschatological Dimension." In *Kierkegaard and Levinas: Ethics, Politics, and Religion,* ed. J. Aaron Simmons and David Wood. Bloomington: Indiana University Press, 2008.

———. *Will as Commitment and Resolve.* New York: Fordham University Press, 2007.

Davenport, John, and Anthony Rudd, eds. *Kierkegaard after MacIntyre.* Chicago: Open Court, 2001.

Dennett, Daniel. *Consciousness Explained.* Boston: Back Bay Books, 1991.

Derrida, Jacques. *The Gift of Death.* Translated by David Wills. Chicago: University of Chicago Press, 1995.

———. *Margins of Philosophy.* Translated by Alan Bass. Chicago: University of Chicago Press, 1982.

Deuser, Hermann. "Evolutionäre Metaphysik als Theorie des menschlichen Selbst. Beiträge zum Begriff religiöser Erfahrung." In *Marburger Jahrbuch. Theologie XVI, Das Selbst in der Evolution,* ed. Wilfried Härle and Reiner Preul, pp. 45–78. Marburg: N. G. Elwert Verlag, 2004.

Dostoevsky, Fyodor. *A Gentle Creature and Other Stories.* Translated by Alan Myers. Oxford: Oxford University Press, 1995.

Dreyfus, Hubert. *Thinking in Action: On the Internet.* Edited by R. Kearney and S. Critchley. Revised edition. New York: Routledge, 2002.

Dreyfus, Hubert, and Jane Rubin. "Kierkegaard on the Nihilism of the Present Age: The Case of Commitment as Addiction." *Synthese* 98, no. 1 (January 1994), pp. 3–19.

Drury, Shadia. *Leo Strauss and the American Right.* New York: St. Martin's Press, 1997.

Dunaway, John. *Simone Weil.* New York: Twayne, 1984.

Dupré, John. *Human Nature and the Limits of Science.* Oxford: Clarendon Press, 2001.

Dupré, Louis. *Kierkegaard as Theologian.* New York: Sheed and Ward, 1964.

Eliade, Mircea. *The Myth of the Eternal Return.* Translated by Willard R. Trask. Princeton, N.J.: Princeton University Press/Bollingen Foundation, 1974.

Evans, C. Stephen. "Faith as the *Telos* of Morality: A Reading of *Fear and Trembling.*" In the *International Kierkegaard Commentary* volume on *Fear and Trembling, and Repetition,* ed. Robert L. Perkins. Macon, Ga.: Mercer University Press, 1993.

———. *Kierkegaard's Fragments and Postscript.* Reprint edition. New York: Humanity Books/Prometheus, 1999.

———. *Kierkegaard's Ethic of Love.* Oxford: Oxford University Press, 2004.

Fenves, Peter. *"Chatter": Language and History in Kierkegaard.* Stanford, Calif.: Stanford University Press, 1993.

Ferguson, Harvie. *Melancholy and the Critique of Modernity: Søren Kierkegaard's Religious Psychology.* London/New York: Routledge, 1995.

Ferreira, M. Jamie. "Immediacy and Reflection in Kierkegaard's *Works of Love.*" In *Immediacy and Reflection in Kierkegaard's Thought,* ed. Paul Cruysberghs and Johan Taels. Louven: Louven University Press, 2003.

———. *Love's Grateful Striving: A Commentary on Kierkegaard's Works of Love.* Oxford: Oxford University Press, 2001.

Frankfurt, Harry. *The Importance of What We Care About.* Cambridge: Cambridge University Press, 1988.

Frazer, Michael L. "Esotericism Ancient and Modern." *Political Theory* 34, no. 1 (2006): 33–61.

Furtak, Rick Anthony. "The Virtues of Authenticity: A Kierkegaardian Essay in Moral Psychology." *International Philosophical Quarterly* 43 (2003): 423–438.

———. *Wisdom in Love: Kierkegaard and the Ancient Quest for Emotional Integrity.* Notre Dame, Ind.: University of Notre Dame Press, 2005.

Garff, Joakim. "Johannes de silentio: Rhetorician of Silence." In *Kierkegaard Studies: Yearbook 1996,* ed. Niels Jørgen Cappelørn and Hermann Deuser, pp. 186–210. Berlin: Walter de Grutyer, 1996.

Gellman, Jerome. "Kierkegaard's *Fear and Trembling.*" *Man and World* 23, no. 3 (1990): 295–304.

Genova, Judith. *Wittgenstein: A Way of Seeing.* New York: Routledge, 1995.

Gill, Jerry H. "Faith Is as Faith Does." In *Kierkegaard's Fear and Trembling: Critical Appraisals,* ed. Robert L. Perkins. University: University of Alabama Press, 1981.

Gilligan, James. *Violence: Reflections on a National Epidemic.* New York: Random House, 1996.

Green, Ronald. "'Developing' *Fear and Trembling.*" In *The Cambridge Companion to Kierkegaard,* ed. Alastair Hannay and Gordon Daniel Marino, pp. 257–81. New York: Cambridge University Press, 1998.

———. "Enough Is Enough! *Fear and Trembling* Is *Not* about Ethics." *Journal of Religious Ethics* 21, no. 2 (1993): 191–209.

———. *Kierkegaard and Kant: The Hidden Debt.* Albany, N.Y.: SUNY Press, 1992.

Grice, Paul. *The Conception of Value.* Oxford: Clarendon Press, 1991.

Grøn, Arne. *Begrebet angst hos Søren Kierkegaard.* Copenhagen: Gyldendal, 1993.

Hadot, Pierre. *Philosophy as a Way of Life.* Translated by Michael Chase. Oxford: Blackwell, 1995.

Hannay, Alastair. "Basic Despair in *The Sickness unto Death,*" Arne Grøn, "Der Begriff Verzweiflung," and Michael Theunissen, "Für einen rationaleren Kierkegaard. Zu Einwänden von Arne Grøn und Alastair Hannay," as well as Hannay's response, "Paradigmatic Despair and the Quest for a Kierkegaardian Anthropology," in *Kierkegaard Studies: Yearbook,* ed. Niels Jørgen Cappelørn and Hermann Deuser, pp. 15–32, pp. 33–60, pp. 61–90, and pp. 149–163, respectively. Berlin: Walter de Gruyter, 1996.

———. *Human Consciousness.* London: Routledge, 1990.

———. "Introduction." In *The Sickness unto Death.* Translated by Alastair Hannay. New York: Penguin, 1989.

———. *Kierkegaard. The Arguments of the Philosophers.* Edited by Ted Honderich. London: Routledge & Kegan Paul, 1982; revised ed., 1991.

———. *Kierkegaard: A Biography.* Cambridge: Cambridge University Press, 2001.

———. *Kierkegaard and Philosophy: Selected Essays.* London: Routledge, 2003.

———. "Kierkegaard and What We Mean by 'Philosophy.'" *International Journal of Philosophical Studies* 8 (2000): 1–22.

———. "Kierkegaard's Philosophy of Mind." In *Contemporary Philosophy: A New Survey, Volume 4,* ed. Guttorm Fløistad, 157–183. The Hague: Martinus Nijhoff, 1983.

———. "Kierkegaard's Present Day and Ours." In *Heidegger, Authenticity, and Modernity: Essays in Honor of Hubert L. Dreyfus,* vol. 1, ed. Mark A. Wrathall and Jeff Malpas, pp.105–122. Cambridge, Mass.: MIT Press.

———. "Proximity as Apartness." In Hannay, *Kierkegaard and Philosophy,* pp. 150–162. London: Routledge, 2003.

Hegel, G. W. F. *Hegel's Science of Logic.* Translated by A. V. Miller. London: George Allen & Unwin, 1969.

Heidegger, Martin. *Being and Time.* Translated by Joan Stambaugh. Albany, N.Y.: SUNY Press, 1996.

———. *Phenomenological Interpretations of Aristotle.* Translated by Richard Rojcewicz. Bloomington: Indiana University Press, 2001.

Hill, Geoffrey. "The Art of Poetry LXXX": Interview with Carl Phillips. *Paris Review* 154 (2000): 272–299.

Hume, David. "My Own Life." In *Essays Moral, Political, and Literary,* ed. Eugene F. Miller, xxxi–xli. Indianapolis: Liberty Fund, 1985.

Husserl, Edmund. *The Idea of Phenomenology.* Translated by Alston and Nakhnikian. Dordrecht: Kluwer, 1964.

Irwin, Terrence. *Plato's Ethics.* Oxford: Oxford University Press, 1995.

Jackson, Frank. "What Mary Didn't Know." In *The Nature of Consciousness,* ed. N. Block, O. Flanagan, and G. Güzeldere, pp. 567–570. Cambridge, Mass.: MIT Press, 1997.

Jacobs, Louis. "The *Akedah* in Jewish Thought." In *Kierkegaard's Fear and Trembling: Critical Appraisals,* ed. Robert L. Perkins. University: University of Alabama Press, 1981.

Johnson, Mark. *Moral Imagination: Implications of Cognitive Science for Ethics.* Chicago: University of Chicago Press, 1993.

Kahn, Ivan. "Melancholy, Irony, and Kierkegaard." *International Journal for Philosophy of Religion* 17 (1985): 67–85.

Kant, I. "Analytic of Pure Practical Reason." In *Kant's Critique of Practical Reason and Other Essays on the Theory of Ethics,* trans. T. K. Abbott. 6th ed. New York: Longmans, Green.

Katz, Claire Elise. "The Responsibility of Irresponsibility: Taking (Yet) Another Look at the Akedah." In *Addressing Levinas,* ed. Sean Nelson, Antje Kapust, and Kent Still, pp. 17–33. Evanston, Ill.: Northwestern University Press, 2005.

Ker, W. P. Introduction. In *Beowulf,* trans. David Wright. New York: Penguin Books, 1957.

Kierkegaard, Søren. *The Book on Adler.* Edited and translated by Howard V. Hong and Edna H. Hong. *Kierkegaard's Writings* XXIV. Princeton, N.J.: Princeton University Press 1994.

———. *Christian Discourses.* Edited and translated by Howard & Edna Hong. Princeton, N.J.: Princeton University Press, 1997.

———. *Concept of Anxiety.* Translated by Reidar Thomte. Princeton, N.J.: Princeton University Press, 1980.

———. *The Concept of Dread.* Translated with introduction and notes by Walter Lowrie. Princeton, N.J.: Princeton University Press, 1957.

———. *Concluding Unscientific Postscript.* Translated by D. F. Swenson and W. Lowrie. Princeton, N.J.: Princeton University Press, 1968.

———. *Concluding Unscientific Postscript to Philosophical Fragments.* Edited and translated by Howard V. Hong and Edna Hong. Princeton, N.J.: Princeton University Press, 1992.

———. *Eighteen Upbuilding Discourses.* Edited and translated by Howard V. Hong & Edna Hong. Princeton, N.J.: Princeton University Press, 1990.

———. *Either/Or.* Edited and translated by Howard V. Hong and Edna Hong. 2 vols. Princeton, N.J.: Princeton University Press, 1987.

———. *Either/Or.* Translated by Alastair Hannay. London: Penguin, 1992.

———. *Fear and Trembling.* Translated by Alastair Hannay. New York: Penguin, 1985.

———. *Fear and Trembling/Repetition.* Edited and translated by Howard V. Hong and Edna H. Hong. Princeton, N.J.: Princeton University Press, 1983.

———. *For Self-examination/Judge for Yourselves.* Princeton, N.J.: Princeton University Press, 1991.

———. *Journals.* Edited and translated by A. Dru. London: Oxford University Press, 1951.

———. *Journals & Papers.* Edited and translated by Howard V. Hong and Edna Hong. Bloomington: Indiana University Press, 1978.

———. *Kierkegaard's Journals and Papers.* Edited and translated by Howard V. Hong and Edna Hong, assisted by G. Malantschuk. 7 vols. Bloomington: Indiana University Press, 1967.

———. *Søren Kierkegaards Papirer.* Edited by P. A. Heiberg, V. Kuhr, and E. Torsting. 2nd enlarged edition by N. Thulstrup. 16 vols. in 22 tomes. Copenhagen: Gyldendal, 1968–1978.

———. *Kierkegaards Samlede Værker.* Edited by A. B. Drachmann, J. L. Heiberg, and H. O. Lange. 14 vols. Copenhagen: Gyldendal, 1901–1906.

———. *A Literary Review.* Translated by Alastair Hannay, London: Penguin, 2001.

———. *The Moment and Late Writings.* Edited and translated by Howard V. Hong and Edna Hong. *Kierkegaard's Writings* XXIII. Princeton, N.J.: Princeton University Press, 1998.

———. *Papers and Journals: A Selection.* Translated by Alastair Hannay. Harmondsworth: Penguin, 1996.

———. *The Point of View.* Edited and translated by Howard V. Hong and Edna H. Hong. Princeton, N.J.: Princeton University Press, 1998.

———. *The Sickness unto Death.* Translated by Alastair Hannay. Abridged and modified. London: Penguin, 1989.

———. *Søren Kierkegaards Skrifter.* Bind 4. Edited by Niels Jørgen Cappelørn, Joakim Garff, Johnny Kondrup, Alastair McKinnon, and Finn Hauberg Mortensen. Copenhagen: G. E. C. Gads Forlag, 1997.

———. *Stages on Life's Way.* Edited and translated by Howard V. Hong and Edna H. Hong. *Kierkegaard's Writings* XI. Princeton, N.J.: Princeton University Press, 1988.

———. *Training in Christianity and the Edifying Discourse Which "Accompanied" It.* Translated by Walter Lowrie. Princeton, N.J.: Princeton University Press, 1967.

———. *Upbuilding Discourses in Various Spirits.* Princeton, N.J.: Princeton University Press, 1993.

———. *Without Authority.* Princeton, N.J.: Princeton University Press, 1997.

———. *Works of Love.* Edited by Howard V. Hong and Edna H. Hong. *Kierkegaard's Writings* XVI. Princeton, N.J.: Princeton University Press, 1995.

Kirmmse, Bruce H. *Encounters with Kierkegaard.* Princeton, N.J.: Princeton University Press, 1996.

Kjaeldgaard, Lasse Horne. "The Peak on Which Abraham Stands." *Journal of the History of Ideas* 63.2 (2002): 303–321.

Knappe, Ulrich. *Theory and Practice in Kant and Kierkegaard.* Berlin: Walter de Gruyter, 2004.

Kundera, Milan. *The Art of the Novel.* Translated by Linda Asher. New York: HarperPerennial, 2000.

Lang, Berel, ed. *Philosophical Style: An Anthology about the Writing and Reading of Philosophy.* Chicago: Nelson-Hall, 1980.

Lawrence, D. H. *Phoenix.* Edited by Edward D. McDonald. New York: Penguin, 1978.

Lepenies, Wolf. *Melancholie und Gesellschaft,* Frankfurt: Suhrkamp, 1969. Published in English as *Melancholy and Society.* Cambridge, Mass.: Harvard University Press, 1992.

Levinas, Emmanuel. "A Propos of 'Kierkegaard Vivant.'" In *Proper Names,* trans. Michael B. Smith, pp. 75–79. Stanford, Calif.: Stanford University Press, 1996.

———. *Totality and Infinity.* Pittsburgh: Duquesne University Press, 1969.

Lingis, Alphonso. *Dangerous Emotions.* Berkeley: University of California Press, 2000.

———. *The Imperative.* Bloomington: Indiana University Press, 1998.

Lippitt, John. *Guidebook to Kierkegaard and "Fear and Trembling."* London: Routledge, 2003.

———. *Kierkegaard and "Fear and Trembling."* London: Routledge, 2003.

Louden, Robert. "On Some Vices of Virtue Ethics." In *Virtue Ethics,* ed. Roger Crisp and Michael Slote, pp. 201–216. Oxford: Oxford University Press, 1997.

Lyons, William. *Matters of the Mind.* Edinburgh: Edinburgh University Press, 2001.

MacIntyre, Alasdair C. *After Virtue.* Notre Dame, Ind.: University of Notre Dame Press, 1981.

———. *A Short History of Ethics.* New York: Macmillan, 1966.

Mackey, Louis. *Kierkegaard: A Kind of Poet.* Philadelphia: University of Pennsylvania Press, 1971.

———. *Points of View.* Tallahassee: University of Florida Press, 1986.

Mackie, J. L. *Ethics: Inventing Right and Wrong.* New York: Penguin, 1977.

———. "The Subjectivity of Values." In *Essays in Moral Realism,* ed. Geoffrey Sayre-McCord, 95–118. Ithaca, N.Y.: Cornell University Press, 1988.

Magee, Bryan. *The Philosophy of Schopenhauer.* 2nd ed. Oxford: Oxford University Press, 1997.

Marino, Gordon. "Anxiety in the *Concept of Anxiety.*" In *The Cambridge Companion to Kierkegaard,* ed. Alastair Hannay and Gordon Daniel Marino. New York: Cambridge University Press, 1998.

Marion, Jean-Luc. *God without Being.* Translated by Thomas Carlson. Chicago: University of Chicago Press, 1991.

———. *Prolegomena to Charity.* Translated by Stephen E. Lewis. New York: Fordham University Press, 2002.

McCarthy, Vincent. *The Phenomenology of Moods.* The Hague: Martinus Nijhoff, 1978.

McDowell, John. *Mind and World.* Cambridge, Mass.: Harvard University Press, 1994.

McLane, Earl. "Rereading *Fear and Tremblin.*" *Faith and Philosophy* 10, no. 2 (April 1993): 198–219.

Molbech, C. *Dansk Ordbog.* Vols. 1–2. Copenhagen, 1833.

Moller, Poul M. "Forberedelser til en Afhandling om Affectation" [Preparations for an Essay on Affection]. In *Efterladte Skrifter af Poul M. Møller* [Posthumous Writings of Poul M. Møller], 3d ed., ed. L. V. Petersen and with a biographical sketch by F. C. Olsen, vol. 3. Copenhagen: C. A. Reitzel, 1855–1856.

Mooney, Edward F. *Knights of Faith and Knights of Resignation: Reading Kierkegaard's "Fear and Trembling."* Albany, N.Y.: SUNY Press, 1991.

———. *On Søren Kierkegaard: Dialogue, Polemic, Lost Intimacy and Time.* London: Ashgate, 2007.

———. "The Perils of Polarity: MacIntyre and Kierkegaard in Search of Moral Truth." In *Kierkegaard after MacIntyre,* ed. John Davenport and Anthony Rudd, pp. 233–263. Chicago: Open Court, 2001.

———. *Selves in Discord and Resolve.* London: Routledge, 1996.

Moore, Kathleen Dean. *Holdfast: At Home in the Natural World.* New York: Lyons Press, 1999.

Mulder, Jack. "Re-Radicalizing Kierkegaard: An Alternative to Religiousness C in Light of an Investigation into the Teleological Suspension of the Ethical." *Continental Philosophy Review* 35: 303–324.

Mulhall, Stephen. *Inheritance and Originality: Wittgenstein, Heidegger, Kierkegaard.* Oxford: Oxford University Press, 2001.

Murdoch, Iris. *Existentialists and Mystics.* New York: Penguin, 1999.

Murphy, Mark. "Divine Command, Divine Will, and Moral Obligation." *Faith and Philosophy* 15 (1998), 3–27.

Nagel, Thomas. "The Absurd." In *The Meaning of Life,* ed. E. D. Klemke, pp. 151–161. New York: Oxford University Press, 1981.

——. *The View from Nowhere.* Oxford: Oxford University Press, 1986.

——. "What Is It like to Be a Bat?" In *Modern Philosophy of Mind,* ed. William Lyons, pp. 159–174. London: Everyman, 1995.

Natanson, Maurice. *The Erotic Bird: Phenomenology in Literature.* Evanston, Ill.: Northwestern University Press, 1997.

Nordentoft, Kresten. *Kierkegaard's Psychology.* Translated by Bruce Kirmmse. Pittsburgh: University of Pittsburgh Press, 1978.

Nussbaum, Martha. "Exactly and Responsibly: A Defense of Ethical Criticism." *Philosophy and Literature* 22 (1998): 364–386.

——. *The Fragility of Goodness.* Cambridge: Cambridge University Press, 1986.

——. *Upheavals of Thought: The Intelligence of Emotions.* Cambridge: Cambridge University Press, 2001.

O'Hear, Anthony. *The Element of Fire: Science, Art, and the Human World.* London: Routledge, 1988.

Outka, Gene. "God as the Subject of Unique Veneration." *Journal of Religious Ethics* 21, no. 2 (1993): 211–215.

Pascal, Blaise. *Pascal Pensées.* New York: E. P. Dutton, 1958.

Pattison, George. *Kierkegaard's Upbuilding Discourses: Philosophy, Literature, Theology.* New York: Routledge, 2002.

——. *The Philosophy of Kierkegaard.* London: Ashgate, 2005.

Pepper, Thomas. "Abraham: Who Could Possibly Understand Him?" In *Kierkegaard Studies: Yearbook 1996,* ed. Niels Jørgen Cappelørn and Hermann Deuser, pp. 211–239. Berlin: Walter de Grutyer, 1996.

Perkins, Robert L. "Abraham's Silence Æsthetically Considered." In *International Kierkegaard Commentary: "Fear and Trembling" and "Repetition,"* ed. Robert L. Perkins, pp. 155–176. Macon, Ga.: Mercer University Press, 1993.

Phillips, D. Z. "Kierkegaard and Loves That Blossom." In *Ethik der Liebe,* ed. Ingolf Dalferth. Tübingen: Mohr Siebeck, 2002.

Piety, M. G. "The Place of the World in Kierkegaard's Ethics." In *Kierkegaard: The Self in Society,* ed. George Pattison and Stephen Shakespeare. London: Macmillan, 1998.

Pons, J. *Stealing a Gift: Kierkegaard's Pseudonyms and the Bible.* New York: Fordham University Press, 2004.

Poole, Roger. *Kierkegaard: The Indirect Communication.* Charlottesville: University Press of Virginia, 1993.

Possen, David. *Søren Kierkegaard and the Very Idea of Advance beyond Socrates.* Ph.D. dissertation, University of Chicago, forthcoming.

Putnam, Hilary. *Reason, Truth, and History.* Cambridge: Cambridge University Press, 1981.

——. *Representation and Reality.* Cambridge, Mass.: MIT Press, 1991.

——. *The Threefold Cord: Mind, Body, and World.* New York: Columbia University Press, 1999.

Quine, W. V. O. "Philosophical Progress in Language Theory." *Metaphilosophy* 1 (1970).

Riker, John. *Human Excellence and an Ecological Conception of the Psyche.* Albany, N.Y.: SUNY Press, 1991.

Roberts, Robert C. "Dialectical Emotions and the Virtue of Faith." In *International Kierkegaard Commentary: Concluding Unscientific Postscript,* ed. Robert L. Perkins, pp. 73–93. Macon, Ga.: Mercer University Press, 1997.

——. *Emotions: An Essay in Aid of Moral Psychology.* Cambridge: Cambridge University Press, 2003.

——. "Existence, Emotion, and Virtue: Classical Themes in Kierkegaard." In *The Cambridge Companion to Kierkegaard,* ed. Alastair Hannay and Gordon Daniel Marino. New York: Cambridge University Press, 1998.

——. "Kierkegaard, Wittgenstein, and a Method of 'Virtue Ethics.'" In *Kierkegaard in Post/*

Modernity, ed. Merold Westphal and Martin Matustik, pp. 142–166. Bloomington: Indiana University Press, 1995.

———. "The Virtue of Hope in *Eighteen Upbuilding Discourses.*" In *International Kierkegaard Commentary: Eighteen Upbuilding Discourses,* ed. Robert L. Perkins, pp. 181–203. Macon, Ga.: Mercer University Press, 2003.

Roberts, Robert C., and W. Jay Wood. *Intellectual Virtues: An Essay in Regulative Epistemology.* New York: Oxford University Press, 2007.

Rudd, Anthony. "'Believing All Things': Kierkegaard on Knowledge, Doubt, and Love." In *International Kierkegaard Commentary: Works of Love,* edited by Robert L. Perkins, 121–136. Macon, Ga.: Mercer University Press, 1999.

———. *Kierkegaard and the Limits of the Ethical.* Oxford: Oxford University Press, 1993.

Ryle, Gilbert. *The Concept of Mind.* London: Hutchinson, 1949.

Sagi, Avi, and Daniel Statman. "Divine Command Morality and Jewish Tradition." *Journal of Religious Ethics* 23, no. 1 (1995): 39–67.

———. "Modern Philosophy and the Neglect of Aesthetics." In *The Philosopher on Dover Beach: Essays,* ed. Roger Scruton, pp. 98–112. Manchester: Carcanet, 1990.

Scruton, Roger. *Sexual Desire: A Moral Philosophy of the Erotic.* New York: Free Press, 1986.

Shorris, Earl. "Ignoble Liars: Leo Strauss, George Bush and the Philosophy of Mass Deception." *Harpers* (June 2004).

Steiner, Rudolf. *Die Rätsel der Philosophie in ihrer Geschichte als Umriss dargestellt* (1914). In *Gesamtausgabe.* Dornach: Rudolf Steiner Verlag, 2002.

———. *The Riddles of Philosophy.* Spring Valley, N.Y.: Athroposophic Press, 1973.

Stendhal. *The Red and the Black.* Translated by Lowell Bair. New York: Bantam Books, 1958.

Strauss, Leo. *Persecution and the Art of Writing.* Chicago: University of Chicago Press, 1988.

TANAKH: A New Translation of THE HOLY SCRIPTURES According to the Traditional Hebrew Text. Philadelphia: Jewish Publication Society, 1985.

Theunissen, Michael. *Kierkegaard's Concept of Despair.* Translated by Barbara Harshav and Helmut Illbruck. Princeton, N.J.: Princeton University Press, 2005.

Tolkien, J. R. R. "On Fairy Stories." In *The Monsters and the Critics and Other Essays,* ed. Christopher Tolkien, pp. 109–161. London: George Allen and Unwin, 1983.

Vacek, Edward Collins. *Love, Human and Divine: The Heart of Christian Ethics.* Washington, D.C.: Georgetown University Press, 1994.

Von Wright, G. H. "Historical Introduction." In Ludwig Wittgenstein, *Prototractatus: An Early Version of Tractatus-Logico-Philosophicus.* London: Routledge & Kegan Paul, 1971.

Walsh, Sylvia. *Living Poetically: Kierkegaard's Existential Aesthetics.* University Park: Pennsylvania State University Press, 1994.

Watson, Gary. "On the Primacy of Character." In *Identity, Character, and Morality,* ed. Owen Flanagan and Amélie Oksenberg Rorty, pp. 449–469. Cambridge, Mass.: MIT Press, 1990.

Westphal, Merold. *Becoming a Self: A Reading of Kierkegaard's Concluding Unscientific Postscript.* West Lafayette, Ind.: Purdue University Press, 1996.

———. "Kierkegaard and Hegel." In *The Cambridge Companion to Kierkegaard,* ed. Alastair Hannay and Gordon Daniel Marino, pp. 101–124. New York: Cambridge University Press, 1998.

———. "Kierkegaard's Religiousness C: A Defense." *International Philosophical Quarterly* 44 no. 4 (2004): 535–548.

———. "The Many Faces of Levinas as a Reader of Kierkegaard." In *Kierkegaard and Levinas: Ethics, Politics, and Religion,* ed. J. Aaron Simmons and David Wood. Bloomington: Indiana University Press, 2008.

Whittaker, John. "The Suspension of the Ethical in *Fear and Trembling.*" *Kierkegaardiana* 4 (1988): 101–113.

Wittgenstein, Ludwig. *Tractatus Logico-Philosophicus.* Translated by C. K. Ogden. Minneola, N.Y.: Dover, 1999.

Wolterstorff, Nicholas. *John Locke and the Ethics of Belief.* Cambridge: Cambridge University Press, 1996.

Zagzebski, Linda Trinkaus. *Virtues of the Mind: An Inquiry into the Nature of Virtue and the Ethical Foundations of Knowledge.* Cambridge: Cambridge University Press, 1996.

Zahavi, Dan. *Self-awareness and Alterity: A Phenomenological Investigation.* Evanston, Ill.: Northwestern University Press, forthcoming.

Zuckert, Michael, and Catherine Zuckert. *The Truth about Leo Strauss.* Chicago: University of Chicago Press, 2006.

Contributors

N. J. Cappelørn is Director of the Kierkegaard Research Center, Copenhagen.

Daniel W. Conway is Professor of Philosophy at Texas A&M University.

John J. Davenport is Associate Professor of Philosophy at Fordham University.

Hubert L. Dreyfus is Emeritus Professor of Philosophy at the University of California, Berkeley.

M. Jamie Ferreira is Professor of Religion at the University of Virginia.

Rick Anthony Furtak is Associate Professor of Philosophy at Colorado College.

Alastair Hannay is Emeritus Professor of Philosophy at the University of Oslo.

Bruce H. Kirmmse is Professor Emeritus of History at Connecticut College. He serves as General Editor of *Kierkegaard's Journals and Notebooks*, Princeton University Press, eleven volumes.

Gordon Marino is Professor of Philosophy at St. Olaf College.

Edward F. Mooney is Professor of Religion and Philosophy at Syracuse University.

George Pattison is Professor of Divinity at Oxford University.

M. G. Piety is Associate Professor of Philosophy at Drexel University.

Robert C. Roberts is Professor in Philosophy at Baylor University.